GENDER !!

M000211485

Series editors:
Pam Sharpe, Patricia Skinner and Penny Summerfield

+>=+=<+

The expansion of research into the history of women and gender since the 1970s has changed the face of history. Using the insights of feminist theory and of historians of women, gender historians have explored the configuration in the past of gender identities and relations between the sexes. They have also investigated the history of sexuality and family relations, and analysed ideas and ideals of masculinity and femininity. Yet gender history has not abandoned the original, inspirational project of women's history: to recover and reveal the lived experience of women in the past and the present.

The series Gender in History provides a forum for these developments. Its historical coverage extends from the medieval to the modern periods, and its geographical scope encompasses not only Europe and North America but all corners of the globe. The series aims to investigate the social and cultural constructions of gender in historical sources, as well as the gendering of historical discourse itself. It embraces both detailed case studies of specific regions or periods, and broader treatments of major themes. Gender in History titles are designed to meet the needs of both scholars and students working in this dynamic area of historical research.

Masculinities in politics and war

Published in our
centenary year
～ **2004** ～
MANCHESTER
UNIVERSITY
PRESS

also available
in the series

+>━●━<+

'The truest form of patriotism':
feminist pacifism in Britain, 1870–1920
Heloise Brown

Noblewomen, aristocracy and power
in the twelfth-century Anglo-Norman realm
Susan Johns

MASCULINITIES IN POLITICS AND WAR

GENDERING

MODERN HISTORY

⁺⊨ edited by ⊨⁺

Stefan Dudink,
Karen Hagemann and John Tosh

Manchester University Press
Manchester and New York

distributed exclusively in the USA by Palgrave

While copyright in the volume as a-whole is vested in Manchester
University Press, copyright in individual chapters belongs to their
respective authors, and no chapter may be reproduced in whole or in part
without the express permission in writing of both author and publisher.

Published by Manchester University Press
Oxford Road, Manchester M13 9NR, UK
and Room 400, 175 Fifth Avenue, New York, NY 10010, USA
www.manchesteruniversitypress.co.uk

Distributed exclusively in the USA by
Palgrave, 175 Fifth Avenue, New York NY 10010, USA

Distributed exclusively in Canada by
UBC Press, University of British Columbia, 2029 West Mall,
Vancouver, BC, Canada V6T 1Z2

British Library Cataloguing-in-Publication Data
A catalogue record for this book is available from the British Library

Library of Congress Cataloging-in-Publication Data
A catalog record for this book is available from the Library of Congress

ISBN 13: 978 0 7190 6521 7

First published by Manchester University Press 2004

First digital paperback edition published 2008

Printed by Lightning Source

Contents

CONTENTS

Figures

Contributors

Stefan Dudink is assistant professor of Gay Studies at the Centre for Women's and Gender and Studies at Nijmegen University, the Netherlands. His research focuses on gender and sexuality in modern Dutch and European political history. He is author of a study on social liberalism in the Netherlands: *Deugdzaam Liberalisme: Sociaal-Liberalisme in Nederland 1870–1901* (Amsterdam, 1997).

Joanna de Groot works in the Department of History and the Centre for Women's Studies at the University of York. Her main interests are in the intersections of gender, ethnicity, sexuality and colonialism between the eighteenth and twentieth centuries and the links between cultural, material, and political elements of these intersections with particular reference to Iran and India. Her published work includes 'The dialectics of gender: women, men, and nationalism in Iran *c.* 1890–1930', *Gender & History*, 5:3 (1993); 'Co-habiting and conflicting identities: women and nationalism in Iran in the twentieth century', in R. Pierson and N. Chaudhuri (eds), *Nation, Empire, Colony* (Bloomington and Indianapolis, 1998); ' "Sex" and "race": the construction of language and image in the nineteenth century', in C. Hall (ed), *Cultures of Empire* (Manchester, 2000).

Karen Hagemann teaches at the Department for History and the Centre for Interdisciplinary Studies on Women and Gender of the Technical University Berlin. Her current research focus on the nation, military, war, and gender in eighteenth–twentieth-century Germany and Europe. Her latest book is *Mannlicher Muth und Teutsche Ehre: Nation, Militär und Geschlecht zur Zeit der Antinapoleonischen Kriege Preussens* (Paderborn, 2002). She is co-editor (with I. Blom and C. Hall) of *Gendered Nations: Nationalisms and Gender Order in the Long Nineteenth Century* (Oxford and New York, 2000) and (with S. Schüler-Springorum) of *Home/Front: The Military and Gender in Twentieth Century Europe* (Oxford and New York, 2002).

John Horne is associate professor of modern European history at Trinity College Dublin. He has published on twentieth-century French social history, comparative labour history, and the history of the Great War. He edited *State, Society and Mobilization in Europe during the First World War* (Cambridge, 1997, new edn, 2002) and is author (together with A. Kramer) of *German Atrocities, 1914: A History of Denial* (New Haven and London, 2001), winner of the Fraenkel Prize for Contemporary History (London). He is currently working on the process of 'cultural demobilisation' after the Great War.

Alice Kessler-Harris is the R. Gordon Hoxie Professor of American History at Columbia University where she is also professor in the Institute for Research on Women and Gender. She has written widely on issues of women and wage-work, including *Out to Work: A History of Wage-Earning Women in the United States* (Oxford, 1983). Her most recent book is *In Pursuit of Equity: Women, Men and the Quest for Economic*

Citizenship in Twentieth Century America (Oxford, 2001). She is currently working on a biography of the American playwright Lillian Hellman.

Marilyn Lake is Professor in History at Latrobe University, Australia. Between 2001 and 2002 she held the Chair in Australian Studies at Harvard University. Her work has appeared in numerous international anthologies in the field of gender and history. Her most recent publications include: *FAITH: Faith Bandler Gentle Activist* (Sydney, 2002); *Getting Equal: The History of Feminism in Australia* (Sydney, 1999); and, with P. Grimshaw and K. Holmes, *Women's Rights and Human Rights: International Historical Perspectives* (Houndmills, 2001).

Joan B. Landes is Professor of Women's Studies and History at The Pennsylvania State University, University Park. Her research engages questions of gender, political culture, and visual cognition in old regime and revolutionary France, and historical and contemporary feminist theory. She is the author of *Women and the Public Sphere in the Age of the French Revolution* (Ithaca, 1988) and *Visualizing the Nation: Gender, Representation, and Revolution in Eighteenth-Century France* (Ithaca, 2001); editor of *Feminism, the Public and the Private* (Oxford, 1998), and co-editor (with L. Lungers Knoppers) of *Monstrous Bodies/Political Monstrosities in Early Modern Europe* (Ithaca, forthcoming 2004).

Jacobus Adriaan du Pisani is professor of History in the School of Social and Government Studies at the Potchefstroom University, South Africa. He has published in the fields of contemporary South African political history and Afrikaner masculinities and is currently involved in team research on aspects of environmental history in African desert margin regions.

Michael Roper is Senior Lecturer in Social and Cultural History at the University of Essex. He has published in the areas of life-story methods, and masculinities in business and war in twentieth-century Britain. He is author of *Masculinity and the British Organization Man since 1945* (Oxford, 1994), and co-editor (with J. Tosh) of *Manful Assertions: Masculinities in Britain since 1800* (London and New York, 1991) and (with G. Dawson and T. Ashplant) of *The Politics of War Memory and Commemoration* (London and New York, 2000). He is currently doing research on the history of child psychotherapy in Britain after 1945, and writing a book on mother-son relationships in Britain during the First World War.

Sonya O. Rose is the Natalie Zemon Davis Collegiate Professor of History, Sociology and Women's Studies at the University of Michigan. She is the author of *Limited Livelihoods: Gender and Class in Nineteenth-Century England* (Berkeley and Los Angeles, 1992), co-editor (with L. Levine Frader) of *Gender and Class in Modern Europe* (Ithaca NY, 1996) and (with K. Canning) of *Gender, Citizenship and Subjectivity* (London, 2002). Her newest book, *Which People's War? National Identity and Citizenship in Wartime Britain, 1939–45,* to be published by Oxford is forthcoming in 2003.

Glenda Sluga is Associate Professor in Modern European History at the University of Sydney. Her most recent publications include *The Problem of Trieste and the*

Italo-Yugoslav Border: Difference, Identity, and Sovereignty in Twentieth Century Europe (New York, 2001) and (co-authored with B. Caine) *Gendering European History*, (London, 2000). She is currently completing a study of the history of ideas of nation, nationality and national self-determination in late nineteenth and early twentieth-century Europe.

Carroll Smith-Rosenberg is Alice Freeman Palmer Professor of History, University of Michigan, with appointments also in the Women's Studies Program and the American Culture Program. She is the author of *Religion and the Rise of the American City* (Ithaca NY, 1971) and *Disorderly Conduct: Visions of Gender in Victorian America* (New York, 1985). Her essay, 'Discovering the Subject of the "Great Constitutional Discussion"', *Journal of American History* (1992), won the prize for best article published that year. Her book in press, *Federalist Capers*, explores the formation of an American national identity during the debates over the ratification of the US Constitution.

John Tosh is Professor of History at the University of Surrey Roehampton. He is the author of *A Man's Place: Masculinity and the Middle-Class Home in Victorian England* (New Haven and London, 1999) and co-editor (with M. Roper) of *Manful Assertions: Masculinities in Britain since 1800* (London, 1991). He is currently working on masculinity and imperial commitment in nineteenth-century Britain.

Barbara Weinstein is professor of Latin American history at the University of Maryland and co-editor of the *Hispanic American Historical Review*. Her research focuses on the social and political history of postcolonial Brazil. Her most recent book is *For Social Peace in Brazil: Industrialists and the Remaking of the Working Class in São Paulo, 1920–1964* (Chapel Hill, 1996). Currently, she is working on a study of the racialisation and gendering of regional identities in twentieth-century Brazil.

Thomas Welskopp is currently guest professor at Georg-August-University, Göttingen. His research focuses on labour and business history, the history of political culture, and on theory and historiography. He is author of *Das Banner der Brüderlichkeit: Die deutsche Sozialdemokratie vom Vormärz bis zum Sozialistengesetz* (Bonn, 2000), and co-editor of *Geschichte zwischen Kultur und Gesellschaft: Beiträge zur Theoriedebatte* (München, 1997).

Acknowledgements

This book began as a conference session organised by Karen Hagemann and Stefan Dudink at the *19th International Congress of Historical Sciences* in Oslo, 2000, entitled 'Masculinity as Practice and Representation'. During the last two years the papers given and comments delivered on that occasion have been extensively rewritten and five further contributions have been commissioned. We should like to thank all the colleagues that have participated in this venture for their intellectual generosity both during and after the original conference session, for their willingness to adapt their papers to the framework we designed for this book, and for putting up with a set of demanding editors. Noam Krieger provided editorial assistance for which we are very grateful, and we are pleased to acknowledge the financial assistance from the Centre for Women's and Gender Studies at Nijmegen University that enabled us to include illustrations in the book. Two chapters draw on previously published material, we thank Cornell University Press and Oxford University Press for permission to use this:

Joan B. Landes' 'Republican citizenship and heterosocial desire: concepts of masculinity in revolutionary France' is adapted from Joan B. Landes, *Visualizing the Nation: Gender, Representation and Revolution in Eighteenth-Century France* (Ithaca and London, 2001). It is used by permission of Cornell University Press.

Alice Kessler-Harris' 'Measures for masculinity: the American labor movement and welfare state policy during the Great Depression' draws on material from Alice Kessler-Harris, *In Pursuit of Equity: Women, Men and the Quest for Economic Citizenship in Twentieth Century America* (New York and Oxford, 2001), chapter 2. It is used by permission of Oxford University Press, Inc.

Stefan Dudink, Amsterdam

Karen Hagemann, Berlin

John Tosh, London

Editors' preface

In this book we aim to demonstrate how a focus on masculinity can contribute to a rethinking of the history of politics and war in the modern world. Our contention is that in this field a gender perspective which foregrounds masculinity is richly productive of empirical and theoretical insights. Focusing on masculinity as both practice and representation and covering the long nineteenth and twentieth centuries, its central objective is to advance our knowledge of both gender history and 'mainstream' political and military histories by demonstrating the extent of their inter-relatedness.

By employing the perspective of the history of masculinity the book shows how politics and war have become the seemingly 'natural' homelands of masculinity – a masculinity that sometimes has been quite explicit, but more often has been elided in the equation of 'man' with 'human' and 'mankind' which conceals masculinity behind discourses of 'general interests' and 'universality'. The contributors analyse the historical processes by which politics and war came to be constructed as 'naturally' – and exclusively – masculine realms. Furthermore, they explore the implications of this focus for traditional historical narratives. How might the histories of politics and war look once the masculine construction of these realms is acknowledged? The nineteenth and twentieth centuries were the period when modern notions of gender difference(s) were constructed, while at the same time modern ideas and practices of war and politics took shape. In seeking to analyse the intersection of these two themes, we ask how modernising tendencies in war and politics were connected with the development of modern notions of gender difference. We want to know how such tendencies reflected and shaped emerging notions of masculinity, and how notions of masculinity produced the gendered practices of – among other things – citizenship and conscription.

This book builds on the fruits of over two decades of women's and gender history. It places the history of masculinity squarely within the field of gender history, and it seeks to apply concepts and methods developed in gender history to the historical analysis of masculinity. This is reflected in the book's structure. After Part I, *Masculinities in politics and war: introductions*, each of the following four parts represents an aspect of gender history's conceptual and methodological apparatus. Part 1 opens with a chapter by Stefan Dudink and Karen Hagemann, who introduce the reader to central themes in the history of masculinity in politics and war in the late eighteenth and the early nineteenth century. They discuss, in particular, the revolutionary equation of universal military service with citizenship. Arguing for a history of masculinity that concentrates of masculinity's specific meanings and political deployments, Dudink and Hagemann highlight the divergent constructions of masculinity produced by the equally divergently shaped dyads of universal military service and citizenship in (post-)revolutionary Europe and America. John Horne takes this history further into the nineteenth and twentieth centuries. His chapter comes with a slight change of focus, since he concentrates on exploring the way in which the study of masculinity might illuminate the history of politics and war, rather than the other way around. He points, among other themes, to the importance of models of fraternity in constituting public life and mediating the struggle for political authority in post-revolutionary society, and to the importance of the male hero in establishing the imagined community of the nation. John Tosh concludes this part with critical reflections on the concept of 'hegemonic masculinity', as it figures in this book and in the wider field of the history of masculinity.

Central to Part II, *Historicising revolutionary masculinity: constructs and contexts*, is gender history's basic assumption that notions of sexual difference are constructed in historically variable and specific contexts, and that the meaning and 'truth' of such notions depend strictly on the epistemological and socio-political nature of these contexts.[1] To historians familiar with gender history this may seem something of a truism. However, the advent of a universalising language of sexual difference in the age of democratic revolutions, and the political uses to which this was put, lends a renewed relevance to the importance of context and historicisation. In chapter 4 Caroll Smith-Rosenberg explores how the eighteenth century's multiple revolutions recast concepts of masculinity and citizenship in the revolutionary United States, leading to a new understanding of masculinity in which racial violence played a central role. In chapter 5 Stefan Dudink charts changing concepts of masculinity and effeminacy in the Dutch age of democratic revolutions, and shows how these intersected with new notions of history and time. Focusing on the visual and political culture of the French revolution, Joan Landes explores the heterosexual underpinnings of revolutionary masculinity in the ways male citizens established their masculinity through real and idealised relationships to women. Karen Hagemann analyses the cult of death for the fatherland in nineteenth-century Germany, in which a 'civilian' concept of 'civic valour' and a military notion of 'combat readiness' competed for prominence. The chapters in this part take seriously the political efficacy of discourses of universal sexual difference, but they also look for the historically specific in the political processes in which supposedly universal notions of femininity and masculinity were crafted.

Most chapters in this book refer, in one way or another, to the gendered construction of the nation, which testifies to the importance of the intersection of gender and nation in modern history. The chapters in Part III, *Gendering the nation: hegemonic masculinity and its others* have masculinity's part in establishing the national 'imagined community' as their main theme.[2] Here gender history's insistence on thinking about masculinity and femininity as *relational* categories comes into play. Masculinity's meanings can be understood only if we analyse them in relation to femininity, other masculinities, and the ambiguous category of effeminacy. R. W. Connell's concept of hegemonic masculinity is particularly relevant here in its focus on a 'culturally exalted' form of masculinity embedded in a set of hierarchic relations with femininity and other, marginalised and subordinate, masculinities.[3] In chapter 8 Joanna de Groot discusses the interplay of masculinity and nation in Iranian political culture of the late nineteenth and early twentieth centuries, considering both its specific nature and how Iranian constructions of manhood and nationhood had features found elsewhere. Jacobus Adriaan du Pisani investigates how Afrikaner nationalism drew on constructions of Afrikaner hegemonic masculinity and its Britsh, Jewish and black others, in its efforts to mobilise support before it came to power in South Africa in 1948. Sonya Rose examines masculinity in Second World War Britain, which contained anti-heroic elements, but was simultaneously defined through the exclusion of 'effeminate' conscientious objectors.

The hierarchical nature of the relations between hegemonic masculinity and its 'others' is a helpful tool for understanding the role of masculinity in constructing the nation. It sheds light on the way masculinity is invoked to establish boundaries between national selves and others. Whereas the feminine can be included in the national self – albeit mostly in a subordinate position – effeminacy is usually placed beyond the line separating self and other and actually helps to create that boundary. The recurrent representation of the national self as masculine and of 'other' nations as effeminate is one example of the work of masculinity in creating the nation. As the chapters in this part show, national(ist) discourses are often more complex, drawing as much on instabilities in constructions of gender as on resolutely binary representations of the differences between men and women. Matters are further complicated by the fact that taking into account masculinity's relations with other categories of gender is not sufficient. Only by placing masculinity in a field of differences that includes categories like race, ethnicity, religion, class, age, marital status, sexuality et cetera, can we fully comprehend its meanings. The chapters in this part do this by a focus on the articulation of the nation through masculinity as it intersected in particular with religion, race, and sexuality.

The chapters in Part IV, *Analysing power relations: the politics of masculinity*, share an emphasis on the symbolic importance of notions of masculinity and femininity. They all address gender's symbolic importance in political and social contexts which seem to be unrelated, or only indirectly related, to the socio-political relations between the sexes. In pointing to this role of gender in the signification and articulation of relationships of power, gender history has opened new paths of inquiry in political history. These chapters seek a delicate balance between an analysis of masculinity as constituting other power relations than those between men and women, and an analysis of masculinity's part in establishing precisely that relationship. They show how masculinity is deployed in divergent struggles, and in all cases the effects of this on the relations between classes, races, states, nations, *and* men and women is highlighted. In her discussion of the founding of the early twentieth-century Australian welfare state (chapter 11) Marilyn Lake addresses how racialised representations of 'civilised manhood' and its entitlement to a living wage were constitutive of both men's power over women and integral to power struggles between men. Alice Kessler-Harris demonstrates that in the American context a labour movement set on preserving its image of independent masculinity became one of the forces hampering the development of the welfare state. In chapter 13 Glenda Sluga investigates masculinity's role in post-First World War peacemaking by showing the impact of ideas about masculinity on the notion of national self-determination and on gender relations in the new world order.

The awareness that constructions of masculinity and femininity signify and articulate various power relations has also influenced historical analyses of gendered subjectivity. It has further strengthened the argument that the relation between discourses of masculinity and femininity and 'real man and women' is always mediated. This room for mediation, negotiation, and manoeuvre is explored in Part V, *Including the subject: masculinity and subjectivity*. The chapters in this part share an ambition to historicise both discourse and experience, without thinking of one of these two as determining the other.[4] Thomas Wellskop writes about the self-fashioning of mid-nineteenth-century German Social-Democrats that focused on a male public sphere where a masculinised notion of political citizenship and revolutionary subjectivity took shape. Barbara Weinstein charts efforts in twentieth-century Brazil to construct 'modern' masculine subjectivities that centred on industrial skill and household headship – efforts that unwittingly opened up possibilities for male workers to contest industrialist policies. In chapter 16 Michael Roper investigates the ambivalently gendered masculine subjectivity of young British soldiers writing to their mothers during the First World War in letters that speak both of manly self-assertion and of less straightforwardly masculine obedience to a moral code of self-diminution. The chapters in this part draw on different theoretical approaches ranging from psychoanalysis to a discourse analysis that emphasises the importance of the appropriation of discourse 'at the juncture between the world of the text and the world of the subject'.[5] They are united, however, by a historical perspective on the compulsive retelling of narratives of masculinity – narratives that never manage to perfectly construct male subjects after their own image.

Notes

1 J. W. Scott, 'Gender: A useful category of historical analysis', *American Historical Review*, 91 (1986), 1053–75.

2 B. Anderson, *Imagined Communities: Reflections on the Origins and Spread of Nationalism* (London and New York, 1991).

3 R. W. Connell, *Masculinities* (Cambridge, 1995), pp. 76–86.

4 K. Canning, 'Feminist history after the linguistic turn: Historicizing discourse and experience', *Signs*, 19 (1994), 368–404.

5 R. Chartier, *Cultural History Between Practices and Representation* (Cambridge, 1988), p. 11.

PART I

*Masculinities in politics and war:
introductions*

1

Masculinity in politics and war in the age of democratic revolutions, 1750–1850

Stefan Dudink and Karen Hagemann

I N 1832 Carl von Clausewitz's *Vom Kriege* (On War) was published. In this treatise the Prussian general argued that war was but an extension of politics by other means. As Clausewitz had died from cholera the previous year, the work appeared posthumously with an introduction by his widow, Marie von Clausewitz, born Countess of Brühl. Modestly, Marie von Clausewitz began by stating that bewilderment at the fact that a female hand dared to preface a work of such nature was entirely justified. However, she asked for her writing and involvement in the publication of her husband's book to be excused. He had not wished to publish the book during his lifetime, she claimed, but had wanted her to do so after his death. Even so, it had taken the persuasion of friends to convince her that Clausewitz's words made it her duty to overcome timidity and to introduce his book to the world.[1] The combined forces of marital obligation, polite society's opinion, and duty had to be invoked for the widow to write an introduction to a book on politics and war – an introduction she partly devoted to apologies for having written it.

Marie von Clausewitz's verbal manoeuvres tell us a lot about the definitions of respectable, aristocratic womanhood in Restoration Prussia. They also tell of masculinity, albeit in a less direct manner. Whereas femininity had to be mentioned explicitly for it to be distanced from war and politics, the masculinity of these latter two domains was quietly assumed. The manly nature of politics and war seemed to require no outspoken confirmation, once the fact that they were not feminine domains was established. This, of course, is something of a pattern in modern history. The exclusion of femininity and women from politics and war produces explicitly gendered discussion, whereas the presence of men and masculinity in these realms is not represented in similarly gendered terms. The essays in this collection address the masculinity of

3

politics and war in modern history. They aim to bring to the surface and unravel masculinity's relations with politics and war, relations that often took on a quality of such self-evidence that masculinity needed not even to be mentioned.

Giving masculinity a history

Let us stay with Clausewitz for a while to see how we might bring masculinity to the surface of history and explore its relations with politics and war. A closer look at *Vom Kriege* makes clear to what extent masculinity was absent from its pages and in what sense it was present. The fame of Clausewitz's work rests on the matter of fact, detached treatment of its subject. *Vom Kriege* was written in a philosophical style that gained it the reputation of being 'realist', in the sense of not being concerned with the moral aspects of war. But the avoidance of moral considerations was not the only rhetorical strategy that underpinned the work's realism. Heroism too was, in a way, absent from the pages of *Vom Kriege*. Clausewitz did write about courage, but he did so in order to dissect it as one of the constitutive elements of war and its operations. This 'objectification' of martial qualities distanced the language of *Vom Kriege* from a discourse on war that sang heroism's praises and emphatically invoked manliness in the process. The modern theory of war acquired its coolly distanced tone of voice by partly renouncing the excited and excitable talk of manly honour, valour, courage, and glory.

It was in the midst of such talk, however, that Clausewitz first expressed his views on the changing nature of war. In 1812, twenty years before the publication of *Vom Kriege*, he had already presented the ideas that were later to form the core of his magnum opus. He then presented them to a Prussian nation engaged in debates over the political and military reforms required to defeat the armies of the French Empire that had so deeply humiliated Prussia. Although strongly divided over the kind of reforms needed, most participants in these discussions brought up the issue of masculinity in their proposals for national regeneration. The humiliation suffered at the hands of the French – presented as a loss of male honour – had to be avenged and the redemption of the nation's masculinity was seen as the precondition for bringing this about. Clausewitz himself became involved in a project of military reform that aimed at a mutual rapprochement of nation and military and also was intended to find an answer to the strategic innovations introduced by the French. In an attempt to make both service in the military more attractive and to introduce the flexibility and mobility that had made the French troops so successful, reformers like Clausewitz set about to modernise notions of soldiering in the Prussian military. Arguing against excessive drill and violently enforced discipline, these reformers propagated an idea of the soldier as an individual with a responsibility of his own, who would fight independently, flexibly and out of intrinsic motivation. In this view manly, individual honour was no longer the prerogative of officers, but also belonged to the common soldier.[2] This was one project among many of recreating a valorous masculinity for the Prussian nation. What is important here, is that the language of masculinity that was so vital to the period of the anti-Napoleonic wars was echoed, some twenty years later, amidst the more sober sentences of *Vom Kriege*. Although we find Clausewitz there referring coolly to military virtue as an 'instrument the power of which one can calculate', we also see him describe this virtue in terms reminiscent of the glorification of masculinity of earlier years. Military virtue was alive, he wrote, in an army 'that has strengthened its physical powers like the muscles of an athlete by practicing deprivation and exertion, that looks at such efforts as a means to achieve victory and not as a curse'.[3] Or we find him speak analytically of audacity as an element in 'the dynamic system of forces' of war, but also valuing it as 'the most noble virtue, the true steel that lends the weapons their sharpness and their shine'.[4]

It is not only in the interstices of an apparently sanitised language of war that manly qualities and virtues reappeared. We also find them at work in the discourses that shaped the socio-political realities Clausewitz aimed to explain. Clausewitz understood, like other people in his time, that war in modern times was waged between nation-states. No longer the exclusive concern of governments and armies, war, he claimed, had since the French Revolution become the business of the nation at large. What the Revolution had done was to make war the affair 'of a people numbering thirty millions, every one of whom regarded himself as a citizen of the State'.[5] The effect of this, Clausewitz wrote, was that no definite limits existed any more to the resources that could be used in war and to the energy with which it could be waged. Clausewitz described this transformation of war that 'liberated it from its conventional limitations' and 'brought it closer to its absolute form', as having its origins in the *political* transformations of the French Revolution.[6] As such this analysis served to underscore Clausewitz's insistence on the unity of politics and war: 'war is an instrument of politics; it necessarily carries its mark'.[7]

At the heart of all of this was Clausewitz's recognition of the increasing entwinement of state and nation since the French Revolution. What is crucial to our interests here is that the processes in which nation and state got entwined were thoroughly gendered. Masculinity in particular was deployed in the various political and military projects that aimed at building the modern nation and at opening up the institutions of the state and of political life to this newly imagined collective entity. The fatherland-loving citizen who self-assuredly demanded to be represented in government; the invocation of the category of the 'people' as sole and supreme source of political sovereignty; the nation claiming the right to self-determination; the national armies created to defend the nation against its adversaries – all of these inventions, that were central to the rise of political modernity, were crafted from materials that invariably included masculinity. If a claim to autonomy – of the citizen, the people, and the nation – was what connected these inventions, masculinity was the trope recurrently invoked to articulate this claim. By the time *Vom Kriege* was written the work of masculinity in helping shape the modern categories of politics and war had been so successful that Clausewitz could make the nation-state, its sovereignty and its will to preserve its independence the central propositions of his book – and no longer explicitly relate them to masculinity.

The chapters in this volume are intended to do more, however, than bring to the surface the part of masculinity in politics and war where it has been elided. They aim to give masculinity a history by analysing, as Mrinalini Sinha puts it, 'its rhetorical and ideological efficacy in underwriting various arrangements of power'.[8] In other words, in addition to pointing out masculinity's part in politics and war, the essays ask *why* masculinity played this part. That question situates the history of masculinity in struggles over power, over claims to political and other forms of authority and legitimacy that were made in gendered terms.[9] This is a history that tries to capture masculinity as it is harnessed to establish, change or defend relations of power. Such a history investigates masculinity's various incarnations by asking which constructions of masculinity were efficacious in underwriting arrangements of power, and which ones were not. What masculinities were invoked, produced, discarded in shaping the autonomy of modern citizens, peoples, and nations? And what relations of power were established, or contested, in this process? These are questions which should follow analyses that show that masculinity was present where at first sight it appeared not to be. They are questions that move beyond establishing masculinity's presence; they give this presence a history.

Politics and war

There are good reasons for no longer adopting the precise formulae
Clausewitz used to write about the relation of politics and war in modern
times. There is too much Hegelian idealism in the statement that the
nature of war is determined by the nature of politics for it to still ring
true. To say that war shapes politics, or to claim that war and politics
are both manifestations of a continuous struggle for power that is
society, sounds more 'realist' these days. But the insight that war and
politics have been relatively inseparable is as important as ever for
understanding modern history, and it is crucial for understanding the
history of masculinity. Many aspects of modern masculinity were forged
in the nexus of politics and war. At the same time the interrelated
nature of politics and war in modern history cannot be properly understood if we do not take into account masculinity's part in establishing
and maintaining this relation.

The 'age of democratic revolutions' ushered in an era in which
major political transformations were preceded by, resulted from, or ended
in war. Not only did war and politics become firmly connected in modern
history, as 'the people' entered the stage of political and military history
their relation changed profoundly, a change closely bound up with –
transformations of – masculinity. Let us examine some of these relations
and developments in more detail as they appeared in the revolution/war
that stands at the beginning of the period covered in this book: the
American Revolution.

War and politics were inseparable in the American Revolution. The
establishment of both national independence and a democratic republic
depended on the outcome of the war with Britain. In turn, that war
itself seemed to embody the political innovations at stake in the conflict. This was – from the perspective of the American colonists – a
'people's war', involving an unprecedented mobilisation of large parts
of the emergent nation against the standing army and mercenaries of
a monarch.

Paradoxically, it was a pre- and early-modern configuration of
politics, war, and masculinity that was at the heart of this first 'modern'
war. The American revolutionaries spoke the language of classic republicanism as it was preserved and reworked in Renaissance and early-
modern Europe. They waged their revolution in the name of, and
fashioned themselves after the model of, the virtuous citizen-soldier
who was willing to sacrifice all for his liberty and that of his republic.[10]
In chapter 4 of this volume Carroll Smith-Rosenberg argues that this

manly political ideal was central to late eighteenth-century European Americans' sense of self and shaped their national identity far into the nineteenth century. Establishing both European Americans' superiority to and continued connection to the mother country, classic republicanism forged the new nation's self image. It was also at the heart of the instability that would characterise this self image as other conflicting political, economic and social discourses – liberalism, fiscal capitalism, gentility – began to intersect with and destabilise classic republicanism's manly political subjectivity.

In keeping with republican notions, the War of Independence was partly fought by militias of volunteers that performed their duties as citizens by becoming soldiers. The militias were important in securing victory for the revolutionaries, in particular when the war became one of guerrilla skirmishes as it did in the South.[11] But the local amateur militias could not win the war by themselves. One of the first decisions of the Second Continental Congress of 1775 was to create a 'Continental Army'. This met with considerable resistance, for in republican thought a standing army figured as the mainspring of tyranny and corruption. Initially, Congress intended the Continental Army to be an army of volunteers, but as the war continued it found itself forced to assent to short-term conscription. Drafting poor men, indentured servants, British deserters and slaves into its ranks, the Continental Army became not exactly a model of manly virtue and independence. In fact, it partly relied on men that most of the time were not even eligible for militia membership.[12] The republican language of the virtuous citizen-soldier retained its prominence in encouraging Americans to take up arms and to justify the war. But the means by which the new United States fought that war had begun to differ dramatically from the militias prescribed in this language.

If we want to chart masculinity's place in the intersection of politics and war of the American Revolution, the first thing to note is the multiplicity of masculinities produced in and productive of this intersection. The republican masculinity of the militias centred around a masculinity of independence that connected the individual citizen to the collective activities of politics and war at the same time that it linked these two activities. The independence of the citizen was guaranteed by his – landed – property. His independence guaranteed that of the militias, and these in turn fought for the liberty and independence of the republic alone and did not obey corrupted and enslaving tyrants. A manly independence stood at the centre of a republican universe that knew of no strict boundaries between individual and collective virtue, or between politics and war. The revolutionaries routinely compared this virtuousness of the militiamen with the corruption of British soldiers, they praised the formers' 'manly spirit' and ridiculed the effeminacy and delicacy of British officers.[13] Critics of the militia feared, however, that what appeared, as manly independence was in fact an unruliness that posed a threat to both effective military organisation and political order. In 1776 George Washington, great advocate of the Continental Army and its first commander, complained that militiamen were 'accustomed to unbounded freedom and no control' and refused to submit to 'the restraint which is indispensably necessary to the good order and government of any army, without which licentiousness and . . . disorder triumphantly reign'.[14] That there was a political side to this unruliness had been demonstrated 1775 when citizen-soldiers in Massachusetts began to question the decisions and authority of the provincial Congress – prompting the Massachusetts Congress to place its armed forces under the control of the Continental Congress.[15] This was a masculinity of disorder and unruliness that had to be disciplined and taught hierarchy and obedience. In this view, manly independence remained indispensable to the revolution, but it was not a quality that, in its desirable form, could simply be presumed to exist in American citizens. Rather, it had to be instilled into them by the state and the military. The decision to introduce conscription even further undermined republican notions of manly independence. The servants, slaves, and poor, coerced to serve in the Continental Army, could be forced to do so precisely because they lacked independence. And yet the independence and liberty of the republic relied as much on them as it did on the manly virtue of the archetypal republican freeholder.

Clearly there were various masculinities at work at the intersection of politics and war of the American Revolution. Equally important as the fact of masculinity's multiplicity, is the way these masculinities were bound up with changing relations of power or attempts to effect such changes. The war between the colonisers and Britain, the struggle among the colonisers over the form of military organisation appropriate to a free republic, the debates over the desirable nature of citizens' sense of independence – in all of these conflicts different notions of masculinity were invoked and at stake. And in all of them the invocation of masculinity was not a matter of mere rhetoric. Discourses of masculinity had a part in shaping tangible social formations: a newly independent republic and nation-state, its specific military organisation and its political relations of inclusion and exclusion.

The masculinities of universal citizenship and general conscription

Masculinities and the power struggles in which they were deployed multiply when we cross the Atlantic and follow the adventures of the manly citizen as he participated in politics and war in (post-)revolutionary Europe. These masculinities need to be studied in the context of the specific relations of power within which they functioned and we have to identify the cultural idioms in which they were framed. This is, of course, an appropriate strategy to historicise gender in general. But it is especially relevant here because of the universalism that began to pervade notions of masculinity, and of masculinity in politics and war in particular, in this period.

In the Dutch Republic local revolutionaries presented the militias of their American colleagues as commendable examples.[16] During the early 1780s the so-called Patriot movement began to oppose the Prince of Orange, whom it accused of usurping power that was not rightfully his. In truly republican style, Patriots propagated the establishment of militias in order to defend liberty against its internal and external enemies and they pointed to the American experience as proof of their convictions. In 1785 John Adams, serving as American ambassador to the Netherlands, wrote in a letter home that the situation in the Republic reminded him of the revolution of 1775. The Patriot party, he wrote, 'views America with a venerating partiality, and so much attached are they to our opposition, that they seem fond of imitating us where-ever they can, and of drawing parallels between the similar circumstances in the two countries'.[17]

Although in many respects traditionally republican, the political discourse of the Dutch Patriot movement also contained elements of a more modern and universalising language of rights and popular sovereignty. The success of the Patriot call to establish militias partly rested on the fact that the militias fitted well into the traditional corporate order of the Dutch Republic. The Patriots appealed to a tradition of citizens carrying arms to protect their towns and villages, and they referred to old and established local and corporate privileges when they tried to form militias against the wishes of the authorities.[18] On the other hand they increasingly spoke of the sovereignty of the people and its natural rights – a language that was closer to a political theory of universal rights than to republicanism's reliance on specific, local and historic rights and privileges.[19]

As Stefan Dudink shows in chapter 5, two divergent notions of masculinity were involved in this tension between traditional republicanism and modern ideas about natural rights and sovereignty. In republican thought masculinity was a precarious disposition that could easily slide into effeminacy and was just as vulnerable to corruption and decay as the republic itself. In the universalising language of sovereignty and natural rights, masculinity appeared as a more secure category, for it was no longer conceived of as intertwined with republicanism's cycles of rise and fall, but with linear historical progress. At the same time masculinity became, in a way, less visible as it began to reside in seemingly gender-neutral concepts like 'citizen of the state' and 'the people'.

[margin handwritten: Men are the norm / the default person]

The Patriot revolution was crushed by the Prince of Orange and his allies in 1787. The democratic experiment would be continued in the Netherlands only after the invasion of French revolutionary troops in 1795. In France from 1789 onward, French revolutionaries introduced new politics and policies that both drew on established ideas about masculinity and would profoundly change them. 'All men are citizens', the leaders of the French Revolution proclaimed. And as France, from 1793 on, got further and further entangled in war with its neighbours, this proclamation of equal citizenship was followed by another one: 'because all men are citizens all men should be soldiers'.

Universal male citizenship and general conscription – and the exclusion of women from them – were vital in making sexual difference a prime difference. These institutions attributed masculinity – and the rights and duties it conferred upon the individual – to all men. As such they helped to make sexual difference *the* difference that surpassed class, regional, religious, and racial differences. As Joan Landes points out in chapter 6, universal male suffrage made it possible for men to enter into relations of equality with other men, with whom they up until that moment only enjoyed relations of superiority or inferiority. At the same time the conflation of male citizenship and military service increasingly virilised masculinity, differentiating it ever more emphatically from femininity. Universal male citizenship and general conscription changed, in the words of André Rauch, 'the masculine condition'.[20]

It is important to see, however, that this was a condition born out of specific political and military circumstances and assembled out of specific cultural materials. As a consequence this masculinity was equally contextually defined – despite a universalising language of nature that had increasingly been invoked in these years to explain and legitimise sexual difference. A closer look at the French and Prussian histories of citizenship and conscription of this period, and a cursory glance at the British experience, shows just how much the new masculine condition differed from place to place, despite the universalising logics of political and military institutions and of ideologies of natural sexual difference.

Both French revolutionaries and Prussian reformers were greatly impressed by the military powers unleashed by the participation of citizens in the American War of Independence.[21] And after their unpleasant encounters with the force of French revolutionary armies, the Prussians had every reason to think of France as both an adversary and an example. Nevertheless, the mutual rapprochement of nation and military took on very different forms on either side of the Rhine – as did the masculinities produced in the process. In 1798 the second Directory introduced conscription as a permanent institution for all unmarried men of ages of twenty to twenty-five. This system of conscription remained in force, with minor adjustments, throughout the Napoleonic years. Before 1798 the successive revolutionary governments had tried their hand at recruiting soldiers by means ranging from calling upon volunteers to the famous *levée en masse* of 1793, but in the end the hunger for new recruits could no longer be stilled by these means.[22]

What is crucial here, is that at the beginning of this road to a forced integration of male citizens into the military stood the 1789 Declaration of (universal) Rights of Man and Citizen. That Declaration had, despite persisting forms of exclusion, opened up the state to the nation's male citizens on an unprecedented scale. In other words: political and civic rights had come before military duties. Large groups of men remained excluded from the full enjoyment of these rights and revolutionary governments after 1793 became ever less generous in this respect. Still, both the pervasive ideological presence and the legal reality of political and civic rights profoundly affected the introduction of general military service. It allowed for a generalisation of the idea of the citizen-soldier, the idea of a male citizen willing to fight and sacrifice for the political community of which he is a full member. It enabled the transformation of this early-modern 'most authoritative fantasy of masculinity' into the modern reality of million's of men's lives.[23]

This reality was always partly state-enforced, and would be so in particular after the introduction of conscription in 1798. The history of draft evasion and of desertion from the revolutionary and Napoleonic armies speaks clearly of the less than voluntary aspects of soldiering during the Revolution and Empire, and so does the history of state repression that followed such attempts to escape conscription.[24] Nevertheless, the notion of fighting voluntarily because one is a full citizen of a revolutionary republic, had for many become synonymous with the revolutionary ideal. As such it was a powerful ideological tool that revolutionaries, describing as volunteers men that been drafted into uniform, even used to legitimise conscription, once the reservoir of volunteers had dried up.[25] Moreover, the idea of the revolutionary citizen-soldier was never just an ideological tool. The representation of the invincible revolutionary armies, consisting solely of zealous and brave believers in liberty, equality and fraternity is undoubtedly mythological. Nevertheless, the presence of a good number of educated revolutionaries and patriotic enthusiasts, as well as the possibility of promotion from the ranks on the basis of merit does account for a part of the success of the revolutionary armies.

Whether reduced to a mere instrument of ideology, or written into soldiers' subjectivity, the discourse of the citizen-soldier revolved around a new and powerful notion of masculinity. This was a masculinity of radical citizenship, defined by an identification with a revolutionary state that was at the same time embodied by this self-same masculinity. In Norman Bryson's words: 'In post-Revolutionary France the state is no longer figured in the king, but in the male body itself, and the body's destiny for glory or defeat is that of the nation as a whole.'[26] This was a masculinity produced in the osmosis of revolutionary state and male citizen, an osmosis that shaped one in the image of the other.[27]

A very different masculinity was produced in the dynamics between the Prussian state and its able-bodied male population, as Prussia looked for ways to counter the military supremacy of France. Three decrees, proclaimed between February 1813 and September 1814, introduced universal conscription and extended it into peacetime. They resulted in what was the most rigid system of conscription in Europe. Whereas the French conscription laws eventually allowed conscripts to 'buy' a substitute, the Prussian regulations continued to rule this out altogether.[28] Conscription in Prussia was a radical affair, that, shaped by military considerations, mirrored the French example and developed it even further.[29]

The universal nature of conscription produced an unprecedented equality between the conscripts from various religious and socio-economic backgrounds – an equality that went against the hierarchical nature of Prussian society. Furthermore, the stress on military duties threatened to make the logic of a necessary link between such duties and political rights enter Prussian political debate. It seemed the Prussian government had unwittingly imported dangerously radical policies into a traditional social order. The army reformers that had pressed for conscription to be introduced were aware of this, but were also clear about their intentions and priorities. For them conscription, and the modernisation of the army in general, were not in any sense political projects. These were exclusively military undertakings, aimed at increasing the military power of the Prussian monarchy. Political reforms in terms of an extension of civic and political rights were not part of the Prussian integration of the male population into the military. The granting of civic and political rights was at the most considered as a means to achieve the patriotic-national mobilisation that was required by the 'people's war' the military reformers aimed for. They were aware that only in this kind of war they would be able to defeat France and its mass armies. This was an integration into the military – and not into a monarchical state.

In Britain the threat and challenge of the French revolutionary armies and Napoleon's empire was met in a different way. The distrust of standing armies among American rebels and continental radicals had its ideological home in Britain. The introduction of universal conscription was out of the question. Nevertheless, after 1789 the British armed forces grew 'at a faster rate than those of any other European power'.[30] Relying to a great extent on men volunteering to serve in the regular army and navy and in volunteer corps, as well as requiring men to serve in the so-called militia, the British state managed to realise an unprecedented mass mobilisation. A 'cult of heroic endeavour and aggressive maleness', that flourished among the upper classes, resounded in propaganda aimed at the lower social strata and in popular ballads and songs.[31] The authorities were aware of the risks of calling upon men from all classes, political backgrounds, regions, and religious denominations to defend the country. They knew demands for political rights were likely to follow from this and indeed they did. Demands for the extension of male suffrage, that would eventually result in the 1832 Reform Act, were all couched in the language of patriotism, a language that large segments of the nation had been taught during the preparation for war against France.[32]

Whereas in France male citizens had entered both the state and the military – allowing for an identity of male citizen and state – in Prussia men were integrated into the military only. That did not make them citizens, but reinforced their status as duty-bound subjects of the King. The realm into which they were welcomed, and where authoritative fantasies of masculinity were to be cultivated, was that of the nation. A German nation was still far from a 'fully articulated' political category and practice and masculinity was to have an important role in making it so.[33] A masculinity of duty, loyal service and sacrifice helped to articulate and shape this vision of a monarchical nation, ultimately embodied by the King.[34]

The realm of the nation also harboured masculinities that were less content with the place they were allotted in this order of things. The army reformers had not been the only ones to argue for a revival of a martial spirit in German men. Civilians had contributed to this discourse as well. In their view the valorous masculinity they aimed to revive was not to be institutionalised in the military, but in militias, that is in civil forms of military organisation. Presenting the war against France as a people's war, these men did locate a valorous masculinity in the realm of the nation, but they also claimed a place for this masculinity in the state. And although they continued to think of the state as monarchic, they did call for an extension of political and civic rights. This was a valorous, civic masculinity that was located in the nation *and* demanded to be represented in the state. It was more and more pushed to the margins of the Prussian discourse on military reforms after the 1813 introduction of general conscription and the final victory over Napoleon in 1815. However, it remained a presence in Prussian and German political history where it would be at the heart of the struggles for the extension of political rights to wider circles of educated and propertied men. In chapter 7 in this volume Karen Hagemann points to the importance of distinguishing between the civilian concept of 'civic valour' and the military notion of 'combat readiness'. She makes clear that from the early nineteenth century on the civilian and the military concepts existed side-by-side and competed. Only in the course of the nineteenth century, and in particular after 1870, did the militarised version assert itself more and more and did a militarised masculinity become hegemonic in Germany.

Masculinity, revolution, war: 1848 and beyond

The European revolutions of 1848/49 make a good case for distinguishing between various forms of masculinity-in-arms and their political uses.[35] Kept alive by liberal politicians and intellectuals who criticised the results of the military reforms and the introduction of conscription, the idea of an armed male citizenry re-emerged in Germany during the 1848 revolution. Members of the Frankfurt parliament argued for the right of German men to carry arms in order to protect both themselves and the fatherland and, in a familiar move, wanted to extend this right to every German man, thus including all men and excluding women from the new democratic political order they envisaged.[36] In the spring of 1848 various German states allowed the establishment of civic militias in an attempt to prevent a radicalisation of the revolution. Opened up to a certain degree to men from lower social strata, these militias were considered by the revolutionaries as guarantees of political and civic liberty and by the authorities as means to channel and control more radical revolutionary demands. In this latter respect they were not always successful, as 'unofficial' militias of labourers, apprentices, and students were created and got into conflict with the police, the military and, sometimes, the established militias. During the late summer and fall of 1848 the counter-revolution set in and militias were either dissolved or their function was limited to policing public order. As revolutionaries resorted to violence in 1849 to get the constitution the Frankfurt parliament had adopted implemented, their troops did not stand a chance against the regular armies they faced. With the repression of the revolution came the end of the militias. The German governments put a stop to the experiments with the militias, and chose to further rely on their armies and police forces.[37] This course of events affected the balance of power between various forms of masculinity-in-arms. In the German states the outcome of the 1848 revolution was an important step on the path toward hegemonic status for a militarised masculinity that had been contending for this status with its civil, valorous brother since the start of the age of democratic revolutions.

In none of the countries where revolution broke out in 1848–49 were revolutionaries successful in seizing state power. Everywhere the representatives of the old regimes reappeared after longer or shorter periods of revolutionary government. A crucial element in the lack of success of the 1848–49 revolutions was the revolutionaries' inability to gain power over the regular military or to build up sufficiently strong troops of their own. From Krakow to Naples, from Paris to Vienna – everywhere revolutionaries were defeated by well armed regular troops that had remained loyal to their governments. Even in Hungary, where the revolutionary government did manage to both build up a sizeable people's army and succeeded in gaining control of the regular troops, the revolution was in the end defeated when Russian troops came to the aid of the Austrian military.[38] This did not mean that a militarised masculinity became the hegemonic model of masculinity in all of these countries in the same way and to the same extent that it did in Germany. After all, not all of them had previously gone through processes of mass mobilisation of the same intensity and scale as had appeared in Prussia. What it did mean was that European states had gradually managed in the years after the fall of Napoleon to undo a highly gendered revolutionary invention – the integration of great numbers of male citizens into the state's military apparatus – of its subversive potential. After the involvement of the military in the July Revolution of 1830, French governments had begun to deliberately depoliticise the military and to increase the distance between army and society by making the former more professional. In 1848 the troops and their officers had no part in revolutionary activities and neither did they hesitate to protect Louis-Napoleon against the insurrection of June 1849.[39] In Prussia the system of conscription continued to be more rigidly enforced than it had in France, even though only a small percentage of all young men liable for military service were drafted. Here too in 1849–49, the military proved thoroughly reliable, at least from the point of view of the conservative forces, during the years of revolution.[40]

If the revolutions of 1848–49 spelled the end for the revolutionary citizen-soldier and showed that the unruly potential of the conscript had been tamed, they did also produce new models of masculine political subjectivity among disgruntled liberals, socialists, and nationalists. These were to cast their shadows over the political history of the nineteenth and early twentieth century, in often-violent confrontations that resulted from another element of the outcome of 1848–49. Modern regular armies had proved capable of defeating any revolutionary movement. This suggested an inversion of the relation between revolution and war that had been established by the French Revolution and that had inspired Clausewitz's famous *dictum*. War did no longer necessarily follow revolution as it had after 1789; the great European war many had feared did not materialise in 1848. The revolutionaries were defeated in small-scale civil wars. In the future, as Jonathan Sperber puts it: 'Revolutions could succeed – or even break out – only when the repressive force of the army had been shattered by military defeat. Henceforth, it was not revolution that would lead to war, but defeat in war that would lead to revolution.'[41] After 1848 Europe's modern national armies, established through strongly gendered discourses and co-producers of a universalising discourse of sexual difference, became the pillars of social and political order. If anything, this made masculinity an even more political and contested category. Both conservative and reactionary forces and liberal, socialist and nationalist movements attempted to appropriate masculinity for themselves.[42] Revolution under these circumstances unleashed a dynamic of politicised masculinity that proved hard to control, as the revolutionary aftermath of the First World War in Germany showed. There military defeat and the break up of social and political order were, more emphatically than before, experienced as a crisis of the gender order and of masculinity in particular. Several of the political projects born out of this perceived crisis of socio-political order/masculinity centred around an ostentatiously virile masculinity to which a near magical power to restore order and to reinvigorate society was attributed. This appeared most dramatically in the infamous right-wing free-corps and in the ideology of *Männerbünde* that pervaded both right- and left-wing political movements.[43] On the left equally formidable powers, albeit to destroy the forces of reaction, were attributed to hyper-masculinity, most graphically represented on socialist and communist election posters in the enormous and muscular allegorical body of the worker, crushing his opponents. By the early twentieth century masculinity had become a hyperbolic political category, both invested with enormous power and the object of intense struggles for power.

Conclusion

The rise of political and military modernity since 1750 intersected again and again with the history of masculinity that, in various guises, helped to produce, as much as it was itself shaped by, new configurations of state and society, politics and war. It might be tempting to think of the years between 1750 and 1850 as a period in which citizenship was masculinised and masculinity became militarised. It is equally tempting to think of this constellation of masculinity, politics and war as a central gender structure of modern, Western society.[44] In a sense this is true. Both successful democratic revolutions and the ones that failed withheld full citizenship from women and established political equality between men; conscription did become the dominant model of military recruitment, and conscription and the right to citizenship were often – if only ideologically – connected. But it is true only if we ignore the differences between the various ways men were integrated into states, militaries and nations, and if we close our eyes to the divergent masculinities that were deployed and produced in the process. To claim that a joint masculinisation of citizenship and militarisation of masculinity are crucial structural features of the history of gender in modernity, is in a way to repeat a mistake that historians of the labour movement and class have for some time now repaired in their field. It is to make one historical trajectory – the French – central and to project this onto other countries. Prussia (rigid conscription, no political rights) and Britain (no universal conscription, initially no political rights) represent other trajectories and other constructions of masculinity in politics and war. What the claim concerning a joint masculinisation of citizenship and militarisation of masculinity also does is to reproduce, rather than critically analyse, the ideological work of masculinity in discourses of universal citizenship and general conscription. The construction of masculinity as a universal category, as a biological given that transcended differences of class, religion, region et cetera, was a powerful ideological asset for political and military projects that aimed at mass mobilisation. But it would be wrong to confuse masculinity's ideological work in such projects with their outcomes.[45] Citizenship was not masculinised to the same extent and it the same way everywhere – and the same thing holds true for the militarisation of masculinity.

The chapters in this book analyse masculinity's work in various political and military projects. They do not reify the nation or privilege the nation as *the* context for writing political and military history. Quite a few actually focus on the construction of the nation through masculinity and several of them investigate the connections and interdependencies in which the seemingly autonomous entity of the nation is embedded. They do highlight, however, the specific and con-textual nature of the military and political projects to the realisation of which masculinity was marshalled and the divergent faces masculinity acquired in the process. They do so because that seems to be a sound intellectual strategy to understand 'universal' masculinity's ideological work in politics and war without getting entangled in it.

Notes

1   C. von Clausewitz, *Vom Kriege: Hinterlassenes Werk* (Berlin, 1999, reprint), p. 13.

2   For Clausewitz's early work see K. Hagemann, *'Mannlicher Muth und Teutsche Ehre': Nation, Militär und Geschlecht zur Zeit der Antinapoleonischen Kriege Preußens* (Paderborn, 2002), pp. 272–4. For the debates over military reforms and the various notions of masculinity involved in them see *ibid.*, pp. 73–96, 304–50; and U. Frevert, *Die kasernierte Nation: Militärdienst und Zivilgesellschaft in Deutschland* (München, 2001), pp. 18–62.

3   Clausewitz, *Vom Kriege*, p. 170 (our translation, SD, KH).

4   *Ibid.*, p. 173.

5   *Ibid.*, p. 667.

6   *Ibid.*, pp. 669, 690.

7   *Ibid.*, p. 690.

8   M. Sinha, 'Giving masculinity a history: Some contributions from the historiography of colonial India', *Gender & History*, 11 (1999), 455.

9   J. W. Scott, 'Gender: A useful category of historical analysis', *American Historical Review*, 91 (1986), 1053–75.

10 J. G. A. Pocock, *The Machiavellian Moment: Florentine Political Thought and the Atlantic Tradition* (Princeton and London, 1975), pp. 506–52; G. S. Wood, *The Radicalism of the American Revolution* (New York, 1992), pp. 95–225.

11 J. Black, *War for America: The Fight for Independence* (Phoenix Mill, 1991), p. 42–3, 56.

12 D. Higginbotham, *The War of American Independence: Military Attitudes, Policies, and Practice, 1763–1789* (New York, 1971), p. 12; P. T. Manicas, *War and Democracy* (Cambridge MA, Oxford, 1989), pp. 103–6.

13 M. E. Kann, *A Republic of Men: The American Founders, Gendered Language, and Patriarchal Politics* (New York and London, 1998), pp. 69–70.

14 G. Washington, 'Letter to Congress, 24 September 1776', quoted in *ibid.*, p. 71.

15 Higginbotham, *War of American Independence*, p. 83.

16 J. W. Schulte Nordholt, *Voorbeeld in de verte: De invloed van de Amerikaanse revolutie in Nederland* (Baarn, 1979), pp. 242–4.

17 J. Adams to A. Lee, 4 September 1785, quoted in *ibid.*, p. 244.

18 M. Prak, *Republikeinse veelheid, democratische enkelvoud: Sociale verandering in het revolutietijdvak, 's-Hertogenbosch 1770–1820* (Nijmegen, 1999), pp. 149–72.

19 S. R. E. Klein, *Patriots Republikanisme: Politieke cultuur in Nederland 1766–1787* (Amsterdam, 1995), pp. 76–88, 195–223.

20 A. Rauch, *Crise de l'identité masculine, 1789–1914* (Paris, 2000), p. 48; J. Landes, see below, p. 97.

21 Both Lafayette and the military reformer A. N. von Gneisenau had fought – on opposite sides – in the American War of Independence. See G. Best, *War and Society in Revolutionary Europe 1770–1870* (London, 1982), p. 54.

22 For overviews of the French road to conscription see: *ibid.*, pp. 77–91; A. Forrest, *The Soldiers of the French Revolution* (Durham and London, 1990), pp. 58–88 and J.-P. Bertaud, *La Révolution armée: Les soldate-citoyens et la Révolution française* (Paris, 1979).

23 The phrase 'most authoritative fantasy of masculinity' is John Barrell's, who used it to denote early eighteenth-century British civic humanism. See J. Barrell, *The Birth of Pandora and the Division of Knowledge* (London, 1992), p. 64.

24 A. Forrest, *Conscripts and Deserters: The Army and French Society during the Revolution and Empire* (New York and Oxford, 1989).

25 Forrest, *Soldiers*, p. 67.

26 N. Bryson, 'Géricault and "Masculinity"', in N. Bryson, M. A. Holly and K. Moxey (eds), *Visual Culture: Images and Interpretations* (Hannover and London, 1994), p. 247.

27 For the political meanings invested in the male body during the French revolution see: T. Crow, *Emulation: Making Artists for Revolutionary France* (New Haven and London, 1995); D. Outram, *The Body and the French Revolution: Sex, Class and Political Culture* (New Haven and London, 1989); A. Potts, 'Beautiful bodies and dying heroes', *History Workshop*, 30 (1990), 1–21; A. Solomon-Godeau, *Male Trouble: A Crisis in Representation* (London and New York, 1997).

28 Forrest, *Soldiers*, pp. 84–5.

29 Hagemann, *'Mannlicher Muth'*, pp. 75–91.

30 L. Colley, *Britons: Forging the Nation 1707–1873* (New Haven and London, 1992), pp. 286–7.

31 *Ibid.*, p. 303.

32 *Ibid.*, pp. 318–19, 334–50.

33 The term is Geoff Eley's, who stresses 'the inchoateness and non-fixity of national meanings and identifications in the nineteenth century' and offers several insights into gender's role in solidifying such meanings and identifications. See G. Eley, 'Culture, nation and gender', in I. Blom, K. Hagemann and C. Hall (eds), *Gendered Nations: Nationalisms and Gender Order in the Long Nineteenth Century* (Oxford and New York, 2000), pp. 27–40.

34 K. Hagemann, 'Of "Manly Valor" and "German Honor": Nation, war and masculinity in the age of the Prussian uprising against Napoleon', *Central European History*, 30 (1997), 187–220.

35 For recent overviews of the events of 1848–49 see W. J. Mommsen, *1848: Die ungewollte Revolution* (Frankfurt am Main, 1998); J. Sperber, *The European Revolutions, 1848–1851* (Cambridge, 1994). From the perspective of women's and gender history see B. Caine and G. Sluga, *Gendering European History 1780–1920* (London and New York, 2000), pp. 75–83.

36 Frevert, *Kasernierte Nation*, pp. 158–9. For an analysis of the claim for male citizens to carry arms as part of the creation of 'institutionalized male political spaces' during the revolutions of 1848–49 see G. Hauch, 'Did Women Have a Revolution? Gender Battles in the European Revolution of 1848/49', in A. Körner (ed.), *1848: A European Revolution? International Ideas and National Memories of 1848* (Houndmills, 2000), pp. 64–81.

37 Frevert, *Kasernierte Nation*, pp. 163–79; R. Pröve, 'Bürgerwehren in den europäischen Revolutionen 1848', in D. Dowe, H.-G. Haupt and D. Langewiesche (eds), *Europa 1848: Revolution und Reform* (Bonn, 1998), pp. 901–14.

38 D. Langewiesche, 'Die Rolle des Militärs in den europäischen Revolutionen von 1848', in Dowe, Haupt, and Langwiesche (eds), *Europa 1848: Revolution und Reform*, pp. 915–32.

39 Best, *War and Society*, pp. 219–21.

40 Frevert, *Kasernierte Nation*, pp. 120–32.

41 Sperber, *European Revolutions*, p. 250.

42 G. L. Mosse, *The Image of Man: The Creation of Modern Masculinity* (New York and Oxford, 1996).

43 N. Sombart, 'Männerbund und Politische Kultur in Deutschland', in T. Kühne (ed.), *Männergeschichte – Geschlechtergeschichte. Männlichkeit im Wandel der Moderne* (Frankfurt and New York, 1996), pp. 136–55; K. Theweleit, *Männerphantasien 1 + 2* (München and Zürich, 2000); Mosse, *Image of Man*, ch. 6.

44 In his analysis of the transformations of European/American hegemonic masculinity over the last two hundred years R. W. Connell calls Clausewitz's *On War* 'a key document' of nineteenth-century masculinity. See R. W. Connell, *Masculinities* (Cambridge, 1995), p. 192.

45 Thembisa Waetjen makes a similar point about the analysis by gender scholars of masculinity's role in nationalism: 'Masculinity may have for gender theory the same metaphoric value it has for nationalism – an overstated cohesion of interest, forces and ideologies.' See T. Waetjen, 'The limits of gender rhetoric for nationalism: A case study from Southern Africa', *Theory and Society*, 30 (2001), 123.

2

Masculinity in politics and war in the age of nation-states and world wars, 1850–1950

John Horne

POLITICS and war are the most traditional fields of historical writing and those used most readily even now to construct the narrative histories that command a wide readership and inform educational programmes. They loom particularly large in the histories of nation-states as these have been written since the eighteenth century. Because politics and war have been the activities of men more than women they are specially suited to exploring the historical nature of masculinity. War and politics turn on issues of power and force. They concern the foundation and maintenance of systems of dominance and the pressures for change that such systems face – pressures that were intense after the late eighteenth-century revolutions. They also involve the cultural representation of dominance – power expressed as authority. Unsurprisingly, war and politics have formed a classic locus for the self-definition of male actors who have seen themselves as bearing power, wielding force, and incarnating authority, whether actual or potential.

Yet because the systems of dominance in question are rarely exclusively or even explicitly concerned with gender, the articulation of masculinity is often indirect. For that reason, as John Tosh argues in chapter 3 of this volume, war and politics offer fertile ground for exploring the notion of 'hegemonic masculinity' as something that concerns more than the power relations of gender, though of course these are central to it. 'Hegemonic masculinity' provides a conceptual tool for examining how other relations of power and authority – racial, colonial, economic, geographic, international – may also be expressed in terms of sexual identity, including antagonistic or subordinate versions of masculinity. The contributions to this volume testify to the value of such an approach.

However, if politics and war illuminate masculinity, the reverse must also be the case. A second purpose of this book is to invite reflection on the ways in which a focus on masculinity might illuminate our understanding of political and military history. The importance of gender lies not only in its own subject matter but also in its ability to cast light on other themes of history and on broader historical synthesis. This essay indicates ways in which the current book points in that direction and suggests some themes for future research.

Power, authority, and the politics of masculine identity

The American and French Revolutions lay at the heart of a process extending to our own day that transformed politics by taking real and symbolic power from monarchic and religious models of fatherhood and reinvesting it in citizenship and the nation. Even without the military dimension, present only in some cases and periods, the redefinition of masculinity provided a potent source of authority in new and reformed political systems. In theory, the self-constituted citizen could be universal, and at moments was taken to be so. In practice, women and many categories of men were excluded from citizenship and deterred from political activism. 'Fraternity' or brotherhood – that 'least understood of the values in the revolutionary triad' according to Lynn Hunt – was an alternative source of political legitimacy to paternalism, but one just as imbued with masculinity and capable of excluding whole categories of men as well as women.[1] Paternal authority itself could be reinvented as the basis of new political systems. Of course, issues other than gender shaped the new forms of political legitimacy. But the conflict over authority that helped define politics after the American and French Revolutions turned on images of masculinity as well as on the power of real men. Indeed, part of the ideological power unleashed by those events came from the way they expanded the repertory of masculine authority.

The legacy of the Revolution in France illustrates this process. A supreme paradox of the French Revolution was how, in spite of the Declaration of the Rights of Man in 1789 whose universality theoretically encompassed women, female political activism was gradually excluded during the Revolution's most radical phase. Political authority was redefined by the ideal of the autonomous and self-constituted male citizen, in whom 'popular sovereignty' was collectively vested, and by the 'fraternity' of male political associations in which active citizenship was played out.[2] Yet while it removed paternal authority from the public sphere by regicide, the Revolution confirmed it in the domestic sphere. After some experimentation with more egalitarian gender relations in the family, the male citizen's authority as 'head of the family' was confirmed by the codification of the civil law under Napoleon.[3] Moreover, the reintroduction of paternalism as a political principle by Napoleon – a self-crowned emperor whose legitimacy and subsequent legend drew on the Revolution and romantic nationalism – demonstrates how the revolutionary process multiplied masculine models of political legitimacy.[4]

The point is driven home by the renewed political upheaval of the mid-nineteenth century. The 1848 revolution repeated the earlier conflict whereby universal rights and suffrage were interpreted in practice as those of the male citizen. Women militants joined the initial burst of revolutionary activism and (in the person of Jeanne Deroin) demanded full citizenship as workers and homemakers. The emergent language of socialism in the 1830s and 1840s, with its insistence that productive labour (including maternity) was the basis of citizenship, underwrote both claims. It is all the more striking, then, that 'universal' suffrage was confirmed as a male preserve, along with male supremacy in the home. Deroin's case to the Provisional Government was dismissed and women's political activity was banned in the second half of 1848.[5] The involvement of women in the Paris uprising against the Provisional Government in June 1848 reaffirmed for moderate Republicans the idea that female political activism was irrational and somehow 'against nature', as did participation by working-class women in the Paris Commune in 1871.[6]

The overthrow of the Republic by Louis-Napoleon Bonaparte in 1851 resulted in the curtailment of male political activism. Napoleon III was a gift to the opposition because he tried to renew his uncle's authority without the latter's military prestige. He was, quite literally, a caricature of martial virility as Republican satire delighted in pointing out, beginning with Victor Hugo's epic poem predicting the humiliation of the new Emperor by God and history. Criticism assuaged the bruised self-image of the Republican citizen whose 'sovereignty' had been usurped by an upstart paternalism. Military catastrophe in 1870 initiated a new form of fraternal Republicanism that remained profoundly hostile to any hint of authoritarianism or even strong government.[7] With the Third and Fourth Republics, it shaped French political culture until the mid-twentieth century. But this meant the continued exclusion of women from electoral politics. Many Republican men were convinced that women were the antithesis of the self-constituted male citizen, being irrational and, what was worse, subordinated to the antagonistic paternal authority of the Catholic Church.

Significantly, the appeal of Catholicism in nineteenth-century France underwent a distinct feminisation, including the cult of female saints, in parallel with the emergence of a secularised politics based on masculine activism and male political associations.[8] Moreover, it is no accident if the Catholic Church, in its effort to contest the politics of liberalism and socialism, should have made the family a prior and divinely ordered source of authority by comparison with the state. The result was a reconstituted politics of Catholic paternalism on the family model, which also allowed a place to female activism based on the celebration of maternity. This message lay at the heart of Social Catholicism inspired by Leo XIII's Encyclical, *De Rerum Novarum* in 1891, and the sociology of Frédéric Le Play, with its emphasis on the family. Consequently, conservative Catholic Republicans were more likely than the secularised left to favour women's suffrage between the two world wars.[9] As much as the supposed weakness of French feminism, it was this battle between different versions of masculine authority, and in particular the ideal of masculinity inherent in French Republicanism, that obstructed the extension of 'universal' suffrage to women for nearly a century, until 1944.

The interplay of masculine authority symbols in the battle between different political regimes might seem distinctly French. Yet the potency of masculinity for regimes that were obliged to reinvent their legitimacy by obtaining increased popular support, or for political movements that tried to achieve this by revolution or reform, was a general feature of the nineteenth and twentieth centuries. Thomas Welskopp, in chapter 14, demonstrates the ideological and rhetorical significance of 'fraternity' to the early Social Democratic movement in Germany as disenfranchised artisans and intellectuals drew on an established tradition of revolutionary oratory to constitute themselves as 'men' and citizens, thereby discursively subordinating women. The tendency remained influential. August Bebel, the principal German socialist advocate of feminism at the end of the nineteenth century, considered that complete female emancipation was a consequence, not a part, of the Socialist revolution, and thus depended on the self-realisation of the male socialist through an epic battle with capitalism. Early twentieth-century Social Democracy was the main ally of the German women's movement in a country in which female participation in national political parties remained illegal until 1908. But its feminism was subordinate to a vision of class emancipation that privileged the male worker.[10]

Framed at its broadest, the hypothesis might be that the two hundred years following the late-eighteenth century revolutions saw the hey-day of 'fraternities' of all types. 'Fraternity' expressed the unprecedented challenge to paternalist sources of political authority because it proclaimed equality of membership and was self-constituted rather than derived from tradition. Whether based on secret rites of initiation or on open membership, brotherhoods proliferated in nineteenth-century Europe and North America (drawing on pre-revolutionary precedents such as the Freemasons), and accompanied attempts at political modernisation in other parts of the world. Some – such as Babeuf's 'Conspiracy of the Equals' and the Carbonari – were clandestine, starting a long tradition of underground organisations aiming at social revolution or national liberation. Others were open and internally democratic and, however restrictive their criteria for membership, acted as microcosms of the political regimes they hoped to create. Trade unionism adapted the tradition to the politics of the workplace and industrial action.

Joanna de Groot, in her study of emergent Iranian nationalism in the late nineteenth and early twentieth centuries, shows how an explicit challenge to paternal authority accompanied political modernisation in this part of Asia. Self-constituted fraternities of different types contested the 'vertical authority of the patriarchal state'. They helped frame a new language of national community and defend that community's vulnerable frontiers against British and Russian encroachment after the First World War. In fact paternalist authority was reaffirmed by the regime of Reza Shah but at the price of internalising the new associative language of nationhood and its combination of traditional and modernising impulses. This dialectic of masculine authority may well be characteristic of modernising nationalism (with its internal contradictions) in twentieth-century Africa and Asia more generally.

Jacobus du Pisani's chapter on the construction of an Afrikaner myth of masculinity indicates how powerful both the secret and open type of fraternal organisation remained in the twentieth century. The *Afrikaner-Broederbond* was literally a secret 'brotherhood' that was paralleled by the public Federation of Afrikaans Cultural Associations, an embryonic representative regime whose masculine ideals and male leadership were assured by the inner influence of the 'brotherhood'. The dual framework had a long pedigree. The Irish Republican Brotherhood (or Fenianism) expressed the conspiratorial, physical force tradition in Irish nationalism from the mid-nineteenth century to the rising of 1916. It overlapped democratically organised cultural and political bodies that acted as the public face of nationalist aspirations. The dual structure was reformulated after 1916. The emergent national movement, Sinn Féin, led to an underground parliament during the War of Independence of which the Irish Republican Army became the clandestine

military wing.[11] The secret brotherhood has continued to enjoy considerable prestige in Irish nationalism due to its monopoly of violence and to
the masculine prestige of the paramilitary patriot. Arguably, this dual
form of fraternity has provided an influential structure for resistance
and national liberation movements in the twentieth century more
generally.

There were many other types of political fraternity – from the club
and voluntary association to municipal assemblies or national parlia-
ments based on male suffrage. These organisations provided much of
the institutional structure of the public sphere whose emergence conditioned political developments in Europe and North America during
the nineteenth century and more widely during the twentieth century.[12]
They also generated the cultural and political assumptions that informed
public life. The point is not that the public sphere remained exclusively
masculine – it did not. Rather it was structured by the increasingly
dense associative life of men and by concomitant ideals of masculinity
that had to be contested by women and by excluded men in a process
that was by no means complete at the end of the twentieth century.[13]
How fraternities of various kinds constituted public life and mediated
the struggle for political authority and representation is one of the ways
in which masculinity informs political history more generally.

Masculinities and the imagined nation

Establishing representative politics was not the same thing as constituting the nation. Especially after the emergence of romantic nationalism
in the late eighteenth century, the nation was seen as coterminous with
society. It embraced women and children, for the family was its primary
cell, and included language and literature, the past and the present. It
was envisaged as the pre-political reality out of which the 'nation-state'
had to be wrought.[14] But that meant formulating a national identity in
order to give the state legitimacy, and the cultural and ideological effort
of imagining the nation in turn allowed a host of claims to be made for
inclusion and recognition by different groups, including women.[15] The
idea of the nation, however, was particularly prolific in male roles and
new formulations of masculinity, and this in turn suggests another
way in which masculinity might illuminate the history of politics and
especially of national political cultures.

Not surprisingly, given the traditional prominence of warfare
for masculine prestige, an updated and idealised version of the soldier
provided one form of masculine claim on the nation, and vice versa.

The volunteer ready to die in defence of the fatherland was the most obvious expression of this idea. The Prussian and German version described by Karen Hagemann, which derived from the 'war of liberation' in 1813 against the Napoleonic occupation of Prussia, proved particularly resilient. It resurfaced as the country faced catastrophe in the total wars of the twentieth century with calls in both 1918–19 and 1944–45 for male volunteers to sacrifice themselves in a last ditch defence of Germany.[16] More generally, it was a powerful myth that portrayed the army as a direct expression of the nation. The equivalent myth deriving from the French Revolution was that of the volunteer of 1792 rising up to repel the Prussians at the battle of Valmy. This remained a powerful image of masculine Resistance used by the Communist Party during the Second World War.[17] In like manner, Garibaldi and his followers in the 1860s incarnated a myth of national self-liberation by the volunteer soldier that remained potent down to the period of Fascism and the anti-fascist Resistance.[18]

The keynote of these and other male myths of nation building was heroism. Valour, sacrifice, and martyrdom were of course not male prerogatives. The nineteenth-century cult of female saints already referred to in a Church concerned to revive and extend its authority after the French Revolution shows this clearly. National heroism on occasions included exemplary women, usually in episodes culled from history (Jeanne d'Arc, Mary Stuart, etc.). Yet men dominated the canon and it may not be too fanciful to argue that nation building required the construction of a secular equivalent of sainthood that disproportionately favoured masculinity as the source of the virtues to be celebrated. Myth cycles, such as the invented legend of Ossian (favoured by Napoleon), which rooted the French nation in a heroic Celtic past, achieved this.[19] The same purpose was served by founding national epics, such as the resistance of the Batavians against the Roman legions celebrated by the Dutch Patriot movement of the 1780s, which is discussed by Stefan Dudink. Arminius, who defeated the Romans in the Teutoberger forest at the beginning of the first century AD, performed a similar function for the cult of the German nation unified by Prussia. Martyrs might also be found in recent history. The boy hero, Barra, who died in the war in the Vendée, and Marat assassinated by a female counter-revolutionary in his bath, were both Revolutionary martyrs – and venerated as such by Jacques-Louis David in a distinctly male aesthetic of heroic beauty of the kind discussed by Joan Landes.[20]

The cult of great men became an integral part of nineteenth-century nationhood. Secular temples bear witness to this. The Panthéon was created in Paris by the Constituent Assembly in 1791 to receive the body of Mirabeau, followed by Voltaire, Rousseau, and Marat. Re-dedicated as a church by the First and Second Empires but secularised again by Republican regimes, the first 'great woman' (Marie Curie) was not honoured until 1995.[21] The aspiration of the Kingdom of Bavaria, which had been created by Napoleon, to achieve German unification in the first part of the nineteenth century required an equivalent shrine to the great men (and occasional woman) of German history and culture. The need was met by the gleaming 'Valhalla' which Ludwig I built at Regensburg, overlooking the Danube.[22] In fact, every emergent nation had its great men whose heroism or genius depended on local circumstances – explorers, pioneers, warriors, statesmen, writers, and scientists. Thomas Carlyle, who was fascinated by the French Revolution, accurately caught the nineteenth-century obsession with male heroism in his influential essay, published in 1840, on heroes and the heroic in history. In it he proclaimed that 'Universal History, the history of what man has accomplished in this world, is at bottom the History of the Great Men who have worked here.'[23]

The positive attributes of national masculine ideals were matched by the negative figures of the internal and external enemy – who might be pictured either as female or as a derided or feared type of masculinity. The bitter satire by French Revolutionaries at the expense of Marie-Antoinette – female and foreign – is a clear example of the former. The latter is illustrated by the mutual dismissal by French and English cartoonists of the other nation during the Revolutionary and Napoleonic Wars by showing it as essentially unmanly. English satire typically portrayed the half-starved and tyrannical *sans-culotte* as a man who could not afford to eat roast beef – a hallmark of John Bull's independent manhood.

The emergence of racial stereotypes later in the nineteenth century provided an enlarged arsenal of masculinity expressing a positive self-image of the race or nation beset by decadent or ultra-masculine men who undermined it within or threatened it by annihilation from without. Jacobus du Pisani shows how the strong male who constituted the subject of Afrikaner nationalism was defined negatively by contrasting types – the treacherous British 'Jingo', the capitalist Jew, the sexually threatening Black. Likewise, Marilyn Lake suggests that the idealised worker, for whom Australian trade unionists demanded a family wage, was seen as a bulwark against submersion by the massed hordes of Asian males, so that supporting the family meant defending 'White Australia'. Although never all defining, the gender dimension of national and racial antagonism was important. Secularised anti-Semitism, for example, is certainly not reducible to its masculine stereotypes, but is inconceivable without them.

Many registers of masculinity could be used to construct the image of the nation. Sonya Rose demonstrates this with her examination of a domestic and deliberately anti-heroic British maleness during the Second World War. This had its roots in the self-image cultivated during the First World War of the 'Tommy' who met the horrors of the western front with irony and a cheerful indulgence in sport and in the music hall.[24] Deployed in conscious opposition to the ultra-militarised masculinity of Nazi Germany, it also stood in marked contrast to the images of imperial manhood prevalent in the press and popular literature at the turn of the century and prolonged by the cult of 'Lawrence of Arabia'.[25] 'National' images of masculinity thus changed with historical circumstances and may well prove to have been as variable as the distinctive forms of 'national feminism' to which historians of the women's movement have drawn attention – and, indeed, may help explain these.[26] Although a good deal of work has been done on the historical construction of national identity, the roles played by gender, and especially masculinity, in constructing the collective subject of the nation have not yet been properly recognised and explored.[27]

Power and authority also took forms that were less obviously based on gender. Rational bureaucratic organisation that administered power impersonally was equally characteristic of modern nation states, providing the discipline and uniformity that translated power and authority into systematic practice. While bureaucracies remained socially and culturally male spheres of action for much of the period, they did not furnish explicitly masculine symbols. Yet moments of crisis such as those brought about by war and revolution in the twentieth century, generated abnormal, 'charismatic' forms of authority (to use Max Weber's categorisation) which were based on the miraculous aura of the leader who promised a religious type of transcendence. Charismatic authority is not intrinsically masculine. But its emergence through the breakdown of national values and identities that had partly been construed in terms of masculinity, and in crises dominated by war, enabled charismatic figures to fashion an unstable political authority in terms of a radically accentuated masculinity. Hitler's power in Nazi Germany drew amongst other things on his promise to unshackle the humiliated masculinity of the defeated nation and to validate mass male sacrifice in the Great War.[28] The role played by masculinity in charismatic leader cults in the twentieth century is a theme with major potential for the history of Fascism and Communism.

War – masculinity by other means?

Masculinity illuminates the history of war and the military no less than that of politics for at least two reasons. The first concerns a point on which I have already touched – the military as a source of masculine authority and a privileged arena of male activity. This general point acquired particular significance following the French Revolution, as discussed in greater detail by Karen Hagemann and Stefan Dudink. The *levée en masse*, or universal military service, first imagined by the embattled leadership of the Convention in 1793 as the counterpart of citizenship, offered the vision of a total mobilisation of the nation for war along lines of gender and age. While the adult male defended the fatherland, women and children manned the home front and old men inveighed against tyrants, according to the decree of the Convention.[29] If politics after the revolutionary era were reshaped in part by new norms of masculinity, war (to adapt Clausewitz's dictum) became masculinity by other means.

The *levée en masse* was important as a political myth because it sought to turn the coercive institution of conscription into the internalised duty of the citizen to serve the nation as a soldier – hence the symbolic importance of the volunteer.[30] The imperative of military modernisation during the nineteenth century imposed some analogous myth of nationalised masculinity on every regime that wished to multiply its armed forces by the introduction of short-term military service. The latter initiated many men into a sense of nationhood. More importantly, it furnished a conception of the nation in which the militarisation of the male population was the ultimate recourse for national defence, and hence survival. The response of the French Third Republic to the trauma of defeat in 1870 by a resurgent rhetoric of the *levée en masse* and the proliferation of military training societies indicates the centrality of militarised masculinity to the political culture of Republicanism down to 1914. The 1905 law that finally made the obligation to military service universal referred directly to the heroic masculine ideal of the revolutionary citizens in 1792–93.[31] In 1914, the mass armies fielded by major continental powers depended on the conscription of most men from the age of twenty to the mid-forties. Such a process was inconceivable without a sense of national cohesion and a regime that enjoyed a measure of genuine support. Myths and ideologies of militarised masculinity were vital in achieving this.

Yet the two world wars resulted in a profound paradox that provides a second reason why masculinity is important for the history of war, particularly in the twentieth century. The politicisation of warfare from the late eighteenth century that turned the nation as a whole into a military resource and potentially delivered mass armies to the battlefield was only one aspect of what some historians have identified as a military revolution that unfolded from 1914 to 1945.[32] The second aspect consisted of technological innovations that industrialised firepower and made the battlefield more destructive than ever before. In 1914–18 this technology also conferred a particular advantage on the defensive, resulting in military stalemate. The encounter of pre-war assumptions about the conduct of war with the reality of the industrialised battlefield not only resulted in unprecedented casualty levels but also destabilised the stereotypes of masculinity that had played an important part in mobilising the populations for war in 1914.[33] We must be careful not to assume that all soldiers were broken by the experience. Most who survived it did so without breakdown. Nonetheless, many men were treated for 'shellshock' or were disabled or disfigured. The war had a profound impact on men's minds and bodies – and it would be surprising if it did not also affect ideas of masculinity.[34]

Michael Roper's discussion of the letters sent to their mothers by young British officers in the trenches reconstructs one emotional and discursive outlet for addressing the gulf between manly patriotism and the experience of combat. Retrospective autobiography provides another, since personal narratives could either avoid or confront this same disparity.[35] Both suggest a more general disturbance. 'Sacrifice' became the mostly widely used trope to express the cost of obeying the norms of militarised masculinity on the battlefield, and it measured a palpable reality for millions.[36] The post-war redemption of that sacrifice in ways that validated the experience of the war, and permitted at least a public form of closure, made masculinity a central dynamic of post-war politics – although it is rarely analysed in these terms. Yet it was a dynamic with varied outcomes. The hundreds of thousands of war memorials erected in the combatant countries in the 1920s replaced the symbolic masculinity that had hitherto expressed the nation with the moral and political capital of millions of real men who had fought and died for it. The cult of the 'great man' was replaced by that of the 'unknown soldier'.[37]

Where the war brought victory, it was possible to incorporate an anti-war message – a reaction against militarised masculinity – into post-war political language. This occurred in Britain, France and the US. The 'patriotic pacifism' that has been seen as characteristic of the bulk of organised French veterans presented a conciliatory and non-aggressive image of manhood. Aristide Briand, the French foreign minister who collaborated with his German opposite number, Gustav Stresemann on diplomatic reconciliation in the mid-1920s, sought to reinvest masculine military values on both sides in collaboration for peace.[38] Yet in the case of defeat, the way was open for a new image of ultra-militarised masculinity, hardened on the industrial battlefield and expressed by the fraternity of the 'front soldier', to be used in the service of revanchist nationalism. Italian Fascism as well as German National Socialism used a radicalised masculinity, rooted in the war, in order to reconstruct a sense of national community.[39]

However, the paradox of total war went further. It soon became apparent that industrial warfare required an economic mobilisation that cut across the ideal of all able men serving in the armed forces. Working-class men were needed in factories and women of all social backgrounds replaced absent men in vital roles. Even as wartime rhetoric validated masculinity by reference to the soldier's 'supreme sacrifice', some men were exempted from risk while women usurped many normal masculine roles in civilian life. Male norms were thus doubly destabilised, by home front requirements as well as by the experience of combat. Furthermore, the battlefield stalemate that dominated the First World War began to show signs of resolution in 1917–18, with the restoration of mobility to firepower (tanks, aircraft, and the tactical integration of specialised arms). The process was completed in the Second World War, by the offensive capacity of the German armed forces and the Allied development of strategic air power. The result was a war of movement that resulted in civilian populations being occupied on a far greater scale than in 1914–18 and directly exposed to aerial bombardment. The distinction between home and fighting front was eroded, with the result that women and children were thrust into the heart of war. This further blurred the notion of war as a privileged arena of male activity.[40]

These unanticipated consequences of twentieth-century warfare doubtless explain why post-war periods experienced sharp tension as the gender order was renegotiated. Masculine authority and male spheres of activity that had been undermined by war were reasserted. A particularly brutal expression of the tendency was the retribution exacted after both world wars on women who were made sexual scapegoats for collaboration with the enemy occupier by having their heads shorn.[41] In more subtle ways, such as those explored by Glenda Sluga in relation to the peace settlement following the First World War, women were assigned a subordinate position based on maternity and denied the status of autonomous national subjects or citizens of the new international order. Yet the post-war reassertion of masculinity was far from being a one-way or uncontested process.[42] More systematic comparative exploration of the political re-stabilisation of normative and actual masculinity after the two world wars and other conflicts is a particularly important area of research.

Paternalism disturbed – employment, welfare, and the expanding state

The current book suggests one further aspect of political history for which the study of masculinity is particularly relevant – the state's involvement in the labour market and social welfare. The nineteenth-century doctrine of separate male and female spheres confirmed male paternal authority over the family while also recognising, and to some extent protecting, the specific place of women within the domestic world.[43] For the same reason the state had special regard for the protection of women and children as it began regulating conditions in industry. In both cases, the state supported domestic masculinity as a foundation of the social order.

The rationalisation of factory production with the second industrial revolution from the 1880s to the 1970s and the development of the state provision of welfare potentially disturbed this model of masculine authority in the working-class family. The pride of the skilled craft and industrial worker, who was invariably a man, came in part from his ability to support his family even if, in industries such as textiles, women and children had a subordinate place in the division of labour.[44] Craft-dominated trade unions had their own version of the 'separation of spheres' in which male differentials in skill and earnings were jealously guarded and the need for married women to work was resented as a threat to the integrity of the working-class family.[45] After the turn of the century 'Taylorism' and 'Fordism' undermined male skill and the threat was compounded by the possibility that the increasingly prominent semi-skilled worker might be an immigrant, a woman, or both. Defending or reconstituting male authority within the family in the transformed world of industrial mass production thus became a key labour and working class issue. It was compounded by the traumatic effect of mass unemployment during the Great Depression of the 1930s.

At the same time, the steps taken by the state to protect workers against the vicissitudes of industrial life (starting with Bismarck's Germany in the 1880s) had the potential either to reinforce or undercut male authority. If the state buttressed the male wage earner by supplementing his income in time of need, welfare paternalism reinforced his role as family breadwinner. If the state independently addressed the needs of women and children, it undermined that role. In fact, the welfare state grew from various impulses and evolved along distinctive lines in different countries, as historians have noted. In addition to the claims of male workers, it reflected feminist demands for recognition of maternity.[46] It also expressed demographic and eugenicist concerns on the part of the state. Stagnant population growth in inter-war France, for example, created deep anxieties about national survival in a state which made family policy and natalism, rather than social class, the primary motive of its welfare system.[47] Nazi Germany placed a premium on the reproduction of the racial community.[48] Soviet Russia in the 1930s replaced an earlier (and limited) belief in gender equality with a strengthened commitment to the proletarian family as a safeguard against social breakdown and as a source of demographic renewal.[49]

Masculinity, especially working-class masculinity, thus emerges as a pivotal issue in the elaboration of welfare and industrial policies by twentieth-century states, although its full significance in this regard has yet to be charted. In the case of the Brazilian workers discussed by Barbara Weinstein in chapter 15, a national system of industrial and vocational education served to reinstate male authority in what was portrayed as a process of economic nation building. The ideal of the separation of spheres was re-emphasised ideologically despite the erosion of skilled male labour through the use of semi-skilled workers, including women, in the engineering industry. This prompts the question of whether enhanced masculine authority in an idealised national community compensated for diminished economic power in other settings. Was it a component of popular authoritarian regimes, from fascism to Peronism? The Nazi regime addressed the humiliation of unemployed workers by promising to reinstate them as breadwinners and sought to humanise work by promoting the 'beauty of labour' through social programmes. The separation of spheres was so central to its social policy that it proved difficult subsequently to mobilise women workers for the war economy.[50] In a very different manner, the worker-based Social Catholicism which emerged in Belgium and France in the inter-war period celebrated an idealised working-class family based on the separation of spheres and the respective dignity of maternity and the male breadwinner in response to industrial transformation and mass unemployment.[51]

The issue emerged with particular clarity as inter-war labour movements confronted economic uncertainty and then Depression. Marilyn Lake shows that Australian male trade unionists fought bitterly and successfully to preserve the 'family wage' that incarnated their claim to economic and sexual predominance within the white working-class family against attempts to dismantle it in favour of separate allowances for mothers and children. Alice Kessler-Harris explores how the American Federation of Labor, which epitomised the ideal of the independent skilled worker, managed to conserve much of that ethos as it reluctantly accepted the need for state unemployment insurance. It succeeded in having the measure channelled through male trade unionism to the exclusion of women, the unskilled, and African-Americans. In both cases, masculinity stands out as a question not just of male self-interest but also of a self-defined 'manliness' (with all its contradictions) around which the considerable defensive power of male organisations was marshalled. Together these chapters pose the question of whether different senses of labour and working class masculinity affected the implementation and operation of the welfare state as it reached maturity in various countries after the Second World War.

Conclusion

It is clear that 'masculinity', like gender more broadly, casts a great deal of light on the history of politics and war. Representative politics created a discursive public space that was filled by new, predominantly masculine voices that construed men in different ways as the source and subject of power and authority. The nation as a collective form of identity was peopled by a host of figures, positive and negative, supplied by varieties of masculinity. War proved deeply paradoxical since it exposed masculine norms to their most extreme test in industrialised combat while relativising them by encompassing women and civilian life. The politics of welfare and industrial rationalisation involved the state directly in the family with the potential to reinforce or undermine masculine domestic authority.

Yet despite the obvious centrality of men to the study of politics and war, only recently has the history of either been written with any reference to masculinity.[52] Past historians might therefore be included in the object of study. History has been written predominantly by men, consecrating their actions with the apparent inevitability of the past. As an academic discipline, it has played an important role in the formation of national identities, political elites, and state bureaucracies. In other words, history (and especially military and political history) has been for much of the period since the eighteenth century a masculine practice addressing male preoccupations.

Historians and history writing bear the imprint of this function. When Theodor Mommsen gave his inaugural address at the University of Berlin in 1874, he concluded that: 'For the German student, his matriculation is still a patent of nobility by which he joins the ranks of the volunteer fighters for right and truth and the freedom of the human spirit.'[53] The association between historical study, national myth, and masculinity could not be clearer. It might be argued that the 'professional' history that emerged in the late nineteenth century (to which Mommsen was a notable contributor) clothed this kind of gendered assumption in a language of 'science' and 'scholarship' that gave it an apparently general validity. Potentially, therefore, a critical reading of the past historiography of war and politics provides an additional, important tool for deciphering the constructions of masculinity discussed in this book.

Notes

1 L. Hunt, *The Family Romance of the French Revolution* (London, 1994), p. 12.

2 *Ibid.*, pp. 153–60; J. Landes, *Women and the Public Sphere in the Age of the French Revolution* (Ithaca and London, 1988), pp. 134–40; P. Rosanvallon, *Le Sacre du citoyen: Histoire du suffrage universel en France* (Paris, 1992), pp. 392–407.

3 The history of divorce legislation is instructive. Revolutionary attempts to introduce a measure of liberty for women were reversed under the Consulate and Empire. I. Wolloch, *The New Regime: Transformations of the French Civic Order, 1789–1820s* (New York, 1994), pp. 312–17.

4 J. Tulard, 'Le Retour des cendres', in Pierre Nora (ed.), *Les Lieux de mémoire* (Paris, new edn, 1997), vol. 2, pp. 1729–53.

5 J. W. Scott, *Only Paradoxes to Offer: French Feminists and the Rights of Man* (Cambridge MA, 1996), pp. 57–89.

6 A. de Tocqueville, *Recollections*, trans G. Lawrence, ed. V. P. Mayer and A. P. Kerr (London, 1970), pp. 136–37; Robert Tombs, 'Warriors and killers: Women and violence during the Paris Commune, 1871', in R. Aldrich and M. Lyons (eds), *The Sphinx in the Tuileries and Other Essays in Modern French History* (Sydney, 1999), pp. 169–82.

7 V. Hugo, 'Les Châtiments', in *Oeuvres Poétiques* (Paris, 2nd edn, 1967), vol. 2, pp. 3–227; P. Nord, *The Republican Moment: Struggles for Democracy in Nineteenth Century France* (Cambridge MA and London, 1995), pp. 11–13.

8 C. Ford, 'Female martyrdom and the politics of sainthood in nineteenth century France: The cult of Sainte Philomène', in N. Aitken and F. Tallett (eds), *Catholicism in Britain and France since 1789* (London, 1996), pp. 115–34.

9 P. Smith, *Feminism and the Third Republic: Women's Political and Civil Rights in France 1918–1945* (Oxford, 1996), pp. 104–62.

10 K. Offen, *European Feminisms, 1700–1950: A Political History* (Stanford, 2000), pp. 165–6; R. J. Evans, *The Feminist Movement in Germany 1894–1933* (London, 1976), pp. 265–75.

11   R. Foster, *Modern Ireland 1600–1972* (London, 1988), pp. 484–502.

12   R. J. Morris, 'Civil society, subscriber democracies, and parliamentary government in Great Britain', in N. Bermeo and P. Nord (eds), *Civil Society before Democracy: Lessons from Nineteenth-Century Europe* (Lanham MD and Oxford, 2000), pp. 124–6.

13   Offen, *European Feminisms*, pp. 182–212.

14   E. Hobsbawm, *Nations and Nationalism since 1780: Programme, Myth, Reality* (Cambridge, 1990), pp. 46–79.

15   G. Eley, 'Culture, nature and gender', in I. Blom, K. Hagemann, and C. Hall (eds), *Gendered Nations: Nationalisms and Gender Order in the Long Nineteenth Century* (Oxford and New York, 2000), pp. 30–1.

16   M. Geyer, 'People as war: The German debate about a Levée en masse in October 1918', in D. Moran and A. Waldron (eds), *The People in Arms: Military Myth and National Mobilization since the French Revolution* (Cambridge and New York, 2003), pp. 124–58.

17   S. Luzzatto, *L'Impôt du sang: La gauche française à l'épreuve de la guerre mondiale, 1900–1945* (Lyon, 1996), pp. 151–7.

18   M. Isenghi, 'Conclusione', in M. Isenghi (ed.), *I Luoghi della memoria: Simboli e miti dell'Italia unita* (Bari, 1996), pp. 572–6.

19   A.-M. Thiesse, *La Création des identités nationals: Europe XVIIIe-XXe siècle* (Paris, 1999), pp. 50–89.

20   A. Soboul, 'Religious feeling and popular cults during the French Revolution: "Patriot Saints" and Martyrs for Liberty', in S. Wilson (ed.), *Saints and their Cults: Studies in Religious Sociology, Folklore and History* (Oxford, 1983), pp. 217–32.

21   M. Ozouf, 'Le Panthéon', in Nora (ed.), *Lieux de mémoire*, vol. 1, pp. 155–78.

22   G. L. Mosse, *The Nationalization of the Masses: Political Symbolism and Mass Movements in Germany from the Napoleonic Wars through the Third Reich* (Ithaca and London, 1975), pp. 53–6; G. L. Mosse, *Walhalla: Official Guide* (Regensburg, 1995).

23   T. Carlyle, *On Heroes, Hero-Worship, and the Heroic in History*, ed. C. Niemeyer (Berkeley and Oxford, 1993), p. 3.

24   J. Fuller, *Troop Morale and Popular Culture in the British and Dominion Armies 1914–1918* (Oxford, 1990), pp. 81–113.

25   G. Dawson, *Soldier Heroes: British Adventure, Empire, and the Imagining of Masculinities* (London and New York, 1994), pp. 167–230.

26   Offen, *European Feminisms*, pp. 213–49.

27   Exceptions include the pioneering study of G. L. Mosse, *Nationalism and Sexuality: Respectability and Abnormal Sexuality in Modern Europe* (New York, 1985); Blom, Hagemann, and Hall's (eds), *Gendered Nations*; and B. Caine and G. Sluga, *Gendering European History, 1780–1920* (Leicester, 2000), pp. 87–116.

28   I. Kershaw, *The 'Hitler Myth': Image and Reality in the Third Reich* (Oxford, 1987), pp. 8–10, for an excellent discussion of Hitler in terms of 'charismatic authority' which does not, however, consider the role played by 'masculinity'.

29   A. Forrest, 'La Patrie en Danger: The French Revolution and the first Levée en Masse', in Moran and Waldron (eds), *The People in Arms*, pp. 8–32.

30   P. Paret, 'Conscription and the end of the Ancien Regime in France and Prussia', in P. Paret, *Understanding War: Essays on Clausewitz and the History of Military Power*

(Princeton, 1992), pp. 53–74; K. Hagemann, 'Der "Burger" als "Nationalkrieger": Entwürfe von Militär, Nation und Männlichkeit in der Zeit der Freiheitskriege', in K. Hagemann and R. Pröve (eds), *Landsknechte, Soldatenfrauen und Nationalkreiger: Militär, Krieg und Geschlechterordnung im historischen Wandel* (Frankfurt and New York, 1998), pp. 74–102.

31 R. Challener, *The French Theory of the Nation in Arms, 1866–1939* (New York, 1955), pp. 28–90.

32 M. Geyer, 'The militarization of Europe, 1914–1945', in J. R. Gillis (ed.), *The Militarization of the Western World* (New Brunswick and London, 1989), pp. 65–102; J. Bailey, 'The First World War and the birth of modern warfare', in B. MacGregor Knox and W. R. Murray (eds), *The Dynamics of Military Revolution 1300–2050* (Cambridge, 2001), pp. 132–53.

33 T. Travers, *The Killing Ground: The British Army, the Western Front and the Emergence of Modern Warfare, 1900–1918* (London, 1987), esp. pp. 37–82; J. Horne (ed.), *State, Society and Mobilization in Europe during the First World War* (Cambridge, 1997), esp. 'Introduction: Mobilizing for "Total War"', 1914–1918', pp. 1–17.

34 Special issue on 'Choc traumatique et histoire culturelle', *14–18 Aujourd'hui-Heute-Today*, 3 (Paris, 2000).

35 A. Thomson, *Anzac Memories: Living with the Legend* (Melbourne, 1994).

36 J. Horne, 'Soldiers, civilians and the warfare of attrition: Representations of combat in France, 1914–1918', in F. Coetzee and M. Shevin-Coetzee (eds), *Authority, Identity and the Social History of the Great War* (Providence and Oxford, 1995), pp. 223–49.

37 G. L. Mosse, *Fallen Soldiers: Reshaping the Memory of the World Wars* (New York and Oxford, 1990), pp. 70–106; D. Sherman, *The Construction of Memory in Inter-war France* (Chicago and London, 2001), pp. 65–103.

38 J. Horne, 'Locarno et la politique de la démobilisation culturelle', in 'Démobilisations culturelles après la Grande Guerre', *14–18 Aujourd'hui-Heute-Today*, 5 (2002), p. 78.

39 K. Theweleit, *Male Fantasies*, trans C. Turner (Oxford, 1987–89); C. Ingrao, 'Etudiants allemands, mémoire de guerre et militantisme nazi: étude de cas', in 'Démobilisations culturelles', *14–18 Aujourd'hui-Heute-Today*, 5 (2002), pp. 55–71; E. Gentile, *The Sacralization of Politics in Fascist Italy* (Cambridge MA and London, 1996), pp. 17–18.

40 K. Hagemann and S. Schüler-Springorum (eds): *Home/Front: Military, War and Gender in Twentieth Century Germany* (Oxford and London, 2003), esp. introduction.

41 F. Virgili, *La France 'virile': des femmes tondues à la Libération* (Paris, 2000), pp. 225–324.

42 M.-L. Roberts, *Civilization without Sexes: Reconstructing Gender in Postwar France* (Chicago, 1994), pp. 213–17; S. K. Kent, *Making Peace: The Reconstruction of Gender in Interwar Britain* (Princeton, 1993), pp. 97–113.

43 J. Tosh, *A Man's Place: Masculinities and the Middle-Class Home in Victorian England* (New Haven and London, 1999), pp. 11–26.

44 P. Joyce, *Work, Society and Politics. The Culture of the Factory in Later Victorian England* (London, new edn, 1982), pp. 111–14.

45 J.-L. Robert, 'Women and work in France during the First World War', in R. Wall and J. Winter (eds), *The Upheaval of War: Family, World and Welfare in Europe, 1914–1918* (Cambridge, 1988), p. 261.

46 S. Koven and S. Michel (eds), *Mothers of a New World: Maternalist Politics and the Origins of Welfare States* (New York and London, 1993), esp. pp. 1–42.

47 S. Pedersen, *Family, Dependence and the Origins of the Welfare State: Britain and France, 1914–1945* (Cambridge, 1993), pp. 412–36.

48 M. Burleigh and W. Wippermann, *The Racial State: Germany 1933–1945* (Cambridge, 1991), pp. 28–35, 267–303.

49 S. Fitzpatrick, *Everyday Stalinism: Ordinary Life in Extraordinary Times: Soviet Russia in the 1930s* (Oxford, 1999), p. 143.

50 T. Mason, *Social Policy in the Third Reich: The Working Class and the 'National Community'* (Providence and Oxford, 1993), pp. 162–4, 349–50.

51 P. Pierrard, *L'Eglise et les ouvriers en France, 1840–1940* (Paris, 1984), pp. 513–39.

52 J. Tosh, *The Pursuit of History* (London, 3rd edn, 2002), pp. 286–9.

53 Quoted in F. Stern (ed.), *The Varieties of History: From Voltaire to the Present* (London, 1956), p. 196. See also B. G. Smith, *The Gender of History: Men, Women, and Historical Practice* (Cambridge MA and London, 1998).

3

Hegemonic masculinity
and the history of gender

John Tosh

THE history of masculinities is a branch of study whose success has outrun its theoretical underpinnings. It began in the USA in the late 1970s as a comparatively modest historicisation of men's sex roles – a history of men as gendered persons. The work of historians like Peter Stearns and Peter Filene placed masculinity on the historical agenda, but it occupied a specialist niche, which scarcely impinged on the concerns of the generality of historians.[1] Since then 'gender' has become a core historical concept, which has challenged and in part overthrown the received wisdom in social, cultural, and political history. No longer can masculinity confidently be located in specifically 'masculine' contexts of work, family, and homosocial networks.[2] Its discursive traces are to be found in every area of culture and society, and are certainly not confined to explicit ideologies of manliness. Within this wider frame historians do not so much attempt 'a history of masculinity' as analyse the relationship between men's gender and the other ways in which their identity and behaviour are structured in specific historical formations.

Nowhere is the potential for the application of a 'masculinity' perspective more promising than in the realm of politics. Whether in identifying the ideological basis of exclusionary practices, or exploring the relationship between civilian and military masculinities, or 'gendering' the body politic itself, historians have deployed masculinity in highly illuminating ways. The political order can be seen as a reflection of the gender order in society as a whole, in which case the political virtues are best understood as the prescribed masculine virtues writ large. Conversely, formal politics may be seen as a dynamic factor in maintaining and strengthening the gender order: the state acts to reinforce masculine norms – for example by imposing military conscription or by conferring tax incentives on men who marry. Together these perspectives articulate the reciprocal relationship between a gendered political realm and a masculinity sustained and disciplined by the state. Alternatively, we may look beyond that comparatively straightforward binary structure to a more complex play of forces, in which masculinity is analysed in its relations of convergence and divergence with other politically charged identities – of race, sexuality, class, and religion.

The broadening historiographical reach of masculinity is an immensely promising development, outstripping the expectations of the early pioneers. But it also demands a great advance in theoretical rigour. A rough and ready notion of sexual difference could serve in the early years of men's history, but much more careful discriminations are needed now. A reading of the current research tends to convey the impression of masculinity as being everywhere in the sense of being freely acknowledged, but nowhere in that it is perceived through a blurred conceptual lens. The more the ubiquity of masculinity is demonstrated and not merely asserted, the greater the need for some theoretical clarity.

This chapter is intended to be an exercise in theoretical stocktaking. It analyses a term which is much favoured in present-day historical writing as carrying a certain theoretical *gravitas*, but which has been subject to very little critical appraisal. It is not hard to see why *hegemonic masculinity* is so frequently referred to. The word 'hegemonic' suggests a structure of control, a hierarchy which allows us to place masculinities in some kind of pecking order. The term also implies that control (even oppression) is in some way integral to masculinity, providing a framework for placing men in relation to women and to those males whose manhood is for some reason denied. There exists a small and cogent body of theoretical analysis. But hegemonic masculinity is most often cited by historians without elaboration, and in a manner which is only loosely connected with current theoretical work. My purpose in this chapter is to identify the current meanings of hegemonic masculinity in historical work, to evaluate the theory itself, and to suggest ways in which it might be reassessed.

The theory of hegemonic masculinity concerns the structure of gender relations. First sketched by R. W. Connell in 1983, the theory has been developed in the writings of a number of sociologists, of whom Connell has been the most influential.[3] It seeks to explain how the political and social order is created in the image of men, and expressed in specific forms of masculinity. The gender structure of society comprises unequal power relations between men and women, and between different categories of men. This structure is maintained not only by force, but by cultural means such as education and the popular media, which establish many of the assumptions of hegemonic masculinity in the realm of 'common sense', where they are particularly difficult to dislodge. Nevertheless instability and change are integral to hegemonic masculinity. Women may challenge the ideology of male supremacy and assert their rights in particular areas like the franchise or the structure of marriage. At the same time, not all men identify with hegemonic masculinity, and may indeed subscribe to practices and values which are incompatible with it; hence the proscription of homosexual behaviour and the resistance of men identifying as gay or 'queer'. Hegemonic masculinity is always in a tense – and potentially unstable – relationship with other masculinities, whether defined in terms of sexuality, class, age, or race.

The theory of hegemonic masculinity has the great merit of addressing the relational complexities of gender (not just masculinity), but its elaboration has for the most part been conducted in the context of contemporary Western societies. Connell, writes primarily as a sociologist in the radical tradition of critiquing capitalism.[4] But the historical implications of hegemonic masculinity are clear. As Carrigan, Connell and Lee have put it, hegemony 'always refers to a historical situation, a set of circumstances in which power is won and held'.[5] Partly because of his early training in the discipline, Connell regards history as indispensable for the understanding of hegemonic masculinity, and in 'The big picture' (1993) he sketched an ambitious overview from the age of the conquistadors in the sixteenth century to the triumph of corporate capitalism in the twentieth.[6] Analysis of the long-term trajectories of masculinity is not, on the whole, something which historians have taken up and developed.

The intellectual and political context

The concept of hegemony extends to the sphere of gender a perspective which was first systematically developed in relation to Marxist theory by Antonio Gramsci during the 1930s. In Gramsci's usage 'hegemony' refers to a domination which goes beyond the exercise of brute force and legal power because it has become embedded in culture; the scale of values which underpins the dominance of the bourgeoisie is deemed right and proper, or else buried beneath the surface of conscious thought; it amounts to the sense of reality by which most people in society order their perceptions. Indeed material enforcement may play a secondary role to the constraining grid of popular culture and everyday morality. In his far-reaching refinement of the classical Marxist tradition, Gramsci argued that the lack of revolutionary commitment among the European masses under Fascism could not be explained solely by the superior force available to the ruling class. Political domination was rooted in a cultural ascendancy which, by providing the only means of 'making sense' of the social order, legitimised the authority of the state. The ruling class had, in effect, won the battle for hearts and minds – until such time as the progressive forces in society could challenge their hegemony by building up an alternative political culture.[7]

Applied to the sphere of gender relations, hegemony denotes both the unequal social relations which empower certain groups of men, and the model of masculinity – often unconscious – which legitimises those relations, convincing the generality of men that there is no other way of 'being a man'. It encompasses not only the highly visible stratification of public life, but the pattern of personal relationships in what is conventionally regarded as 'private' life. In this sense the successful maintenance of hegemonic masculinity clearly depends, as Connell puts it, on 'the ability to impose a definition of the situation, to set the terms in which events are understood and issues discussed, to formulate ideals and define morality'.[8] From this perspective the role of the mass media in taking up and reinforcing the dominant expressions of masculinity is clearly central to the maintenance of hegemonic masculinity in modern societies.

The Gramscian inheritance is also reflected in the political stance of some of the theorists who have discussed hegemonic masculinity. Just as Gramsci aimed to equip Communists with the understanding of bourgeois hegemony which would enable them to challenge it successfully, so the anti-sexist men's movement and the gay liberation movement set themselves the task of destabilising hegemonic masculinity. Indeed Connell's intervention might be construed as an attempt to promote the contesting of hegemony, by raising consciousness about its pervasive power.

But if Gramsci helps to explain the structural character of hegemonic masculinity, he is no help as to its content. Here the most significant influence has been the concept of patriarchy. This was the dominant theoretical perspective of second-wave feminism during the 1970s and 1980s. At its simplest, 'patriarchy' was a convenient shorthand for male domination. In a speculative vein, some theories of patriarchy sought to explain the origins of sexual domination in early human history.[9] But historically speaking, much the most fruitful aspect of this phase of feminism was the demonstration of how patriarchy operated in a range of social contexts in which women's subordination was clearly central. Key areas were the sexual division of labour, power relations within the family, the double standard of sexual conduct, and the exclusion of women from formal political institutions. These topics furnished much of the agenda of women's history during the pioneer phase, as the early work of Joan Scott or Judith Walkowitz demonstrates.[10]

Since the 1980s the concept of patriarchy has been subject to a great deal of searching critique, not least from feminists. Originating in a politics of protest against oppression, it has been pointed out that patriarchy tends to lock women into the role of victim and to demonise all men as agents of that oppression. Given its ideological provenance, the term is so morally loaded that it is said to impose a rigid polarisation on a field of social relations which in reality is much more complex. It is also objected that patriarchy has little explanatory power because, in claiming to account for all aspects of gender inequality from the state down to the household, it ends up explaining nothing; and because it similarly ranges across all periods in a misplaced quest for the eternal principles of women's subjection.[11] Not all of these criticisms are fair. The alleged over-generalisation of patriarchy is precisely what makes the notion so valuable, because it emphasises how comprehensive the principle of male supremacy has been in most recorded societies. The criticism of ahistoricity is also wide of the mark. Most proponents of patriarchy did not say that there had been no change over time, merely that patriarchy had endured as an underlying principle of social stratification. One could maintain this position without, for example, denying the transition from scriptural to scientific patriarchy during the Early Modern period.[12]

The debt of hegemonic masculinity to this strand of feminist thought is clear. Connell's rationale in advancing the theory was precisely to demonstrate the structural and ideological links between masculinity in its multiple forms and the unequal distribution of power between the sexes: 'most men benefit from the subordination of women, and hegemonic masculinity is the cultural expression of this ascendancy'.[13] Hegemonic masculinity has proved to be a particularly sophisticated and adaptable development of some of the key ingredients of patriarchy. It does not brand all men as the upholders of patriarchy. The central place which the theory accords to *masculinities* means that it is sensitive to historical variation, and much less likely to apply a blunt instrument to all periods and cultures. Moreover the Gramscian inheritance means that *hegemony* implies far less permanence than patriarchy; it invites challenge and contestation, as those whom it oppresses seek to topple it and to replace it with a differently ordered hegemony. Above all, the theory of hegemonic masculinity shows how the maintenance of patriarchy actually *depends* on unequal relations between different masculinities. An early acknowledgement of this perspective was made by Heidi Hartmann in 1979: 'patriarchy is a set of social relations which has a material base and in which there are hierarchical relations between men and solidarities among them, which enable them to control women'.[14] But the close focus of hegemonic masculinity on those hierarchical relations and solidarities, and on the structural relations between them, goes far beyond the agenda of patriarchal theory. Here the prime debt of the concept of hegemonic masculinity is to gay liberation.

From the vantage point of the twenty-first century the main impact of gay liberation may appear to have been the popularisation of the view that masculinity is a matter of individual preference, based on a range of choices as regards sexuality and lifestyle. But the gay theorists of the 1970s and 1980s were as much, if not more, concerned with power as with choice. Drawing on the insights of Foucault, they argued that homosexuality was a social construction, whose emergence during the second half of the nineteenth century said as much about the dominant forms of masculinity as about gay men themselves. Jeffrey Weeks in particular explored the relationship between gay identity and compulsory heterosexuality (as well as the historical evidence for common cause between homosexuals and feminists).[15] He and other gay historians emphasised how heterosexual masculine identities came to depend on the demonisation of 'the homosexual' as a means of defining boundaries and policing deviants. Heterosexuality could not be compulsory for women, but optional for men; and it had to be suppressed among young men in order to maintain the prime patriarchal institution of marriage. And, as Eve Kosofsky Sedgwick has emphasized in an influential passage, gay sex introduces rivalry and jealousy into ranks of men, and thus weakens their solidarity in defence of patriarchy; collectively men observe a homophobia at times bordering on panic because team loyalty must prevail over intimacy.[16] Within patriarchal assumptions the logic of the state in visiting the severest penalties on homosexual behaviour is therefore compelling.

The notion that men are ranked according to their sexual orientation, and that the fear of 'deviant' sexuality is systematically employed to discipline not only sexual deviants but other marginal masculinities, is fundamental to hegemonic masculinity. 'Pacifists and pansies' – one of the many wartime slurs on the manhood of conscientious objectors in Britain – expresses this point perfectly.[17] But hegemonic masculinity is potentially a more comprehensive theory of gender than either patriarchy or gay theory. Theories of patriarchy tend not to differentiate between masculinities; gay theory, while premised on the existence of patriarchy, does not address the whole range of masculine practices which oppress women. Both gay theory and feminist theory view the dominant forms of masculinity from the perspective of those at the receiving end, as it were; hegemonic masculinity takes on board these critical perspectives, but explores their implications for the behaviour and experience of the majority of men who either uphold hegemonic masculinity or collude in it as silent beneficiaries. Thus we see how the core practices of hegemonic masculinity discriminate against men as well as women. The social primacy accorded to the male breadwinner marginalises not only the working wife but also the househusband. Compulsory heterosexuality has the consequence of disparaging the single woman, as well as outlawing homosexual practices. The sexual subordination of the married woman is maintained by persecuting the 'errant' wife and by holding the cuckold up to ridicule. The list of such complementarities could be extended.

Hegemonic masculinity in historical analysis

Historians, as noted already, tend to employ the term 'hegemonic masculinity' somewhat uncritically: if they draw on Connell at all, they do so selectively, and they rarely explain or critique their use of the term. But two meanings recur. First, hegemonic masculinity is taken to stand for those masculine attributes which are most widely subscribed to – and least questioned – in a given social formation: the 'common sense' of gender as acknowledged by all men save those whose masculinity is oppositional or deviant. Physical strength and practical competence are standard components, as Connell himself emphasised in his original formulation; other recurrent features include sexual performance and the capacity to protect and support women.[18] The identification of a cluster of hegemonic attributes does not, of course, mean that all men conform to them in practice: many men will be physically below standard or unable to maintain domestic dependants. But it is a measure of hegemony that such men feel that they should struggle to attain these goals, and that to the extent that they fall short of them they do not count in their own eyes as 'men'. Masculine attributes which are hegemonic in this generic sense tend to be enduring, giving rise to the assumption that gender identification is 'above' or anterior to other social categories, following independent trajectories of development and change, and perhaps scarcely changing at all.[19]

But hegemonic masculinity is not confined to these features of the gender *longue durée*. In fact, as several contributors to this volume note, hegemonic masculinity typically embraces elements which are much more contingent. One of the characteristic features of national crisis is that it may bring about drastic change in the socially acceptable ways of being a man. During the French Revolution, as Joan Landes reminds us, the right to bear arms signified not merely a state commitment to the *levée en masse*, but a new and highly public constituent of universal masculinity. One feature of the French drive for European ascendancy was that that same identification of masculinity with military values evolved in other countries which were obliged to resort to mass conscription. The effect was particularly marked in Prussia where, as Karen Hagemann explains, death for the fatherland was elevated as a heroic possibility for all men, in a new hegemonic model of military masculinity.[20] Sonya Rose graphically documents the impact of national crisis on hegemonic masculinity in her account of the transition from peacetime to total war in Britain in the 1940s. During the 1920s and 1930s the aggressive and belligerent masculinity of the First World War had been superseded by a quieter, more domestic, and anti-heroic style. While these virtues were patently inappropriate with the return of war in 1939, the renewed hegemony of martial values was tempered by a cult of stoic good-humoured 'ordinariness' which matched the role of civilians on the home front. In Rose's account hegemonic masculinity, far from being an enduring monolith, is contingent and volatile.

But whether founded on changing circumstance or long-term structures, the examples of hegemonic masculinity discussed so far are defined according to the gender norms to which most men subscribe, whether or not they fully enact them. This might be called the minimalist interpretation of hegemonic masculinity. The second usage has a sharper political edge. It identifies hegemonic masculinity as the masculine norms and practices which are most valued by the politically dominant class and which help to maintain its authority. How far a given political order succeeds in this respect must depend on the extent to which the hegemonic norms and practices are taken up by the generality of men, so in practice there is a blurring between this category and the first one. But analytically it helps to keep them distinct. Connell describes the hegemonic masculinity of contemporary capitalist societies as based on calculative rationality and technical expertise; it reflects the ascendancy of the bureaucrat and the businessman, in place of the landed class whose code of honour was hegemonic until the revolutionary era beginning in the late eighteenth century.[21] In some instances the implication is clear that hegemonic codes of manhood served to strengthen the power and security of the governing class. Mark E. Kann has described such a situation in the early years of the American Republic, where the founding fathers sought to restore a proper hierarchy after the upheaval of war by promoting hegemonic norms of masculinity. 'By controlling the criteria for male elevation and degradation, elites who join hegemony to manhood significantly strengthen their ability to secure men's consent and quiescence.'[22] In periods of emerging national identity or of national resistance, this dominant masculinity is likely to become a metaphor for the political community as a whole and to be expressed in highly idealised forms. In *The Image of Man* (1996) George Mosse identified the fusion of physical beauty with inner moral virtue as the masculine ideal of European bourgeois nationalism, and traced its permutations from the late eighteenth century up to the 1990s.[23]

This identification of hegemonic masculinity with the dominant class has important implications for the armed services. In order for the state to have secure control of the means of violence, there must be a reliable stream of recruits into the armed forces with the appropriate values and capacities; and there must be a broad popular acceptance of the military as being necessary and even laudable. Both these considerations tend towards a convergence between military and civilian codes of masculinity. As Michael Roper's analysis of officers' letters home during the First World War shows, the experience of combat tested the masculinity of combatants in unforeseen and deeply ambivalent ways. But these contradictions were lost in the popular rendering of military life. The soldier was idealised though a variety of cultural mediums, including adventure fiction, military journalism, and uniformed youth movements. In Edwardian Britain the army stood for a hegemonic masculinity that valorised the trained and powerful body and invoked high ideals of courage and sacrifice.[24]

At the same time, it is worth emphasising that the notion of a hegemonic masculinity applies not only to elites, but to subordinate classes. Many features of the dominant masculinity will be imposed on other social groups, either by compulsion or through the pressure of social prestige. But subordinate groups have, to a greater or lesser extent, been structured around their own masculine codes which may vary significantly from those at the top. Indeed, the political prospects of those social groups which lie outside the circle of power have often hinged on the coherence of their gender codes. A classic example is the professional and commercial men of early nineteenth-century England: Leonore Davidoff and Catherine Hall analyse their blend of hard work, sobriety, and domesticity during a period when social and political ascendancy still belonged to the landed elite, but when the 'middling sort' was gradually taking on the mantle of a hegemonic middle class.[25] Working-class politics offers a particularly fascinating arena in which to explore these issues. Thomas Welskopp shows how the Social Democrats – the largest working-class political party in nineteenth-century Germany – rejected the bourgeois standard of private property and domestic patriarchy; instead they developed a masculine culture of associations and assemblies, in which manliness was tested in the cut-and-thrust of public debate. Comparable patterns can be found in the extra-European world. In twentieth-century Brazil, according to Barbara Weinstein, labour unions struggled hard to preserve the activist character of the male worker, as against the self-controlled, compliant worker whom the employers tried to create. Marilyn Lake shows how during the early twentieth-century Australian working men adapted their definition of masculinity to take account of new conditions of industrial bargaining: the family or living wage, instead of being just a negotiating ploy, was re-articulated as 'a right that was understood to inhere . . . in manhood itself'.[26] And in a particularly striking instance, Alice Kessler-Harris shows how the commitment of the American labor movement to the ideal of manly independence caused it immense difficulty in accepting sorely needed state assistance during the Great Depression.

But we need to be clear what is being claimed here. Masculinity has often furnished governing elites with a powerful rhetoric for dignifying the political order: a case in point is the adaptation of metaphors of masculinity to correspond with the priorities of the peace-making process in 1919, as described by Glenda Sluga. In many societies which exclude women from any formal political role, political virtue will be conceptualised in masculine terms, in a discourse which reflects hegemonic conventions and practices. For example Kathleen Wilson (in her fine study of eighteenth-century politics) has referred to 'the masculinist model of English virtue'; we can be sure that there was a masculinist model of French virtue, Prussian virtue, and so on, even if other aspects of national identity were conceptualised in feminine terms (as in the motherland).[27] Sonya Rose remarks that 'hegemonic masculinity and wartime Britishness were of a piece'.[28] Comparable identifications were made by nationalists in societies outside Europe, as Joanna de Groot demonstrates in her analysis of civic manliness in Iran during the era of imperialist intervention. What is not clear from such accounts is how far the dominant masculinity of a given nation or class was also to do with sustaining and defending gender hegemony as such.

This is where Connell's distinctive take on hegemonic masculinity is so illuminating. He demonstrates rather more clarity, rigour, and political cutting edge than the historical approaches described so far. By defining hegemonic masculinity as those norms and institutions which actively serve to maintain men's authority over women and over subordinated masculinities, he offers a coherent structural framework of broad application. Hierarchies between women and men and hierarchies among men are seen as interdependent. Carrigan, Connell, and Lee were particularly concerned to stress the complicity of hegemonic masculinity in the oppression of gay men.[29] Indeed hegemonic masculinity has been given the alternative label of 'hierarchic heterosexualism' by one commentator.[30] This emphasis has been echoed by several historians of the nineteenth century, alert to the consequences of hegemonic strategies towards homosexual men, which were so harsh and so formative of modern sexual politics.[31]

But the central structuring principle of hegemonic masculinity, according to Connell, is power over women. The attributes which it prescribes are those which confirm the power and prestige of men at the expense of the opposite sex: typically strength, self-reliance, bread-winning capacity and sexual performance. Connell makes a threefold distinction to reflect the variable relation between hegemonic masculinity and patriarchy.[32] Firstly, the mark of an unmediated hegemonic masculinity is the readiness to impose authority over women without scruple. Secondly, most men draw back from consistently or openly enforcing their power as a sex, while at the same time benefiting from the prevailing structure of gender relations: theirs is a complicit masculinity, cashing in on the patriarchal dividend. Thirdly, there are substantial categories of men whose values or behaviour are at odds with patriarchal order. For example physically weak men are marginalised because they lack the resources to enforce face-to-face patriarchal relations; young men are disciplined because their sexual excesses threaten to bring patriarchy into disrepute; and gay men are oppressed because they subversively advertise an alternative to the heterosexual norm. As Carrigan, Connell, and Lee have put it, 'it would hardly be an exaggeration to say that hegemonic masculinity is hegemonic insofar as it embodies a successful strategy in relation to women'.[33]

Evaluation

The most original and creative phase in formulating a theory of hegemonic masculinity took place fifteen years ago. How well has the theory worn, and how solid a foundation does it provide for further historical work? Connell and his associates, who made the key conceptual advance in the 1980s, had in mind a primarily materialist model. Not for nothing was Connell's most influential work called *Gender and Power*. His rationale was to illumine (and hopefully transform) practices of power and oppression in the family, in work, in schools, and in politics. The study of history held for him a broadly emancipatory appeal.[34] The work collected in this volume takes a rather different tack. The dominant approach is to examine the historical specifics of masculinity through the study of discourse and representation: the construction of identities, the making and unmaking of heroes, the articulation of national character, and so on. The contributors draw on a distinguished pedigree. One thinks of Graham Dawson's study of Henry Havelock and T. E. Lawrence as masculine exemplars, and Abigail Solomon-Godeau's analysis of representations of the male body during the period of the French Revolution.[35] In this volume the chapters by Carroll Smith-Rosenberg, Joan Landes, and Stefan Dudink make up an impressive set of variations on the theme of masculine civic virtue as it was represented during the transition to democracy and nationalism. Their sophistication is evidence of the continuing vigour of the 'cultural turn' in historical studies.

But here, as in other branches of history, the cultural turn entails loss as well as gain. It subordinates practice to representation; it prioritises the cultural 'moment' over a longer time perspective; above all, it often obscures the material foundation of structures of difference. The majority of cultural historians do not see their practice as being at odds with the earlier 'social' approach, and they do not discount the significance of the material basis of power and inequality.[36] At a theoretical level it may be true to say that social relations do not exist apart from the production of cultural meanings; but in actual historical work the outcome can be a curiously detached kind of cultural analysis. Because Gramsci laid such emphasis on the cultural dimensions of hegemony, it has too readily been assumed that hegemonic masculinity is a cultural phenomenon *tout court*. But hegemony is also about lived social relations – about experience as well as representation. Thomas Welskopp's chapter is a telling illustration of this point. The 'contentious masculinity' of Social Democrats in mid-nineteenth-century Germany was formed not only through tropes and images, but through a collective experience of fraternalism and an active, exclusionary misogyny. The Social Democrats' practice of an active citizenship took place in the forum of the public debate, from which women were rigorously excluded. Debate resembled

war: manliness was equated with standing up for one's principles, refus-
ing compromise, driving one's adversary from the floor. In Welskopp's
account the debates were critical to working-class masculinity less because
of their discursive content than because of the *activity* of debate – the
competitiveness, the aggression designed to secure a total rout, and the
pronounced misogyny.

But if Connell's approach is a salutary reminder of the material
basis of gender relations, questions must be asked about its range of
application. In *Masculinities* (1995) hegemonic masculinity was offered
as the central gender concept for the understanding of today's societies,
and as the basis of an ambitious reinterpretation of two hundred years
of Western history.[37] Two objections are particularly relevant to the
historical understanding of politics and war. In the first place, it is never
convincingly demonstrated why patriarchy should take precedence over
all other structuring principles, to the extent that Connell affirms. One
can accept the profoundly hierarchical character of masculinities, and
the investment of men in power and dominance, without concluding
that maintaining power over women is the deciding imperative. The
logic of a dominant code of masculinity may be to uphold class power,
or to consolidate the ascendancy of one religious denomination over
another, and in these cases power over men may be more significant
than power over women. In colonial societies great pains were taken to
impose a polarised discourse of gender, in which the masculinity of the
colonisers was affirmed and celebrated at the expense of the standing
of the colonised. This is the argument of Mrinalini Sinha in her study of
nineteenth-century Bengal; the manhood of the Bengalis was disparaged,
not because they were unreliable agents of patriarchy, but because the
lowering of their self-esteem was a condition of secure colonial rule.[38]
Jacobus Du Pisani deals with a particularly complex situation in his
chapter on South Africa. He shows how during the 1930s and 1940s the
Afrikaner cultural elite developed a manly ideal of the hard-working,
God-fearing, and self-reliant farmer, ready and able to re-live the heroism
of the *bittereinder* ('bitter-ender') who had held the British at bay a
generation earlier. But the same masculine self-image also served to
belittle the manhood of the African majority, and this became brutally
apparent when the Nationalist Party came to power in 1948.

Connell's global survey of masculinities properly acknowledges the
complex gender regimes to be found in colonial society and the way
in which the manipulation of masculine imagery was an ideological
support for colonial domination, but these dimensions feature much
less in his theoretical exposition.[39] The gist of much work in recent years

Critique of Connell

is that hegemonic forms of masculinity have sustained different structures of power in different historical formations, and that the priority
which Connell gives to patriarchy is over-stated. Thus Smith-Rosenberg
demonstrates the role of hegemonic masculinity in maintaining the political ascendancy of the 'republican gentleman' in the Anglo-American
world of the eighteenth century. Welskopp, Lake, Weinstein and Kessler-
Harris analyse hegemonic masculinity as an expression of class politics
near the bottom of the social scale; Rose, de Groot, Dudink and
Hagemann place it in the frame of national identity. In fact it is becoming
clear that the notion of a unlinear link between hegemonic masculinity
and one hierarchical axis may not be the most useful way of characterising the actual distribution of power. Masculinity is better seen as one
of a number of hierarchical principles which operate together to define
the lineaments of the social order: in Sinha's words, we recognise
masculinity to be 'constituted by, as well as constitutive of, a wide set of
social relations'.[40]

Connell's heavy stress on the dynamic of patriarchy is open to a
second objection, which is that it drastically simplifies the homosocial
dynamic – that is to say, the considerations which govern men's relations
with each other *as men*. In all societies men practice a range of activities
and honour specific masculine values which have nothing to do with
the maintenance of patriarchal control. It is here that the dialectic of
comradeship and competition is played out.[41] Strength, self-reliance,
bread-winning capacity, and sexual performance are all in their different
ways patriarchal attributes, but they are also celebrated among men in
ways which have as much to do with peer-group standing as with sexual
dominance; and those who fail to come up to scratch are not simply
dysfunctional shock-troops in the sex war; they are condemned as 'less
than men'. The work ethic has been a fundamental masculine value in
modern bourgeois societies. In its classic form it served to justify and
intensify the gulf between industrious man and decorative woman, but
this was incidental; without question its prime appeal lay in the promise
it held out of material success and social prestige. Again, men's clubs
and fraternities reinforced women's exclusion from the public sphere,
but they were chiefly valued by their members for other reasons: for
their networking potential, the opportunity to enjoy a 'men's culture',
and as a means of cultivating class solidarity.[42] In short, the pecking
order among men cannot be explained simply in terms of their differ-
ential contribution to the upholding of sexual domination.

The military sphere is particularly crucial to this argument. Of course
men's monopoly of institutionalised force has bolstered their ascendancy

over women, both in a material sense and because it lent conviction to the myth of male invincibility. Moreover military values have often been promoted as a response to perceived threats to male dominance. During the era of the New Imperialism in late nineteenth-century Britain, the partial militarisation of hegemonic masculinity served to bolster the indispensability of manly attributes at a time when women's educational and social advances appeared to pose a challenge to traditional patriarchal assumptions.[43] But the patriarchal framework does not begin to provide an adequate explanation for the intimate links between militarism and masculinity. Historically men have been kept in a state of readiness for warfare in order to defend a community which encompassed women as well as men. The vigour and courage prized by men were not only a basis for claiming gender privilege, but a potentially mortal burden, in many instances cutting off life before the privileges of manhood had been acquired.[44] The shared danger of death and the mutual dependence of soldiers in moments of peril explain why fraternal comradeship – the love of soldiers – has been such a pronounced feature of most armies.[45] The patriarchal dividend of military masculinity is clear, but it is far from being a sufficient explanation. To say that in the final analysis the gendered pecking order among men exists because of its bearing on the power dynamic between men and women is a very large claim which is far from being borne out by the historical record. Here, at least, the first (or minimalist) definition of hegemonic masculinity, as those attributes most widely subscribed to by the generality of men, makes for less distortion.

Conclusion

Hegemonic masculinity was the much-needed development of a theoretical base in masculinity studies when it was first sketched twenty years ago. It brought into sharp focus the structural relationship between men's power over women and the distinctions commonly observed (and enforced) between men. Its value does not lie primarily in identifying what the generality of men subscribed to at a given time, or in revealing the gender practices of the ruling elite, though each of these approaches has a contribution to make. The theory of hegemonic masculinity has proved its worth because it keeps the power relations of gender always in view, and it reminds us that structures of sexual dominance operate at several levels, all of which must be identified and understood in their complementary relations. A generation of research in history and allied disciplines has been stimulated by notions of hegemonic masculinity.[46]

As with every model of social analysis, the elegance and coherence of the theory was purchased at the cost of schematic oversimplification. The inherent distortions have become steadily more evident over the past decade. For scholars who have signed up to the 'cultural turn' hegemonic masculinity is too heavily implicated in the materialism and determinism of *marxisant* social history. For those who are drawn to the postmodern fragmentation of sexual identities it smacks too much of the naïve sexual politics of socialist feminism. The outcome of these intellectual developments is that the cultural manifestations of hegemonic masculinity are now given much greater emphasis, and its place in the social and political order has been diversified, revealing the implication of masculinity in the maintenance of power structures besides patriarchy. But multivalence and contingency can, in turn, be overplayed. The virtual absence of 'patriarchy' from the scholarly lexicon at the present time points to a disconcerting shift away from those deep-set and enduring inequalities between men and women which informed scholarly work in the 1970s and 1980s. To analyse historical masculinities in broadly cultural terms without attending to the relations of material power between men and women is no less distorting that to focus exclusively on the patriarchal rationale of hegemonic masculinity. The challenge for our subject is to convey the imperatives, contradictions, and ambiguities of masculinity as they were realised in historical experience. We can only accomplish this if we strive to integrate the materialist insights of a generation ago with the beguiling subtleties of cultural interpretation today.

Notes

My thanks to David Tjeder, Stefan Dudink, Karen Hagemann and Michael Roper for their helpful comments.

1 P. G. Filene, *Him/Her/Self: Sex Roles in Modern America* (Baltimore, 1974); P. N. Stearns, *Be A Man! Males in Modern Society* (New York, 1979).

2 As asserted, for example, in J. Tosh, 'What should historians do with masculinity?', *History Workshop Journal*, 38 (1991), 184–7.

3 R. W. Connell, *Which Way Is Up?* (Sydney, 1983), pp. 27–32, 41, 58–62; T. Carrigan, B. Connell, and J. Lee, 'Hard and heavy: Toward a new sociology of masculinity', in M. Kaufman (ed.), *Beyond Patriarchy: Essays by Men on Pleasure, Power and Change* (Toronto, 1987), pp. 139–92; R. W. Connell, *Gender and Power* (London, 1987); R. W. Connell, *Masculinities* (Cambridge, 1994).

4 It should be noted, however, that Connell first trained as a historian. His interest in history is evident in his writings, especially 'The big picture: Masculinities in recent world history', *Theory and Society*, 22 (1993), 597–623.

5   Carrigan, Connell and Lee, 'Hard and heavy', p. 181.
6   Connell, 'The big picture'.
7   A. Gramsci, *Selections from the Prison Notebooks* (London, 1971), esp. pp. 12–13; 53–60; 261–4; R. Williams, *Marxism and Literature* (Oxford, 1977), pp. 108–14.
8   Connell, *Gender and Power*, p. 107.
9   G. Lerner, *The Creation of Patriarchy* (New York, 1986).
10 L. Tilly and J. Scott, *Women, Work and the Family* (London, 1978); J. M. Walkowitz, *Prostitution and Society in Victorian England* (Cambridge, 1981).
11 This started with S. Rowbotham, 'The trouble with patriarchy', in R. Samuel (ed.), *People's History and Socialist Theory* (London, 1981).
12 J. M. Bennett, 'Feminism and history', *Gender and History*, 1 (1989), 251–72.
13 Connell, *Gender and Power*, p. 185.
14 H. Hartmann, 'The unhappy marriage of Marxism and Feminism: Towards a more progressive union', in L. Sargent (ed.), *Women and Revolution* (Boston, 1981), p. 14. See, also C. Cockburn, *Brothers: Male Dominance and Technological Change* (London, 1983), p. 125.
15 J. Weeks, *Coming Out: Homosexual Politics in Britain from the Nineteenth Century to the Present* (London, 1977); J. Weeks, *Sex, Politics and Society: The Regulation of Sexuality since 1800* (London, 1981).
16 E. Kosofsky Sedgwick, *Between Men* (New York, 1985), ch. 1.
17 S. Rose, see below, p. 189.
18 Connell, *Which Way Is Up?*, p. 27.
19 I discuss this point more fully in J. Tosh, 'The new man and the old Adam: Emerging themes in the history of English masculinities, 1750–1850', in T. Hitchcock and M. Cohen (eds), *English Masculinities, 1660–1800* (London, 1999), pp. 236–8.
20 See also K. Hagemann, 'Of "manly valour" and "German honor": Nation, war and masculinity in the age of the Prussian uprising against Napoleon', *Central European History*, 30 (1997), 187–220.
21 Connell, 'The big picture', pp. 607–10; Connell, *Masculinities*, pp. 186–94.
22 M. E. Kann, *The Republic of Men: The American Founders, Gendered Language, and Patriarchal Politics* (New York, 1998), p. 28.
23 G. L. Mosse, *The Image of Man* (New York, 1996).
24 On Britain, see H. J. Field, *Toward a Programme of Imperial Life: The British Empire at the Turn of the Century* (Oxford, 1982), and J. M. McKenzie (ed.), *Popular Imperialism and the Military, 1850–1950* (Manchester, 1992). For a perceptive general discussion of masculinity and the military, see D. H. J. Morgan, 'Theater of war: Combat, the military and masculinities', in H. Brod and M. Kaufman (eds), *Theorizing Masculinities* (Thousand Oaks CA, 1994), pp. 165–82.
25 L. Davidoff and C. Hall, *Family Fortunes: Men and Women of the English Middle Class, 1780–1850* (London, 1987).
26 M. Lake, see below, p. 211.
27 K. Wilson, *The Sense of the People: Politics, Culture and Imperialism in England, 1715–85* (Cambridge, 1995), p. 203.
28 Rose, see below, p. 186.
29 Carrigan, Connell and Lee, 'Hard and heavy', pp. 170–6.
30 A. Brittan, *Masculinity and Power* (Oxford, 1989), p. 188.

31 Weeks, *Coming Out*; Weeks, *Sex, Politics and Society*; K. Plummer (ed.), *The Making of the Modern Homosexual* (London, 1981); A. Sinfield, *The Wilde Century* (London, 1994).

32 Connell, *Gender and Power*, pp. 183–6; and *Masculinities*, pp. 77–81.

33 Carrigan, Connell and Lee, 'Hard and heavy', p. 180.

34 See, especially Connell, 'The big picture'.

35 G. Dawson, *Soldier Heroes: British Adventure, Empire and the Imagining of Masculinities* (London, 1994); A. Solomon-Godeau, *Male Trouble: a Crisis in Representation* (London, 1997).

36 An important exception is Patrick Joyce. See his 'The end of social history?', *Social History*, 20 (1995), 73–91.

37 Connell, *Masculinities*, pp. 186–98.

38 M. Sinha, *Colonial Masculinity: The 'Manly Englishman' and the 'Effeminate Bengali' in the Late Nineteenth Century* (Manchester, 1995).

39 Connell, *Masculinities*, pp. 194, 197–8.

40 M. Sinha, 'Giving masculinity a history: some contributions from the historiography of colonial India', *Gender & History*, 11 (1999), 446.

41 M. Donaldson, 'What is hegemonic masculinity?', *Theory and Society*, 22 (1993), 643–57.

42 M. A. Clawson, *Constructing Brotherhood: Class, Gender, and Fraternalism* (Princeton, 1989); J. Tosh, *A Man's Place: Masculinity and the Middle-Class Home in Victorian England* (London, 1999), pp. 127–36.

43 J. Tosh, 'Imperial masculinity and the flight from domesticity in Britain, 1880–1914', in T. Foley *et al.* (eds), *Gender and Colonialism* (Galway, 1995), pp. 72–85.

44 D. D. Gilmore, *Manhood in the Making: Cultural Concepts of Masculinity* (New Haven, 1990), pp. 223–4, 229–30.

45 See P. Fussell, *The Great War and Modern Memory* (New York, 1974), esp. ch. 8, for a classic account.

46 See, for example, A. Cornwall and N. Lindisfarne (eds), *Dislocating Masculinity: Comparative Ethnographies* (London, 1994); M. Vale de Almeida, *The Hegemonic Male: Masculinity in a Portuguese Town* (Providence, 1996).

PART II

*Historicising revolutionary masculinity:
constructs and contexts*

4

The republican gentleman: the race to rhetorical stability in the new United States

Carroll Smith-Rosenberg

T HE nineteenth century was the child of the 'Long Eighteenth Century's' many revolutions: the political revolutions that gave birth to the American, French, and Haitian republics; the national revolutions that produced the United States and Haiti as the first modern post-colonial states; the fiscal and industrial revolutions that shaped modern capitalism; the consumer revolutions that informed bourgeois cultures and identities. Over the century that followed, these revolutions intersected, transforming Western society, engendering modern concepts of the republican state, citizenship, capitalism – indeed modernity itself.

Revolutions are not gentle instruments. They disrupt societies, fracture families, decentre identities. Disdaining old truths, they lay bare the contradictions that lie at the heart of a culture's ideological foundations. This essay explores the ways the eighteenth-century's multiple revolutions recast concepts of masculinity and citizenship, leading ultimately to a new understanding of masculinity in which racial violence played a central role. To explore these issues, I have chosen to focus my analysis on a particularly rich site of political and social transformations, the revolutionary United States as it took form during the closing decades of the eighteenth century. The United States was the first modern republic in a world of monarchies, the first post-colonial nation in a world of empires.[1] Presenting their new self-image to a watching – and sceptical – world, European Americans represented themselves as radically new freedom-loving republicans and, simultaneously, as legitimate heirs of Europe's Enlightenment culture and imperial ventures. How did they harmonise these varied presentations of self? The figure of the republican gentleman, I will argue, personified the ideological contradictions the new Americans faced.

While novelty and contradiction characterised the new United States, isolation did not. Eighteenth-century European Americans lived within an Atlantic world shaped by the relentless flow of peoples, goods, practices, and political discourses across the Atlantic's broad expanse. To study the new American nation, therefore, we cannot limit our gaze to the North American mainland. Rather, we must broaden our vision to ponder the new nation's interaction with and dependency upon Great Britain, Africa, and the African diaspora, especially as that diaspora was shaped by the plantation slavery economies of the West Indies.[2] Certainly British republican and imperial discourses shaped the new nation, its understanding of republican citizenship and of gender. Equally relevant, of course, was the impact the commercial, fiscal, and consumer revolutions had on these understandings. Lastly, we cannot understand freedom and citizenship without understanding their polar opposites, slavery and racial disenfranchisement.

A starting point: the republican world of Augustan England

As freedom-loving and loyal citizens of the British Empire, eighteenth-century European Americans cut their political teeth on the hard biscuit of classic republican discourse. From its origins in Aristotle's writings, through Machiavelli's adaptations to Bolingbroke's political revisions, classic republicanism depicted the virtuous citizen as a *zoon politikon*, a political animal who dedicated his life and fortune to the well being of his state and the protection of his nation's liberty. Modelling himself upon images of Spartan and Roman warriors, he prided himself on his virility, courage in battle, and manly self-control.[3] Eschewing the fashionable luxuries the consumer revolution so temptingly held out, he was an aesthete depending on no one for favour or advancement. He was his own man, and that man was, at heart, pre-modern and pre-commercial.[4]

Increasingly, classic republican discourses associated political corruption with economic change – especially the economic changes associated with the fiscal revolutions of the late seventeenth century. Classic republic thought, John Pocock tells us, became obsessed with the dangers the late seventeenth century's fiscal revolution posed to the economic and social foundations of the British state and the republican subject as a *zoon politikon*.[5] Stability and order, a return to a golden age of economic self-sufficiency and subjective transparency, came to seem as central to the maintenance of civic virtue as the defence of liberty itself. Classic republican discourses, as scripted in Augustan Britain and disseminated among Britain's North American settler colonists, were nostalgic – fearful of commerce and the new culture of civility.[6]

Fiscal and political changes in Augustan Britain certainly gave classic republicans a great deal to be concerned about. To pay for the imperial and commercial wars Britain engaged in, Walpole and his political successors transformed England's national debt into a marketable property. The honour of the state was no longer a good to which one dedicated one's life and fortune. It had become a fiscal opportunity tied to speculation in commercial paper and corporate stocks. A new source of wealth emerged along with a new class of economically and politically powerful men.[7] Enter the speculator, the venture capitalist and his political allies – the new men of paper and place. Exit the virile *zoon politikon*, his manly dedication to state service, his Spartan asceticism.

The speculator and fiscal capitalist were thus the first faces modernity presented to England's landed gentry, faces classic republicans vociferously condemned. Classic republican texts excoriated the new men of fiscal capitalism as denizens of a passionate and venal world driven by fantasy, cathected with desire and characterised by instability and uncertainty. They lusted for political power, these critics railed, gambled their way to great fortunes and then squandered those fortunes on luxurious, sybaritic life styles. They were corrupt and effeminate.[8]

Merchants and commerce played more ambivalent roles within classic republican scripts. The value of their landed estates, the source of the gentry's claims to economic, and hence political, independence and civic virtue, depended on the price of agricultural goods and hence on trade and events occurring in ports around the world. The gentry responded with nervous suspicion and deep ambivalence to the circumscribing of their virtue by men and processes beyond their control. Trade, they consoled one another, was productive, linked to their own and their nation's prosperity and imperial dominance. It was allied to science and invention. It expanded Englishmen's knowledge of the world.[9] But trade depended on credit, which hung upon opinion. It fed upon fantasy and desire. It introduced virtuous British citizens to the luxuries of the 'Orient', led them into debt, the alienation of their estates, economic and political dependency. It effeminised them.[10]

Of course, classic republicans could not hold back the tides of change. Throughout the long eighteenth century, England's merchants expanded their trade routes until England's commercial sway stretched from India and China through the East Indies and Africa to the Caribbean and North America. Thus positioned, British merchants heaped the riches of the world upon the wharves of London, Bristol and Liverpool. From there they flowed through the arteries of trade into distant towns and villages and then across the Atlantic to the Caribbean and North

America. Indeed, North American merchants played a critical role in Britain's commercial revolution. Their ships carried the sugar and spices of the Caribbean to North American markets and British ports. By the mid-eighteenth century, North American ship builders, sail and barrel makers, country shopkeepers and rugged Western farmers had become willing participants in Britain's commercial revolution – and, with profits gained through commerce, in her consumer revolution as well.[11] Trade beckoned the English gentleman and his European American emulators to enter a world in which polite ceremonies, fashionable consumption and theatrical display signed class status and social respectability.[12] And so a second face of modernity presented itself – that of the eighteenth-century gentleman. It was a comely face, refined and delicate.[13]

No two figures could have been more dissimilar than the classic republican *zoon politikon* and the eighteenth-century gentleman of grace and wit. Of course, there were similarities. Both were men of wealth, leisure, and education, familiar with the classics and the histories of great republics and empires. But there the similarities ended. The classic republican, as we know, disdained urbanity and material display. His world was political and martial. In contrast the fashionable eighteenth-century gentleman's world revolved around balls, salons and tea tables. Beauty and grace, the sentiments and fashion held centre stage in that world – as did the gentlewoman.

Indeed the most telling difference between the classic republican world and the world of eighteenth-century gentility was the place women held in each. Classic republicanism had banished women from the world of politics, insisting that their lack of physical strength, rational self-control and independent, landed wealth prevented them from being virtuous republicans. Women, they claimed, corrupted the pure world of male public service and love of liberty. They would lead men into a far more dangerous world of unrestrained desire and fantasy, extravagance and corruption. And worse, they would effeminise men, make them womanly in manners and sentiments.[14] In contrast, the eighteenth-century discourses of gentility and *politesse* place women at the centre of a world of elegant culture and carefully choreographed heterosociality.[15] The eighteenth-century gentleman sought always to please and charm – especially the ladies. To accompany ladies at balls, the gentleman became an accomplished dancer and knowledgeable about music. To entertain them at tea parties, he played an instrument, composed a bit, made himself familiar with the latest play, the newest novel. Most especially, he cultivated the arts of polite conversation.[16] Because ladies abhorred confrontation, so did the gentleman. Because political and religious

disputes lay outside their purview, only the rudest of men would introduce them. In short, performing for ladies' accolades made a man a
refined gentleman – the antithesis of the rugged *zoon politikon*.[17]

By the late eighteenth century it was clear that understandings of
what it meant to be a gentleman had changed radically. Far from being
an independent ascetic fierce in defence of liberty and at war with
modernity and urbanity, the ideal gentleman had become a devotee of
fashion, carefully trained to perform the fashions of the day with grace
and elegance. Of course, it was the gentleman and his abettors, the men
of commerce, capital, and speculation, who would carry the new day.
In so doing, they redefined understandings of masculinity, making
gentility and refinement critical to the practice of virtuous citizenship.

They could not have accomplished these transformations if the
only political discourse available to them was the discourse of classic
republicanism. Gradually, over the 'Long Eighteenth Century', Lockean
liberalism came first to challenge and then to replace classic republicanism as the premier political discourse of Great Britain and later of the
United States. In many ways, one could say Lockean liberalism turned
the classic republican world upside down. The virtuous liberal citizen was
less concerned with fiercely defending his state and far more concerned
with preserving his private property from the incursions of that state.
He made privacy a right, self-interest his driving force.[18] The parallels
between the eighteenth-century gentleman and the eighteenth-century
liberal citizen are striking. Both defined themselves in counter-distinction
to the state. Both saw the state as a source of political corruption, the
domain not of gentlemen but of professional politicians, bureaucrats,
and political operators. Both valorised domestic space, private virtues
and refinements, and a world far removed from the agora. While the
eighteenth century's repeated imperial wars made patriotism an accoutre-
ment of fashion – from time to time – the sentiments and feelings
remained critical components of the eighteenth-century gentleman's
presentation of self to the world.

This last point is particularly telling in terms of the engendering
of citizenship and the republican state. The sentiments had long been
considered the domain of women. As we have seen, embracing com-
plaisance, the culture of gentility made refined feelings and the consideration of others' feelings one of the principal marks of a gentleman.
Liberalism similarly valorised the sentiments, in part, at least, as a
response to one of classic republicanism's most telling criticisms – that
liberalism's focus on individual rights did little to create a sense of social
cohesion.[19] If service to the state was no longer the citizen's highest

duty, if the virtuous citizen was driven by his own private interests, classic republicans asked, what would hold society together and promote social cohesion? The liberal answered – the gentleman's refined sentiments. The private individual, witnessing another's need or an act of injustice in the private sphere, would sympathise with the sufferer and deploy the property his self-interest had led him to acquire to relieve human misery. This feeling gentleman, in his turn, would be observed by others who, in their turn, would also be inspired to sympathise with the poor and with victims of injustice. Social connections would multiply. The circulation of feelings among people would create a new, voluntary – and *apolitical* – form of social bonding and cohesion. The tasteful display and delicate performance of suffering thus became key to the new liberal social order. Modernity had become spectacular and the world feminised.[20]

Interacting, liberalism and gentility reconstituted the citizen as a private man of feelings and refinement who rather than serving and protecting the state demanded the state serve and protect him. Concepts of masculinity and of virtuous citizenship expanded to include the sympathies, culture, and grace. The liberal gentleman's feelings were as tender as those of women, his sense of grace and civility as delicate. Suffering little children to come unto him, he unashamedly embraced a world of domesticity and affection. The binary distinction between masculinity and femininity began to erode at the same times as modern society split into public and private arenas, the one led by a potentially corrupt and tyrannical bureaucracy, the other, private world filled with voluntary acts of charity and a thousand points of light. The modern citizen and the modern man were formed within these new binary oppositions.

Sea changes and Atlantic transformations: the post-colonial experience

The ideological conflicts British liberalism helped resolve proved far more complex when played out on the far side of the Atlantic. The United States of America's ideological heritage and post-colonial status were central to this complexity. Let us begin with that heritage. Classic republicanism was far more central to late eighteenth-century European Americans' sense of themselves as both republicans and white 'Americans' than it was to late eighteenth-century Englishmen's sense of themselves as Englishmen. Classic republican rhetoric helped revolutionary European Americans shape an image of themselves as freedom-loving republicans who had fought valiantly to protect their liberty against British tyranny and corruption. Wielding classic republicanism's ringing phrases, re-volutionary European Americans presented themselves both at home and in the courts of Europe as brave 'Sons of Liberty' and heroic states-men.[21] While the Revolutionary War introduced economic and social changes far more attuned to liberal capitalism than to a classic republican pre-modern vision of the world, post-revolutionary European Americans could not easily discard the political discourses that had played so central a role in their self-fashioning. Classic republicanism remained a significant political discourse and a central component of European Americans' national identity far into the nineteenth century.[22] Classic republicanism forged the new nation's self-image as 'The Land of the Free and the Home of the Brave'.

But the emotional and psychological significance of classic repub-licanism to European Americans' sense of self went still deeper. To understand this significance we must think of European Americans as the first post-colonials of the modern Western world. As such, they had to struggle simultaneously to establish their difference from, indeed their superiority to, the mother country they had just defeated in a bloody revolution – and their continued connection to that mother country. Classic republicanism helped them do both.

Continuing their embrace of the classic republicanism their fathers had inherited from Augustan Britain, they could represent themselves as the true heirs of Britain's tradition of liberty and political responsibil-ity, a heritage classic republicans traced back to the *Magna Carta*. At the same time, classic republican rhetoric permitted European Americans to position themselves as superior to a Britain they increasingly repre-sented as corrupt and degenerate – the Britain of corrupt politicians, a standing army, and rotten boroughs. Taking chapter and verse from the great classic republican texts of Augustan England, European Americans argued that the British country gentry had ceded political control to political placemen who were subject at all times to the pres-sures of patronage and self-interest. Political factions governed parlia-ment. Mercenaries fought her battles. All had occurred, European American patriots continued, because the British gentry had succumbed to the temptations of fashionable life. Devoting themselves to private pleasures and public display, they had forfeited their claims to political power and civic virtue. It was European American patriots, not corrupt British politicians, who now held up the beacon of liberty to the world. As virile heirs and protectors of ancient British liberties, European Amer-icans could not be discounted as savage residents of a savage land.[23]

Race and virility thus fused to form the heart of America's new national self-image.

Having wedded themselves to classic republican rhetoric, did European American then turn their backs on the fiscal innovations espoused by eighteenth-century England – along with its culture of gentility and consumerism? No. As the eighteenth century progressed, they embraced both with growing fervour. Here, then, is where we find ideological confusions escalating, subjectivities decentring and fragmenting. The very post-colonial pressures that made classic republicanism a critical rhetorical theme in the new nation also encouraged European Americans to embrace Britain's culture of gentility and consumerism. To present themselves as men of civility and sophistication – and thus as the cultural equals of Europe's elite – European Americans had to make the culture of gentility, its refinements, courtesies, and ceremonies their own. They had to insist that European Americans were as refined, educated, and talented as Europeans. Otherwise, Buffon's assertion that the impact of America's climate and geography would gradually reduce European Americans to a state of savagery – like the native Americans who prowled America's woods and planes – would appear to be true. Thus the post-colonial European American found himself in the trying position of having simultaneously to embrace the rhetoric of classic republicanism and the practices of the culture of gentility.[24] At one and the same time, he had to present himself as a *zoon politikon* and an eighteenth-century gentleman of refinement and polish. His performance of his American subjectivity, so newly, tentatively formed was at heart divided and unstable.

Social and economic realities further complicate our picture – and further fracture the new 'American' identity. That European Americans knew full well that the new nation, especially north of the Mason-Dixon Line, could claim few gentlemen 'to the manner born', only exacerbated ideological and subjective tensions. The English eighteenth-century gentry had to work hard to learn the graces demanded of the new gentleman, but they never doubted their status as gentlemen. They might appear to the London *bon ton* as rude and rustic, as Squire Westons given to drinking heavily and sleeping with their dogs, but they knew at all times that their social status rested on real incomes generated by their landed estates and a history of ruling their shires that they liked to think went back centuries.[25] European Americans possessed no such surety. The new republic's economic and social elite knew itself to be, by British standards, decidedly new and of middling class. Even New York State's patroon elite, families who traced their wealth and social status to extensive seventeenth-century land grants, were deeply involved in trade and manufacturing. European American gentlemen were far more like characters from a Charles Dickens novel than like those who inhabited Jane Austen's world. A century later, Henry James would keep what they manufactured a dark and humiliating secret, one that marginalised them within refined European society.[26]

Knowing all this, elite European Americans worked overtime to establish their status as gentlemen of culture and social polish. Thomas Jefferson brought 145 rolls of hand-painted French wallpaper with him on his return from Paris in the 1780s. Robert Morris, American's richest merchant and leading Federalist, imported a French dancing master and three Parisian cooks. Leading merchants and manufacturers built elegant Regency-style town houses and country estates with carefully designed romantic vistas and British names.[27] 'Life became a continuous performance', social historian Richard Bushman points out, 'perpetually subject to criticism. Everyone and virtually everything could be brought to judgement before the bar of refinement and beauty. Not only was criticism directed outward to others, but people had to watch themselves through the eyes of others. They had to perform for themselves and suffer from their own self-criticism. Performance was unrelenting.'[28] At all times, European American performers felt the breath of Europe's 'Others' at their backs and of European disdain upon their faces.[29]

The race to rhetorical stability

Occupying a dangerous and unstable middle ground, these new Americans had to work determinedly to fashion a unique sense of personal and national self out of an unstable mix of conflicting political, economic and social discourses: classic republicanism, liberalism, the discourses of gentility and respectability, the Protestant Work Ethic, fiscal capitalism, rugged individualism, American Exceptionalism. How were the new Americans to weave these disparate discourses and ideologies into a unified whole?; to present themselves to the world as coherent national subjects?; to stabilise the uncertain fusion of manliness and refinement on which their post-colonial identity rested?

Internally fragmented and contradictory subjects assume the appearance of coherence when juxtaposed to multiple others, who through their difference serve to consolidate and bestow an appearance of cohesion upon the fragmented subject. The more contradictory and unstable the ideologies that construct an identity, the more insistent the mechanisms constructing those others become. Internal contradictions, rejected or hated aspects of the subject, are projected outward onto negatively constructed others who exist in 'Manichaean' opposition to a now empowered and purified self. They serve as foils against which the uncertain subject is consolidated and mobilised. 'Identities are constructed through, not outside of difference', Stuart Hall argues, and continues:

> Throughout their careers, identities can function as points of identification and attachment only *because* of their capacity to exclude, to leave out, to render 'outside', abjected. Every identity has at its 'margin', an excess, something more. ... it is only through the relation to the Other, the relation to what it is not, to precisely what it lacks, to what has been called its constitutive outside that the 'positive' meaning of ... identity can be constructed.[30]

Enslaved African Americans and Native American warriors epitomised the 'excess', the 'abjectness' that lurked at the margins of the 'new American' identity, as they lurked at the periphery of white homes, in slave cabins or along the frontier. Negatively figured, they were imaginatively called forth by the new national press to stabilise European Americans' unstable senses of self. Their dark bodies setting off European American whiteness, their barbaric ways framing European American civility, they spotlighted European Americans' genetic and cultural connectedness to Europe. At the same time their stark otherness helped obscure the ideological confusions and rhetorical contradictions that undercut white Americans' sense of a coherent national identity.[31] 'The literature of the United States has taken as its concern the architecture of a *new white man* ... The process of organizing American coherence through a distancing Africanism became the operative mode of a new cultural hegemony', Toni Morrison argues in her critical volume *Playing in the Dark*. 'Africanism [by which Morrison means white figurations of African Americans and of blackness] has become', she continues,

> both a way of talking about and a way of policing matters of class, formations and exercises of power, ... meditations on ethics and accountability. Through the simple expedient of demonising and reifying the range of colour on a palette, American Africanism makes it possible to say and not say, to inscribe and erase, to escape and engage, to act out and act on, to historicize and render timeless. It provides a way of contemplating chaos and civilization, desire and fear, and a mechanism for testing the problems and blessings of freedom.[32]

Economic self-interest reinforced ideological patterns. Throughout the eighteenth century slavery was a driving economic force not only in the American south, but in the north as well. The provision trade to the plantation/slave economies of the West Indies provided northern merchants, farmers, and artisans with a critically important market. Ship carpenters, sail-makers and stevedores built ships for the West Indian trade. New York City sugar refiners, rum distillers, candy manufacturers – and their employees – depended on West Indian sugar for their livelihoods. Without the profits made in the West Indian trade, northern merchants would not have been able to trade with Great Britain or to import the exotic luxuries from India and China that proclaimed the north's urban elite refined gentlemen and ladies. The north's prosperity, spiralling population, displays of cultured refinement along with the pleasures northerners derived from the possession of exotic goods – none would have been possible without slavery. The freedom-loving American republican depended upon plantation slavery for his economic prosperity, prized possessions, and, most centrally of all, his very sense of self.[33]

Nor was slavery an unknown institution in the north. Throughout the colonial period, slavery had been a well-entrenched social and economic institution in the north. Indeed it continued to be so well into the nineteenth century. Although by the mid-1780s, states north of Maryland had abolished slavery, abolition, especially in the Middle Atlantic states, was a gradual process.[34] As a consequence, for years after the Declaration of Independence was proclaimed and the Liberty Bell rung, slaves were everywhere in the north. They worked as skilled urban artisans, agricultural labourers, domestic servants, hucksters, stevedores, and mariners. In livery, they marked elite social standing in Philadelphia and New York.[35]

As representations of African Americans helped stabilise 'Americans'' new national image, so did representations of Native Americans. Urban political magazines and newspapers, religious sermons, and political speeches all represented Native Americans as brutal savages unfit to claim sovereignty over the lands they had long roamed. No other genre presents this image more tellingly than the captivity narrative, one of eighteenth- and early nineteenth-century America's best-selling genres. Captivity narratives presented the Native American as the savage antithesis of the pious and civilised European American, the dark mirror image of the enlightened white man. No native nobility illuminates captivity narratives' representations of Native Americans. Rather, they present Native Americans as dark creatures of the night. Native Americans 'skulk' across inhospitable landscapes devoid of human habitation. They tomahawk, murder women and children, burn farms to the ground, loot and steal. 'To be cast into the Power of Savages, who, from Infancy are taught a hardness of Heart, which deprives them of the common Feelings of Humanity, is enough to intimidate the firmest Mind', one captivity narrative begins – and continues: 'but when we hear of helpless Women and Children torn from their Homes, and dragged into the Wilderness, we shudder at the Thought and are bound to acknowledge our infinite Obligations to the Almighty, that we are so much more enlightened than these unhappy Wretches of the Desert'.[36] 'The great and continuing popularity of these narratives, the uses to which they were put and the nature of the symbolism employed in them are evidence that the captivity narratives constitute the first coherent myth-literature developed in American for American audiences', Richard Slotkin tells us.[37] They helped define the European American as a civilized, virtuous and coherent national subject.

Beginning with the late eighteenth century and continuing through much of the nineteenth century, European Americans wove these three faces of modernity – the face of the capitalist, the face of the genteel and feeling man, the face of the white racist – in and through their self-representations as virtuous republicans, the equals, indeed superiors, to Englishmen and Europeans. Out of this inharmonious fusion of contradictory discourses, European Americans constituted their self-image as modern republican citizens and modern men. The result continues to be an internally contradictory and inherently unstable national identity. Is this a fourth face modernity presents to the world – the face of self-doubt and inner confusion?

Notes

1 It may seem particularly bold, especially in a European publication, to assert the United States as the first modern republic. What about the Netherlands? But the United States was the first republic that formally disavowed a monarchy. And it was definitely the first modern post-colonial nation. In the twenty-first century, as the military and fiscal power of the United States encircles the globe, thinking of the United States as a post-colonial nation may be difficult. But the key to the United States' self image lies in this very contradiction. The United States has always seen itself simultaneously as a post-colonial nation, born of its brave revolution against British tyranny, and the legitimate heir to Britain's political culture and Britain's Empire in America. To this day, the United States uses its self-image as a freedom-loving nation formed in the forge of revolution to mask its imperial desires. The fact that, unusual among post-colonial nations, it shared a racial identity with its former coloniser facilitated its adoption of Britain's imperial agenda.

2 For just a few explorations of the economic, cultural and ideological interdependencies of the Atlantic world see, for example: J. Roach, *Cities of the Dead: Circum-Atlantic Performance* (New York, 1996); and R. Blackburn, *The Making of New World Slavery: From the Baroque to the Modern 1492–1800* (London, 1997).

3 J. G. A. Pocock's monumental *Machiavellian Moment: Florentine Political Thought and the Atlantic Republican Tradition* (Princeton, 1975) offers the definitive exploration of classic republican thought as it took form in seventeenth- and eighteenth-century Great Britain and was then transposed to North America. See especially ch. xii.

4 *Ibid.*, chs xiii and xiv.

5 *Ibid.*, p. 423.

6 *Ibid.*, ch. xv.

7 J. Brewer, *The Sinews of Power* (London, 1989); R. Roberts and D. Knyaston (eds), *The Bank of England, 1694–1884* (New York, 1995); A. N. Porter and R. F. Holland (eds), *Money, Finance and Empire, 1790–1960* (London, 1985).

8 *Ibid.*, ch. xiii and xiv, *passim*. See, as well, J. P. Greene, 'The concept of virtue in late colonial British America', in R. K. Matthew (ed.), *Virtue, Corruption, and Self-Interest: Political Values in the Eighteenth Century* (Bethlehem, 1994), pp. 17–54.

9 I. Kramnick, 'Corruption in eighteenth-century English and American political discourse', in Mathews, *Virtue, Corruption and Self-Interest*, pp. 55–75. For a lengthy discussion of Britain's landed gentry's ambivalent attitudes toward trade see Pocock, *Machiavellian Moment*, ch. xiii.

10 C. Davenant, *Works, vol. II* (London, 1699), p. 275. Quoted in Pocock, *Machiavellian Moment*, p. 422.

11 See, for example, D. Hancock, *Citizens of the World: London Merchants and the Integration of the British Atlantic Community, 1735–1785* (Cambridge, 1995); P. K. Liss, *Atlantic Empires: The Network of Trade and Revolution, 1713–1826* (Baltimore, 1983); J. H. Plumb, *The Birth of a Consumer Society: The Commercialization of Eighteenth-Century England* (Bloomington, 1982); R. Porter, *English Society in the Eighteenth Century* (Harmondsworth, 1982); L. Weatherill, *Consumer Behavior and Material Culture in Britain, 1660–1760* (London, 1988); M. Berg, *The Age of Manufactures: Industry, Innovation and Work in Britain, 1700–1820* (Oxford, 1985).

12 For the rise of a consumer economy and culture see, for example, N. McKendrick, 'Introduction', ch. II: 'The commercialization of fashion', and ch. III: 'Josiah Wedgwood and the commercialization of the potteries', in Plumb (ed.), *The Birth of a Consumer Society*; and P. Borsay, *The English Urban Renaissance: Culture and Society in the Provincial Town 1660–1770* (Oxford, 1989).

13 For the classic discussion of the culture of gentility in eighteenth-century Europe see N. Elias, *The History of Manners*, trans. E. Jephcott (New York, 1982); and N. Elias, *Power and Civility*, trans. E. Jephcott (New York, 1982).

14 For various examples of classic republicanism's dismissal of women see Pocock, *Machiavellian Moment*, pp. 465, 475 and *passim*. See, as well discussions in L. Kerber, *Women of the Republic: Intellect & Ideology in Revolutionary America* (Chapel Hill, 1980); R. M. Smith, ' "One united people": Second-class female citizenship and the American quest for community', *Yale Journal of Law & the Humanities*, 1:2 (May, 1989), 229–93. For a comparison with European political attitudes towards women see J. B. Landes, *Women and the Public Sphere in the Age of the French Revolution*

(Ithaca, 1988); L. Hunt, 'The many bodies of Marie Antoinette: Political pornography and the problem of the feminine in the French Revolution', in L. Hunt (ed.), *Eroticism and the Body Politic* (Baltimore, 1991), pp. 108–30; and G. Fraisse, *Reason's Muse: Sexual Difference and the Birth of Democracy*, trans. J. M. Todd (Chicago, 1994).

15 See, for example, A. Vickery, *The Gentleman's Daughter: Women's Lives in Georgian England* (New Haven, 1998); H. Barker and E. Chalus (eds), *Gender in Eighteenth-Century England: Roles, Representations and Responsibilities* (London and New York, 1997); and R. W. Uphaus and G. M. Foster (eds), *The Other Eighteenth Century: English Women of Letters 1660–1800* (East Lansing, 1991). For the situation in France see D. Goodman, *The Republic of Letters: A Cultural History of the French Enlightenment* (Ithaca, 1994).

16 For the classic analysis of the culture of *politesse* see N. Elias, *The History of Manners*; and N. Elias, *The Court Society*, trans. E. Jephcott (New York, 1983).

17 D. S. Shields, *Civil Tongues and Polite Letters in British America* (Chapel Hill, 1997). For discussions of male gentility as it was performed in Great Britain, see, for example, P. Carter, 'Men about town: Representations of foppery and masculinity in early eighteenth-century urban society', in Barker and Chalus (eds), *Gender in Eighteenth-Century England*, pp. 31–57. In no way did the classic republican and the man of gentility differ more radically, John Pocock tells us, than in the basis of their self-knowledge, their understanding of themselves. The new ways and new values had altered the basis of the citizen's self-knowledge. The classic republican, his political independence, grounded on land holdings which all could see and none could alienate, Pocock explains, 'knew himself to be a citizen and knew how to play his role and take decisions within the *politeia* or *modo di vivere* of a republic'. He 'knew and loved [him]self in . . . relation to a *patria, res publica* or common good'. The classical republican's self-esteem (his *amour de soi-meme*) was based on the firmness of this knowledge. The man of gentility, consumerism and display, in contrast, was governed by '*amour-propre*', that is, by a self-love that depended 'on the figure one cut in one's own eyes and those of others'. Within the eighteenth century's world of capitalism and consumerism, a man's worth was no longer measured in hectometres planted, bushels of grain harvested, or rents received in solid specie. It rested, rather, on his projecting an appearance of credibility, respectability and polish. Surety about oneself and others disappeared. The new gentlemen, the classic republican concluded, was an actor, a performer, dependent on his audience, governed not by reason and self-restrain but by self-love and the desire to shine in society. In early modern England, the terms actor and counterfeit had been synonymous. The aura of the counterfeit continued to hang over the eighteenth-century gentleman – at least in the opinion of classic republicans Pocock, *Machiavellian Moment*, p. 464.

18 For discussions of liberal humanism, see C. B. MacPherson, *The Political Theory of Possessive Individualism: Hobbes to Locke* (Oxford, 1962); R. M. Smith, *Civic Ideals. Conflicting Visions of Citizenship in U.S. History* (New Haven, 1997); and R. A. Ferguson, *The American Enlightenment, 1750–1820* (Cambridge Mass, 1997). See, as well, M. B. Becker, *The Emergence of Civil Society in the Eighteenth Century* (Bloomington, 1994); J. Appleby, *Economic Thought and Ideology in Seventeenth-Century England* (Princeton, 1978); and S. M. Dworetz, *The Unvarnished Doctrine: Locke, Liberalism and the American Revolution* (Durham, 1990).

19 R. Smith, 'The Toquevillian thesis reconsidered', unpublished essay.

20 The literature on the sentiments is voluminous. For one fine example see J. Ellison, *Cato's Tears and the Making of Anglo-American Emotions in Press* (Chicago, 1999).

21 See Pocock, ch. xv, 'The Americanization of virtue', in *Machiavellian Moment*, pp. 506–52; and G. Wood, *The Creation of the American Republic, 1776–1787* (New York, 1969).

22 G. Wood, *The Radicalism of the American Revolution* (New York, 1993) and Smith, *Civic Ideals*.

23 *Ibid.*

24 For discussions of the translation of an Anglo-European discourse of civility and politesse within a United States' context see Shields, *Civil Tongues*; and R. Bushman, *The Refinement of America: Persons, Houses and Cities* (New York, 1993).

25 See, for example, A. Vickery, *The Gentleman's Daughter: Women's Lives in Georgian England* (New Haven, 1998).

26 E. Blackmar, *Manhattan for Rent, 1785–1850* (Ithaca, 1989); C. Matson, *Merchants and Empire: Trading in Colonial New York* (Baltimore, 1998); T. M. Doerflinger, *A Vigorous Spirit of Enterprise: Merchants and Economic Development in Revolutionary Philadelphia* (Chapel Hill, 1986). For the psychological implications, see K. A. Lockridge, 'Colonial self-fashioning: Paradoxes and pathologies in the construction of genteel identity in eighteenth-century America', in R. Hoffman, M. Sobel, and F. J. Teute (eds), *Through a Glass Darkly: Reflections of Personal Identity in Early America* (Chapel Hill, 1997), pp. 274–339.

27 Doerflinger, *A Vigorous Spirit*; Matson, *Merchants*; M. M. Lovell, 'Bodies of illusion: Portraits, people and the construction of men', in R. St. George (ed.), *Possible Pasts: Becoming Colonial in Early America* (Ithaca, 2000) pp. 270–301.

28 Bushman, *The Refinement of America*, p. xiv. See, as well, T. H. Breen, 'An empire of goods: The Anglicization of colonial America, 1690–1776', *Journal of British Studies*, 25 (October, 1986), 467–99; Shields, *Civil Tongues*; T. Westcott, *The Historic Mansions and Buildings of Philadelphia with Some Notice of their Owners and Occupants* (Philadelphia, 1877).

29 For an exploration of the role American literature played in this process, see J. Gardner, *Master Plots: Race and the Founding of an American Literature, 1787–1845* (Baltimore, 1998).

30 S. Hall, 'Introduction: Who needs identity?', in S. Hall and P. Du Gay (eds), *Questions of Cultural Identity* (London, 1996), pp. 5–6.

31 Two late eighteenth-century political magazines in which these representations were commonplace were *The American Museum*, published by radical Irish exile Mathew Carey, and *The Columbian Magazine and Monthly Miscellany*, the most elegant of the late eighteenth-century political magazines. For a survey of this literature see C. Smith-Rosenberg, 'Discovering the subject of the "Great Constitutional Discussion"', *Journal of American History*, 79:3 (1992), 841–73.

32 Toni Morrison, *Playing in the Dark: Whiteness and the Literary Imagination* (Cambridge, MA, 1992), pp. 7–8, 14.

33 Matson, *Merchants, passim.*; Doerflinger, *A Vigorous Spirit, passim.*

34 Most states freed only those African Americans born after a date named in the emancipation legislation – and then required those freed to serve a lengthy

apprenticeship, usually twenty years or more, in order to recompense their owners for the cost of having purchased and raised them.

35 G. Nash, *Forging Freedom in the Formation of Philadelphia's Black Community 1720–1840* (Cambridge, 1988); and G. Nash, *Race, Class and Politics: Essays on American Colonial and Revolutionary Society* (Urbana, 1986).

36 A collection of captivity narratives by Mathew Carey published in 1794. *Affecting History of the Dreadful Distresses of Frederic Mannheim's Family: To which are added, the Sufferings of John Corbly's Family: An Encounter between a White Man and Two Savages: Extraordinary Bravery of a Woman: Adventures of Capt. Isaac Stewart: Deposition of Massey Herbeson: Adventures and Sufferings of Peter Wilkinson: Remarkable Adventures of Jackson Johonnot: Account of the Destruction of the Settlements at Wyoming* (Philadelphia, 1794). Carey and other magazine editors included excerpts from captivity narratives in their political magazines. These descriptions circulated widely among the new nation's reading public.

37 R. Slotkin, *Regeneration Through Violence: The Mythologie of the American Frontier, 1600–1860* (Middletown CT, 1973), p. 95. Slotkin presents detailed accounts of a number of such captivity narratives, *passim*. For another discussion of early captivity narratives see C. Smith-Rosenberg, 'Captive colonizers: Ambivalence and an emerging "American" identity', *Gender & History*, Special Issue on Gender, Nationalism and National Identity, 5 (Summer, 1993), 177–95.

5

Masculinity, effeminacy, time: conceptual change in the Dutch age of democratic revolutions

Stefan Dudink

THE political transformations of the late eighteenth century changed masculinity as much as masculinity was harnessed to bring about these changes. This chapter is concerned with masculinity's role in one specific transformation that occurred in the rise of modern political culture. Between 1750 and 1850, as Reinhart Koselleck and others have pointed out, political concepts were invested with a sense of profound historical change. In these years concepts that had been embedded in cyclical notions of history and time acquired new meanings as they were embedded in notions of linear historical development.[1]

'Revolution', for instance, had traditionally been used to refer to a cycle of successive forms of government. This cycle was thought of as closed. The set of possible political regimes was limited, and it was unthinkable to break out of the revolving wheel of political life into a radically new and open future. In the course of 'the age of democratic revolutions', however, the concept became connected with a leap into the future that had earlier been beyond the horizon of historical expectations. From then on, revolutions no longer necessarily led back into a limited set of known political regimes. When intertwined with a linear notion of history, revolution could denote a step forward, straight into a brand new political future.[2] In the process 'democracy' was transformed. It was no longer a – reprehensible – stage in an inevitable cycle of political decline and fall. It became a goal to be reached in the course of a linear history of political progress. The concept 'progress' itself articulated the underlying sense of historical development and change that increasingly pervaded political discourse.[3]

In this chapter I examine this kind of conceptual change as it intersected with and emerged into changing concepts of gender, and of masculinity in particular. Early modern concepts of masculinity and femininity were perhaps not conceived in cyclical terms exactly, but they definitely were not the unchanging, naturalised categories of identity they were to become in the course of the nineteenth century.[4] Early modern masculinity was not a reassuringly fixed category that came with the possession of a male body. Rather, it was a precarious disposition easily lost, for it could always slide into effeminacy. Masculinity was defined not so much in terms of a given difference from femininity, as in terms of a dangerous proximity to effeminacy.[5] Clad in (imported) soft and shining fabrics, overexcited by reading (French) novels, and lacking honesty due to a desire to please (the ladies), effeminacy was what both defined masculinity and simultaneously threatened to undo it.

This precarious masculinity was central to various political narratives that were explicitly cyclical. Republicanism was such an explicitly cyclical ideology, in which the republic appeared as both the most desirable and the most vulnerable political form, inevitably doomed to fall once it had achieved greatness. Masculinity's precariousness played no small part in this narrative, for it was the perceived loss of manly virtue in a republic's citizens that set off the demise of the commonwealth at large.

What happened to concepts of gender when, in the years around 1800, cyclical political narratives were gradually pushed to the margins of political discourse and replaced by narratives of a linear nature promising historical development and progress? Although not much work has yet been done on this theme, it seems that, unlike other concepts, masculinity and femininity were not invested with notions of historical development. Rather they were, in a sense, placed outside history and change. As supposedly natural and biological phenomena, masculinity and femininity appeared as the opposites of history, beyond time and place, not subject to the laws of history, not shaped by social forces. But although the concepts themselves escaped historicisation, they did become the markers of progress and civilisation. Only advanced societies were supposed to have organised their social, political, moral, and cultural life in accordance with true notions of sexual difference. Societies that did not abide by the rules of nature in this domain were, or would become, backward. So, to a certain extent, masculinity and femininity did become goals at a horizon of historical development. The concepts themselves, however, were firmly shielded from history.[6]

In the following I will take a closer look at aspects of the early phase of this process of conceptual change in the Dutch age of democratic revolutions, 1780–96. Conceiving of masculinity as a trope of political discourse and focusing on 'its rhetorical and ideological efficacy', I want to chart the part of masculinity in shaping modern political culture in the Netherlands, as both this culture and masculinity were gradually pervaded by a sense of historical development and change.[7]

Republic to empire

Unlike most other European states, the Dutch state of the *ancien régime* was not a monarchy, but a republic, a federation of provinces that was the product of the sixteenth-century Dutch revolt against the Spanish King.[8] This republic was a highly decentralised state that prided itself on its political and civic liberties, but nevertheless harboured monarchical tendencies at the heart of its constitutional system. In the republic, princes of the House of Orange occupied the post of 'Stadholder'. Officially the servant of the provincial estates and the Estates General, the Stadholder was appointed by these provincial and national 'representative' bodies and received his powers from them. In practice, however, these powers were of such a nature that they allowed the Stadholder to become the most powerful person in the republic. In particular the fact that Stadholders were appointed commanders of the navy and army, and could themselves appoint numerous local and other officials gave them, depending on individual skill and political circumstances, considerable influence. As a result, much of the political history of the republic was a history of continuous struggle over political power and privileges between Stadholder and provincial estates and Estates General.

From the 1780s onward this struggle for power radically changed character when traditional calls for restoration of old privileges from the estates and other local bodies became entwined with political arguments of a more radical, democratic kind. The so-called 'Patriot movement' politicised complaints about economic and moral decline that had been voiced in Dutch enlightened public opinion for over fifty years. Appropriating terms as 'patriot(ism)', 'liberty', and 'fatherland', the Patriot movement claimed to speak for the nation as a whole, but expounded a specific political programme. Accusing the Stadholder of usurping power that belonged to 'the people' and its proper representatives, the Patriots pointed to the Stadholder and his clients as obstacles on the road to national recovery. They called for democratisation as a part of a wider programme to regain economic prosperity and international power. In the course of the 1780s Patriotism transformed Dutch political culture and turned into a revolutionary movement that came close to overthrowing the Dutch *ancien régime*.[9]

Harking back to traditional republican concepts of civic virtue and citizenship, the Patriots called for Dutch citizens to arm themselves, to form local militias, and thus prepare to defend liberty – invariably presented in female allegorical form – against her attackers from within and without. Militias were established all over the country and in 1787 the conflict with the Prince of Orange became so heated that civil war seemed inevitable. The Patriot militias, however, did not stand a chance against the Stadholder's troops and his Prussian allies. Defeated and fearing persecution many Patriots went into exile in France.

Having witnessed the French Revolution, these refugees returned with or following French troops in 1795. Now it was the Prince's turn to leave the country as Patriots established the 'Batavian Republic'. The new regime came with important changes, such as a National Assembly elected by all male inhabitants over twenty years of age and a unitary constitution that replaced the Republic's federative political structure. State and Reformed Church were separated ending the exclusion of dissenters and Catholics from holding public offices, and the 'Jewish nation' was granted full citizenship. The Batavian Republic soon fell prey to irresolvable political conflict, however, and after having gone through several coups it came under ever-stronger French tutelage. Having made his brother King in 1806, Napoleon occupied the country in 1810.

The masculinity of Dutch Patriotism

Dutch historiography has been haunted for a long time by the contradictory views of past and future in Dutch political discourse in the age of democratic revolutions. The question whether political debate was dominated by traditional arguments over the correct interpretation of the constitutional past, or was waged in the modern language of natural rights, has proven particularly vexing. More recently, historians have begun to consider this contradiction as constitutive of Patriot political language. A language of restoration of old rights and privileges, and of abiding by the old constitution, was traditional in the sense that it had provided the vocabulary used in the recurrent political struggles between Stadholders and provincial estates and Estates General. It was traditional too in its drawing on assumed historic rights and practices, and in its claim to full restoration of these. Accompanying this traditional political vocabulary, however, was a modern and modernising language of natural rights and of popular sovereignty in particular. The voices of English dissenters like Richard Price and Joseph Priestley and of the American revolutionaries resounded in Dutch Patriotism, sometimes contradicting its traditional tenets, but often merging into an unsettling call for political change.[10]

Patriotism was dangerous and powerful precisely because of the way it appropriated traditional political language in order to refashion and use it in subversive ways. Nowhere was this more apparent than in Patriotism's dealing with the Republic's founding language. Republican concepts of liberty, of the manly virtue of republican citizens eager to defend liberty against attacks from within and outside, of the ever present threat posed by luxury, corruption and effeminacy to the republic's virtue and its continued existence – all of these were dangerously restyled as Patriots painted them with the brush of popular sovereignty. What had traditionally been conceived of as the political duty of a limited group of men, was now presented as the duty and right of 'the people'. Traditionally, republicanism conceived of the political activity of male citizens in terms of the distribution of rights and privileges in a hierarchical, corporate social order. In some ways Patriotism built on corporatism and it also regularly presented itself as the protector of order against the unruly classes. However, it claimed to speak on behalf of the 'sovereign people' as well. Although Patriots defined this category only tentatively, it certainly included more men than that of 'the citizens' in traditional republicanism. The people were entitled by (natural) right to deal with the enemies of liberty, to expose and root out corruption, and to take up arms in these pursuits. Most dangerous of all, the people had the right to continuously make its sovereign power felt.[11]

A crucial element of Patriot political ideology and practice was the call to citizens to arm themselves. From its very beginning the Dutch Patriot movement had stressed that liberty could be maintained only if citizens were willing to take up arms and to defend the free republic against both its external and internal enemies. In the early 1780s internal and external enemies had become almost of a piece. Patriots accused the Stadholder of monarchical aspirations and – as a relative of the British royal family – of betraying the country's interests to Britain. For the Patriots the armed resistance of American citizen-soldiers against the British tyrant was an example worthy of imitation. Many Dutch citizens answered this call and soon militias – the so-called Free Corps – were established in numerous towns and villages. Their members fashioned themselves after the model of the citizen soldier, bought the colourful uniforms the militias wore, and participated in the prominently public exercises.[12]

The contradictory and hybrid nature of Patriot politics surfaced in the militias too. In many ways the militias were traditional organisations. They grew out of the corporate nature of Dutch *ancien régime* society, claimed to build on historic practices and regulations and spoke the stern language of republican virtue.[13] At the same time their political activities regularly overstepped the boundaries of republican ideology and practice to enter a world where popular sovereignty was being shaped. Militias were used to exert political pressure and often played a decisive role when Patriots tried to take over and reform local governments. National conventions of militias were held that resembled meetings of a national, representative assembly. The militias themselves were organised democratically, chose their own officers, and were open to members of all religious communities – practices that were often presented as blueprints for wider political reform.

The languages of republicanism and popular sovereignty were entwined in the Patriot rhetoric of the militias. The notion of masculinity deployed, however, seemed largely traditional and embedded in cyclical notions of political time. In truly republican manner the flood of brochures, pamphlets, and poems advertising the need for citizens to arm themselves presented the founding of militias as a re-masculinisation of both individual citizen-soldiers and the nation at large. The effeminacy that characterised the nation in its then enfeebled and corrupted state was to be left behind; a virtuous masculinity to be regained.

Addressing the 'manly and valorous' members of the militia in the city of Zwolle in 1784, Patriot leader Joan Derk van der Capellen claimed that it was a pure chimera for an 'unarmed, defenceless or effeminate people' to try and maintain its liberty. After all, history had taught: 'That Liberty can be protected only by the nation itself. That citizens are her natural body-guard.'[14] In 1783 the author of the best-selling Patriot treatise *De Vryheid* (Liberty) argued at length that the defence of liberty required first and foremost that Dutch male citizens take up arms. People that 'have succumbed to luxury, lechery and effeminacy, that do not know what liberty is, and do not in the least desire it' could perhaps afford to teach their sons how to dance. 'The offspring of the citizens of a free commonwealth', however, had to be taught how to use sabre and rifle.[15] Patriot poet J. Bellamy spelled out the narcissistic rewards of arming oneself to an imagined male audience in 1783. 'Dolled up noblemen' paraded in front of 'women's mirrors'; the citizen soldier caught his own gaze in the shine of his sabre:

> Does not your noble heart beat stronger
> Does not your manly countenance shine
> Do you not feel your Liberty
> When you see yourself in arms?[16]

This was effeminacy – and masculinity – republican style. This was effeminacy as republicanism's privileged metonym, able to conjure up the entire chain of cause and effect of decay as republicanism envisaged it: commerce-wealth-luxury-weakness-corruption-tyranny.[17] Patriots deploying this trope in late eighteenth-century Holland built on the power it had by that time acquired in Dutch Enlightened public opinion. The economic and moral decline of the republic had been the central issue in the numerous 'Spectatorial' magazines published throughout the century and in the culture of sociability that was the home of Dutch Enlightenment. To a certain extent the republican chain of cause and effect structured public debate as it evolved in Spectators and Enlightened societies. The country's perceived economic decay was attributed to a decay of morals that had set in when passionate extravagance replaced a calmly controlled and calculated way of dealing with acquired wealth. Thus commerce itself – the source of the country's prosperity – was not so much condemned, as was the inability to control passions in the face of the wealth it produced. Despite this departure from republican orthodoxy, effeminacy figured centrally in Dutch Enlightened lamentations about the country's decline. It captured crucial elements of the Enlightened critique of Dutch eighteenth-century morals and played a part in the making of a Dutch national identity through this critique. Invariably associated with the adoption of French tastes and manners, 'effeminacy' figured centrally in a negative definition of 'Dutchness'.[18] It helped to define what the nation had once been and could again become: a nation of productive, frugal men, self-controlled, modestly dressed in garments made from fabrics produced in Dutch workshops. When Patriots decried the nation's effeminacy, as in their propaganda for the militias, this critique acquired a profoundly political nature, and so did the masculinity that Patriotism wished to redeem. The manly citizen-soldier, admiring his reflection in the sabre he had learned to handle, was a thoroughly politicised character, his masculinity invested with political radicalism.

This was, however, as J. G. A. Pocock writes, 'a precarious and threatened mode of self-affirmation'. History was of a circular nature in the republican universe, '[g]iven the spatio-temporal finitude and instability of any republic'.[19] All republics went through an inevitable cycle of rise and decline. The manly virtue at the foundation of the flourishing of republics was a disposition that all too easily evaporated in the heat produced by wealth, luxury and hubris. Once overcome, effeminacy continued to pose a threat to the masculinity of the virtuous citizen, who was always at risk of unwittingly producing the preconditions for the loss of manly virtue in himself or in others. Masculinity, at the mercy of the irresistible force of cyclical time, was either lost or recently redeemed. Its seemingly secure possession was in fact a temporary state, requiring nothing less, in Pocock's words, than 'heroic virtue if not a special grace'.[20]

In many respects Dutch Patriots lived in a republican universe with its assumptions about circular history and time. Even their cherished militias – strongholds of regained masculinity – did not exist outside the cycle of rise and fall. Jacobus Kok's 1784 history of militias and Free Corps in the Netherlands was intended to support the Patriot militias by providing them with a long and impressive history. Kok rejoiced in the current growth of the number of militias in the country. He presented this as an expression of 'a noble desire to maintain Liberty' and praised the militia members' masculinity.[21] This he sharply contrasted with earlier periods when military enthusiasm among Dutch citizens had faded. The narrative of his history was not one of straightforward progress, however. Kok wrote of the past in terms of the ebb and flow of historic cycles. The rise of commerce in the mid-fifteenth century, he noted, had come with dangerous luxury. 'Exquisite and endless meals; extravagant dress, both among the male and the female sex . . . occasioning lechery of every kind' had made Dutchmen lose a martial spirit that until that time had been strong and vigorous. Soon they were at the mercy of a despotic ruler and his standing army.[22] This was all in the past, but the cyclic nature of Kok's narrative implied this could all too easily become the future again as well. Some critics already discerned the seeds of future decay in the behaviour of militia members. They warned militiamen to avoid 'every sign of excess' in their doings in order not to fuel their opponent's hope for a steady 'decay' of the militias.[23] The cult of the uniform among the militia members was a particularly discomforting sign of excess for such critics. In 1783 one of them wrote about 'feeble little captains' wearing their uniforms to 'plays, concerts [and] dinner parties'. He accused them of constantly making changes to their uniform, so as to look better than their fellow-soldiers. There was, he concluded, a reprehensible element of *fashion* in the enthusiasm for the militias.[24] The militias could signal a regained manly virtue, but also mirror society's effeminate desires and morals. They could stop and reverse the republic's corruption, as well as signal its impending decay.

Batavian valour in a commercial republic

Both regaining and maintaining a manly civic disposition could be aided by examples of heroic virtue. Republican ideology reserved a special place for the *exemplum virtutis*, the tale of male heroism derived from Greek or Roman history and deemed worthy of emulation. Dutch Patriotism was no exception in this respect. It too drew on laudable examples of heroism and self-sacrifice from the classics. But it seemed to prefer its own, 'national' inventory of heroes. The advent of modern nationalism pushed classical heroism from the centre of the republican pantheon and replaced it with a home-grown variety.[25] In Dutch republicanism, the tribe of the Batavians provided heroism of such national ancestry. This tribe was supposed to have come to the Netherlands form Germany in the first century BC and to have successfully revolted against the Romans in the years AD 69–70. Love of liberty and valour in defending it had been attributed to the Batavians since the invention of the 'Batavian myth' in the early sixteenth century. The myth was reinvented several times and put to various political uses in the two centuries that followed. But in its various reincarnations valour, heroism, and love of liberty remained the tribe's crucial features, qualities that supported a republican sense of self in the Dutch republic.[26]

The Patriots too drew on this myth in order to justify their political program. In a pamphlet published anonymously in 1781, Joan Derk van der Capellen had written that the Batavians valued their liberty and knew how to protect it. They had never handed over their sovereignty to anybody, had taken important decisions democratically in assemblies where all men would appear in arms, and in times of war had chosen leaders that could also be removed from their posts again.[27] In his 1784 speech for the Zwolle militia, van der Capellen claimed that the Batavians had maintained their liberty because they had, through military exercise, continued to be men.[28] This capacity to preserve a virtuous and valorous masculinity was what made the Batavian hero a perfect *exemplum virtutis*.

Tacitus' *Germania*, written around AD 98, was the main historical source of the Batavian myth. Throughout Europe the *Germania* and Tacitus' *Annals* provided the historic material for the making of national identities based on 'tribal virtue'. To German nationalists Tacitus bequeathed the heroic figure of Arminius, or Hermann, destroyer of three Roman legions and still celebrated by publicists and dramatists during the wars of liberation of 1813–15.[29] In the Netherlands the Roman writer's description of the free, liberty-loving, and martial peoples of Germany – including the Batavians – resounded directly or indirectly in most references to the Batavians' excellence. Rich in references to the relations between, and the occupations and characteristics of, German men and women, the book lent itself particularly well to drawing lessons from a glorious past in gendered terms.[30] In a footnote to a 1714 Dutch translation of the *Germania*, that would be reprinted throughout the century, the name Germany itself was said to derive from a Teutonic combination of the words *Ger* and *Man*, meaning: 'in every respect . . . a man: as if they [the Teutons] intended to say, that the German or Teutonic men, rightly bore the title *Men* because of their sturdiness and manly valour, . . . everything about them testified to complete masculinity'.[31]

With the Patriots especially, the lines where Tacitus praised the Batavians warlike nature did not go amiss. In modern English translation these lines read: 'Of all these races the most *manly* are the Batavi'.[32] Seventeenth- and eighteenth-century Dutch translations usually referred to the fact that the Batavians' *valour* surpassed that of the other German peoples.[33] Patriots clearly understood this valour to be a manly quality. In a chapter on Batavian valour from his 1784 history of the Batavians, E. M. Engelberts called on Dutch men to regain the 'manly valour' of their forefathers. He acknowledged that the effeminacy and cowardice among the majority of Dutch men made this a difficult feat to accomplish, but nevertheless insisted on its necessity.[34]

In Patriot representations the Batavians appeared as possessing an extraordinary and lasting manly virtue. This was supposed to originate from the fact that their history was one of relative stasis. Depicted as self-supporting and agrarian, Batavian society did not suffer from the debilitating effects of commerce and urban civilisation. As opposed to Athenians and Romans, the Batavians were 'far removed from enfeebling moral corruption, that unfortunate fate of many people, once civilisation degenerates into cowardly effeminacy', Patriot historian P. Loosjes wrote in 1783.[35] Outside the grip of the cycle of rise and decay, Batavian masculinity had the capacity to make cyclical time stand still. Batavian manly virtue came from a context that seemed to make it possible to securely possess this masculinity and its beneficial political effects.

But how to emulate this masculinity in the urbanised, commercial world that was the late eighteenth-century Dutch Republic? The histories of Batavian society that Patriots relied on were ambiguous about the possibility of reviving Batavian dispositions in the present. On the one hand these were moralising treatises, their authors clearly set on reforming their audience with the help of historical example. On the other hand these histories contradicted such ambitions. They combined a call to follow historical example with elements of a theory of history that assumed that such a return to historical virtue was impossible. The emergence of a 'modern' historical consciousness could be detected in between the lines praising Batavian morals and manners.[36] These histories had been influenced by 'philosophical history', that enlightened approach of the past that described and explained societies' transitions from one stage to the next in a *linear* historical narrative.[37] The linear notions of history and time that 'philosophical history' rested on did not allow for a return to past morals and manners. These had thrived in social and political contexts that belonged to a past that was not retrievable. Patriots had turned to the Batavians in the hope they could halt the cycle of rise and decay. Patriot historians answered their call, but at the same time threatened to open up vistas of linear history that placed Batavian virtuous masculinity beyond Patriots' reach.

Philosophical history did not go well with the historical assumptions of republican politics. This was particularly so when the new history took the form of a linear narrative of civilisation's progress. From this perspective the austere republic – let alone its Batavian archetype – appeared archaic and primitive.[38] This was exactly the line of attack adopted by some of the Patriots' opponents. They argued that the Dutch republic was a modern, commercial society. Its highly developed division of labour did not allow for citizens engaged in commerce and industry to become soldiers. Patriot calls to revive the martial ardour of the Batavians amounted to an attempt at going back to an earlier state of socio-economic development and civilisation. But the spirit of commerce could no longer be replaced by that of the citizen-soldier. The fanatics who proposed to do so would only produce chaos, discord, and an end to the blessings of living in a free and advanced society.[39] During the 1780s conservative publicist and advocate of a moderate interpretation of Enlightenment thought, Elie Luzac, ridiculed Patriots' use of the Batavian example and suggested that the militias aimed to violently introduce a 'North American form of government'.[40] Patriots had praised the citizen-soldiers' masculinity; one opponent labelled them 'effeminate heroes', effeminacy in this case denoting a lack of manly civilisation and manly self-control in particular – a masculinity that had fallen victim to the sovereignty of the passions.[41]

Restoration to revolution

The Patriot revolution ended in 1787, when the Stadholder managed to crush it, assisted by Prussian troops. The Stadholder's supporters referred to these events as a 'blessed revolution' – a choice of words that pointed to an understanding of revolution in a framework of repetition and return. For the Patriots there was less cause for celebration. Many of those that did not leave the country were to be imprisoned or punished with the loss of their positions. Among those was the Reformed minister and professor of theology, IJsbrand van Hamelsveld. This radical Patriot had preached Patriotism from the pulpit and even had called upon the male members of his flock to take up arms. Forced to resign his offices after 1787, Van Hamelsveld became a professional writer and translator. In 1791 he published *The moral condition of the Dutch nation, at the end of the eighteenth century*, a voluminous lamentation on the moral decay of Dutch society. Although very close to the narrative of decay that undergirded both the Spectators' and the Patriot complaints about national decay, Van Hamelsveld's book differed from those in that his narrative bordered on that of a prophecy of doom. The narrative of decay had always been intended to inspire moral reform and, through it, recovery; in various explicitly eschatological phrases and passages Van Hamelsveld came close to suggesting the unavoidable fall of the country.[42] Comparing the body politic to the mortal physical body, Van Hamelsveld concluded that there were differences between the two, but only of a minor nature. This gave the sick body politic some chance for recovery, but not much. The moral decay might be such that a country's 'recovery must be deemed impossible and its end unavoidable'.[43] In that respect the Netherlands, and Europe more generally, were not in promising shape. Its peasantry, although by nature strong, was becoming enfeebled. Its cities were peopled by 'effeminate beings, already old in the prime of their lives . . . that have the excesses they have indulged in to thank for their weakness'.[44] In his darkest hour, this Patriot feared he saw cyclical time transforming into a linear path to doom. For him effeminacy no longer was a warning sign, urging citizens to improve their ways; it had become the ill-shaped companion of the messengers announcing the end of time.

Perhaps to Van Hamelsveld's surprise, he and the Dutch republic lived to see, in January 1795, the invasion of the republic by French troops that brought a moderate revolution to the Netherlands. In 1796 he became a member of the National Assembly that was elected by the country's male inhabitants of over twenty years of age. In his opening address of 1 March 1796 the Assembly's president, Pieter Paulus, suggested that the latest revolution and the establishment of a National Assembly marked a profound break with the past. In less than a year, he claimed, the revolution had achieved more than had been realised in the two hundred years that preceded it. The 'greatest men among our forefathers' had wished for the dawn of true liberty, but had never been able to imagine its actual arrival for it had simply been too magnificent – but here it was.[45]

Similar views were expressed by Cornelis Zillesen in his history of the events of 1795–96, published two years later. 'The revolutions of our time are without historical precedent', Zillesen wrote. He located their origins in civilisation's progress, a progress that was expressed in a growing sense of self-worth among citizens who had become aware of their natural rights. The enemies of revolution might claim that natural rights spelled nothing but disorder; but they were actually grounded in the progress of civilisation and morality.[46]

Looking back in 1796 to the 'Batavian revolution', Patriot and remonstrant minister Cornelius Rogge had also adapted philosophical history's faith in linear progress to a Patriot political stance. He described revolution as a way to bring political life in tune with the progress of civil society. In this account the old political order appeared as out of date and the sense of self-worth of emancipated citizens as the product of a modern, evolved society. Addressing an imagined audience of political rulers Rogge wrote:

> One has to keep abreast of the taste, the spirit of one's age. People now speak a different language than they spoke a hundred years ago . . . Rulers who want to remain in an age that has passed and want to pull back their subjects that have moved ahead will see the leash being torn and will die in the shock. The people know their rights and sense their worth: the humblest wage earner feels that he too is a human being, a member of Society and a citizen of the State. Rulers, look upon them and treat them as such.[47]

Revolution occurred when rulers ignored the sign of the times and ruled as if society and their subjects' sense of self had not changed. Revolution brought politics in tune again with an evolved society. Rogge cleverly inverted the argument that had presented Patriotism as archaic and the political structure of the republic as modern. In this politicised use of linear history 'effeminacy' as the counter-concept that defined masculinity disappeared to the background of political discourse. Masculinity, as a result, became an 'unmarked' category, residing in seemingly gender neutral concepts like 'the people', 'a member of Society', and 'a citizen of the State'. However, despite his appropriation of linear history for Patriotism, Rogge could not help devoting a few paragraphs to revolutions as the means to revitalise societies that had become effeminate, lecherous, and idle as a result of luxury and wealth. Apparently he thought it wiser not to totally rely on society's linear progress towards political liberty. The spectre of effeminacy still provided a powerful rhetorical trope for those who wanted to make male citizens aware of the precarious nature of both their masculinity and the liberty that depended on it.

Conclusion

After the French invasion of 1795 and the subsequent revolution, many Patriots left behind the specific ideological mix of republicanism and sovereignty they had prepared in the 1780s. They embraced a self-consciously modern and modernising political language of popular sovereignty and natural rights. However, as historian Niek van Sas has remarked, the discursive framework that enabled the Dutch to take leave of their *ancien régime* had been produced in the years 1781–87. In these years the Patriot movement established the groundwork for a new political culture on which they could build again after 1795.[48]

The masculinity of a decidedly early-modern provenance that I discussed in this chapter had been a prominent element of Patriot political culture of the 1780s. Although this was a masculinity that had been embedded in cyclical notions of political time, it had helped establish the discursive space in which a new masculine subjectivity could later be assembled, the masculinity of the modern political subject that was aware of his rights and dignity as a member of society and a citizen of the state. Effeminacy, and all it implied about politics as a cyclical process rather than a matter of progress, was a particularly powerful political concept. As opposed to philosophical and other histories of linear progress, effeminacy, and the cyclical notions of political time that it conjured up, provided strong incentives for political self-fashioning and political action. It implied that masculinity – and the political liberty it supported – could never be assumed but always had to be guarded or regained, and therefore it called for permanent vigilance and constant action. The power of effeminacy also resided in the fact that those who abhorred it had to constantly invoke it in order to make clear just how corrupted and reprehensible it was. This, of course, was a characteristic effeminacy shared with many other negatively connoted concepts that denoted that which was 'other'. Effeminacy, however, was an 'intimate other', a danger residing in the history of the political community and the individual citizens themselves, a danger that could always return and the blame for which could not be securely projected onto other communities.

Modern political culture came with new male characters that shared an orientation toward a bright new future, and whose masculinity crucially contributed to their power to lead their political communities toward that future. The revolutionary hero, engaged in acts of self-creation and of the creation of new political institutions, exemplified one of these novel political subjectivities, one that was defined by an ability to lead society into a *man*-made and open-ended future.[49] Another was the zealous nationalist, who, in Anne McClintock's words, 'represent[s] the progressive agent of national modernity (forward thrusting, potent and historic), embodying nationalism's progressive, or revolutionary principle of discontinuity'.[50] Historians of gender have generally associated the appearance of these new, future-oriented, male characters in modern political culture with the rise of modern, biologised, and binary notions of sexual difference. We do well to notice, however, that in the years around 1800 these new political men had only very recently distanced themselves from a concept of political masculinity that centred on the fragility of masculinity, and in which this precarious masculinity had been linked with cyclic notions of political time. If I am right this pre-modern concept of masculinity was even instrumental in creating the space out of which new political man could emerge. The men of modern political culture had every reason to hurry toward the future: early modern effeminacy was right at their heels.

Notes

This chapter is part of a research project on masculinity and nation in the Netherlands, 1780–1848, that is funded by the Netherlands Organization for Scientific Research (NWO). I should like to thank Mieke Aerts, Karen Hagemann, Gary Price, Jane Rendall, and John Tosh for very helpful comments on an earlier version.

1 R. Koselleck, 'Einleitung', in O. Brunner, W. Conze, and R. Koselleck (eds), *Geschichtliche Grundbegriffe: Historisches Lexikon zur politisch-sozialen Sprache in Deutschland* (Stuttgart, 1972), pp. xiii–xxvii; R. Koselleck, *Vergangene Zukunft: Zur Semantik geschichtlichen Zeiten* (Frankfurt am Main, 1979).

2 K. M. Baker, 'Revolution', in C. Lucas (ed.), *The French Revolution and the Creation of Modern Political Culture, II: The Political Culture of the French Revolution* (Oxford, 1988), pp. 41–62; J. Dunn, 'Revolution', in T. Ball, J. Farr, and R. L. Hanson (eds), *Political Innovation and Conceptual Change* (Cambridge, 1989), pp. 333–56; Koselleck, *Vergangene Zukunft*, pp. 67–86.

3 Koselleck, 'Einleitung', see esp. xvi–xvii.

4 C. Honegger, *Die Ordnung der Geschlechter: Die Wissenschaften vom Menschen und das Weib, 1750–1850* (Frankfurt and New York, 1991); T. Laqueur, *Making Sex: Body and Gender from the Greeks to Freud* (Cambridge MA and London, 1987); L. Schiebinger, *The Mind Has No Sex: Women in the Origins of Modern Science* (Cambridge MA and London, 1989).

5 M. Cohen, *Fashioning Masculinity: National Identity and Language in the Eighteenth Century* (London and New York, 1996), p. 9.

6 I draw here on the work of Ute Frevert who has tested Koselleck's analysis of conceptual change in 1750–1850 for the concepts of masculinity and femininity using German dictionaries and encyclopaedias. U. Frevert, *"Mann un Weib, und Weib und Mann" Geschlechter-Differenzen in der Moderne* (München, 1995), pp. 55–66. See also K. Hausen, 'Family and role-division: The polarisation of sexual stereotypes in the nineteenth century – an aspect of the dissociation of work and family life', in R. J. Evans and W. R. Lee (eds), *The German Family: Essays on the Social History of the Family in 19th- and 20th-Century Germany* (London, 1981), pp. 51–83.

7 The words in quotation marks are Mrinalini Sinha's. See M. Sinha, 'Giving masculinity a history: Some contributions from the historiography of colonial India', *Gender & History*, 11:3 (1999), 455.

8 For overviews of the developments described in this section see R. Aerts, 'Een staat in verbouwing: Van republiek naar constitutioneel koninkrijk 1780–1848', in R. Aerts *et al.* (eds), *Land van kleine gebaren: Een politieke geschiedenis van Nederland 1780–1990* (Nijmegen, 1999), pp. 11–95; J. Israel, *The Dutch Republic: Its Rise, Greatness and Fall 1477–1806* (Oxford, 1998); M. C. Jacob and W. W. Mijnhardt (eds), *The Dutch Republic in the Eighteenth Century: Decline, Enlightenment, and Revolution* (Ithaca and London, 1992).

9 N. C. F. van Sas, 'The patriot revolution: New perspectives', in Jacob and Mijnhardt (eds), *The Dutch Republic in the Eighteenth Century*, pp. 91–119.

10 S. R. E. Klein, *Patriots republikanisme: Politieke cultuur in Nederland 1766–1787* (Amsterdam, 1995); W. R. E. Velema, 'Contemporaine reacties op het patriotse politieke vocabulaire', in H. Bots and W. W. Mijnhardt (eds), *De droom van de revolutie: Nieuwe benaderingen van het Patriottisme* (Amsterdam, 1988), pp. 32–48; W. R. E. Velema, 'Vrijheid als volkssoevereiniteit: De ontwikkeling van het politieke vrijheidsbegrip in de Republiek 1780–1795', in E. O. G. Haitsma Mulier and W. R. E. Velema (eds), *Vrijheid: Een geschiedenis van de vijftiende tot de twintigste eeuw* (Amsterdam, 1999), pp. 287–303.

11 Klein, *Patriots Republikanisme*, pp. 76–88, 195–223; Velema, 'Vrijheid als volkssoevereiniteit'.

12 Israel, *Dutch Republic*, pp. 1101–7; Klein, *Patriots Republikanisme*, ch. 5; Sas, 'The Patriot Revolution', p. 113–15; H. L. Zwitzer, 'De militaire dimensie van de patriottenbeweging', in F. Grijzenhout, W. W. Mijnhardt, and N. C. F. van Sas (eds), *Voor vaderland en vrijheid: De revolutie van de patriotten* (Amsterdam, 1987), pp. 27–51.

13 M. Prak, *Republikeinse veelheid, democratische enkelvoud: Sociale verandering in het revolutietijdvak, 's-Hertogenbosch 1770–1820* (Nijmegen, 1999), pp. 149–72.

14 J. D. van der Capellen tot den Pol, *Aan het volk van Nederland: Het democratisch manifest van Joan Derk van der Capellen tot den Pol 1781*, eds W. F. Wertheim and A. H. Wertheim-Gijse Weenink (Weesp, 1981), p. 152.

15 *De Vryheid* (Amsterdam, 1783), p. 274.

16 Zelandus (J. Bellamy), *Vaderlandsche gezangen van Zelandus* (Utrecht, 1783), p. 83.

17 For effeminacy, its range of meanings in eighteenth-century culture, and in republican political thought in particular, see, Cohen, *Fashioning Masculinity*; L. Dowling, *Hellenism and Homosexuality in Victorian Oxford* (Ithaca and London, 1994), pp. 5–12; M. Peace and V. Quinn (eds): 'Luxurious sexualities: Effeminacy, consumption,

and the body politic in eighteenth-century representation', *Textual Practice*, 11:3 (1997).

18 J. Kloek and W. W. Mijnhardt, *1800: Blauwdrukken voor een samenleving* (Den Haag, 2001), pp. 73–8, 165–78; D. Sturkenboom, *Spectators van hartstocht: Sekse en emotionele cultuur in de achttiende eeuw* (Hilversum, 1998), chs 3 and 4.

19 J. G. A. Pocock, *The Machiavellian Moment: Florentine Political Thought and the Atlantic Tradition* (Princeton and London, 1975), p. 466.

20 *Ibid.*

21 J. Kok, *Oorsprong, aanwas, geschiedenissen, voorrechten en tegenwoordigen staat der Nederlandsche schutterijen, en exercitiegenootschappen* (Amsterdam, 1784), p. vi.

22 *Ibid.*, pp. 44–50.

23 *Redenvoering aan de gewapende burgerij in Nederland* (Utrecht, 1784), p. 91.

24 *Wie wil er mee soldaatje speelen? Of: Samenspraak gehouden in de roef, tusschen een Amsterdamsch en een Utrechtsch burger, vaarende van Utrecht op Amsterdam* (n.p., 1783), pp. 7, 13–15.

25 Martin Thom, focusing primarily on France, situates this 'transfer of value from the ancient city to the barbarian tribe' in a somewhat later context, i.e. after the French revolution, and during the years of transition between the Enlightenment and Romanticism. M. Thom, *Republics, Nations and Tribes* (London and New York, 1995), pp. 1–10.

26 E. O. G. Haitsma Mulier, 'De Bataafse mythe in de patriottentijd: *De aloude staat en geschiedenissen der Vereenigde Nederlanden* van E. M. Engelberts', *Tijdschrift voor Geschiedenis*, 19:1 (1992), 16–34; E. O. G. Haitsma Mulier, 'De Bataafse mythe opnieuw bekeken', *Bijdragen en Medelingen betreffende de Geschiedenis der Nederlanden*, 111:3 (1996), 344–67; I. Schöffer, 'The Batavian myth during the sixteenth and seventeenth centuries', in J. S. Bromley and E. H. Kossmann (eds), *Britian and the Netherlands, Some Political Mythologies: Papers Presented to the Fifth Anglo-Dutch Historical Conference* ('s-Gravenhage, 1975), pp. 78–101.

27 J. D. van der Capellen, *Aan het volk van Nederland: Het patriottisch program uit 1781*, H. L. Zwitzer (ed.), (Amsterdam, 1987), p. 19.

28 Capellen tot den Pol, *Aan het volk*, p. 152.

29 Thom, *Republics*, pp. 212–14.

30 For an excellent analysis of conflicting late eighteenth-century English and Scottish interpretations of *Germania* that focus on women's status and position see J. Rendall, 'Tacitus engendered: "Gothic feminism" and British histories, *c*. 1750–1800', in G. Cubitt (ed.), *Imagining Nations* (Manchester and New York, 1998), pp. 57–74.

31 *Antiquitates Germanicae, of hoogduitsche oudtheden: Waar in de gelegentheid en zeeden der Germaanen, beschreeven door Tacitus, naaukeurig verklaart en met printverbeeldingen opgeheldert worden: Benevens H. Grotius verhandeling van de oudtheid der Batavische republyk* (Amsterdam, 1714), pp. 8–9. This translation was reprinted in 1728 and 1756.

32 Tacitus, 'Germania', trans M. Hutton, rev. E. H. Warmington, in *Tacitus I: Agricola, Germania, Dialogus* (Cambridge MA and London, 1970), p. 175 (italics added).

33 A translation of 1636, that was first printed in 1684 and reprinted throughout the eighteenth century, used the word *vroomheit* which in modern Dutch means piety, but is probably best translated as virtue since in seventeenth- and eighteenth-

century usage it could be used to refer to both valour, righteousness, and piety. C. Cornelius Tacitus, 'Boeksken van de gelegenheit, zeeden, en volken van Germanië', in *Pieter Corneliszoon Hooft: Alle de gedrukt werken 1611–1738* (Amsterdam, 1972), p. 497. In a translation from 1800 the Batavians had become the *dapperste* (most valorous) of all these peoples, H. van Wijn, *Historische en letterkundige avondstonden ter opheldering van eenige zeden der Nederlanden; bijzonderlijk in derzelver daaglijksch en huislijk leeven; en van de stand der Nederduitsche dichtkunde, sedert de vroegste tijden, tot aan het begin der zestiende eeuwe* (Amsterdam, 1800), p. 77.

34 E. M. Engelberts, *De aloude staat en geschiedenissen der Vereenigde Nederlanden, II* (Amsterdam, 1784–1799), p. 409.

35 P. Loosjes, *Characterkunde der vaderlandsche geschiedenisse* (Haarlem, 1783), p. 61. See also Engelberts, *Aloude staat, I,* pp. 386–8.

36 E. O. G. Haitsma Mulier, 'De achttiende eeuw als eeuw van het historisch besef', *De Achttiende Eeuw,* 26:2 (1994), 150–2. Haitsma Mulier, 'Bataafse mythe in de patriottentijd', 28–30. Haitsma Mulier, 'Bataafse mythe opnieuw bekeken', 363–5.

37 D. R. Kelley, *Faces of History: Historical Inquiry from Herodotus to Herder* (London and New Haven, 1998), ch. 8; S. Stuurman, 'Tijd en ruimte in de verlichting: De uitvinding van de *filosofische geschiedenis*', in M. Grever and H. Jansen (eds), *De ongrijpbare tijd: Temporaliteit en de constructie van het verleden* (Hilversum, 2001), pp. 79–96. Because of its attention to the means of subsistence of the German tribes, Tacitus' *Germania* was crucial to the conception of the famous 'four stages theory' that was the main intellectual home of the new linear notion of historical development. See, for example, R. L. Meek, *Social Science and the Ignoble Savage* (Cambridge, 1976), pp. 12, 34, 66.

38 A. O. Hirschman, *The Passions and the Interests: Political Arguments for Capitalism before its Triumph* (Princeton, 1977), pp. 58–63.

39 Velema, 'Contemporaine reactie', pp. 39–43; W. R. E. Velema, *Enlightenment and Conservatism in the Dutch Republic: The Political Thought of Elie Luzac* (Assen and Maastricht, 1993), pp. 161–9.

40 *Ibid.,* p. 168.

41 *De Spiegel der vryheid, waar in ten klaarsten word getoont hoe gemakkelyk de verlooren vryheid zonder oprigten van vry-corpsen of het wapenen der burgeryen weerom gevonden kan worden* (n.p., 1783). For effeminacy as the unmanly rule of the passions, see D. Sturkenboom, 'Historicizing the gender of emotions: Changing perceptions in Dutch Enlightenment thought', *Journal of Social History,* 34:1 (2000–1), 65–6; Sturkenboom, *Spectators van hartstocht,* pp. 151–5.

42 R. H. Kielman, "Geloof mij', het einde nadert': Tijdbesef en toekomstperspectief rond 1800', *Leidschrif,* 14:2 (1999), 127–53, 148–9; N. C. F. van Sas, 'De verbeelding en de macht: IJsbrand van Hamelsveld in het Studiehuis der Restauratie', in E. O. G. Haitsma Mulier, L. H. Maas, and J. Vogel (eds), *Het beeld in de Spiegel: Historiografische verkenningen: Liber amicorum voor Piet Blaas* (Hilversum, 2000), pp. 181–9.

43 Y. van Hamelsveld, *De zedelijke toestand der Nederlandsche natie, op het einde der achttiende eeuw* (Amsterdam, 1791), p. 10.

44 *Ibid.,* p. 59.

45 *Dagverhaal der handelingen van de Nationaale Vergadering representeerdende het volk van Nederland, I* (Den Haag, 1796), p. 5.

46 C. Zillesen, *Geschiedenis der Vereenigde Nederlanden, nevens de voornaamste gebeurtenissen in Europa, II* (Den Haag, 1798), pp. 262–8.

47 C. Rogge, *Tafereel van de geschiedenis der jongste omwenteling in de Vereenigde Nederlanden* (Amsterdam, 1796), pp. 7–8.

48 Sas, 'Patriot Revolution', p. 118.

49 J. G. A. Pocock, *Politics, Language and Time: Essays on Political Thought & History* (London, 1971), pp. 273–6.

50 As opposed to women, who in nationalist discourse 'are represented as the atavistic and authentic body of national tradition (inert, backward-looking, and natural), embodying nationalism's conservative principle of continuity'. A. McClintock, *Imperial Leather: Race, Gender and Sexuality in the Colonial Contest* (New York and London, 1995), p. 359.

6

Republican citizenship and heterosocial desire: concepts of masculinity in revolutionary France

Joan B. Landes

THE passage from absolute monarchy to republican nationhood in the revolutionary circumstances between summer 1789 and July 1794 radically altered the relationship between the French men and their state. The bold achievement of the equal rights of citizenship and universal male suffrage upset longstanding barriers of property, religion, and literacy. Even the privilege of race was challenged when the national legislature voted for emancipation in February 1794, thereby affirming the massive slave rebellion on the vital French colony of Saint-Domingue, present-day Haiti. Citizenship in these years was suffused with symbolic, moral, and political content. To be a citizen meant actively participating in public life, whether by way of civic oath-taking, political action, or military service. As the revolutionary leader Maximilien Robespierre emphasised as early as 1791, 'to be armed for his personal defence is the right of every man without distinction; to be armed for the defence of the nation (*la patrie*) is the right of every citizen'.[1] The cultivated worldliness or *honnêteté* (politeness, tact, fairness, and honest conduct) preferred by old regime elites was supplanted by the intermingled values of domesticity and patriotism. 'To be an *honnête homme*', as one revolutionary pamphleteer explained to a citizen of Philadelphia, 'one has to be a good son, a good husband, and a good father, and . . . bring together every private and public virtue . . . That is where you will find the true definition of patriotism.'[2]

Universal male suffrage offered men the possibility of realising relations of equality with other men, with whom they had traditionally enjoyed only relations of superiority or inferiority. But, at the same time, masculinity was becoming increasingly virilised, in large part because of the conflation of male citizenship and military service resulting from the outbreak of foreign war in April 1792 and civil conflict, most dramatically following the March 1793 counter-revolutionary insurrection in the region of the Vendée. The *levée en masse* – in effect, the appeal to all men to serve in defence of their country – was much more than a mechanism for efficient military enrolment. First introduced in August 1793, it radically transformed the 'masculine condition'. As André Rauch argues: 'What had been the *métier* of some – carrying arms – became the characteristic of all, a quality that distinguishes the man from the child, from the woman, but also from the sick and the old.'[3]

Not only were men granted rights in the political sphere, which were refused to all women because of their sex, but at the same time two routes were shut down by which adult women (and their female children) had formerly been able to experience military life: female soldiering, and the very old custom of camp following. In the event that a woman was found to have fought in the revolutionary armies, including perhaps some hundred women who are thought to have fought under concealed identities, she was usually congratulated on her service and impeached to return home to resume the modest role suitable to her sex. On the home front, male politicians also denied appeals by women to carry arms in defence of their homes and the nation at large.[4] In this context, Robespierre's formulation regarding the citizen's right to bear arms is striking for the way in which it binds citizenship to patriotic duty and connotes the double-edged endowment of the male citizen's new identity. As the mechanism of the *levée en masse* demonstrates, the nation simultaneously gives and takes from its citizens; it grants rights even as it makes unprecedented demands, above all in asking the citizen to risk his life in its defence. Yet only one category of citizen was entitled to occupy this charged zone of subjectivity, one of enormous danger but also potential power.

The preamble of the democratic Constitution of Year III reveals how closely masculinity and rights were tied under the democratic republic, but also signals the powerful emotional webs by which the Republic hoped to bind the male citizen to family life: 'No one is a good citizen if he isn't a good son, good father, good brother, good friend, good spouse.'[5] By examining the representations of citizenship in revolutionary visual and political culture, I aim to explore the heterosocial underpinnings of revolutionary masculinity. Virile, agonistic action in public and military life afforded male citizens the opportunity to excel against their equals and their adversaries. But just as importantly, male citizens established their masculinity through real and idealised relationships to women. In this respect, men played out their role as heterosexual subjects in the intimate domain and as citizens of the nation-state.

Male identity and nationalism

We might think of republican citizenship and the citizen army as laboratories in which men achieved and displayed aspects of a virile masculinity, the mark of their distinction from the effeminising forms of masculinity that republicans associated with the Old Regime. Yet even as virility was performed, it was simultaneously placed at risk, physically as well as sexually – whether as a failure to be sufficiently strong in deed and stoic in action, or because of an unseemly display of affection for another man, thereby revealing too much about the homoerotic drives behind brotherly love. To be less than a man was to be effeminised, that is, made to occupy the degraded position of a woman in a gendered social hierarchy. From a republican perspective, however, effeminacy had further connotations. To be unmanned was also to be suspected of preferring languorous, perverse, docile, or non-reproductive sexual acts, transgressions attributed to the nobility and recalcitrant clergy by republicans.

The gender dynamics of French nationalism are best seen in the context of what Benedict Anderson terms a deep, horizontal community. As Anderson asserts, 'Ultimately, it is this fraternity that makes it possible, over the past two centuries, for so many millions of people, not so much to kill, as willingly to die for such limited imaginings.'[6] George Mosse addresses nationalism's special affinity for male society, and relates the concept of respectability to the legitimisation of men's dominance over women.[7] Likewise, the idealisation of motherhood and the corresponding 'exclusion of all nonreproductively-oriented sexualities from the discourse of the nation' are aspects of the 'virile fraternity' or 'distinctly homosocial form of male bonding' favoured by nationalism.[8]

In the first instance, homosocial attractions among men serve to bind men not just to each other but to the nation. Underscoring this point, studies of French high art of the 1790s identify a proliferation of feminised images of male beauty, intended for a male viewer, at the moment when a virile and fraternal version of nationalism was being forged. Thomas Crow perceives a 'single sex frame of reference' among painters of the period, whereby artists were 'asked not only to envisage military and civic virtue in traditionally masculine terms, but were compelled to imagine the entire spectrum of desirable human qualities, from battlefield heroics to eroticised corporeal beauty, as male'.[9] As Abigail Solomon-Godeau cautions, however, the fascination with the sensual ephebe or the androgyne in neoclassical art production coexisted with misogynistic and homophobic public discourses, 'which are signaled

by their obsessive invocation of the threat of effeminacy and emasculation'. In addition, she adds, such feminised forms of male subjectivity
– 'non-phallic' or 'castrated' – may accompany and even work to shore
up male power by incorporating the threat posed by women to the
patriarchal gender order. From Solomon-Godeau's vantage point – which
is echoed by André Rauch's observation of 'the precariousness of the
male position' – 'the imagery of feminised and vulnerable manhood is
as much an index of the resilience of patriarchy as it is a sign of its
fragility'.[10] Certainly, the metaphors of brotherhood and friendship
signal the ways in which fraternally-oriented men acknowledge other
men's equality. Yet as Geneviève Fraisse observes, the circle of friendship
was not meant to include women, for fear that love, a private sentiment,
would come to be confused with friendship, a public sentiment springing from love of humanity. As an example of the refusal of what she
terms 'the logic of similitude and identity', Fraisse refers to the views
of the eighteenth-century author Étienne Pivert de Sénancourt, who
affirmed that 'if girls do the same things as boys, if women have the
same rights as men, if identity between men and women supplants their
difference, love will be destroyed for the sake of friendship, a terrible
prospect'.[11]

In the second instance, however, women do not occupy only a position of dread in the revolutionary imagination. They are also cherished,
loved, and allegorised, as is apparent in Pierre-Nicolas Beauvallet's
pen and ink drawing *Allégorie de la Liberté* (Figure 1). The pose of this
graceful, though colossal Liberty, clothed in a clinging garment, evokes
the celebrated *Farnèse Flora*, a Roman replica of an original Greek sculp-
ture, likely known to the artist from an engraving or a plaster cast.
Liberty is a marvellously eclectic composition, carrying the conventional
attributes of Liberty, Abundance, Commerce, Vigilance, and Prudence.
The artist has chosen to represent her in a self-absorbed pose. Looking
at her own image in the mirror she holds, Liberty simultaneously resists
and invites the spectator's interest. Additional evidence suggests that
Beauvallet appreciated and knew well how to exploit the power of the
female body. Thus, in its description of an allegorical statue that
Beauvallet contributed to the *Lycée des Arts* at the end of the decade,
the *Journal des inventions et découvertes* reported:

> She is modestly dressed [*pour la décence*]; but her nude arms express
> the ease with which she needs to act with all the power and energy
> that a great number of circumstances demand! . . . Although for the
> most part draped, it is with discernment and such taste that the artist

1   *Allégorie de la Liberté*, P.-N. Beauvallet (1795)

has skilfully added new beauty by hiding almost nothing of what the nude would offer, if she were not veiled.[12]

By clothing the demure *Allégorie de la Liberté* in a revealing antique robe, Beauvallet similarly succeeds in legitimating the spectator's desire as itself a virtuous act. Liberty's wetly draped garment, the curl of hair at her neck, dropping toward her discretely exposed right bosom, her youth, and her beautiful proportions all work to elicit the very gaze that her look denies.

Schooling the patriotic citizen

Leave Your Arrow and on Some Familiar Tunes Learn My Cherished Moral; Be No Longer the Son of Venus, Become the Lover of the Father-land (Figure 2) sheds light on who the subject of that look might be, showing how erotic life might become a school for patriotism or, conversely, how patriotism might teach a practice of love. A figure of Republic/*La Patrie* instructs Cupid (the small child) to serve the nation rather than Venus, the goddess of love. In the mythological sources, Cupid is the son of Venus and Mercury, the winged messenger of the gods. Transposed onto the scene of national identity, it is no accident that the subject who is asked to become the lover of the Fatherland is a boy. It is he who has a doubly difficult but doubly rewarding task to accomplish. He must sublimate his love for his mother and also break the chains of frivolous, unbridled love. On the one hand, he is asked to become a man – independent of an overly needy dependence on the mother who could, if not properly distanced, smother his independent will. On the other hand, maturity describes the arc of the citizen's moral development, for to break with infantile love is to repudiate past habits. In the revolutionary context, there is no mistaking the fact that the past signifies Old Regime libertinism which is very often deemed to be a consequence of women's dangerous exercise of power, a theme cleverly exploited in Choderlos de Laclos's novel *Liasons Dangereuses*.

Thus, the republican nation asks its citizens to get over the old erotic games, once the pastime of the idle rich, especially of its overly pampered and pleasure-seeking women. Instead, the nation calls for citizens who will submit themselves willingly to the disciplined passion and chastened love appropriate to a virtuous moral order. Cupid's moral lesson, the practice of republican patriotism, does nevertheless offer women a place in the reconstituted polity as the face of the Republic. As a man, Cupid will have become 'the lover of the Fatherland [*La Patrie*]'. Yet his

Laisse ta flèche, et sur des airs connus
apprends ma morale chérie.
ne sois plus le fils de Vénus;
deviens l'amour de la Patrie.

...Päs.

2   *Leave your arrow and on some familiar tunes learn my cherished moral;*
be no longer the son of Venus, become the lover of the Fatherland (ca. 1793)

attachment to his mother remains: the fatherland is as a mother to its citizens. It has the character of a mature not an infantile love, even though Cupid's lesson hints that an unacknowledged spring of patriotism may well be incestuous desire. In the revolutionary context of male fellowship and heightened fraternal love, the representation of the nation as a female body is itself an important aspect of the disciplinary project of what Michel Foucault would have called 'bio-power'. Much like a woman in Freud's Oedipal scenario, the patriotic male subject learns to sublimate his passion for the same; in this case, a desire for other men's bodies. By taking the female body of Republic as his lover, the citizen is interpellated into the normative context of family life on which the Republic depends.

Virile nationalism and the female body of Republic

In these images we come closer to understanding the place of women within the political erotics of the republican nation-state. While it is clear that patriotic love can and does take a homoerotic form, we are left to consider how public and private passions also affect a heterosexual investment in the nation's body. One of the most enduring puzzles of French politics remains why such a virile nationalism should have chosen a woman's face for its emblem. Certainly, there are plentiful examples in revolutionary print culture of overly powerful female political per-sonifications. In such cases, one is tempted to see the female figure of Republic as a cross-dresser, perhaps even an occasion for the manifesta-tion of homosocial desire. But to see *La Patrie* as nothing but a cross-dresser, a mask for the masculine (collective) subject of the nation and its virile values, would be to miss the logic by which the alluring body of woman becomes a site for men's patriotic investments.[13] In this case, the circuit of heterosexual desire between the seductive feminised object of the nation-state and the male patriotic subject is best seen as char-acteristic of what Doris Sommer has termed 'the mutual incitement of love and country'. As Sommer explains, 'If there were no erotic or sentimental investment in the state, if our identities as modern sexually defined subjects did not take the state to be a primary object and there-fore the partner on whom our identity depends, what could explain our passion for *la patria*?'[14]

Rousseau's sentimental appeal to maternal love as an anchor of patriotism points directly to this consolidation of heterosexual and familial investments in the nation's body. In 'Consideration on the Government of Poland', he metaphorises the infant's love for his mother, which he regards as the strongest of all human emotions, to patriotic longings. Thus, the baby/patriot's first and last sight are of his mother and of his 'mother' country:[15]

> It is education that must give to souls a national shape, and guide their opinions and tastes so that they will be patriotic out of inclination, out of passion, out of necessity. A baby first opening its eyes must see the mother country [la patrie] and until death must only see her. The true republican sucks love of his mother country [la patrie] with his mother's milk, that is to say, laws and liberty. This love makes up his entire existence, he sees only the mother country [la patrie], he lives only for her, as soon as he is alone, he is nothing; as soon as he has no more mother country [patrie], he is no longer, and if he is not dead, it is for the worse.[16]

Rousseau's formulation of the intuitive sources of patriotism, rooted in every man's infancy, was widely endorsed by revolutionary Jacobins. For them, as Patrice Higonnet observes, 'the *patrie* was every Jacobin's mother', 'la patrie . . . la mère commune'. As Abbé Grégoire pronounced on the occasion of the festival for Simoneau, 'The love of one's *patrie*' is 'almost innate'.[17] A print celebrating the Constitution of 1793 reprises the lessons learned by Rousseau's patriot, while simultaneously revealing the proximity of male society to republican patriotic ideals. *The Fatherland Instructs Its Children, She Receives All of Them in Her Bosom and Reason Enlightens Them* (Figure 3) shows *La Patrie* instructing one child, another Cupid-like figure, in the lessons of the Constitution and the Rights of Man. A sunburst above the Panthéon (inscribed with the word 'Reason') radiates with three principles of revolutionary fraternity: Adore the eternal (one), love your brothers, and cherish your country. The print instantiates woman as an allegory of the Republic/*La Patrie*, but it addresses men. It exhorts male patriots to act as citizens of the nation, to regard other men as brothers within the fellowship of citizenship, and to embrace the nation as one would a lover. As elsewhere, the female figuration of the nation underscores the extent to which 'love and patriotism may evoke the same rush of belonging and possession'.[18]

Rousseau points out that to be without the national object to cherish and love is to suffer a kind of civic death: 'as soon as he has no more mother country [patrie], he is no longer, and if he is not dead, it is for the worse'.[19] Certainly, Rousseau did not mean that a citizen should remain rooted to his place of birth. To the contrary, travel in the company of his tutor is an essential ingredient of Rousseau's imagined citizen Emile's education. Similarly, the politically motivated or socially

La Patrie instruit ses enfans,
elle les recoit tous dans son sein,
et la Raison les eclaire.

vueverdo fecit

3   *The Fatherland instructs its children, she receives all of them in her bosom and Reason enlightens them (ca. 1793)*

ambitious man of the revolutionary generation might travel to the largest town in his region and ultimately to Paris, the epicentre of political and social life, a delicious irony given Rousseau's pronounced contempt for the French capital and his deep suspicion of urban life in its totality. The hapless recruit was also bound to be a traveller, obliged to venture far from home, fighting in defence of France or on behalf of fellow patriots in external wars of liberation. Ordinary men – those tied by custom or necessity to the land and provincial life – were thus afforded extraordinary opportunities, which in the past would have been possible only for the very wealthy, those who emigrated or entered household service far from home, and those whose profession enabled them to travel, such as soldiers, sailors, merchants, peddlers, or explorers.

Everyman's heroism

Two images, some years apart, show how women and men are differentially positioned in relation to emerging notions of national identity. *Devotion to the Fatherland* (Figure 4) is a complex allegory of patriotism which captures the mood in 1793 accompanying the passage of the *levée en masse*. The second work, a painting by Guillaume Guillon-Lethière, *The Fatherland in Danger* (Figure 5) from 1799 belongs to another period of heightened patriotism, when the French faced the threat of invasion from the countries of the second coalition, England, Austria, and Russia. Following a series of defeats and the failure of peace negotiations, the Directory unleashed a campaign to prepare the population for war and self-defence. Borrowing the iconography of Year II with its ardent patriotism, artists supported the government's renewed recruitment campaign. In his review of *The Fatherland in Danger* for the Salon of 1799, the influential republican art critic J.-B. P. Chaussard celebrated Lethière's patriotism.[20] Whereas images of the early 1790s often featured plaintive women, tearfully seeing their husbands off to war, in both these works a stalwart spousal farewell accommodates the demands of war. Both images portray what Philippe Bordes terms the viewpoint of advanced republicans of the period, that women do have a role to play in the national community, as fully-fledged citizens (*citoyennes*).[21] But that in turn requires taking the nation's interests as prior to self or family interest.[22] In the ideal situation, as we see in Lethière's portrayal, there ought to be no conflict between private and public life.

Moreover, these two works evidence the close association between what Karen Hagemann terms '"patriotism" – defined as spontaneous and self-sacrificing "love of country" – "valor" . . . and "manliness" '.[23] They demonstrate the role played by images in mobilising the population for war, while underscoring how heroic male action – ultimately, death on the battlefield – is predicated on men's ability and willingness to define themselves in relation to the historically unprecedented demand of universal conscription. Of course, republicanism from the Greeks through the Renaissance city states is tied to the notion of a self-governing community of men under arms, its hallmark being the citizen militia not an army directed by aristocrats and staffed by mercenaries. However, no prior experiment in republican or democratic self-government resorted to universal service, instead restricting citizenship to men of property and birthright. Accordingly, the *levée en masse* dramatically altered men's eligibility for military service, and was even adopted by neighbouring states like Prussia, which nonetheless refused to follow France in granting all men the vote. That it was possible to demand service without democratic rights is a good measure of the power of national ideology in eliciting men's service.

Manliness required an implicit heroics, a willingness to risk one's life in order to defend and serve Republic/*La Patrie* in the double sense of protecting one's homeland and home, both of which were represented in French nationalism as feminine. *La patrie* has multiple connotations, the fatherland, but also homeland, native land, and mother country. The gender of the French noun motivates a feminine identification, whereas *patrie* from the Latin *patria*, from *patrius*, refers to the fatherland. However, it is important to note the efficacy of such doubled gender associations in evoking an emotional response to patriotic calls. To borrow a metaphor from the economic sphere, if a shared possession of the nation (*la patrie*) serves as the common coin of national identity, then we might think of *La Patrie*'s feminine body as a sort of surplus value in the sphere of representation – realised in and through the heroic actions of masculine men on her behalf. Hagemann's characterisation of German nationalism in this period, forged in relationship to French aggression, is equally descriptive of the French. In both cases, there was an intimate connection between universal conscription, patriotism, and heroic death:

> the sacrifice of death confirmed the reality of the fatherland which needed to be liberated, or created in the first place . . . The new element here was not the cult of heroes as such, but rather its democratisation and nationalisation. With universal conscription, the veneration and commemoration of heroes also had to be universalised if the same willingness to fight and die was expected of all men.[24]

4 *Devotion to the Fatherland*, P. A. de Machy, after A. Talamona (ca. 1793)

In *Devotion to the Fatherland* (Figure 4), a seated figure of Republic/ *La Patrie* receives the donations of the French people, most poignantly men's avowal to die on her behalf and woman's willingness to offer the next generation in service to the state. In a forceful gesture of dedication, while holding the hand of a second child, a mother raises up her infant son, foreshadowing the fateful moment when he too will lay down his life for the fatherland. Two soldiers volunteer for service, while a woman burns incense. The raised infant is echoed by the oath-taking gesture of the soldier on the far right, who is being embraced by a woman, as another man, shown twisting in Republic's direction, reaches out, appearing to pull her into the ambit of state law and civic duty. Of all the subjects in this print, only this woman looks away from Republic, caught between patriotic duty and female concerns, between love for the state and love for the individual. The iron-willed young man, like his fellow soldier, exhibits no such ambivalence. He is resolved to fight, and if necessary to die for his country. Accordingly, this print plays out the gender division between virile men and sentimental women, which David so famously translated onto canvas in *The Oath of the Horatii* and *Brutus*.

Female reluctance is once again overwhelmed by the force of men's commitment. Women do have a role to play within the nation, as witnessed by the two women left and centre, one offering her sons to Republic's cause, the other burning incense to commemorate their valiant actions. Women's citizenship is qualified, however; her status is second to that of men. Women's role is to support, enable, and memorialise the sacrificial deeds of men. In this way, *Devotion to the Fatherland* affirms a model of heroic masculinity, one in which men act and possess the right to defend (the body of) the nation. The allegorical representation of the fatherland is not a quaint holdover from an older iconography but an affirmation of the centrality of the female body to the defence of home and homeland in democratic nationalism.

The *Fatherland in Danger* (Figure 5) exploits similar themes. Women are shown encouraging their husbands and brothers to enrol. A colossal statue of Republic/*La Patrie* is seated high above this farewell scene in an indeterminate port city, as a fleet is about to depart. In one hand Republic holds two smaller figures of Liberty and Equality, while her other hand rests on a bundle of fasces, symbol of unity and power. *La Patrie* looks down upon the populace, her prominent bosom testifying to the nation's nurturance of its citizenry. Lethière has blended Italianate, Gothic and Renaissance architectural styles, while in the distance an imaginary antique city looms. In much the same manner, he juxtaposes contemporary and antique garb, incorporating popular and political dress styles during the Directory. By infusing patriotic content into generic subject matter, he hopes to elevate landscape painting to the rank of history painting, to universalise the Revolution's significance. There

5 *The Fatherland in Danger*, G. Guillon-Lethière (1799)

is even one Black among the assembled crowd, an acknowledgement of the abolition of slavery by the Convention in 1794, and a gesture of amity by France toward her former colonies.

The painting's focal point is the embracing couple, accompanied by their nursemaid and child. The husband's position in the real world of politics and military affairs is underscored by his military dress, whereas the wife's antique robe suggests her affinity with the monumental statue of Republic. Like Republic, she serves as a symbol of the homeland, an emblem of the nation's domestic peace and accord. In contrast, the soldier/husband is a liminal figure. His actions marry the family to the national realm. He embraces his wife, while simultaneously gesturing to his companions-in-arms that he will heed the nation's call to arms. This confluence of private and public life, as Bordes explains, is pivotal to the artist's conception: 'The happy association between the expression of private affections and patriotic sentiments is one of the most powerful springs of the whole work, having led Chaussard to declare that love and glory were "two truly French passions".'[25]

Moreover, at Republic's feet another important scene unfolds, as several women raise up their infants. The children's outstretched arms, like their mother's waves of farewell, mime the men's raised swords, the latter serving as a tribute to the popular ceremonies of revolutionary oath taking. As in *Devotion to the Fatherland*, men's patriotic avowals resonate with the younger generation, even those who have not yet reached the age of reason. A young woman in the foreground is depicted carrying rifles, not for herself or other women but on behalf of men who alone have the privilege of laying down their lives on Republic's behalf. Women and children, though not subjects in their own right, are nonetheless interpellated into the scene of republican citizenship, as the cherished objects of republican citizens. As a consequence, men's embrace of Republic is echoed in their love for their wives and children. In Lethière's portrayal, there is no conflict between intimacy and patriotism. Rather they comprise the two faces of nationalism.

Every citizen as a lover

Citizenship is frequently described as the compilation of rights belonging to insiders and denied to outsiders of a particular nation-state. Yet rights and privileges by themselves cannot describe the arc of feeling attaching the citizen to the nation. As this exploration of revolutionary culture suggests, the citizen also inhabits an imaginary temporal and spatial realm in which the national body elicits a passionate response from its subjects. And in this imaginary realm, as in the symbolic sphere of language or in the domain of the 'real', to borrow a psychoanalytic topography, not all citizens are created equal. Apart from the divisions between patriots and their enemies, no more salient difference existed within the national body during the 1790s than that between men and women, *citoyens* and *citoyennes*. Among the many things that a citizen learned in his practice of citizenship was the value of masculinity, which in turn allowed a man to claim the right to possess the nation and to risk his life on its behalf. At the same time, male sexual passion was tied to fatherhood in the republican codes of domesticity and family.

Alongside female representations, there exist numerous other significations of the French nation – the *tricolor*, the *bonnet rouge*, the *coq*, the *pré-carré* or four-square map of France, the *Marseillaise*, and the Declaration of the Rights of Man and Citizen.[26] While any of one these abstractions might trigger strong emotions, none had the power of the embodied female figure to evoke feelings of affection and intimacy. Visual fictions were at once a holdover of traditional French Catholic and monarchical culture, but they also became the means by which a new political culture was forged. As Maurice Agulhon grasps, 'Once the State became collective and anonymous, it lost the means to be emotive unless it proved possible to reawaken devotion for the ideal that was its inspiration, namely Liberty, or the Republic, (the principles are linked, the names more or less interchangeable). But for Liberty or the Republic to be loved, was it not more or less necessary for them to be personified?'[27] Men were encouraged to love the nation as man to wife, lover to beloved. Certainly their manhood was affirmed as citizens of the French state, but so too was their heterosexuality insofar as erotic norms within the family life were duplicated within the political sphere. In the imagined landscape of the nation, family and state – or as the republican critic Chaussard put it, love and glory – were mutually sustaining. Far from being a simple reversal of the scorned body politic of monarchical France, the repetitive imagery of a female Republic helped to anchor patriotism in passionate feelings and in the realm of the imagination, thereby tapping the citizen's infantile desires for a female body while directing those feelings toward a legitimate female object: in the personal sphere, a wife, in the political realm, the state. Among the most profound and enduring changes wrought by the Revolution, despite subsequent political transformations, was the democratisation, nationalisation, and (even) universalisation of norms of masculinity in a manner that would have been unthinkable within old regime France. But such generosity did not extend to women, those beings who were held to be different by nature.[28]

Certainly this was an age when effusive manifestations of brotherly love were encouraged, but male camaraderie and affection were also tamed within the logic of family life and social reproduction. As the feminine iconography of the nation makes clear, men's fellowship was no substitute for their loyalty to the body of the nation, which not so coincidently took a female shape. As for women, they too had investments in the nation, including the self-flattery that is born of mimesis – seeing one's face in the body of Republic. Yet in such identifications, there is nothing of the heroic subjectivity that animated men's self-longings.

Conclusion

In this exploration of revolutionary visual and political culture, I have sought to establish the profound impact of democratic republicanism on male subjectivity, and, in turn, the extent to which masculine values influenced republicanism. Revolutionary visual culture contributed to the destruction of absolutism and to forging new roles for men in both the intimate and public sphere. The depiction of the nation as an alluring female body helped to eroticise patriotism and to bind male subjects to the nation-state, at the very moment when they were being asked to sacrifice life and limb on the nation's behalf. Both universal citizenship and universal military service were in the first instance, and for some time thereafter, the privilege of men, and predicated on the defence of the national body and the home bodies within its borders, by definition women and children. Although much has changed in the two centuries since the Revolution, it is of some interest that the French Republic, or more familiarly *Marianne*, still wears a feminine face (and body): in recent decades, that of movie stars and models such as Brigitte Bardot, Catherine Deneuve, and Laetitia Casta, who once declared that her breasts were raised on butter and *crème fraîche*. Interestingly, Casta was the first *Marianne* to be selected by a vote of the 36,000 mayors of France – a body of officials still overwhelmingly male in composition. As the spokeswoman of the Association of French Mayors remarked, explaining their choice: 'Well, perhaps because she's the prettiest. And Marianne is, of course, usually represented as a bust. Casta obviously has the nicest bust of them all.'[29]

Notes

1 Maximilien Robespierre, le 27 avril 1791, cited in D. Godineau, *Citoyennes tricoteuses: Les femmes du peuple à Paris* (Paris, 1988), p. 119.

2 Cited in P. Higonnet, *Goodness Beyond Virtue: Jacobins During the French Revolution* (Cambridge MA, 1998), p. 136.

3 A. Rauch, *Crise de l'identité masculine, 1789–1914* (Paris, 2000), p. 48.

4 See D. Godineau, *The Women of Paris and Their French Revolution*, trans K. Streip (Berkeley, 1998); D. G. Levy, H. B. Applewhite, and M. D. Johnson (eds), *Women in Revolutionary Paris, 1789–1795: Selected Documents Translated with Notes and Commentary* (Urbana, 1979); and J. B. Landes, *Women and the Public Sphere in the Age of the French Revolution* (Ithaca, 1988).

5 Cited in G. Fraisse, *La controverse des sexes* (Paris, 2001), p. 86.

6 B. Anderson, *Imagined Communities: Reflections on the Origin and Spread of Nationalism* (London, 1991, rev. edn), pp. 6–7.

7 G. L. Mosse, *Nationalism and Sexuality: Middle-Class Morality and Sexual Norms in Modern Europe* (Madison, 1985), cited in A. Parker, M. Russo, D. Sommer, and P. Yaeger, 'Introduction', in A. Parker, M. Russo, D. Sommer, and P. Yaeger (eds), *Nationalisms and Sexualities* (New York and London, 1992), p. 6.

8 A. Parker, M. Russo, D. Sommer, and P. Yeager, 'Introduction'. See also M. Sinha, *Gender and Nation* (American Historical Association: Women's and Gender History in Global Perspective Series, forthcoming).

9 T. Crow, *Emulation: Making Artists for Revolutionary France* (New Haven, 1995), p. 2. See also W. Davis, 'The renunciation of reaction in Girodet's *Sleep of Endymion*', in N. Bryson, M. A. Holly, and K. Moxey (eds), *Visual Culture: Images and Interpretations* (Hanover NH, 1994), pp. 168–201. For a contrasting reading of *Endymion*, cf. E. Lajer-Burcharth, *Necklines: The Art of Jacques-Louis David* (New Haven, 1999), p. 253.

10 A. Solomon-Godeau, *Male Trouble: A Crisis in Representation* (New York, 1997), pp. 40–1; Rauch, *Crise*, p. 251. See also A. Potts, 'Beautiful bodies and dying heroes', *History Workshop*, 30 (Autumn 1990), 1–21; A. Potts, *Flesh and the Ideal: Winckelmann and the Origins of Art History* (New Haven, 1994); S. Dudink, 'Cuts and bruises and democratic contestation: Male bodies, history and politics', *European Journal of Cultural Studies*, 4:2 (2001), 153–170; and R. A. Nye, *Masculinity and Male Codes of Honor in Modern France* (Berkeley, 1998).

11 Fraisse, *Controverse*, p. 49.

12 *Journal des inventions et découvertes*, no. 2, vendémiaire an IV (octobre 1795), 136–7, cited in P. Bordes and A. Chevalier (eds), *Catalogue des peintures, sculptures et dessins* (Vizille, 1996), p. 200.

13 I argue in my *Visualizing the Nation: Gender, Representation, and Revolution in Eighteenth-Century France* (Ithaca, 2001) that an iconographic explanation of this phenomenon is insufficient, not least because it is by no means self-evident why Old Regime allegorical traditions were carried over into the revolutionary culture. Nor do the masculine and feminine representations of Republic, or Republic's active and passive poses, simply reflect changing political circumstances or women's fortunes within the Revolution. For the latter position, see L. Hunt, *Politics, Culture, and Class in the French Revolution* (Berkeley, 1984); M. Agulhon, *Marianne into Battle: Republican Imagery and Symbolism in France, 1789–1880*, trans J. Lloyd (Cambridge, 1977); Aghulhon and P. Bonte, *Marianne: Les Visages de la République* (Paris, 1992).

14 D. Sommer, *Foundational Fictions: The National Romance of Latin America* (Berkeley, 1991), pp. 41, 32.

15　In the following passage I translate *la patrie* as 'mother country' rather than 'fatherland' in order to underscore the gendered resonances of the ties between mother love (*l'amour de sa mère*) and love of country (*l'amour de sa patrie*). Although French syntax, like that of other Romance languages, certainly facilitates this understanding, Rousseau has in mind much more than a simple grammatical connection. As the passage indicates, he is describing the relationship between the male patriot and his mother – that is, mother country.

16　J.-J. Rousseau, *Considérations sur le Gouvernement de Pologne et sur sa réformation projetée* (April 1772), in C. E. Vaughan (ed.), *The Political Writings of Jean Jacques Rousseau*, vol. 2 (New York, 1962), p. 437.

17　Higonnet, *Goodness Beyond Virtue*, pp. 144, 352, n. 2. Abbé Grégoire cited in *ibid.*, p. 144.

18　Sommer, *Foundational Fictions*, p. ix.

19　Rousseau, *Considération sur le Gouvernement de Pologne*.

20　See J.-B. P. Chaussard, *La Décade philosophique, littéraire et politique*, 10 vendémaire an VIII (2 octobre 1799), pp. 41–2.

21　'citoyennes responsables à part entière.' *Catalogue*, p. 92.

22　Writing in the wake of the French Revolution, the German philosopher Hegel exhibited many of Rousseau's worries about women's divisive role in political and ethical life. Woman's place is confined to the family, which Hegel conceived of as an ethical community, but of an inferior kind. Whereas the state achieves universality, family life always retains its particularistic character. Men do learn to interact ethically within the family, wherein love animates relationships between members. But unlike women, they also leave the family to experience the individualism of civil society. Only then is the highest level of unity achieved, when men reunite to form the ethical community of the state. Lacking both civil and political rights, women's lives are confined to the private sphere of the family, their ethical lives impoverished as they will never learn to take the standpoint of the whole. At best they can achieve only a partial whole – a love for one's own husband, children, and a defence of family interest. But as resistance to the demands of the state in the arena of military service underscores, the family's desire to protect its members can be at odds with the state's need to defend itself. See G. W. F. Hegel, *Philosophy of Right*, trans T. M. Knox (London and New York, 1952).

23　K. Hagemann, 'Of "Manly Valor" and "German Honor": Nation, War, and Masculinity in the Age of the Prussian Uprising Against Napoleon', *Central European History*, 30:2 (1997), 189.

24　Hageman, 'Manly Valor', 218–19.

25　Bordes and Chevalier (eds), *Catalogue*, p. 92.

26　For a recent account of French nationalism, see D. A. Bell, *The Cult of the Nation in France: Inventing Nationalism, 1680–1800* (Cambridge MA, 2001). On French emblems, see M. Pastoureau, *Les Emblèmes de la France* (Paris, 1998). For Vauban's contribution to the creation of France's geometrical, ordered, national boundaries, see P. Sahlins, *Boundaries: The Making of France and Spain in the Pyrenees* (Berkeley, 1989), pp. 68–71; and C. Mukerji, *Territorial Ambitions and the Gardens of Versailles* (Cambridge, 1997), pp. 248–99. On the Gallic cock, see Pastoureau, 'The Gallic cock', in P. Nora (ed.), (English-language edn. L. D. Kritzman) *Realms of Memory:*

The Construction of the French Past, vol. 3, Symbols, trans A. Goldhammer (New York, 1992), pp. 405–32. On the *Marseillaise,* see M. Vovelle, 'La Marseillaise: La Guerre ou la paix', in P. Nora (ed.), *Les Lieux de mémoire, vol. 1, La République* (Paris, 1984) pp. 85–136; and L. Mason, *Singing the Revolution: Popular Culture and Politics, 1787–1799* (Ithaca NY, 1996), pp. 93–103. In *Imagined Communities,* Benedict Anderson discusses how maps achieve logo status in anticolonial nationalisms, but the same could be said of their European forerunners.

27 Agulhon, *Marianne,* p. 31. Furthermore, in rhetorical style, allegories were customarily introduced and addressed as persons. For people unacquainted with the allegorical tradition of classical culture or its conventions, Liberty may have been likened to a festival queen or a patron saint – also represented by a statue, carried in procession as a bust, and addressed in hymns.

28 For a recent discussion of this paradox in the context of Enlightenment thought, see S. Steinberg, 'L'inégalité entre les sexes et l'égalité entre les hommes: Le tournant des Lumières', *Esprit,* 273 (mars-avril 2001), 23–40.

29 Cited in D. Ollivier, 'Liberté, Egalité, 36C: Why was a pneumatic Victoria's Secret model chosen as the embodiment of the French Republic?', www.salon.com (19 February 2000).

7

German heroes: the cult of the death for the fatherland in nineteenth-century Germany

Karen Hagemann

'No man is too good to die a sacrificial death for the freedom and honour of his nation', stated the heading of an article that appeared in January 1933 in the *Völkische Beobachter*, the central organ of the National Socialist Party. The article introduced a reprinted 1912 biography on Theodor Körner – a young man 'of good middle-class family' who despite being at the beginning of a promising career as a playwright in Vienna and happily engaged to be married, volunteered for military service after Prussia declared war on France in March 1813.[1] Körner fought with the legendary Lützow Freicorps, wrote a large number of popular war songs within a short period of time and died in one of his corps' first great battles in August 1813.[2] Up to the National Socialist era, commemorative texts extolled him repeatedly as *the* 'German boy hero' par excellence who willingly died for the fatherland. The high points of Körner commemoration, like the specific form they took, mirrored changes in historical conditions. Not only were memories of Körner and other 'German heroes' kept alive above all in times of heightened militarism and nationalism – especially in the years before the First and Second World War – but also his image was transformed over the course of the nineteenth century from a 'valorous' and 'freedom-loving' 'son of the middle class' with German-national views to a soldierly hero.[3]

Theodor Körner was one of many 'warrior heroes' accepted into the pantheon of 'German heroism'. Like Körner, all of these 'heroic men' were constantly being reconstructed in the national memory. Their gender played a central role here because national constructs of heroism are always based on, and at the same time fundamentally shape, hegemonic concepts of masculinity.[4] 'Heroes' were thus presented as the manliest of men. They were supposed to act as role models for 'average men' and in this way define the norms of masculinity to which the state, the military and society aspired. Heroic masculinity is thus always ideal-typical masculinity, much desired but rarely attained in 'heroic times'. The myth of death for the fatherland was consistently at the heart of the collective commemoration of national 'warrior heroes'. The 'fallen' were supposed to assume a prominent place in the pantheon of heroes because they had given their lives *voluntarily* for the nation in a by definition 'just' war. It went without saying that they had fought for only the loftiest objectives, the 'honour' and 'liberty' of 'home and fatherland'.[5] The hero, the nation, masculinity, and war were constructed in this myth as a mental unit, which would have been unthinkable without the unifying argument of 'just' war. Only the circumstance of a 'just' war legitimised manly heroic commitment, including the ultimate sacrifice. This self-sacrifice for a higher life formed the core of the myth of death for the fatherland and thus of the image and cult of the 'warrior hero'.

The myth of death for the fatherland, which reached in Prussia and Germany an initial peak during and after the so-called Wars of Liberation of 1813–15, was neither new nor specifically German. Its roots extend back to the ancient Greek and Roman republics, which had glorified it in their own heroic legends.[6] With the formation of nation-states it became a central component of many modern national cultures. As Benedict Anderson famously put it, the willingness to *die* for the nation, to sacrifice one's body, memorialised in poetry and monuments, became the extreme heroic form for the suturing of the male individual and the nation.[7] With the introduction of universal male conscription, it experienced its first heyday everywhere, regardless of the concrete political and military system, not least because it was 'universalised' for the first time in the context of national wars.[8] The broad mass of men who were called up for military service for the first time, but above all the opinion leaders of the bourgeois male elites, could be mobilised for this new form of national war on the basis of universal conscription only if death on the battlefield was glorified as an 'act of freedom' and an heroic 'truly manly deed'. Valour (*Wehrhaftigkeit*), as the readiness to defend family, home and fatherland, was now declared a cardinal virtue for *every* man. It was no coincidence that the myth became a central element of the hegemonic image of masculinity for the first time in Revolutionary France, which had intro-duced the *levée en masse* in the context of the Revolutionary Wars. Now it was declared that all men who fell in war could die a 'hero's death' and be honoured in the national memory as 'warrior heroes'. Previously, this 'title of honour' had been bestowed only upon aristocratic men, above all military leaders.[9]

The age of national wars was also the age of the emergence and formation of modern civil society (*Bürgergesellschaft*) whose core for middle class men consisted of the principles of equality before the law, individual liberty, fraternity and patriotism, defined as spontaneous and self-sacrificing 'love of country'.[10] At first glance these principles seem to conflict with the expectation of manly valour, at least such a conflict has been constructed in historiography.[11] This construct rests on the equating of 'valorous' with military: the 'civilian' concept of 'civic valour' (*bürgerliche Wehrhaftigkeit*) is not distinguished from the military concept of 'combat readiness' (*militärische Kampfbereitschaft*) and as a consequence the 'citizen as national warrior' is equated with the soldier, the 'man of arms'. I would like to show in the following that this is a narrow perception from the perspective of the age of world wars. From the beginning, both models – the 'civilian' concept of 'civic valour' and the military concept of 'combat readiness' – existed side by side and competed in the cult of death for the fatherland. Only during the long nineteenth century, above all in the Wilhelmine period, did the militarised version of the cult of heroes assert itself more and more in Germany, and in this context the hegemonic image of masculinity also became militarised.

This chapter will trace that development. The focus of analysis is on the period of the wars against Napoleon between 1806 and 1815, when the model of the patriotic valorous man, at whose centre the myth of death for the fatherland stood, was formulated with a broad impact for the first time in its various versions and conveyed through symbols, rituals and ceremonies. The deployment of these cultural representations and symbolic practices was central to the dissemination of the myth and its accompanying model of masculinity, since they spoke directly to the male subject and his view of himself as a man through the emotions.[12] Because Prussia, alongside Austria, was the leading German power in these wars, and the first territorial state to introduce universal conscription at the beginning of the conflict, and since the ideas and practices that developed in this context shaped the cult of death for the fatherland in the long term, the Prussian monarchy will be the focus of attention here. After analysing the formative period of this cult, I will then trace the broad lines of development up to the First World War.

Universal conscription and patriotic-national mobilisation

On 10 March 1813, six days before the official declaration of war against France, the Prussian king Frederick William III decreed the introduction of the 'Iron Cross', the first 'military badge of honour' to be awarded for 'soldierly bravery' without regard to social status. With this medal, common soldiers, militia members and volunteers could be recognised as war heroes alongside noble commanders-in-chief, generals and officers.[13] On 5 May 1813 the Prussian monarch also ordered 'the establishment of a lasting monument' for the soldiers who had lost their lives 'in the struggle for independence and the fatherland'. The decree determined, first, that 'any warrior who met his patriotic death while performing a heroic deed' should be honoured on a 'simple plaque' erected at the public expense in the regimental church. Second, all soldiers who had 'died on the bed of honour' were to be remembered in their home parishes on memorial plaques that bore the inscription 'Died for King and Country from this Parish' as well as the names of all the local war dead. Third, a church 'funeral rite' was ordered for after the end of the war to commemorate all of the 'warriors' who had died a 'hero's death'.[14] With these two decrees, at the beginning of the Wars of Liberation Frederick William III already instituted a broad programme for the national cult of heroism, which he additionally confirmed in his 23 May 1813 proclamation 'To the Prussians!', in which he decreed: 'Every Prussian who meets his death for his country dies a hero, and every Prussian who returns should be honoured for his gallant spirit and heroism.'[15]

It was no accident that the reverence for and commemoration of heroes attained great importance during and after the Wars of Liberation. After the short Austrian-French war of 1809, these were the first wars in German history to be conducted on the basis of universal conscription with an army of allied troops in which volunteers and militiamen from all walks of life fought side by side with linesmen. The dramatic defeat of the Prussian-Saxon army in 1806–7 had so thoroughly shaken the foundations of the Prussian state and military system that the king and the ruling elites were forced to make fundamental changes in the state and military administrations. One central project was the introduction of universal conscription. Despite extensive disagreements over the con-crete details, it was widely considered – well beyond the circles of army reformers – to be a precondition for the longed for revenge, victory over Napoleonic France. Two decrees of February and March 1813 finally introduced universal conscription into Prussia, which was then continued for peacetime in the Law Concerning Compulsory Military Service of September 1814. Since than all Prussian men between seventeen and forty who were subject to compulsory military service were obliged to serve in the militia as an independent military organisation alongside the standing army.[16]

Much resistance had to be overcome before compulsory military service could be instituted in practice. A broad patriotic national mobilisation was necessary. Male 'citizens' as civilian members of a federation of subjects had to be turned into 'citizens of the state' who accepted responsibility and were prepared not merely to make any material 'sacrifice' for the 'Prussian nation' but also, in the case of war, to do their duty by taking up arms and defending 'homeland' and 'fatherland'. This mobilisation was to be achieved through intensive propaganda for a 'valorous manly stance', which revolved around the myth of a heroic and honourable 'death for the fatherland'. It was above all the state, the military and the Lutheran church that celebrated this myth in ceremonies and rituals honouring and commemorating heroes. But they were supported by a veritable flood of patriotic national publications from middle-class authors. What was new in this period was not the myth of 'death for the fatherland' as such and its celebration, but rather its increasingly patriotic and national overtones, and above all, its universalisation. Now that every man of military age was supposed to be a 'defender of the fatherland' who might die in battle, death 'on the field of honour' had to be celebrated, glorified and made socially acceptable for *all soldiers*. This was where the myth of 'death for the fatherland' came in.[17]

The cult of the death for the fatherland

In Prussia the myth of the 'hero's death' had already been propagated in patriotic literature, above all poetry and sermons, during the Seven Years' War from 1756–63.[18] It was only during the French Revolution, however, that it came to be celebrated extensively in ritual and ceremony. While in France, as a result of the strict separation of church and state maintained after the Revolution, it developed into a civil religion of sacrifice, in Prussia and other parts of Germany it assumed a Christian form from the beginning.[19] But regardless of this circumstance, and despite all political differences between France and its enemies, it centred on the idea of sacrificial death as the highest form of masculine loyalty to the nation.

In the German-speaking lands, the medium par excellence for the broad dissemination of the myth of death for the fatherland was and remained poetry. During and after the Wars of Liberation patriotic national songs and poems became *the* popular mass medium. Thousands of songs and poems were composed during and after the Wars of Liberation. Their main addressees included volunteers, militiamen and

linesmen. The allied troops were one of the main sites of their distribution in oral and written form.[20] The most common poetic topoi during
the wars of 1813–15 included their exaltation as a 'just and holy war' and
the glorification of death in battle as a 'blood sacrifice' on the 'altar
of the fatherland'. These poems made use of the old Christian idea of the
sacrificial death: the 'warrior' was stylised as a Christian martyr following
the model of Jesus himself. His blood, his wounds and his death were
interpreted as the expression of true Christianity and equated with great
self-sacrifice and a deep capacity for suffering. At the same time, this
sacrificial death was regarded as a sign of the most profound patriotism.
The 'national warrior' as a patriotic martyr found true fulfilment only
in death on the battlefield.[21] These poems repeatedly emphasise that the
true 'German hero' made his sacrifice freely. Accordingly, the popular
term 'freedom' assumed a double meaning in the poems: on the one
hand, following antique notions, it signified the individual freedom to
sacrifice for the fatherland, and on the other, it referred to the collective
freedom from external servitude and oppression.[22] Since internal and
external freedom, understood in this manner, were considered to be
a central characteristic of 'manliness' and 'honour', a man must 'fear
disgrace and servitude more than death' and be prepared at any moment
to embrace joyfully his sacrificial death. Only in this way could he claim
to be a 'man of honour' and thus a 'true man'.[23]

Similar images were also disseminated in numerous sermons
during and after the Wars of Liberation, which have survived in printed
form. Apart from poetry, sermons were the most widespread medium
of patriotic national propaganda at this period. Lutheran clerics proved
themselves loyal servants of the Prussian state and, whether at the front
or at home, they proclaimed the duty of every Christian to make a
patriotic sacrifice. Military chaplains in particular never tired of invoking the myth of 'death for the fatherland'. After all, it was one of their
foremost duties to awaken the 'pious, brave and cheerful spirit' of
volunteers, militiamen and soldiers. At home as well clerics were busy
processing the myth in their sermons. Their chief aim in so doing was
to strengthen the patriotic readiness to sacrifice of men and women on
the home front. One of their main demands was the willingness to
send young male relatives proudly off to war.[24]

Next to lyric poetry, sermons and the print media a wealth of
newly invented symbols, rituals and festivals conveyed the myth of the
'sacrificial death for the fatherland'. Countless patriotic national festivals
and rituals were celebrated all over Prussia during and after the war
years. These included swearing in ceremonies and consecrations of the

flag as well as celebrations of thanksgiving and victory and local commemorations.[25] In addition, after the final victory over Napoleon in July
1815 two special festivals – the peace festival of 18 January 1816, and the
commemoration of the dead on 4 July 1816 – were held, as stipulated in
the royal decrees from the beginning of the war. Both served to honour
and commemorate the heroes of the struggle.[26]

The Festival of Thanksgiving for the Peace organised on a grand
scale by the government, local authorities, the military and the church
seem to have taken place in all Prussian parishes.[27] As at other, similar,
occasions in the past that had celebrated victory, the centrepiece of the
festival was a thanksgiving service with a *Te Deum*, heralded the night
before by a prolonged ringing of bells. In most towns, the church service
began or ended with a military parade or solemn procession in which
those invested with the iron cross, wearing oak or laurel wreaths, were
accorded a place of honour.[28] In their speeches, local worthies – especially middle-class men such as schoolteachers and pastors – called for a
lasting commemoration of these 'German heroes' as the only means of
keeping their manly and valorous stance alive among coming generations
of men. Therefore, as the official *Gazette of the Royal Kurmark Administration* reported in March 1816:

> In several towns patriotic pastors, schoolteachers or other men
> recounted to the assembled youth the history of the wars and the
> deeds of our compatriots in the field, in order to explain to them the
> meaning of this holiday and awaken in their hearts the early seeds of
> patriotism. In other places pastors publicly read out the names of all
> those who fell as sacrifices and began to record the collected news of
> their deeds and fates in the parish chronicle.[29]

In order to keep the 'heroic memory' alive in the long term, smaller
local war memorials were also consecrated within the framework of the
peace festival. Planting young oak trees and erecting iron crosses were
especially popular forms of commemoration.[30]

Equally important for the invention of the tradition of the cult of
heroic death for the fatherland was the Festival in Commemoration of
the Dead. The responsible Department of Public Worship and Education
set out the programme in great detail. It decreed that the central event
was to be a memorial service with a collection, preceded by an hour of
bell ringing during which all business had to cease. Even the liturgy,
sermon texts, and prayers for the ceremony were carefully stipulated.[31]
The festival in commemoration of the dead was celebrated and accepted
as a collective memorial service of the 'Prussian nation'. The church

service was extraordinarily well attended everywhere. Most people, including those who had lost no relatives themselves, dressed in mourning. All of the sermons that have come down to us emphasise on the one hand that it was only in relief for war victims that the community could demonstrate its 'active recognition' of their great sacrifice; the families must be compensated for the debt that could no longer be repaid to the fallen men themselves.[32] On the other hand, they called upon 'men and boys' to preserve the self-sacrificing achievements of the 'fallen heroes' and to follow their example, ever ready to fight bravely in their defence.[33]

With the introduction of the Iron Cross and these and other festivals and rituals, the Prussian monarchy, in co-operation with the military, the Protestant church and middle-class 'patriots', provided the blueprint for a long-lasting tradition of the cult of death for the fatherland. This cult, with its images, pathetic language, symbols, and rituals was available wherever and whenever it was needed. During and after the Wars of Liberation it fulfilled three important functions. First and foremost, the cult served to mobilise the desperately needed patriotic and national readiness to fight and sacrifice, which, with the introduction of universal conscription, had to be demanded not only of all potential conscripts, but also, for the first time, of the entire 'Prussian nation'. This nation was cast as a 'people's family' (*Volksfamilie*) in which *every 'Prussian'* – men and women, young and old, rich and poor – had their specific patriotic national sacrifice to make and duties to perform. Moreover, the cult was intended to help society to deal with the grief of the dead soldiers' families by acknowledging their 'sacrifice' and at the same time commemorating the 'heroism' of their fallen warriors. The main message was that the fallen soldiers lived on not only in the memory of their families, but also in that of the 'nation', which grieved along with them, thus at once guaranteeing the immortality of the fallen and comforting those left behind. Last but not least, the cult was used to construct Prussia and Germany as a 'manly nation'. Recalling the heroic sacrifices of earlier generations and presenting them to future generations as models was intended to create national continuity, of which there were two versions after 1813. In the literature of regional-state patriotism, which dominated the Prussian discourse in the years 1813–15, this attempt referred primarily to the heroic military tradition that had been founded under Frederick the Great. In the less influential German national line of argumentation, in contrast, this attempt referred mainly to the imagined heroic Germanic tradition. While the first position was associated from the beginning with a model of disciplined 'soldierly combat readiness' shaped more by military and state interests, the second was initially linked to a 'civilian' concept of 'citizen valour'.

Images of patriotic valorous masculinity

A model of patriotic and valorous masculinity centred around the myth of death for the fatherland was propagated at the same time as the myth itself.[34] This model revolved around the notions of 'love of liberty', 'honour' and 'fraternity', 'piety' and the 'fear of God', 'strength', 'bravery' and 'loyalty', but above all 'readiness to sacrifice', 'patriotism', and 'valour'. It united the old values of Prussian soldierly honour and officer's virtue and Christian middle-class ethics with new notions of sentimental heroic Romanticism and manly citizen participation. The patriotic poetry addressed to the German and Prussian men going off to the Seven Years' War and the counter-revolutionary Wars of Coalition between 1792 and 1795 had already demanded patriotism and valour as central masculine virtues. What was new during the Wars of Liberation of 1813–15 was the striking ubiquity of the image of the patriotic-valorous man. While previously it had only been one model of masculinity among others, in the years between 1806 and 1815 it became a 'hegemonic model'. At bottom, this model was intended to motivate men not previously subject to conscription to perform military service and to put them in a frame to mind to fight, kill and die willingly 'for the fatherland'. It was for this reason that the idea of patriotic valour was so central. Men were addressed as fathers of families, citizens of their towns and Prussian or German patriots who were now called upon to liberate and defend family, home and fatherland (defined as Prussian and/or German) and to risk their lives voluntarily in the process. The trio of family, home and fatherland linked the personal interests of male individuals with the collective interests of the Prussian state and the German nation.[35]

At the period of the Wars of Liberation, the broad influence of the model of patriotic-valorous masculinity appears to have been promoted in particular by its formulation in four different generation- and stratum-specific versions, which were associated with competing political and military ideas: the 'citizen as national warrior', the 'German boy hero', the 'Christian militia man' and the 'man of arms'. The image of the 'citizen as national warrior', with its German national overtones, founded the tradition of a 'civilian' concept of 'civic valour'. This image spoke to the educated middle-class man as head of household and 'citizen of the state', calling upon him to defend his 'fatherland' and promising more political rights in return. These rights, however, the prospective 'citizens' should get *after* they had fulfilled their military duties. Moreover the political demands were modest. First and foremost aims were next to a united 'federative nation state' (a German league of territorial states), the freedom of the press and of assembly, and corporative representative bodies in the communes and the territorial states.[36] For the overwhelming majority of early liberal protagonists of this variant of the model of masculinity, moreover, it was self-evident that only educated and propertied men of the Christian faith could be accorded these political rights after the end of hostilities, and that next to all women also men of the 'working classes' and Jews were to be excluded. 'Citizenship' was thus linked in a specific way with 'valour'. For most, this political concept of masculinity went hand in hand with a rejection of large standing armies. They argued for universal conscription in the form of a militia, which would be trained regularly and deployed only in case of war.[37]

The heroic romantic image of the 'German boy hero' who sought to liberate the 'German fatherland' by means of his voluntary 'blood sacrifice', and to erase the disgrace brought upon it by the 'inactive', rationalistic generation of fathers, spoke particularly to young volunteers. The mainly young, educated propagandists of this generation-specific variant of the model of the 'citizen as national warrior' presented voluntary military service as a form of masculine self-realisation and a rite of initiation into manhood. In war young men could prove their valour and thus their manliness, and in this way secure a right to equal civil and political participation in the post-war 'fraternal community' of adult men – as future fathers of families and 'citizens of the state'. In wartime – in the face of death – they were the equals of older men (unlike in peacetime society). This specific form of equality was the basis of the notion, so popular in war poetry, of the 'fraternity' and 'comradeship' of *all* men at war.[38] The heroic romantic image of the 'German boy hero' was also based on the civilian concept of 'civic valour', but, since political demands played a far smaller role here than in the variant of the 'citizen as national warrior', it tended to be more open to 'militarisation', that is, to being co-opted by the military.

The image of the 'Christian militia man', strongly marked by regional-state patriotism, appealed mainly to simple members of the militia and territorial reserves. It was directed towards 'uneducated' men of the lower strata and primarily propagated the readiness to fight and sacrifice, the fear of God, discipline and loyalty. Here too, the manly obligation to protect family, home, and 'fatherland' was defined as the core responsibility of every man, but without any promise of and demand for increased political participation. The regional patriotic and military image of the 'man of arms' referred to a new type of linesman envisioned by army reformers, one who no longer fought on the basis of obedience and drill, but rather out of a self-determined devotion to king and country. This image was closely related to the image of the 'Christian militia man'. For army reformers, the 'Christian militia man' was simply an inexperienced and less qualified 'man of arms'.[39] Both models were thus variants of the model of disciplined 'soldierly combat readiness', which would become increasingly dominant as the nineteenth century wore on, and which was linked from the beginning with a position of loyalty towards the state.

What all four variants of the hegemonic model of 'valorous-patriotic masculinity' shared, despite their differences, was the idea that a 'true man' must be ready, if the situation demanded it, to die a hero's death for the fatherland, and to do so willingly. All versions of the new model were also constructed as counter-models to the 'Gallic foe', who was described as 'degenerate' and 'effeminate'. From the inner-German perspective, they were opposed both to the complementary image of virtuous and domestic, in short, 'truly German' femininity, and to the masculine counter-images of the 'loot-hungry mercenary', the 'cowardly scoundrel', the aristocratic 'Francophile', and the 'unchristian Jew'. These counter- and complementary images were apparently intended not only to serve the purposes of patriotic national mobilisation and to increase military fighting strength, but also to stabilise masculine self-confidence.[40] Only against the backdrop of the counter- and complementary images specific to the time could masculinity in general and manly heroism in particular be effectively defined and dramatised, for they are always relational.

The construction of the 'German national character' in gender- and socially specific terms was closely tied to the construction of a polarised notion of 'sex-specific character'.[41] The two processes shaped and reinforced each other reciprocally. The central qualities now attributed to all men because of their very 'nature' were 'activity', 'force', 'valorousness', 'courage', and 'strength', but also 'creativity' and 'passion'. The dichotomous and hierarchical view of gender, which claimed universality through its grounding in 'anthropology', provided an excellent basis for the political objective of militarising concepts of masculinity, since the male canon of virtues was already essentially defined in terms of martial and active traits.[42] The whole construction corresponded to altered political and military demands, since it legiti-mised the required manly virtues above all as 'natural', thus for the first time claiming universal validity across social boundaries. In this way it was the perfect accompaniment to the introduction of *universal* conscription.

Traditions and changes

After the period of the Wars of Liberation, the model of a polarised gender order became ever more firmly anchored in the German middle classes. It became part of the underlying structure of modern 'bourgeois society', reinforcing the idea that 'manliness' and 'courage', 'strength', 'industry', 'valour', and 'patriotism' were inextricably linked. This idea appears to have been accepted even by early liberals, who rejected all forms of standing army and the militarisation of society. Since this image of masculinity demanded 'valour' only in case of attack, that is, when family, home and fatherland were in need of defence, it was unnecessary for adult men to emphasise or flaunt the manly virtue of 'valour' much during peacetime. In this time the civilian masculine virtues of the citizen were more in demand.[43] This was particularly evident immediately after the war of 1813–14 in the 'warrior reception' festivities that were initiated and organised by the local authorities in towns and villages all over Prussia and northern and western Germany in order to welcome the returning volunteers and militiamen home. The entire ceremonial served two main purposes: to thank the 'liberators' and 'saviours' of the fatherland, and to reintegrate them symbolically into bourgeois civil society. That is why the festivities had a wholly unmilitary character and resembled large and cheerful family gatherings featuring rich food, colourful flower arrangements, music, and dancing. They represented, as it were, a ritual of 'release' from things military that civil society deemed necessary.[44] In poetry written for these festivities the returning 'defenders of the fatherland' were addressed as heads of household, breadwinners and citizens.[45] They were supposed to return to the civilian manly virtues of industry, responsibility and devotion to the common good and to display once again their 'domesticity' – a virtue that, along with 'sensibility' (*Empfindsamkeit*), was not simply attributed to early nineteenth-century middle-class men in exceptional cases, but expected of them.[46] 'Domesticity' and 'sensibility' were regarded not merely as fundamental virtues of loving and caring fathers and husbands, but also as prerequisites for patriotism and valour. For only a man who loved his own family, home, and fatherland from the bottom of his heart would be prepared to risk his life to protect and defend them. Only later in the nineteenth century, in the context of the militarisation of the model of the 'patriotic-valorous' man, did men have ever fewer opportunities to cultivate these virtues openly. They were no longer compatible with the military concept of 'soldierly combat readiness'.

To be sure, in the nineteenth century rhetorical declarations of the willingness to defend the fatherland had been a constant refrain during peacetime. They were repeatedly affirmed above all in the many ceremonies held after 1815 and 1871 to commemorate the victories and 'fallen heroes' of past wars.[47] A growing number of war memorials also served the 'cult of heroes'; while around 1800 there had been only eighteen such monuments to individuals, by 1883 the number had grown to more than eight hundred.[48] The organisers of these ceremonies and donors to memorials fell back not just on the repertoire of symbols, rituals and forms developed during the wars of 1813–15, but also on the pathos-laden phrases surrounding the commemoration of heroes that arose at the time. The poems and songs from the war years 1813–15 in particular enjoyed continuing popularity well into the twentieth century in schools and in middle-class men's organisations such as the *Turner* (gymnastic clubs), *Sänger* (choirs), and *Burschenschaften* (patriotic student associations).[49] After 1815, however, it was initially deemed neither necessary nor desirable to integrate the 'heroism' of the war years 'into everyday civilian practice as a permanent leitmotif'.[50] In middle-class everyday life the veneration of heroes was limited to literature, art, and music, monuments, rituals, and ceremonies.[51]

The cult of heroes was cultivated more systematically only by the military, whose influence on young men of all social classes rose markedly with the more consistent enforcement of universal conscription after the 1860s, the schools, and the burgeoning field of children's literature.[52] Schoolbooks and boys' literature in particular promoted the explicit training and veneration of heroes.[53] Male youths were reminded over and over again of the model of the 'boy heroes' of the Wars of Liberation, who, like Theodor Körner, had answered the Prussian king's call in 1813 and streamed out of their schools, university lecture-halls and workshops to volunteer for military service.[54] The focus on male youth in the 'training of heroes' was no accident. Since they would bear the burden of a future war, it was chiefly of them that the state and society would demand combat readiness and heroism. Young men were thus always a main target group of the propaganda surrounding war heroes. War was presented to them over and over again as the true test of genuine manliness.

Only in the context of the increasing militarisation of German society after the wars of 1870–71, which reached a preliminary high point before the First World War, was increasing value placed upon a 'manly-military habitus' in the everyday peacetime lives of adult middle-class men. The 'civilian' ideal of masculine 'valour' was replaced more and more by that of 'soldierly combat readiness' characterised by military discipline. This is evident among other things in the growing influence of nationalist and militarist men's associations. The *Kriegervereine* (associations of reservists) in particular underwent a veritable boom throughout Germany beginning in the 1870s. By the end of the nineteenth century they had more than 1.5 million members. In terms of sheer numbers, they were the largest associational movement.[55]

But in Wilhelmine Germany too it was above all young men who strove to revive heroic masculinity. As the thirty-year-old professor Max Weber put it in his 1895 inaugural lecture in Freiburg, they longed to distance themselves from their 'success-drunk and peace-thirsty fathers', who rested on their military laurels from the 'wars of unification', and were searching for fields in which to prove their manliness.[56] Max Weber was not the only man at the end of the nineteenth century to criticise his unheroic, dull, and prosaic fathers and forefathers and to press for the renewal of national heroism in the struggle for an 'imperial grandeur' appropriate to Germany. The emergent middle-class youth movement also held dear the ideal of a fighting hero who would sacrifice himself bravely in the service of an imperial 'Greater Germany'. Readers of the youth movement journal *Wandervogel* in 1906, for example, were told: 'A struggle has broken out over the preservation of the best forces of our people. German manliness, inwardness and loyalty, love of fatherland, pleasure in the craft of arms . . . We want to aid in educating youths and men who are prepared to live and, if necessary, to die, for the fatherland. And the latter is still the main thing.'[57] The associations gathered under the umbrella of the *Jungdeutschlandbund* (Young Germany Federation), which counted nearly 750,000 members in 1914, propagated similar ideas.[58] The young men who belonged to these organisations never doubted that they could become heroes and live the ideals of courage and bravery to the fullest only in the 'heroic times' of war. Only in war, they believed, could they experience manly 'comrade-ship' in its true form.

The old idea of war as a catalyst for national unity, renewal and taking a bold, manly stand (*Ermannung*), which had already been popular in the years between 1806 and 1815, began to meet with increasing acceptance among middle-class men in Wilhelmine Germany. After the turn of the century even older academics came to believe more and more in the necessity of a new war for masculine cultural renewal. For that reason quite a few of them welcomed the beginning of the First World War, which they justified quite self-evidently after the shots fired at Sarajevo as a 'defensive war'. In *Die deutsche Erhebung von 1914* (The German Uprising of 1914), for example, an historical study that appeared shortly after the beginning of the war and linked 'the German uprisings of 1813, 1848, 1870 and 1914', the respected Berlin professor of history Friedrich Meinecke wrote:

> Now death for the fatherland, that ancient sacrifice . . . has once again acquired for us a new and eternal meaning. [This sacrificial death] signals a sacred springtime for all of Germany. In the years before, we were apparently irreparably divided and frequently weary and despairing about the unhappy hatred between classes and confessions and the threats to our intellectual life. Now we are suddenly lifted above all barriers, a single, mighty, deep-breathing life-and-death community of the people.[59]

Similar ideas were also propagated in the many popularly written commemorative books that appeared in large editions before and during the First World War on the occasion of the hundredth anniversary of the Wars of Liberation of 1813–15.[60] Only against the background of these Prussian and German lines of tradition can we explain the heroic enthusiasm with which above all young men from educated middle-class circles volunteered for military service in August 1914.[61] Among their role models were the volunteers of 1813–14, youthful heroes such as Theodor Körner. Patriotic military education by the state, the army, and bourgeois society had born fruit.

Conclusions

With the myth of 'death for the fatherland' and its representation in the rituals and festivals of the national cult of heroism, in the years before and during the 'Wars of Liberation' the state and military in Prussia, in collaboration with the Lutheran church and with the willing support of the producers of topical patriotic literature, established a tradition that not only became a lasting component of the national political culture of Prussia and Germany, but also strongly influenced, and was influenced by, the formation of gender images. In this context, the new model of 'patriotic valorous masculinity', which corresponded to the altered political conditions of a national 'society of state citizens' with universal conscription, became hegemonic for the first time, securing male power in the state by tying the political rights of the citizen to military service. The concrete form of this model changed over the nineteenth century.

It was transformed more and more from a 'civilian' concept of 'citizen valour' into a model of disciplined 'soldierly combat readiness' shaped by the interests of the military and the state. Yet the core idea remained the same: when their country needed to be defended, 'real' men had to display an 'heroic spirit' and to fight and die willingly for the 'honour' and 'liberty' of the 'fatherland'. Society fell back upon this model and the images, symbols, rituals and ceremonies associated with it above all in times of crisis and war. In this way, together with the introduction of universal conscription, lastingly influential collective pathos formulas and symbolic forms of heroic masculinity were made available. It was precisely the long tradition of these cultural representations and practices that created continuity and certainty in the restless years before, during, and after wars. Their adaptation to the new times ensured their continued acceptance. This well-balanced mixture of tradition and change made the cult of death for the fatherland and the notions of masculinity conveyed along with it so very effective. The main targets of these images and practices were always young men upon whom – and this is often overlooked – the greatest burden of 'war work' rested, and of whom the greatest 'blood sacrifice' had to be demanded in wartime. For that reason, it was above all among them that the military, schools, and middle-class associations, but also the arts and literature, sought to keep alive the 'heroic spirit' in the 'inter-war periods' of the long nineteenth century in Germany.

Notes

I would like to thank Pamela Selwyn for her translation and Stefan Dudink and John Tosh for their comments on earlier versions of this chapter.

1 *Völkischer Beobachter*, 31 (31 January 1933). On the cult of heroes in National Socialism, see Sabine Behrenbeck, *Der Kult um die toten Helden: Nationalsozialistische Mythen, Riten und Symbole 1923–1945* (Cologne, 1996).

2 K. Berger, *Theodor Körner* (Bielefeld and Leipzig, 1912).

3 R. Schilling, 'Die soziale Konstruktion heroischer Männlichkeit im 19. Jahrhundert: Das Beispiel Theodor Körner', in K. Hagemann and R. Pröve (eds), *Landsknechte, Soldatenfrauen und Nationalkrieger: Militär, Krieg und Geschlechterordnung im historischen Wandel* (Frankfurt am Main and New York, 1998), pp. 121–44; R. Schilling, 'Die "Helden der Wehrmacht" – Konstruktion und Rezeption', in R.-D. Müller and H.-E. Volkmann (eds), *Die Wehrmacht: Mythos und Realität* (Munich, 1999), pp. 550–72; R. Schilling, 'Kriegshelden': Deutungsmuster heroischer Männlichkeit in Deutschland 1813–1945* (Paderborn, 2002).

4 On the concept of 'hegemonic masculinity' developed by R. W. Connell see his *Masculinities* (Berkeley, 1995); as well as chapter 3 by John Tosh in this volume.

5 G. L. Mosse, *Fallen Soldiers: Reshaping the Memory of the World Wars* (Oxford, 1990).

6 M. C. Bowra, *Heldendichtung: Eine vergleichende Phänomenologie der heroischen Poesie aller Völker und Zeiten* (Stuttgart, 1964); E. Mai and A. Repp-Eckert (eds), *Triumph und Tod des Helden: Europäische Historienmalerei von Rubens bis Manet* (Cologne, 1987); H. M. Blitz, *Aus Liebe zum Vaterland: Die Deutsche Nation im 18. Jahrhundert* (Hamburg, 2000).

7 B. Anderson, *Imagined Communities* (London and New York, 2nd edn, 1991), pp. 9–10.

8 The term 'democratised', which Ute Frevert uses in this context seems to me to be euphemistic. U. Frevert, 'Herren und Helden: Vom Aufstieg und Niedergang des Heroismus im 19. und 20. Jahrhundert', in R. van Dülmen (ed.), *Erfindung des Menschen: Schöpfungsträume und Körperbilder, 1500–2000* (Vienna, Cologne and Weimar, 1998), pp. 323–44.

9 R. Koselleck and M. Jeismann (eds), *Der politische Totenkult: Kriegerdenkmäler in der Moderne* (Munich, 1994).

10 'Patriotismus', in *Conversationslexikon oder Enzyclopädisches Handwörterbuch für gebildete Ständ*, vol. 9 (Altenburg, 1817), pp. 306–7; R. Vierhaus, ' "Patriotismus" – Begriff und Realität einer moralisch-politischen Haltung', in R. Vierhaus, *Deutschland im 18. Jahrhundert: Politische Verfassung, soziales Gefüge, geistige Bewegungen* (Göttingen, 1987), pp. 96–109; G. Birtsch (ed.), *Patriotismus* (Hamburg, 1991).

11 See, for example, Frevert, 'Herren und Helden'; or Schilling, 'Soziale Konstruktion'.

12 S. Wenk, 'Gendered representations of the nation's past and future', in I. Blom, K. Hagemann, and C. Hall (eds), *Gendered Nations: Nationalism and Gender Order in the Long Nineteenth Century* (Oxford and New York, 2000), pp. 63–77.

13 K. Hagemann, *'Mannlicher Muth und Teutsche Ehre': Nation, Militär und Geschlecht zur Zeit der Antinapoleonischen Kriege Preußens* (Paderborn, 2002), pp. 449–54.

14 *Preußischer Correspondent*, 37 (4 June 1813).

15 'An die Preußen!, Friedrich Wilhelm III', Löwenberg, 23 May 1813, in *Preußischer Correspondent*, 34 (30 May 1813).

16 Hagemann, *Mannlicher Muth*, pp. 75–91.

17 *Ibid.*, pp. 340–9, 497–508.

18 Blitz, *Aus Liebe*.

19 M. Jeismann, *Das Vaterland der Feinde: Studien zum nationalen Feindbegriff und Selbstverständnis in Deutschland und Frankreich* (Stuttgart, 1992), pp. 152–8.

20 Hagemann, *Mannlicher Muth*, pp. 340ff.

21 K. Hagemann, 'Of "Manly Valor" and "German Honor": Nation, war and masculinity in the age of the Prussian uprising against Napoleon', *Central European History*, 30 (1997), 187–220.

22 G. Kaiser, *Pietismus und Patriotismus im literarischen Deutschland: Ein Beitrag zum Problem der Säkularisation* (Wiesbaden, 1961), pp. 109ff.

23 F. Jacobs, *Deutschlands Ehre: Dem Andenken der in dem heiligen Kriege gegen Frankreich gefallenen Deutschen gewidmet* (Gotha, 1814), p. 5.

24 C. W. Spieker, 'Der Tod fürs Vaterland, dargestellt durch Beispiele aus der Geschichte: Eine Rede vor einem Bataillon Landwehr im Freien gehalten, September 1813', in C. W. Spieker, *Gebete, Predigten und Reden: Zur Zeit der Erhebung des Preußischen Volks gegen die Tirannei des Auslandes, im Felde und in der Heimath gehalten* (Berlin and Leipzig, 1816), p. 236.

25 Hagemann, *Mannlicher Muth*, pp. 457–97.
26 See also for the following, *ibid.*, pp. 497–508.
27 *Amts-Blatt der königlich kurmärkischen Regierung*, 13 (29 March 1816), p. 123.
28 *Ibid.*
29 *Ibid.*
30 *Ibid.*
31 *Königsberger patriotische Predigten aus den Jahren 1806–16 von Dr. Ludwig Ernst Borowski, Erzbischof der Evangelischen Kirche, Generalsuperindendent in Preußen*, ed. with an introduction by D. A. Uckeley (Königsberg, 1913), pp. 142–55.
32 *Amts-Blatt der königlich kurmärkischen Regierung*, 19 (6 May 1814), p. 179.
33 *Vossische Zeitung*, 151 (17 December 1816).
34 See, for the following, Hagemann, 'Manly Valor'.
35 K. Hagemann, ' "A Valorous *Volk* Family": The nation, the military, and the gender order in Prussia in the time of the anti-Napoleonic wars, 1806–15', in I. Blom, K. Hagemann, and C. Hall (eds), *Gendered Nations*, pp. 179–205.
36 Hagemann, *Mannlicher Muth*, pp. 289–303.
37 *Ibid.*, pp. 289–303, 324–31.
38 *Ibid.*, pp. 331–40.
39 *Ibid.*, pp. 306–24.
40 *Ibid.*, pp. 222–71.
41 K. Hausen, 'Family and role-division: The polarisation of sexual stereotypes in the nineteenth century – an aspect of the dissociation of work and family life', in R. J. Evans and W. R. Lee (eds), *The German Family: Essays on the Social History of the Family in 19th- and 20th-century Germany* (London, 1981), pp. 51–83; L. Schiebinger, *Nature's Body: Gender in the Making of the Modern Sciences* (Boston, 1993).
42 U. Frevert, 'Geschlecht – männlich/weiblich: Zur Geschichte der Begriffe (1730–1990)', in Frevert, *'Mann und Weib, Weib und Mann': Geschlechter-Differenzen in der Moderne* (Munich, 1995), pp. 29ff.
43 R. Pröve, ' "Der Mann des Mannes": Civile Ordnungsformationen, Staatsbürgerschaft und Männlichkeit im Vormärz', in K. Hagemann and R. Pröve (eds), *Landsknechte*, pp. 103–21; U. Frevert, 'Das Militär als "Schule der Männlichkeit": Erwartungen, Angebote, Erfahrungen im 19. Jahrhundert', in U. Frevert (ed.), *Militär und Gesellschaft im 19. und 20. Jahrhundert* (Stuttgart, 1997), pp. 145–73; G. L. Mosse, *The Image of Man: The Creation of Modern Masculinity* (Oxford and New York, 1996).
44 Hagemann, 'Mannlicher Muth', pp. 475–81.
45 See, for example, M. Claudius, 'Lied für die heimkehrenden Vaterslandsverteidiger', *Deutsche Blätter*, 5:82 (10 September 1814), 126–27.
46 There was no conflict as constructed by, among others, Anne-Charlott Trepp. See A.-Ch. Trepp, 'The private lives of men in eighteenth-century central europe: The emotional side of men in late eighteenth-century Germany (theory and example)', *Central European History*, 27 (1994), 127–52; A.-Ch. Trepp, *Sanfte Männlichkeit und selbständige Weiblichkeit: Frauen und Männer im Hamburger Bürgertum zwischen 1770 und 1840* (Göttingen, 1996).
47 E. Trox, *Militärischer Konservativismus: Kriegervereine und 'Militärpartei' in Preußen zwischen 1815 und 1848/49* (Stuttgart, 1990); S.-L. Hoffmann, 'Mythos und Geschichte:

Leipziger Gedenkfeiern der Völkerschlacht im 19. und frühen 20. Jahrhundert', in E. François, H. Siegrist, and J. Vogel (eds), *Nation und Emotion: Deutschland und Frankreich im Vergleich 19. und 20. Jahrhundert* (Göttingen, 1995), pp. 111–32; J. Vogel, *Nationen im Gleichschritt: Der Kult der Nation in Waffen in Deutschland und Frankreich, 1871–1914* (Göttingen, 1997).

48 M. Lürz, *Kriegerdenkmäler in Deutschland, vol. 1: Die Befreiungskriege, vol. 2: Die Einigungskriege* (Heidelberg, 1985); Koselleck and Jeismann, *Der politische Totenkult.*

49 D. Düding, *Organisierter gesellschaftlicher Nationalismus in Deutschland (1808–1847): Bedeutung und Funktion der Turner- und Sänger-Vereine für die deutsche Nationalbewegung* (Munich, 1984); S. Goltermann, *Körper der Nation: Habitusformierung und die Politik des Turnens, 1860–1890* (Göttingen, 1998); D. Heither, *Blut und Paukboden: Eine Geschichte der Burschenschaften* (Frankfurt am Main, 1997); D. Klenke, *Der singende 'deutsche Mann': Gesangsvereine und deutsches Nationalbewußtsein von Napoleon bis Hitler* (Münster, 1998).

50 Ute Frevert presupposes this and in so doing overlooks the precise construction of the model, see Frevert, 'Herren und Helden', p. 326.

51 Bowra, *Heldendichtung*; Mai and Repp-Eckert, *Triumpf und Tod*; Frevert, 'Herren und Helden', pp. 327ff.

52 K. Saul, 'Der Kampf um die Jugend zwischen Volksschule und Kaserne', *Militärgeschichtliche Mitteilungen*, 9 (1971), 97–143; U. Frevert, *Die kasernierte Nation: Militärdienst und Zvilgesellschaft in Deutschland* (Munich 2001), pp. 193–301.

53 M. Christadler, *Kriegserziehung im Jugendbuch: Literarische Mobilmachung in Deutschland und Frankreich vor 1914* (Frankfurt am Main, 2nd edn, 1979).

54 See, for example, T. Welter, *Lehrbuch der Weltgeschichte für Gymnasien und höhere Bürgerschulen*, Part 3: *Geschichte der neueren und neuesten Zeit* (Münster, 1861), p. 370.

55 K. Saul, 'Der "Deutsche Kriegerbund": Zur innenpolitischen Funktion eines nationalen Verbandes im kaiserlichen Deutschland, *Militärgeschichtliche Mitteilungen*, 6 (1969), 95–159; T. Rohkrämer, *Der Militarismus der 'kleinen Leute': Die Kriegervereine im Deutschen Kaiserreich, 1871–1914* (Munich, 1990).

56 M. Weber, 'Der Nationalstaat und die Volkswirtschaftspolitik', in M. Weber, *Gesammelte politische Schriften* (Tübingen, 2nd edn, 1958), pp. 21–5.

57 Quoted in W. Mogge, 'Wandervogel, Freideutsche Jugend und Bünde', in T. Koebner *et al.* (eds), *'Mit und zieht die neue Zeit': Der Mythos der Jugend* (Frankfurt am Main, 1985), p. 183.

58 Saul, 'Der Kampf', pp. 97ff.

59 F. Meinecke, 'Die deutschen Erhebungen von 1813, 1848, 1870 und 1914', in F. Meinecke, *Die deutsche Erhebung von 1914* (Stuttgart, 1914), pp. 28–9.

60 Hagemann, *Mannlicher Muth*, pp. 47ff.

61 J. Verhey, *The spirit of 1914: Militarism, myth and mobilization in Germany* (Cambridge, 2000).

PART III

Gendering the nation:
hegemonic masculinity and its others

8

'Brothers of the Iranian race': manhood, nationhood, and modernity in Iran c. 1870–1914

Joanna de Groot

HE last decade has seen the emergence of a lively historiography on formations and re-formations of categories of 'masculinity' and 'nation' and their roles in the era of modernity. Cultural histories of the defining of particular 'nations' and of the complex construction of 'manliness' in different historic settings have opened up discussion and understanding of the varied processes, relationships, and institutions which established and maintained 'manhood' and 'nationhood'.[1]

The discussion on the interplay of gender and 'nation' in Iranian political culture/cultural politics during the later nineteenth and early twentieth centuries which follows here will address themes of identity and inclusion developed in studies of other societies. It will take a comparative approach and consider both how Iranian constructs of manhood and nationhood had features found elsewhere (not least because of Iranian contacts with non-Iranian experiences and ideas) and how such constructs drew on specifically Iranian circumstances and resources. The point of departure will be the view that just as Iranian cultural politics/political culture were rooted in particular Iranian experiences, resources, and assumptions, so their histories shared features and developments experienced and created in many societies involved in the trajectories of modernity. The story of the formations and re-formations of ethnicity and masculinity in Iran from the 1870s to 1910s is neither mysteriously unique, exotic, or isolated from stories of nationalism and masculinity elsewhere, nor identical with Indian, French, Egyptian, or Irish stories. As others have commented they were all 'in' modernity but each one differently and distinctively.

Formations of Iranian modernity

The conditions within which distinctive discourses of manhood and nationhood emerged in Iran in the later nineteenth century can well be approached within this framework. Like people in other parts of the world, those in Iran confronted transformative challenges arising from the altered impact of material factors, state power, and external influences upon their lives during that century. Iranians in this period experienced the policies of a new dynasty (the Qajars) seeking to secure itself amid powerful indigenous interests and external pressures. As in many communities around the world, Iranian cultivators, traders, craft producers, and businessmen found themselves dealing with material changes associated with new technologies of communication (telegraph, steam, print) and with the growth of money power and of forces of competitive production over which they had little control. Iranians' incorporation into networks of international exchange and investment centred outside Iran, and their exposure to the imperial and strategic rivalries of the Tsarist and British empires paralleled the experiences of peoples in India, Africa, China, or southeast Asia with French, Dutch, or British colonial and entrepreneurial interests. Like counterparts in the Ottoman empire, Japan, Russia, or Egypt, government officials, entrepreneurs, and intellectuals in Iran tested and debated the alternatives of ignoring, resisting, adapting, or accepting the new opportunities and threats they encountered. To this extent nineteenth-century Iranians participated in the global developments characterising modernity as both agents and recipients.[2]

However, equal attention should be given to specificities in the situation of those Iranians. Unlike Indians, Xhosa, Maoris, or Egyptians they were not exposed to direct colonial rule nor were they involved with European economic interests with the same degree of intensity, since such involvement was limited by material and political constraints. Iranians evolved their own distinctive practices for brokering tensions between dynastic and regional or sectional power, between localised material self-sufficiency and extended exchange networks, between cultural diversity, religious pluralism, and communal identity and larger structures of religious and political authority. Thus while the impact of European manufacturers and demands for Iranian raw materials or carpets as well as for diplomatic, commercial, and territorial concessions was a real feature of nineteenth-century Iranians' experience this impact was demonstrably uneven. It was characterised by varied and shifting patterns of adaptation, resistance, and indifference or ignorance among cultivators, merchants, court circles, nomadic pastoralists, intellectuals, land and office holders, and religious specialists. The diversity and resilience of various communities and interests, rooted in material and political relations of power and interdependence, and the cultural resources of custom, language, religion, and origin stories, flavoured the responses of these communities to economic, political, and cultural change.[3]

Established constructions of ethnicity and gender were embedded in the culture, politics, and material life of these varied communities. 'Manliness' was enacted in the practical arrangements assigning males particular tasks and delimiting particular spheres of activity (*bazar* business, religious and legal office, public, professional, and political association) as distinctively male. The warrior/hunter/raider/protector of pastoralists' encampments, the elders and leaders of cultivation teams in villages, the workshop master, religious specialist, or *luti* (street tough) in a town, were identities grounded in these enactments and the deployment of such types as normative. Similarly linguistic, religious, or other cultural differences as well as actual or fictive kinship links shaped the identities, rivalries, and lifestyles of communities and sectional groupings. The distinctive language dress and customs used to identify Kurds or Baluch, the marriage patterns, and narratives of kinship or shared pasts which connected or divided communities and occupational groups typified widely used strategies for asserting shared interests and identities. Central to Iranians' constructions of identity was their acceptance of ethnic diversity as a normal social reality, expressed in popular proverbs and descriptions of regions of Iran by educated men, and seen as a source of both solidarity and conflict.[4]

The cultural evidence for these formations of masculinity and ethnicity is, not surprisingly, biased towards urban, privileged, and educated sections of society, but can also be traced in wider areas of cultural practice. The gendered commemoration of the dead on tombstones in the Bakhtiari areas of west/central Iran signified females by combs and males by lions, guns, or swords. Streets and neighbourhoods in Iranian towns sustained a male culture of gangs of toughs with their own *argot*, customs, and dress codes, using 'manly' physical force as protectors/bullies in their neighbourhoods or in feats of strength as street entertainers and patrons of *zurkhanehs* (houses of strength) for gymnastic exercise. They linked their identities and activities to ideals of *javanmardi* (youngmanliness) and *pahlavanat* (knightliness) expressed in popular versions of the traditions of Muslim mystical brotherhoods and poetic tales of chivalry and heroic combat recounted in teahouses and *zurkhanehs*.[5] Similar constructions of a shared past and culture affirmed group identities by celebrating and giving an ethnic flavour to narratives of lineages, customs, and histories. Such narratives might be unstable and shifting, but they combined with reference to distinctive features of custom and lifestyle to express the particular identity of these people. Depictions of common descent, of distinctive beliefs or customs, and of linguistic differences established a range of particularised and ethnicised identities within 'Iran'. These overlapped with other identities based on diversity of belief, on shared residence or occupation, or on status/class ideals of noble descent, corporate and kin loyalties among 'ulama (religious specialists) and bureaucrats, and pious artisan identity among (male) craft producers.

Religion also played a significant role in elite and popular constructions of masculinity and femininity. Quranic verses, the sayings and traditions of the prophet Muhammad and the Imams (the lineage of hereditary spiritual leaders acknowledged by Shi'a Muslims) and religious terminology contrasted the authority and rational power of men with women's dependency, 'weakness', and lack of judgement. These religious elements supplemented extensive proverbial, moral, and anecdotal constructions of gender difference and hierarchy, associating masculinity with assertive, authoritative, and protective roles in families, productive activities and communities, controlling the conduct and work of female and younger male subordinates. They also centred gender discourses around sexual honour (namus) where the purity/chastity (ismat/iffat) of women was seen as needing defence and enforcement by men, even if in practice sexual conduct was policed by women. Male responsibility for female sexual virtue and the familial character of honour and reputation which could be compromised by lapses in that virtue were features in the sexualisation of male patriarchal identities. Official and popular support for the enforcement of patriarchal control of sexuality are evidenced in the actual and symbolic punishments involving physical and sexual assault and officially managed but participatory public spectacle as penalties for violations of codes of sexual conduct.[6] The political spin placed on issues of sexual misconduct was interestingly signified in the mixed meanings given to the term fitna, which combined notions of rebellion and disorder with the idea of seduction and female sexual assertion or promiscuity as offences against marital and familial order, inscribing the sexual in the political and vice versa. While this pervasive concern with sexual honour has often been discussed as part of restrictive formulations of female propriety and subordination, its significance in the inscription of masculinities as intimately linked to the maintenance of sexual and familial honour should not be ignored.

The emergence of gendered discourses of nationhood

Significantly, while these well-established views of gender, ethnicity, and religion could have quite close linkages, with notions of 'proper' masculinity or femininity being located in 'our' community, neither had much connection with concepts of 'Iran' or 'nation'. The term 'Iran', poetically opposed in geographical terms to 'Turan' (notionally areas of Central Asia) in epic tradition, was primarily a literary concept used in educated discourse, like the notion of 'Iranian' identity which was used in contrast to 'Arab', 'Turk', or 'Afghan'. That usage often appeared in association with distinctions between Sunni and Shi'a Muslims (since Shi'ism had been the official religion of the Iranian state since the sixteenth century and the dominant practice by the seventeenth) and with assertions of cultural superiority. The term *vatan* (homeland), later to be used by nationalists to signify the 'national' homeland, was more likely to be used in the sense of 'birthplace' in a particular locality, city, or region. The term *mellat*, which was to come to mean 'nation/ people' in nationalist discourse, had previously been used in the sense of a community or religious group. It reflected traditions of self-organisation and self-definition among religious, occupational, and residential communities and of patterns of power in which dynastic regimes and government officials pursued their aims through negotiation with representatives of vested interests and local groupings.

It is in this context that we should consider the emergence of significantly gendered discourses of nationalism in Iran during the later nineteenth century. The most overt stimulus for these discourses was the challenges faced by the Iranian state in the era of modernity. The Qajar dynasty had succeeded in establishing some kind of hegemony in Iran between the 1790s and the 1830s. However, military defeats, loss of territory, and adverse treaty settlements showed the real deficiencies of the regime in the face of the assertive imperial and strategic interests of the Tsarist and British empires in Central Asia and India respectively. The treaties which registered loss of Iranian territory also granted Europeans commercial privileges, reinforcing their other competitive advantages in capitalistic production, investment, and exchange within the global networks of trade and money which also increasingly impacted on Iran. By the later nineteenth century the protests and criticisms of merchant/entrepreneurs were added to the concerns of intellectuals and government officials over the ineffectiveness of the Qajar regime in its expected role as protector of the 'guarded domains' of Iran and the well-being of its subjects. The association of these new difficulties with the increasing presence of European goods, and to a limited extent European people, in urban centres gave them the cultural and ideological twist of confrontation between indigenous/Muslim and alien/infidel interests. This narrative of confrontation gained force as Iranians of the official, elite, and commercial classes encountered new views of social, legal, and educational reform as diplomats, migrants, and travellers in the Tsarist and Ottoman empires, and Western Europe and used them to develop their own views on these matters as they affected Iran.[7]

Concerns with the problems of the material and political vulnerability of Iranians and with the possibilities for new approaches to reducing that vulnerability formed the terrain on which a new language of nation/homeland/patriotism was initially constructed. By the 1860s and 1870s, a polemical/prescriptive literature of reform aimed at government circles argued for the adoption of new forms of military and administrative organisation with associated legal and educational modernisation in terms not just of the needs of the dynasty but of the interests of the *vatan/mamalek* (lands) of Iran. 'Iran' began to be depicted as a nation/homeland needing defence or improvement using images which moved away from acknowledgement of the many diverse communities and cultures within the state towards the idea of a single 'nation'. The Shah himself, in an evolution of the old established trope of the ruler as protector and guarantor of prosperity, began to refer to the 'homeland' for which he was responsible. As *Akhtar*, a Persian language journal published by Iranians in Istanbul argued in 1877, *vatan* was more than a birthplace, but the 'country and sum total of existence', with a 'soul' grounded in the social fabric and community of residents and hence worthy of love. It transmuted old religious ideas, based on sayings of Muhammad, of love of homeland as part of faith and mystics' notions of the spiritual homeland to which souls aspire into a call to love *vatan* as part of ones own self-esteem since it sustained human dignity, achievement, and honour, even human essence itself. In the same series of articles the physical entity of *vatan* as territory was supplemented by the language of bodily and personal identity as it becomes a beloved or a victim, that is, an object of attachment and concern. Interestingly, discussions of patriotism also acquired a gendered flavour as writers like Akhundzadeh made it the attribute of 'zealous *men*' (using a term which combined a sense of both secular and religious enthusiasm) or spoke of the 'sons of the homeland' who constituted the *mellat*.[8]

By the 1880s and 1890s, these literary interventions were growing in volume and intensity as reformers, who had focussed their energies on influencing court and government circles, became frustrated with their lack of success and began to place their patriotic calls for reform on a more oppositional footing. They increasingly invoked not just the 'nation' as homeland and land of Iran but 'people' (*mellat*) which they opposed to the despotic power of the Shah and his government (*doulat*). This move to a populist/democratic notion of the *mellat* and its demand for freedom and progress reflected the influence of French constructions of the nation-as-people which developed in uneasy conjunction with a statist discourse of state-led modernisation and national strengthening owing much to Russian, Prussian, and Ottoman models. Napoleon and Bismarck were favoured heroic images of the period.[9] Use of the term *mellat* sidestepped other concepts like 'subject' or 'tribe', conveying a sense of community and shared culture from its older usages into the new language of nationalism. Indeed it usefully, if dangerously, resolved the question of whether the *mellat* of Iran was to be defined by Shi'a Muslim religious affiliation. This unstable ambiguity expressed the tensions between the intelligentsia's growing critiques of religion and religious specialists (*mullas, 'ulama*) as obstacles to national progress and their awareness that religious views and values powerfully motivated many Iranians and that sections of the *'ulama* were also vocal critics of government. It also reflected the continuing use of religious language and images as cultural resources even among secularising and anti-clerical writers and activists, and the role of indigenous as well as 'foreign' traditions of radical criticism.

Manhood and national renewal

The arguments and ideas about 'nation' and 'people' being developed at that time were largely produced within male homosocial milieux of officeholders and intellectuals. These were spheres from which women were absent. This is not to say that there were not educated, culturally and intellectually active women. Rather what needs to be understood are the constraints and separations between women's cultural practices and the formative experiences which produced male public intellectuals (religious or secular), office holders and political activists. Intellectual and political exchanges, alliances, and disagreements took place within male discussion circles, patronage networks, and professional settings. These ranged from traditional personalised groupings around learned or influential men, like the ideologue Jamal-ad-Din 'al-Afghani' or the reformist official Mushir-ad-douleh, to the more co-ordinated *anjumans* (societies) formed to debate and pursue reforming causes from the 1890s onwards.[10]

In such milieux visions of a strong and reformed *vatan* focused on masculine domains of government and formal education. After an early emphasis on military reform, nationalists of the later nineteenth century looked to the overhaul of administration and in particular to modernising the law and education as the means to reform and liberate the potential of Iranian society. This reflected the reformers' analysis of the 'successes' of European entrepreneurs and governments as springing from a mixture of properly enforced legal rights and obligations, and the application of 'modern' rational and technical expertise to all areas of life. As the reformer and sometime minister Mirza Husein Khan Mushir-ad-douleh put it, 'what Iran needs . . . today are *men* with experience and know-how' (my emphasis).[11] Whether in general exhortations or more elaborated schemes, the 'national' well-being of Iranians (political, moral, and material) was associated with reforming/creating a public education system teaching science, reason, and technical and commercial skills in a modern curriculum.

Just as they argued that education would release the potential of (male) Iranians for progress and resistance to foreign domination, so too these patriotic writer-activists stressed the role of law as a liberating and strengthening force. Accountable systematised, and fully implemented legislation would, in their view, free up economic innovation and underpin active citizenship. Law, according to an essay of 1871, was the 'one word' which would unlock progressive change; it was the title of the campaigning journal, *Qanun*, published by Malkom Khan during the 1890s; it lay at the centre of Talibov's argument that 'if we had the rule of law (*qanun*) we would be *masters* (sic) of knowledge, wealth, order, and independence'.[12] Again there was a significant shift away from advocacy of the government adopting legal reform in pursuit of its interests and duty towards arguments that the rule of law would benefit Iranian people as autonomous citizens and promoters of freedom and progress, tasks at which Shah and government had failed. The emergence of increasingly oppositional nationalist discourses circulating among the intelligentsia and merchant classes in various print forms focused attention on the spheres of government and economic vulnerability to European power and of institutional change in law, education, and administration which were coded as male. The rescue and rebuilding of the *vatan* and *mellat* were to be tasks for a new masculine patriot citizenry.

The masculinity of nationalist projects was even more explicitly expressed in a range of bodily and emotive depictions which imaged the *vatan* as a wounded/sick patient or endangered/violated girl or mother requiring the medical care or chivalric devotion of patriotic male healers/ lovers/sons. As nationalist discourses offered more outspoken censure and oppositional alternatives to the Qajar *doulat*, now implicated in the despoilment/malaise of the homeland by its succumbing to foreign diplomats and concession hunters and failure to pursue reform, so they took on these male patriotic responsibilities for the *mellat*. Older discourses which presented the Shah as a father/shepherd of a subject flock whose personalised authority was marked by reference to his divinely endowed radiance (*farr*) were shifted in two significant ways. Itself responding to the new internal and external pressures for change, the regime created a growing number of public and official *loci* of state action and authority distinct from the personal power of the Shah, including an expanded bureaucracy and apparatuses for regulating and supervising the poor, sick, and disorderly. The shape and energy of government and even its sovereignty were no longer linked to the ruler alone. This opened up a terrain on which responsibility for the homeland could be claimed by those speaking for the re-imagined *mellat* as the proper custodians of the 'national' interest. The image of the all-powerful Shah/father was replaced with that of the *vatan*-loving/ worshipping sons/lovers coming to the aid of the beleaguered or diseased homeland as expert healers, honourable protectors, and patriotic renewers. New languages of 'modern' expertise, historic pride, and filial and fraternal duty combined the emotive and erotic appeal of devotion to beloved (*aziz*) Iran with the authority of reference to rational and progressive agenda of justice and productivity and with familiar tropes of religion and family honour.[13]

The crucible of political upheaval

The years 1905–11 saw the intensification of the contest between government and 'people' in a period of political upheaval including the grant of a constitution (1906), a royal anti-constitutional coup (1908), and its reversal by constitutionalists (1909) whose success was then undermined by elite manoeuvrings, Russian and British intervention, and divisions among the constitutionalists themselves. This heightened political atmosphere generated rapid expansion in political activity (demonstrations, *bazar* closures, occupying buildings, civil conflict) and in political organisation ranging from local *anjumans* (societies) of urban activists, merchant and craft groups, even peasants, to social democrat bodies with international connections. This was accompanied by an explosion of political writing and cartoons including *shab-namehs* ('night-letters', i.e. clandestine leaflets fly-posted or distributed at night on city streets), pamphlets, and newspapers offering extended political commentary and analysis, vigorous satire, and impassioned exhortation. A political class gathering in the newly formed national *Majlis* (Assembly) created by the constitution and in the new parties and associations began to connect to larger constituencies as well as to negotiate relationships with the powerful vested interests represented by propertied and ruling elites and leading *'ulama*. This situation gave powerful impetus to the development and deployment of nationalist, reformist, patriotic, and radical leftist argument and imagery in which appeals to well-established, culturally widespread gender codes and reactions entwined with proliferating depictions of homeland and people by both pro- and anti-constitutionalist authors.[14]

As in the reconfiguring political culture of the French Revolution in the 1790s, or of anti-colonial activity in Egypt or Bengal at the turn of the twentieth century, the deeply resonant tropes of family and sexuality, of spiritual, sexual, and brotherly love were powerful resources in Iranian political culture and cultural politics.[15] Central among those tropes were those of the beloved, sick, dishonoured, endangered, idealised *vatan* embodied as a feminised lover/mother able to appeal to the honour, patriotism, and filial or patriarchal concerns of Iranian men as they were already embedded in political discourse. Just as the educated propagandists of the years before 1905 had elaborated a gendered and embodied homeland as an object of patriotic male reformers' love, concern, and activism, so popular street songs in Tehran, the capital city, sexually satirised the newly acceded Muzaffar-ad-din Shah as 'sister Muzaffar' the nursery-maid.[16]

Under the impetus of political upheaval and division, foreign intervention and territorial invasion, and civil conflict the theme on which these image-makers now focused was that of 'the homeland in danger'. New publications and more traditional preaching and propaganda supporting the constitution, nationalism, and reform urged patriotic 'sons' or 'brothers' (and sometimes gender-neutral 'children') as Iran's citizen people to defend these ideals from Shah, court, 'reactionaries', and foreign enemies and develop the homeland. Opponents of new forms of government and political activity, with their hostility to established interests, mobilised their support around the threat to indigenous traditions, notably religious norms and legal practice, using modern pamphlets and publicised telegrams as well as older techniques of preaching and formal religio-legal pronouncements. It is significant that just as supporters of opposed political positions contended on shared terrains of expression (pulpits, the press, telegrams, and street gangs) so they also contended for use of similar political imagery. The most studied area of contested imagery is that of Shi'a Islam, claimed by both pro- and anti-constitutionalists as a source of motifs of struggle and martyrdom, of 'national' cultural authenticity or of hallowed tradition under threat.[17] More central to the discussion here were changing appropriations of tropes of gender and sexuality through which diverse and opposed versions of 'nation,' 'state', and 'people' could be expressed and deployed to gain support. Such depictions contributed not only to complex and sometimes contradictory views of gender hierarchy and differences but also to the process whereby Iranian constructions of masculinity were reinforced and transformed.

Representations of danger to Iran and Iranians, whether from foreign intervention and the Shah's despotism, or from the 'godlessness' and 'anarchy' of constitutionalists, took a number of gendered forms. The image of a sick and endangered 'mother *vatan*' invoked related images of the protective and also 'expert' patriots who would heal and defend the homeland with their masculine courage and command of knowledge. In 1907 one journal *Tarraqi* (Progress) argued that the dying and ignorant body of *vatan* could only be revived by 'vaccinations' of knowledge. Significantly that body was also described as 'sacred', linking familiar tropes of holiness and devotion to the 'modern' tropes of disease and cure, and the argument targeted the failures of government ministers accused of 'poisoning' the homeland, while the duty of patriots was to 'cure' it.[18] The vertical authority of the patriarchal state is here challenged on behalf of the fraternal, comradely, horizontal alliance of the patriot *mellat*. The other focus of criticism was the 'foreigners' (Arabs, Turks, Mongols) who had invaded and damaged Iran in the past and the unsuitability of their modern successors as intruders (British, Russian, Ottoman) as physicians for the nation. The crises in the social and political 'body' of Iran, it concluded, needed indigenous 'skilful physicians and knowledgeable doctors' for their cure. Such a cure was depicted as a process of moral and political recovery in which the inherent nobility and conquering tradition 'ingrained in Iranian blood' would be manifest in resistance to foreigners and rejection of the luxury and apathy currently debilitating government and people.[19] The entwining of male codes of nobility and rationality with ethno-racial ideas of blood inheritance is used to create a moralising reformist patriotism in which past glories inspire healthy purgative regeneration of 'national' fibre and ending of 'debility'.

If one way of representing the endangered mother-*vatan* was through metaphors of illness, there were more directly gendered responses to invasions by Ottoman and Russian troops from 1907, the carving out of 'spheres of influence' in Iran for the Russians and British in the Anglo-Russian convention of 1907, and the slide to civil war between pro- and anti-constitutionalists. This introduced militaristic and confrontational features into political life which foregrounded questions of 'national' autonomy and integrity and the need to assert and defend them, tasks and circumstances which called up powerful associations with masculinity. One highly visible expression of these associations was the rhetoric of *namus* (honour) which upheld the distinctive role of men as custodians, arbiters, and defenders of female and family honour which came into increasing use. Before 1905, an earlier generation of political writers had already presented their views of Iran's difficulties in the face of foreign interference and invasion, whether Arabs in the seventh century or Russians in the nineteenth, in terms of the dishonouring of the 'Iranian family/nation' by the sale or rape of women. In a text depicting the development of a young Iranian boy, designed as a plea for reform through the acquisition of 'useful knowledge' by Talebov the threat of foreign domination is signified by forcing 'our' women to go unveiled and the suppression of the Muslim call to prayer so the sleep of European women will be undisturbed.[20] The obverse of this image of Iranian subjugation through the violation of women was the call to patriot sons of the mother-*vatan* to show their 'manliness' by resisting and repelling these offences against their honour.[21] The theme of male control over and protection of women was a common terrain on which the politics of change was developed and contested among religious, secular, popular, establishment, and oppositional participants, confirming the key place of masculinity on this terrain.

As the political situation intensified after 1906 so the discourses of manhood, sexual honour, and sexuality itself intensified with real possibilities of political and territorial disintegration stimulating vehement evocations of the enemies of mother-*vatan* as rapists to be repelled by the 'zeal' (*gheyrat*) of patriotic Iranians. This language combined historic meanings of personal religious devotion and the defence of patriarchal honour with new images of passion for freedom, nation, and progress. The incursion of Ottoman troops into western Iran in 1907 provoked an impassioned response in journals like *Musavat* (Equality) which spoke of adulterers threatening the purity of the mother-*vatan* and attacking the Shah's preoccupation with 'love-play' and the 'woman-like' inaction of Iranian men. A leaflet of 1908 entitled *Warning letter to the popular societies of Iran* used the trope of Iranian women facing sexual abuse from Russian soldiers and even forced to sell sexual services to comparable effect. It makes a rhetorical challenge to male sensibilities in which the abused women embody national/familial honour whose protection is the responsibility of Iranian men:

> Are they not your honour? . . . Are they not your sisters? Are they not the wives of your brothers in religion? Are you not in charge of protecting Iranians' honour? . . . Russian soldiers take these wretched ones and dishonour them . . . If you have any sense of virtue protect your honour . . . Oh you shameless ones! What has become of you?[22]

Here we have both an interesting tension among contesting views of women (as extensions of male honour, as sister-equals in the national family, as vulnerable victims), and a clear articulation of linked dimensions of masculinity and patriotism. The duty to protect the honour/women of the national brotherhood, bonded by shared religion, required political and armed struggle against the sexualised Russian threat to 'Iranian' soil. The growing conflict is a terrain where male virtue is shown in combat and where the brotherhood of Iranian patriots would replace the discredited paternal power of the monarchy which had allied itself with Russian troops to fight the constitutionalists. 'Oh brothers of the Iranian race', wrote a Shirazi in one of the new journals *Nida-yi Vatan* (Call of the Homeland) in January 1908, calling on compatriots to realise the need of their 'kind mother'.[23] Appeals to patriotic and civic manliness and love (in all its filial, erotic, religious, and political meanings) proliferated as the civil war and Russian military intervention intensified. Constitutionalist activists in Azerbaijan in north-west Iran, a centre of much radical politics and fighting, called on other Iranians who took pride in the 'chivalry and bravery of their forefathers' to join them in 'the pursuit of the lost beloved, the nation and its new institutions, now under attack. Moving from moral/ religious exhortation ('resistance in Islam has always been the special duty of men') to sexually explicit rhetoric ('Is it that in these lands men and men's balls have been destroyed? Are all men dead and have non-men taken their place?') the writer equates lack of concern with the fate of the *Majlis* and constitution with lack of manly honour and courage. Men who stay out of the conflict are called cowards who have left the 'realm of manhood' and are scorned for their lack of *javanmardi* (youngmanliness), zeal or bravery and for preferring 'a life . . . lower and viler than that of the women of the earth' to acting to save the homeland.[24]

A *shab-nameh* of August 1908 took these references to patriarchal honour and street masculinity in a more explicitly religious direction. In the midst of the civil war and Russian invasion of Azerbaijan it turned to a powerful and widely influential image, that of the slaughter of one of the founding leaders of the Shi'a community, the third Imam, Husein, and his family at the battle of Karbala, near modern Baghdad, in October 680. The narratives and depictions of this moment of suffering and martyrdom for the Shi'a faith which developed over later centuries, and particularly in Iran from the time of the Safavid dynasty (1501–1722) came to permeate public and private religious practice and discourse among Shi'a believers. By the nineteenth century, annual commemoration of the Karbala events included street processions of male devotees cutting and beating themselves, performances of 'passion plays' enacting the story by amateur and professional performers with elite patronage, and private gatherings for mourning prayers and recitations. References to the hero Husein and the villains Yazid and Shimr his opponents had become familiar and widely used means to invoke ideals of redeeming virtue (Husein was seen as an intercessor for believers) and oppressive tyrannical evil. Outside the annual period of commemoration prayers, sermons, and sayings took up the drama and characters of Karbala as a dominant paradigm of the struggle between good and evil, and the moral and political power of suffering, martyrdom, and devotion to a just cause. What has been called 'the Karbala paradigm' was a powerful and pervasive cultural resource, not only in the domain of religious identity and solidarity, but also as a *political* paradigm for registering commitment and criticising injustice and oppression.[25]

In the *shab-nameh* in question the struggle and suffering of the Karbala martyrs (men and women) are used as an image for the courage and suffering of Azerbaijani women who fought 'like male lions' to defend their honour thereby impugning the masculinity and Shi'a credentials of male readers who failed to join the struggle for the constitution:

> You have witnessed the events of Karbala. Your Muslim zeal has become Jewish abjectness. You [who are] less than women have fallen short and gone to sleep . . . Oh you shameless ones, less than women, less than dogs . . . Did you not think that not all Iranians have the temperaments of women or worship anti-Christ like you?[26]

What is interesting here is the slippage from praise for women who displayed 'male' qualities in defending their honour, thereby shaming the men whose 'proper' task this was, to denigration of Muslim men by likening them to 'inferior' women and Jews. Men are urged simultaneously to right injustice, resuscitate their manhood, and rescue national and sexual honour by acting as manly patriots in defence of the embattled 'nation', constitution, and 'people'. These exhortations sat alongside parallel and contradictory formulations celebrating women's courage rather than their inferiority, and sometimes hinting that patriotic and constitutionalist ideals and projects might include female as well as male protagonists. Such contradictions are a reminder that in a period of political crisis and innovation gender roles and identities might be substantive as well as symbolic issues in the shifting conflicts over power in political institutions and access to political activity and agency. While recent scholarship has understandably and appropriately approached contested gender issues form the perspective of women's experience and changing agency, it should also be understood as constitutive of changing and contested masculinities.[27]

Late nineteenth-century polemicists had evoked the weaknesses of Iran and calls to remedy them in terms of the abused and sickly female body needing the courage, devoted love, and modern intellectual skills of patriotic reformist lover/sons. Constitutionalist politics between 1905 and 1911 appeared as sexual/moral dramas in which secularism was depicted as the onset of sexual corruption of men by 'improper' women who evaded proper male control, and government oppression, like foreign invasion, was presented (in a letter to a leftist journal of 1910) as attacking Iranian 'chastity'.[28] Questions about the status and education of women, and the impact of women's own activism, organising and ideological contributions after 1906 were substantive and divisive issues, but also important symbolic signifiers of other processes and controversies. They provided images and rhetoric expressing the extended engagement of Iranians with modernity through the nineteenth century, and then the sharper contests and crises of the early twentieth century as the categories 'man'/'manliness', 'woman'/'femininity', 'politics', 'state', and 'people' underwent reshaping. The remaking of each of these categories was entwined with the remaking of the others. Within this complex cultural field the political significance of masculinity was *intensified* by the linkages, uncertainties, and changes around it and the refashioning of manhood and the refashioning of politics, patriotism and government were mutually interdependent.

Conclusion

Narratives of the making/remaking of constructions of manhood and nationhood in Iran from the onset of 'renewalism' among intellectuals and officials in the 1860s, to the wider upheavals of contestation over political representation and national emancipation between 1905 and 1914, need to address several themes.[29] One is the emergence of political cultures and activities which included a widening range of Iranians in discussions, enactments, and imaginings of 'masculine' and 'Iranian' identity. While this might stimulate innovative developments and combinations in Iranian views of manhood and nationhood rooted in the 'modern' discourses of state, ethnicity, and 'people', and of reforming rational masculinity, inherited forms and resources still had continuing and powerful roles. Legacies of popular and religious constructions of sexual and gender relations and norms were as significant as the emergent emphasis on nationalism, social justice, and statist reform, and the defence of historic male privilege, however legitimised, was central as the scoping of new meanings for manhood. This uneven and complex blend of co-habiting and sometimes conflicting elements was deployed differently by different groups of Iranians but arguably was a shared resource which was to play a role throughout the twentieth century. The emergence of more intrusive and centralised state initiatives in education, transport, and administration as well as of more inclusive media influences and centralising forces in the economy between the 1920s and the 1970s enabled the transmission of this resource across many social divides. The interest of the narratives of manhood and nationhood which emerged in the preceding decades thus lies as much in their importance for twentieth-century histories of Iranian modernity, as in their intrinsic significance for an understanding of the period.

The other interest of these narratives is in the wider setting of histories of nationalisms and masculinities. The interplay between the distinctively local features of Iranian discourses on these themes and those which occur elsewhere illustrates the pervasiveness of gendered discourses of nationhood and masculinised constructions of patriotism as well as to common tendencies to draw on history, customs, and ideas of ethnicity and culture to shape such constructions and discourses. Students of gender and/or nationalism in French, Indian, Russian, Egyptian, or Irish contexts (to name but a few) will recognise these patterns, as they might recognise the entwining of manhood and nationhood with the discourses of reason, progress, state power, and productivity which are associated with modernity. They will equally recognise the distinctive and particular characteristics of Iranian experience just as they do in those other cases. The specific forms and roles of Shi'a Islam, of social relations in Iranian towns, nomadic encampments or villages, and of kinship, court politics and local power structures as well as of intellectual and communal life all fed into the processes which 'produced' Iranian versions of masculinity and nationalism. So too did the particular character of Iranian contacts with social and political developments in Russia, India, western Europe, and the Ottoman empire, through which of course the exchanges and insights which linked Iranian experiences to those of others took place. What this piece of historical narrative has sought to convey, is both the chronological process of development which shaped Iranian versions of manhood and nationhood, and the rich texture of their complex engagement with Iranian specificities and with the more widely shared features of modernity.

Notes

1 See, for example, K. McLelland, 'Masculinity and the "representative artisan" in Britain 1850–1880', in M. Roper and J. Tosh (eds), *Manful Assertions: Masculinities in Britian since 1800* (London and New York, 1991); K. McLelland, 'England's greatness the working man', in C. Hall *et al.* (eds), *Defining the Victorian Nation: Class, Race and Gender and the British Reform Act of 1867* (Cambridge, 2000); M. Sinha, *Colonial Masculinity: The 'Manly Englishman' and the 'Effeminate Bengali' in the Late Nineteenth Century* (Manchester and New York, 1995); M. Girouard, *The Return to Camelot: Chivalry and the English gentleman* (New Haven, 1981); G. L. Mosse, *Nationalism and Sexuality: Respectability and Abnormal Sexuality in Modern Europe* (Madison WI, 1985); G. L. Mosse, *The Image of Man: The Creation of Modern Masculinity* (New York and Oxford, 1996); C. Moscovici, *Gender and Subject-Citizenship in Nineteenth Century French Literature and Culture* (Lanham MD, 2000); D. Outram, *The Body and the French Revolution: Sex, Class, and Political Culture* (New Haven, 1989). C. Hall *et al.*, *Defining the Victorian Nation*; A. Burton, *Burdens of History: British Feminists, Indian Women, and Imperial Culture, 1865–1915* (Chapel Hill, 1994); C. Hall, *Civilising Subjects: Metropole and Colony in the English Imagination* (Cambridge, 2002); M. Agulhon, *Marianne into Battle: Republican Imaginery and Symbolism in France, 1789–1880* (New Haven, 1981); L. Hunt, *The Family Romance of the French Revolution* (London and New York, 1992); J. W. Scott, *Only Paradoxes to Offer: French Feminists and the Rights of Man* (Cambridge MA, 1996); P. Chatterjee, 'The nationalist resolution of the woman question', in K. Sangari and S. Vaid (eds), *Recasting Women: Essays in Colonial History* (New Brunswick NJ, 1990); P. Chatterjee, 'Colonialism, nationalism, colonized women: The contest in India', *American Ethnologist*, 16:4 (1989), 622–33; Special issue 'Gender and Nationalism', *Gender & History*, 5:3 (1993).

2 On Iranian nineteenth-century involvements with modernity and global influences see J. Foran, *Fragile Resistance: Social Transformation in Iran from 1500 to the 1979 Revolution* (Boulder CO, 1993), part 2; J. Foran, 'The concept of dependent development as a key to the political economy of Qajar Iran', *Iranian Studies*, 22 (1989), 6–56; G. Neshat, 'From *bazar* to market', *Iranian Studies*, 14 (1981), 53–85; D. Gillard, *The Struggle for Asia: A Study in British and Russian Imperialism* (London, 1977).

3 See G. Gilbar, 'The persian economy in the mid 19th century', *Die Welt des Islams*, 19 (1979); E Abrahamian, *Iran Between Two Revolutions* (Princeton NJ, 1982); Foran, *Fragile Resistance*.

4 See W. Floor, 'The guilds in Iran', *Zeitschrift der Deutschen Morgenlandischen Gesellschaft*, 126 (1975), 99–116; W. Floor, 'The political role of the *lutis*', in N. Keddie and M. Bonine (eds), *Modern Iran: The Dialectics of Continuity and Change* (Albany, 1981); H. Layard, *Early Adventures in Persia and Susiana* (London, 1886); M. Sheil, *Glimpses of Life and Manners in Persia* (London, 1856); J. B. Fraser, *Narrative of a Journey into Khorasan* (London, 1825); E. Eastwick, *A Journal of Three Years' Residence in Persia* (London 1864); A. Amanat, 'In between *madrasa* and marketplace: The designation of clerical leadership in modern Shi'ism', in S. Arjomand (ed.), *Authority and Political Culture in Shi'ism* (Albany, 1988).

5 See A. Fathi, 'The role of the "rebels" in the constitutional movement in Iran', *International Journal of Middle East Studies*, 10 (1979), 55–66; Floor 'Political role of the *lutis*'.

6 Examples are in C. J. Wills, *The Land of the Lion and the Sun* (London, 2nd edn 1891), p. 122; UK Foreign Office Papers, London (hereafter FOP), FO60/vol. 212, memo Stevens, Tehran to Clarendon, London, October 1886.

7 See A. Amanat, *Pivot of the Universe: Nasir ad-din Shah and the Persian Monarchy 1831–1896* (London, 1997), chs 9–10; D. Gillard, *The Struggle for Asia*; H. Algar *Religion and the State in Iran, 1785–1906: The Role of the Ulama in the Qajar Period* (Berkeley CA, 1969), chs 9–14; Amanat, 'In between *madrasa* and marketplace'; M. Bayat, *Iran's First Revolution: Shi'ism and the Constitutional Revolution of 1905–1909* (New York and Oxford, 1991), chs 1–4; Foran, *Fragile Resistance*, ch. 5; G. Nashat, *The Origins of Modern Reform in Iran, 1870–80* (Urbana Ill., 1982); S. Bakhash, *Iran: Monarchy, Bureaucracy and Reform nder the Qajars, 1858–1896* (London, 1978); F. Kashani-Sabet, *Frontier Fictions: Shaping the Iranian Nation* (Princeton NJ, 1999), chs 1–3.

8 'The love of homeland is part of faith', *Akhtar* (The Star), 3:8 (28 February 1877), 1–2; 'Again what should be said about the homeland', *ibid.*, 3:9 (7 March 1877), 1–2.

9 Bismarck was given admiring treatment in journals like *Sharaf* (Honour) in 1884 and *Sharafat* in 1898; the image of Napoleon was transmitted via reports from Iranians who visited Napoleonic France and translations of Bourienne's *Memoires* into Persian in the 1830s whereby it came to the attention both of Nasir ad-Din Shah and of reformist officials; see comments in Amanat, *Pivot of the Universe*, p. 487, n. 41; Kashani-Sabet, *Frontier Fictions*, pp. 93, 96–7 quoting Husein al-Musavi, *Treatise on the Creation of a Civilised Nation (Mellat)* (written 1898) and Mirza Saleh Shirazi, *Travel Account* (in Persian, written 1824, pub. Tehran, 1985).

10 See Bakhash, *Iran*; N. Keddie, *Sayyid Jamal ad-Din 'al-Afghani'* (Berkeley CA, 1972); F. Adamiyat, *Ideas of Freedom and the Beginning of the Constitutional Movement in Iran* (in Persian, Tehran, 1981); H. Algar, *Mirza Malkum Khan: A study in the History of Iranian Modernism* (Berkeley CA, 1973).

11 Letter to Mirza Sa'id Khan, 6 August 1866, quoted in G. Nashat, *Origins of Modern reform*, p. 145.

12 Mirza Yusef Khan Mustashar ad-Douleh, *One Word* (written 1871, pub. Tehran, 1985); Talebov, *Ahmad's Book*, vol. 2, p. 136.

13 See M. Tavakoli-Targhi, *Refashioning Iran: Orientalism, Occidentalism and Historiography* (Basingstoke, 2001), pp. 118–23.

14 Accounts of the 'constitutional revolution' are summarised in Foran, *Fragile Resistance*, pp. 170–94, and Abrahamian, *Iran Between Two Revolutions*, ch. 2. Fuller treatments are in Bayat, *First Revolution*, and Afary, *Constitutional Revolution*. Useful contemporary material is in E. G. Browne, *The Persian Revolution* (London, reprint, 1966) and Nazim al-Islam Kermani, *History of the Awakening of the Iranians* (written 1910, pub. Tehran 1978).

15 Compare L. Hunt, *Politics, Culture and Class in the French Revolution* (Berkely CA, 1984); Hunt, *The Family Romance*; D. Outram, *The Body and the French Revolution*; M. Badran, *Feminists, Islam and Nation: Gender and the Making of Modern Egypt* (Princeton NJ, 1992); B. Baron, 'The construction of national honour in 19th century Egypt', *Gender & History*, 5 (1993), 244–55; B. Baron, 'Mothers morality and nationalism', in R. Khalidi *et al.* (eds), *The Origins of Arab Nationalism* (New York, 1991); P. Chatterjee, *Nationalist Thought and the Colonial World: A Derivative Discourse* (London, 1986); P. Chatterjee, *The Nation and Its Fragments: Colonial and Postcolonial Histories* (Minneapolis, 1993).

16 FOP, FO65/vol.1529, quoted in 'Report on Tehran', October 1896.

17 Bayat, *First Revolution*, chs 5, 8–10; V. Martin, *Islam and Modernism: The Iranian Revolution of 1906* (London, 1989); Afary, *Constitutional Revolution*, chs 4, 5, 11.

18 'Concerns of the glorious ministry', *Tarraqi* (Progress) (16 April 1907), 1–2.

19 'Discovering the illnesses of the homeland and the diagnosis of Iran', *Rahnema* (The Guide), 1–2 (August, 1906), 5–7, 7; *ibid.*, 7–13 (September 1907), 5–7, 6–7, 10–11, 5, 3–4, 4–5; *ibid.*, 18–19 (February, 1908), 6; *ibid.*, 23–4 (April–May, 1908), 5–6.

20 Talebov, *Ahmad's Book*, vol. 1, p. 99.

21 Examples are in *Qanun*, (written 1890s, facs. edn, Tehran, 1978), issue 1, p. 3, issue 7, p. 1, issue 10, p. 2, issue 12, and the narrative 'The Strange Dream and Peculiar Discovery', serialised in the Cairo-based Persian language journal *Parvarish* (Development) between June and November 1900, sensitively discussed by A. Najmabadi, 'The Erotic *Vatan* (Homeland) as Beloved and Mother', *Comparative Studies in Society and History*, 39:3 (1997), 442–67, as well as in Kermani's work and journals like *Akhtar*.

22 Nazem al-Islam Kermani, *History of the Awakening*, vol. 1, pp. 610–11.

23 'Letter from Shiraz', *Nida-yi Vatan* (Call of the homeland) (12 January 1908), 4.

24 'The call of Azerbaijan to the protected lands of Iran', *Musavat*, 27 (January 1909).

25 On the 'Karbala paradigm' see M. Momen, *Introduction to Shi'a Islam: The History and Doctrines of Twelver Shi'ism* (New Haven, 1985), chs 2–3 and pp. 240–3; M. Fischer, *Iran from Religious Dispute to Revolution* (Cambridge MA, 1980), pp. 12–27, 170–80; J. Calmard, 'Le mecenat des representations de Ta'ziye', part 1, in *Le Monde Iranien et l'Islam: Sociétés et Cultures*, vol. 2 (Genève, 1974), part 2, pp. 73–126 and vol. 4 (Genève, 1976–7), pp. 133–62; P. Chelkowski (ed.), *Ta'ziyeh: Drama and Ritual in Iran* (New York, 1979); E. Bosworth and C. Hillenbrand (eds): *Qajar Iran: Political, Social and Cultural Change* (Edinburgh, 1983), chs 12–13.

26 Kermani, *History of the Awakening*, vol. 2, pp. 224–6.

27 See Afary, *Constitutional Revolution*, ch. 7; A. Najmabadi, 'The Erotic *Vatan*'; A. Najmabadi, '*Zanha yi-millat*: Women or wives of the nation', *Iranian Studies*,

26 (1993–4), 51–71; A, Najmabadi, *The Story of the Daughters of Quchan: Gender And National Memory in Iranian History* (Syracuse, 1998); B. Bamdad, *From Darkness into Light: Women's Emancipation in Iran*, trans F. Bagley (Hicksville NY, 1977), ch. 3; Paidar, *Women and the Political Process*, chs 2–3.

28 'Letter from the city', *Iran-I No* (New Iran) (May 1910), 4.

29 A term used as a more focused alternative to the overworked 'modernisation' by Monica Ringer in her *Education, Religion, and the Discourse of Social Reform in Qajar Iran* (Costa Mesa CA, 2001).

9

Hegemonic masculinity in Afrikaner nationalist mobilisation, 1934–48

Jacobus Adriaan du Pisani

Views about the Afrikaner people vary considerably, but there is general agreement that the Afrikaners were highly successful in the twentieth century. They managed to mobilise political power and hold on to that power in spite of the fact that they constituted a shrinking minority of the South African population. The rise of Afrikaner power has been investigated from different angles, including that of religiously inspired ideology, racial/ethnic mobilisation, and the formation of class alliances.[1] Thus far Afrikaans historians have not perceived gender as particularly relevant to issues of politics and power in Afrikaner society.

This chapter investigates the role of masculinity in the mobilisation of Afrikaner power. It focuses on the construction of Afrikaner hegemonic masculinity in the fourteen years (1934–48) immediately preceding the National Party election victory, which brought nationalist Afrikanerdom to power in South Africa. In this period a new Afrikaner hegemonic masculinity, which would be a dominant force in apartheid South Africa, emerged. The forces and agents which shaped it, the strategies employed in its construction, and the way societal change impacted upon it are discussed. I will show how Afrikaner hegemonic masculinity was constructed around particular symbols, how myths played an important role in its construction and how alternative masculinities were marginalised by silencing or stigmatising them.

Between defeat and victory: the quest for *volkseenheid*

After their defeat by the British in the Anglo-Boer War (1899–1902) Afrikaners were for some decades engaged in defining their place and role in South African society. In an industrialising and modernising

South Africa processes of urbanisation, social transformation, and political mobilisation resulted in changing living conditions, lifestyles, modes of thinking, ideologies, and political orientations in Afrikaner society. In 1910 the former British colonies and Boer republics were integrated into the Union of South Africa. Blacks were excluded from effective participation in mainstream politics in the country. Although they formed less than a third of the total South African population, the white population was politically dominant.

After 1910 the main contest in white politics was between a more inclusive South Africanism, promoting political collaboration between the Afrikaners and moderate English-speaking South Africans, and a more exclusive Afrikaner nationalism, directed towards restoring Afrikaner *volkseenheid* (national unity) as a tool to gain political power and realise the aim of restoring an Afrikaner republic. Several party political reorientations occurred in government and opposition ranks, but between 1914 and 1934 the South African Party of Generals L. Botha and J. C. Smuts was the flag-bearer of South Africanism, while the National Party of General J. B. M. Hertzog represented Afrikaner nationalism.

From 1924 the National Party was the senior partner in a coalition government, but the 1930s was a period of political division in Afrikaner nationalist ranks. When the National Party merged with the South African Party in 1934 to form the United Party, the Afrikaner right wing, under the leadership of Dr D. F. Malan broke away to form the 'Gesuiwerde' Nasionale Party (Purified National Party). After the 1934 elections the United Party emerged as the governing party and the (Purified) National Party as the official opposition. Henceforth nationalist Afrikaners regarded not only pro-British 'imperialists' and 'jingoes' as their political enemies, but also the *Smelters* who had merged in the United Party.

In the late 1930s several right-wing political groups with national-socialist leanings (e.g. the *Ossewa-Brandwag*, *Gryshemde* and *Nuwe Orde*) were established, posing a potential threat to the (Purified) National Party's claim to be the political home of nationalist Afrikanerdom. The Afrikaner section of the white population found themselves divided in several moderate and right-wing political groupings. The National Party (first under the name 'Gesuiwerde' Nasionale Party and later *Herenigde Nasionale Party of Volksparty*) persisted in its efforts to achieve the greatest possible political unity among Afrikaners. Their efforts were eventually rewarded with the election victory of 1948, after which the National Party ruled for forty-six years until 1994.

Hegemonic masculinity, national identity, and political power

Robert Connell applied Gramsci's concept of hegemony to the field of masculinity studies by developing the theoretical concept of hegemonic masculinity.[2] Hegemony refers to the cultural dynamics through which a specific group attains and maintains a leading position in society. Hegemony is the outcome of contestation and is not static, but historically mobile. Any system of hegemony is by definition liable to insecurity.[3]

In Afrikaner society much contestation was involved, particularly in the 1930s and 1940s, in the construction of Afrikaner hegemonic masculinity. Apart from party political divisions the Afrikaner nationalist elite had to contend with the division between traditionalist rural communities and modernising urban communities, class distinctions, and provincialism. The Afrikaner nationalist ideal of masculinity, which gradually attained and consolidated a position of hegemony, was a construct of that emergent middle-class version of Afrikaner intellectualism known as Christian-Nationalism and espoused by Afrikaner 'cultural leaders', including ministers of religion, academics, journalists, and politicians.

The *Afrikaner-Broederbond*, a secret all-male elite organisation established in 1918 to promote Afrikaner interests, played a crucial role. Because this organisation was instrumental in the construction of the Christian-National ideology its membership requirements give an indication of the core values of Afrikaner hegemonic masculinity at the time. Financially independent, white, Afrikaans-speaking, Protestant men (by implication adherents to the Calvinist version of Christianity and members of any of the three big Afrikaans churches) over the age of twenty-five could become members if their proposers could confirm their irreproachable character and their commitment to their fatherland, language and culture.[4] These explicit requirements, combined with other implicit elements, such as heterosexuality and political conservatism, represented the Afrikaner nationalist 'manly ideal'.

As several scholars have pointed out masculinity plays a decisive role in the construction of the nation as 'imagined community'.[5] In Afrikaner society, like in most cultures, there was a close connection between hegemonic masculinity and nationhood. The male elite, who in the 1930s and 1940s were mostly members of the *Afrikaner-Broederbond*, regarded the creation of the nation as 'men's business' and took the initiative in this regard. The emergence of the Afrikaner nationalist ideology, the mobilisation of Afrikaner power and the construction of a hegemonic form of Afrikaner masculinity were closely related processes. Hegemonic masculinity and national identity were mutually constitutive.

Hegemonic masculinity is often deployed to establish other forms of hegemony, such as hegemonic forms of nationhood. It is a vital element, in terms of Gramsci's notion of hegemony, of an ideology that helps to merge divergent economic, political, intellectual and moral goals. Such an ideology may be used by one social group to join the interests of another group to its own and to establish in this process hegemony over a third party. This is precisely the type of process that occurred in Afrikaner society in the 1930s and 1940s. Afrikaner hegemonic masculinity was used as part of an ideology to merge divergent Afrikaner interests and goals in order to establish hegemony over the English speaking and black populations.

Dana Nelson, in her study of the relationship between white manhood and national identity in the United States, emphasises the ideological coordination in that country of nation, manhood, and whiteness. She uses the term 'national manhood' to signify an ideology that has linked a fraternal articulation of white manhood to civic identity.[6] There are some remarkable similarities in the way that white masculinities in the United States and South Africa were constructed. In both cases there was a need to cultivate sameness and to manage difference to reach a unifying standpoint for national identity. At a particular historical moment in each country the abstracting identity of white manhood was transformed into a supraclass ideal for guaranteeing national identity. In both countries white manhood's identification with national unity worked historically to restrict others from achieving full entitlement.

A series of masculine images, discussed in different sections of this chapter, linked the 'manly ideal' to the national ideals of Afrikanerdom. By promoting these masculine images Afrikaner leaders constructed a complex of interlinking national ideals. In concrete visual terms this expression of national ideals through masculine images could also be seen in the architecture of monuments commemorating the Great Trek (the Voortrekker Monument in Pretoria) and the Anglo-Boer War (the Women's Memorial in Bloemfontein), which symbolised masculine strength, faith, and striving.[7] These monuments became Afrikaner shrines where, from time to time, commemorative events were held to honour the heroes and keep the national ideals alive. In the Afrikaner culture, in the same way as in other cultures, the nationalist elite used the 'manly ideal' as an inspirational image that might be taken to symbolise the nation, alongside the national anthem and the national flag.

Among the strategies of exclusion and inclusion used in Afrikaner nationalist mobilisation were the management of differences among

Afrikaner men and the merging of different perceptions and expressions of masculinity in such a way that the desired *volkseenheid* was achieved. As an auxiliary strategy cultural brokers used negative stereotyping of other masculinities to make Afrikaner men conscious of their sameness, in contrast to *volksvreemde* elements threatening their identity. These strategies, which linked Afrikaner hegemonic masculinity and national identity, are now analysed in more detail.

Exclusion: Afrikaner hegemonic masculinity and its 'others'

In masculinity studies – and in gender studies in general – the 'other' has become an important theoretical concept. Connell has indicated how masculinity can be negatively constructed by the production of the 'other'.[8] David Glover and Cora Kaplan point out that dangerous 'countertypes' may pose a threat to the 'manly ideal'.[9] In contrast to the 'self' within the context of the dominant or hegemonic form of masculinity, the 'other' may include categories such as women, homosexuals, effeminate men, and men from other races, ethnic groups, social classes, ideological orientations, and religions.

From the vantage point of the emergent hegemonic masculinity in the 1930s and 1940s Afrikaner men regarded all of these categories to some extent as 'others'. English and black men were perceived to pose the greatest threat to Afrikanerdom at the time and othering centred round the concepts of *verengelsing* (anglicisation) and *rasvermenging* (miscegenation). Let us investigate some of Afrikaner masculinity's others.

Imperialists, jingoes, and capitalists: the English-Jewish 'conspiracy' against Afrikanerdom

The memory of the Anglo-Boer War as the climax of the struggle between British imperialism and Boer republicanism was kept alive in Afrikaner nationalist circles. For the older generation of Afrikaners, who had experienced the hardship of the Anglo-Boer War and Milner's Anglicisation policies after the war the English were still enemy number one and they blamed the English for all the suffering of the Afrikaner *volk* in the past.[10]

Oudstryders (Anglo-Boer War veterans) projected the image of the burghers on commando as one of men amongst men and natural warriors – courageous, tough, with excellent riding and shooting skills, and veldcraft. The heroic *bittereinder* warrior who had fought courageously against the might of British imperialism to the bitter end was one of the primary images of Afrikaner nationalist masculinity.[11] In contrast popular legend, through hundreds of anecdotes circulating in Afrikaner society, portrayed the *kakies* (Tommies) as unheroic softies who could not ride and shoot properly and who were not tough enough for the harsh South African conditions.[12] Afrikaans historiography, which in main consisted of a male national narrative, portrayed Boer leaders such as President Paul Kruger, Generals Christiaan de Wet and Koos de la Rey, and *Vader* Dr J. D. Kestell as men of God, who believed in the divine mission of the Afrikaner *volk*. In contrast General (later Lord) Horatio Kitchener and other British commanders were depicted as unscrupulous imperialists who would not hesitate to use any means to win the war.

Afrikaner nationalists argued that if the Boer forces had pursued their initial successes more energetically, if the British had not broken the unwritten agreement not to use blacks in a combat role in a 'gentlemen's war', if the despicable *joiners* (Boer traitors) had not helped the British against their own people, and if it was not for Kitchener's scorched earth policy and the rounding up of Afrikaner women and children in concentration camps, which broke the spirit of resistance, Britain would never have won the war. The war had not been won by courageous battle, but by 'methods of barbarism'. This was the picture of Boer masculinity as being physically and morally superior to British masculinity engraved through war diaries, history books, literature, and later also films upon the minds of generations of young Afrikaners. In right-wing circles this mythical image has persisted even up to this day.

Nationalist Afrikaners branded all people who lived in South Africa, but put their loyalty to Britain above their loyalty to South Africa, as jingoes.[13] From its establishment the National Party used the term 'jingoism' as part of its political rhetoric to cast suspicion on any person who dared to express pro-British sentiments. Not only the Dominion Party, but also the South African Party and later the United Party, were accused of harbouring jingoistic elements. Newspaper cartoons portrayed the alienness of the jingo by the clothes he was wearing – cap, check jacket, and knickerbockers.

By the 1930s the younger generation, who had no first-hand experience of British political oppression, especially those living in urban areas, were less anti-English. The old contrast between the tough, almost crude, *burger* and the physically clumsy and somewhat effeminate *kakie* had lost its effectiveness among more sophisticated and culturally refined urbanised Afrikaner men. In the South African cities, where the English culture was then dominant, Afrikaners adopted aspects of the English traditional lifestyle. Quite a number of urban Afrikaners married English spouses and embraced the English culture.[14] Sarah Gertrude Millin observed in the 1930s that the more refined young urban Afrikaners could barely be distinguished from English South Africans.[15]

For Afrikaner nationalist leaders this was a worrying trend, which they perceived as a battle for the 'soul' of the Afrikaner. In order to counter *verengelsing* and promote the Afrikaner *volksaard* (national character) the *Afrikaner-Broederbond*, through its public arm, the *Federasie van Afrikaanse Kultuurvereniginge* (FAK – Federation of Afrikaans Cultural Associations), initiated a network of alternative Afrikaans institutions, such as the *Voortrekkers* (a youth movement) the *Afrikaanse Nasionale Studentebond* (a student association), and several others. These organisations were not necessarily all-male organisations, but the all-male *Broederbond* initiated their establishment and monitored their development, and down to the local level men were dominant in leadership positions within them. In order to transmit 'traditional' Afrikaner values to the youth, particularly young boys and men as the future *volksleiers* (national leaders), *Christelik-Nasionale Onderwys* (Christian-National Education) was developed.[16]

In the *Smelterstyd* (the period of the Hertzog-Smuts merger, 1934–39) Afrikaner nationalist politicians portrayed pro-British masculinities as a mythical *volksvreemde* conspiracy between British imperialists, English jingoes, and Jewish capitalists, which allegedly stood in the way of Afrikaner advancement. The conspiracy imagery was used as a bogey to promote *volkseenheid*.

Anti-Semitism, which had not been a feature of Afrikaner ideologies before, started taking root among Afrikaners. At a time when many Afrikaners experienced financial hardship in an economy dominated by British and Jewish capital, the capitalist Jew was regarded with suspicion as the enemy of the Afrikaner *volk*. The National Party used the 'Jewish question' as a campaign issue in the 1938, 1943, and 1948 elections, and barred Jews from National Party membership in 1940. Right-wing Afrikaner organisations (such as the *Gryshemde*) were openly anti-Semitic. Like other anti-Semitists they regarded the Jewish man as morally weak, unmanly, and effeminate. The National Party, competing for right-wing support, branded *Brits-Joodse imperialisme* (British-Jewish imperialism) as enemy of the Afrikaner.[17] The basic message of National Party politicians and the Afrikaans newspapers supporting them remained the same: Stay away from British-Jewish capitalism, jingoism and imperialism, and from any Afrikaner leader who associates himself in any way with their cause. Particularly after the formation of the United Party in 1934 the 'pure' Afrikaner was warned not to join the *Smelters* in a *volksvreemde* alliance.

Republicanism, expressed in the ideal of the re-creation of an Afrikaner republic, was a rallying point for Afrikaner nationalists with anti-British sentiments.[18] They regarded the period between the Great Trek and the Anglo-Boer War, when the Boer republics of Transvaal and the Orange Free State had thrived, as the golden age of Afrikanerdom. A gallery of male *volkshelde* (national heroes), who assumed almost godlike proportions, came into existence in popular culture.[19] The pioneering *Voortrekker*, who had trekked into an unknown interior to rid himself of British rule, was next to the *bittereinder* Boer warrior the most prominent metaphor of heroic masculinity.[20] The commemoration of the republican past reached a climax in 1938 with the *Voortrekkereeufees* (Great Trek centenary) during which Afrikaner history was invoked in the form of anti-British motifs from the Great Trek and the Anglo-Boer War. The republican ideal was linked to the 'manly ideal' in Afrikaner nationalist thinking. It was assumed that when the republican ideal was realised the Afrikaner *volk*, temporarily emasculated by British imperialism, would attain adult manhood, the type of defiant manhood personified by the *Voortrekker* and *bittereinder*, and take its rightful place among the nations of the world.

In the late 1930s Afrikaner nationalists saw the imminent war in Europe as a threat to Afrikaner republicanism and argued that South Africa as autonomous dominium had the right to remain neutral in a war in which Britain would be involved. Cartoonists of Afrikaans newspapers used a variety of masculine caricatures to give visual expression to their opposition to South Africa's participation in such a war. It was inconceivable that Afrikaners would once again be drawn into a war of imperial Britain. Yet the unthinkable became a reality. It came as a shock to Afrikaner nationalists when at the start of the war Hertzog and Malan's neutrality motion was defeated in parliament, Smuts became prime minister, and South Africa entered the Second World War on the British side.

Anti-British feelings once again flared up in Afrikaner nationalist ranks. Not all Afrikaners took an anti-war stance. In fact Afrikaners made up a third of the South African forces that fought on the Allied side.[21] Those Afrikaners who opposed South African participation in the war used the injustice suffered by the Afrikaners at the hand of the British in the Anglo-Boer War as justification for their view.[22] Afrikaner supporters of the war effort and particularly the *rooilissies* (those who signed up to fight under Montgomery in North Africa) were branded, almost like the *joiners* in the Anglo-Boer War, as *hanskakies*, i.e. henchmen of the British imperialists.[23]

Smuts emerged, even more than before, as a major enemy of Afrikaner nationalism. Cartoons in Afrikaans newspapers usually portrayed him grotesquely in military uniform or as a midget next to the huge figure of John Bull.[24] These cartoons depicted Smuts as not a great man, but a little man, subservient to British imperial interests and thus the antipole of Afrikaner nationalist masculinity.

On the pro-Nazi side several Afrikaner national socialist movements emerged, the largest being the *Ossewa-Brandwag* (OB). Its military structure was based on the Boer commando system, it was a staunchly patriarchal organisation, and its views were ethnically exclusive. The OB had similar ideological traits (e.g. antimodern conservatism and anticommunism) and used the same type of symbols and masculine *Blut und Boden* imagery as the German Nazis, but claimed to be anti-British rather than pro-Nazi.[25] The extremist *Stormjaer* (storm-trooper) wing had a macho image and committed anti-government acts of sabotage, reminiscent of the Rebellion of 1914.[26] They regarded Jopie Fourie, who had been executed by the Botha government for his activities during the Rebellion, as martyr and role model. In pro-government circles their behaviour was regarded as naive playing at war, but in right-wing circles it was seen as heroic deeds on behalf of the Afrikanerdom.[27]

Black peril: black men and uncontrollable sexuality

In a period of simultaneous white and black urbanisation urban Afrikaners had fears of being swamped by blacks. By 1936 just over 30 per cent of the total South African population lived in the urban areas. On the Witwatersrand, the biggest urban area around Johannesburg, the black population more thàn doubled from 304,000 in 1921 to 620,000 in 1936. During the Second World War influx control was relaxed, black urbanisation further accelerated, and between 1936 and 1946 the black urban population almost doubled once again.[28] Massive black urbanisation, which posed a real threat to white workers, was the most controversial issue in post-war white politics.[29]

The National Party used the *swart gevaar* (black peril) slogan effectively in political campaigns and its propaganda had undeniably racist undertones. D. C. Boonzaier, cartoonist from 1915 to 1940 of *Die Burger*, the foremost Afrikaner nationalist newspaper, often exploited the black peril theme in his cartoons. He portrayed white fears of being swamped by blacks by using images such as a black volcano or a black wave threatening to wash the whites away. Blacks were depicted in some of his cartoons as half-naked barbarians, suggesting that the Christian white civilisation was under threat.[30]

Afrikaans books published in the 1940s to supply an academic or quasi-academic justification for racial separation expressed racism in terms of fear of miscegenation and its potential negative impact on the white population.[31] Some texts portrayed the *Boerevolk* as a pure white race with a holy duty to protect their racial purity at all costs.[32] Physical aversion of Afrikaners to blacks was quite common. A whole arsenal of negative attributes were associated with blacks in Afrikaner thinking: they were regarded as dirty, contaminated by disease, ugly, dim-witted, lazy, brutal, etc. The black man was regarded as primitive, uncivilised, immature. These negative physical and spiritual attributes were the antithesis of the Afrikaner ideal of masculinity and were employed to bolster the mental picture among the Afrikaners of blacks as an inferior race with whom one could not mix without being degraded. The Afrikaner had to protect his women against the uncontrollable sexuality of the black man.

National Party propaganda, such as election posters and political cartoons in newspapers, often used female images to portray threats against the Afrikaner nation, particularly the perceived threat of miscegenation. In the 1938 election campaign a National Party electioneering poster showed a despondent-looking white woman sitting in front of a house with cracking walls and broken windows. Her black husband was leaning lazily against the wall, his hands in his pockets, with their mixed-blood children playing in front of them. The caption called upon voters to support the National Party to protect the *volk* against mixed marriages.[33]

To whip up emotions racial fears and the gender card were often mixed in political cartoons published in newspapers supporting the National Party. On the eve of the 1948 election a cartoon appeared in *Die Transvaler*, which showed a white woman standing on a small island surrounded by a black ocean threatening to engulf her. One of the words written on the dark waters was *gelykstelling* (racial integration). Her two small children were clinging to her dress on which was written 'South Africa'. She was lifting her hands in despair, pleading for help.[34] This type of propaganda was successful. Threatened with displacement and with their occupational mobility restricted most of the Afrikaner workers, instead of voting for the Labour Party, in 1948 decided to support the National Party with its promises of racial barriers. Support by Afrikaner workers in urban constituencies had a decisive impact and swung the election results in favour of the National Party.

Inclusion: managing difference in Afrikaner society

Large-scale Afrikaner urbanisation started towards the end of the nineteenth century and reached its climax between the 1920s and the 1940s.[35] For the first generation of urbanised Afrikaners, who had their roots in the rural farming communities and who were in many cases forced off the land and into urban labour as a result of rural impoverishment, the *volksvreemde* English-dominated city was a hostile environment, where they had to fight for material survival. The poor white problem reached critical proportions in the 1920s and was further aggravated by the worldwide depression and droughts in the early 1930s.[36]

As a result of their negative experience of urban life Afrikaners harked back to a romanticised rural past. For many years after the majority of Afrikaner men had ceased to be farmers the puritan image of the simple, honest, steadfast, religious, and hard-working *boer*, who had earned a claim to the land through the cultivation of his farm and his love for the soil of the fatherland, remained the dominant representation of Afrikaner masculinity. Afrikaner masculinity, threatened by the modern hegemonic masculinity of the pro-capitalist English elite, who controlled the business sector in the cities, retained its conservative and anti-modern tendency for quite a while.[37]

The second generation of urban Afrikaners came to accept the city as their home. As more Afrikaners flocked to the cities an Afrikaner urban culture evolved.[38] Afrikaans enclaves were formed in residential areas in the cities and social organisation centred round Afrikaans churches and schools. Despite this relative isolation modernising influences gradually transformed the urban Afrikaners' lifestyle and way of thinking.[39]

Urbanisation was in more than one way a crisis point for the Afrikaner nationalist elite in their efforts to construct a hegemonic masculinity and an inclusive Afrikaner nation. It caused Afrikaner society to become much more diverse than before. An important trend in Afrikaner masculinity was its increasing sophistication, associated with rising levels of education. More education also meant more critical attitudes. The new generation of poets, the so-called *Dertigers* (Generation of Thirty–there was only one woman among them) were the most prominent source of *lojale verset* (loyal resistance) against narrow-minded Afrikaner nationalist conformism under the banner of *volkseenheid*.[40]

In the shaping of Afrikaner nationalist ideology a fierce ideological battle was waged in Afrikaner intellectual circles in the 1930s.[41]

How was difference amongst Afrikaners to be managed in such a way as to make them aware of their sameness and to bind them together in a broad political movement? The National Party, Afrikaans churches, schools, and a network of Afrikaans organisations formed a *volksfront* (national front), which promoted *volkseenheid* under the banner of the Christian-National ideology. An elite of male leaders in the *Afrikaner-Broederbond* dominated this front.[42] A strong partnership between the *Afrikaner-Broederbond* and the National Party was forged. The leaders of these two organisations worked hard on strategies to include all those Afrikaners who they identified as the in-group in their envisaged *volkseenheid*. Step by step they moved closer to their ideal, overcoming several setbacks.[43]

A good example of how socio-economic trends were used to build *volkseenheid* was the issue of poverty. Earlier poor white Afrikaners had often been treated with distaste as a weak link that might enfeeble the white population. This changed in the course of the 1930s. The 'Purified' National Party, concerned that poor whites might be lost to the Afrikaner nationalist cause, started emphasising that poverty could not be ascribed to any defect or inferiority inherent in the Afrikaner nation, but was the result of conquest, dispossession and exploitation by British imperialists since the Anglo-Boer War.[44]

Poverty was depicted in a positive light in Afrikaans writings. In Afrikaans novels (such as Jochem van Bruggen's *Ampie* and D. F. Malherbe's *Hans-die-Skipper*) and stories in Afrikaans popular magazines the nobleness of poverty, personified by male heroes, was often the main theme. Material poverty was associated with spiritual wealth. It was believed that the man with moral power could hold his own against hardship and poverty and retain his decency. The poor man's capacity to be as good an Afrikaner as anyone else was not doubted.[45]

From the mid-1930s, precisely at the time when poor whiteism was disappearing, the Afrikaner elite converted the *volksvreemde* Jew into a scapegoat that could be blamed for the economic hardship befalling the Afrikaner and cultivated the perception that the Jews stood in the way of Afrikaner economic advancement. This is an example of how negative stereotyping of 'others', i.e. alternative masculinities, was used to make Afrikaner men conscious of their 'sameness' in contrast to *volksvreemde* elements threatening their identity. During the 1938 centenary celebrations of the Great Trek the poor white question was elevated to new prominence and Afrikaner poverty was linked to all the suffering of the *volk* in the past. The strongest unifying and mobilising nationalist appeal that emerged from the celebrations was the dedication to rescuing the Afrikaner poor or the so-called *Reddingsdaad* idea under the slogan *'n volk red himself*[46] (a nation saves itself).

The focus was now on the urban setting. Afrikaner nationalist propaganda contrasted the desperate poor Afrikaner, looking in vain for work, on the one hand to the prosperous Englishman or Jew and on the other hand to the black worker with whom he had to compete for economic survival. Anglicisation and miscegenation posed a threat to him. 'After 1939', writes Taylor, 'poverty was invested with heroic dimensions'.[47] The poor became, for the National Party and the *Afrikaner-Broederbond*, *ons armes* (our poor), thus incorporating them into mainstream Afrikaner nationalism.

Researchers focusing on class analysis attribute the remarkable growth of the National Party to the successful promotion of a shared *volkskapitalisme*, by which a powerful alliance between urban and rural classes in the Afrikaner population was forged.[48] The incorporation of the white urban working class into nationalist Afrikanerdom was significant. In the cities the labour movement posed a potential threat to Afrikaner nationalism and Afrikaner hegemonic masculinity. Afrikaner nationalist leaders realised that class divisions could dilute the ethnic identity of the Afrikaner and weaken Afrikaner nationalism.[49] Therefore they deliberately incorporated Afrikaner urban working class men in the nationalist movement and in formulations of hegemonic masculinity. The leaders emphasised the egalitarian nature of Afrikaner society and rejected class distinctions as artificial.[50] The notion that less sophisticated forms of manual labour performed by men was inferior, was rejected. All types of labour were necessary to maintain the *volksgemeenskap* (national community) and any kind of work was noble as long as it was devoted *volksdiens* (service to the nation).[51] An alternative Afrikaner nationalist trade union movement was set up.[52] The aims of the newly established Christian-National unions were, apart from normal trade union functions, to sever the link between Afrikaner workers and class-based unions, and to get their support for Afrikaner nationalism.[53]

Malan and his *Gesuiwerde Nasionale Party* had to take the changes in Afrikaner society into account, but could not neglect the interests of the Afrikaner rural farming communities, because they were still the backbone of the National Party supporters, particularly in the Cape Province. Despite their rural roots the new Afrikaner intellectual and political elite of the 1930s and 1940s were urban middle-class Afrikaners.[54] Their objective was to accommodate rural and urban Afrikaners in one nationalist movement. To fuse traditional and modern imagery they used the concept of the Afrikaners' *Tweede Trek* (Second Trek), this time to the cities.[55] In his Day of the Covenant speech at Blood River in 1938 Malan used this concept to call upon Afrikaners to 'conquer' the cities. The opportunity had to be taken to carry the Afrikaner *volksaard* (national character) into the cities, instead of adopting a 'translated' English civilisation.[56]

The elite ameliorated the process of forging a class alliance between rural and urban sections of the Afrikaner population, representing a break with the past, by shrouding it in traditionalism.[57] 'The cities', writes H. Giliomee, 'had to be captured for the Afrikaners, not only for the wage and salary earners, but also for the entrepreneurs in trade, industry, mining and finance'.[58] At a *volkskongres* in Johannesburg in 1947 urbanisation was described as a *mylpaal* (landmark) and a *keerpunt* (turning point) in the history of the Afrikaner. Afrikaners had to abandon negative attitudes towards the city and seize the opportunity to expand the *volkslewe* (national life). The Afrikaner needed to take up the challenge and come into his own in the city by upholding his traditions and *volksaard*.[59]

In the merging of rural and urban Afrikaner masculinities into a unified movement the *Voortrekkereeufees* played an important role. An *ossewatrek* (ox-wagon trek) was organised. Several wagons followed different routes through the country. Local communities celebrated their arrival in towns with festivals, culminating in a huge closing ceremony at Monumentkoppie in Pretoria, the site where the Voortrekker Monument would be constructed.[60] Afrikaner nationalist leaders, exploiting the emotional potential of the celebrations to promote *volkseenheid*, revived and in some cases invented traditions and symbols of the past. Many Afrikaner men grew beards and wore *Voortrekker* clothes, thus confirming their Afrikanerness in a show of solidarity at a time when the hegemony of Afrikaner nationalist masculinity had not yet been ensured, particularly not in the urban centres. The celebrations were designed to stimulate Afrikaner historical consciousness and strengthen Afrikaner nationalist identity.

McClintock refers to the *Eeufees* as a 'spectacle of invented tradition and fetish ritual' and regards it as the decisive moment in the construction of Afrikaner national identity, which paved the way for the 1948 assumption of power. She indicates how the Afrikaans-speaking petit bourgeoisie professionals and intellectuals in the *Broederbond* assumed the role of 'cultural brokers and image-makers' to create through the spectacle of the celebrations, in a style similar to the Nüremberg rallies of the Nazis, the 'illusion of a collective identity'. Because of their economic insecurity at the time the Afrikaners were particularly susceptible to this type of social engineering. The middle class 'cultural brokers' had to function through a sentimental culture sufficiently accessible to the lower strata. By capturing the confluence of the modern and the archaic they enabled the Afrikaner workers to overcome their feelings of industrial dislocation. They managed to paper over the myriad regional, gender and class tensions threatening *volkseenheid* and overcome the rival mythologies of socialism and South Africanism.[61]

Conclusion

In the period under survey urbanisation brought modernising influences into play in Afrikaner society. Elements of the urban lifestyle were incorporated into traditional perceptions of masculinity. Lifestyles and expressions of masculinity diversified. Because of more social and economic contact with other groups in the cities ethnic and racial issues featured more prominently in Afrikaner thinking. Nationalist leaders emphasised the dangers of *verengelsing* (anglicisation) and *bloedvermenging* (miscegenation).

This chapter has shown how images of masculinity, such as the hardworking and honest Afrikaner farmer, the heroic *bittereinder* Boer warrior, *ons armes*, the family man as good provider, the imperialist British jingo, the capitalist Jew, and the supposedly inferior black, assumed mythical proportions in Afrikaner nationalist thinking. Afrikaner nationalist propaganda juxtaposed starkly contrasting images with emotive appeal: the jingoist British imperialist thwarting the republican Afrikaner's legitimate claim to self-determination; the poor Afrikaner urban worker at the mercy of the exploitative capitalist Jew and Englishman; the uncivilised black hordes swamping the white Christian civilisation. These images were linked to the values and national ideals of the Afrikaner, such as political self-determination, patriotism, being a chosen people with a divine mission, building an own future through hard work.

In order to come closer to *volkseenheid*, Afrikaner nationalist mobilisation led to a larger measure of conformism within the organised Afrikaner establishment and in representations of masculinity. Because of the strong ethnic identification among Afrikaners individual critical thinking was not welcomed and both personal needs and group values were subjected to the cohesion of the group and its members. Hence the high level of respect for leaders and authority, the adherence to rules, the self-image of moral superiority, and the tendency to place people in separate compartments by classifying them as 'different' or 'other'.[62]

A cartoon which appeared in *Die Burger* on 18 May 1938 portrayed the ideal response of the Afrikaner nationalist to the temptation to join the United Party. In the cartoon Hoggenheimer, an anti-Jewish and anticapitalist caricature created by Boonzaier, tries to lure the Afrikaner away to the United Party, but the proud and upright Afrikaner looks him right in the eye and says '*Nee, ik bly Nasionaal*' (No, I stay National), and continues on the road of Nationalism. By dissociating himself from the 'other' he confirms his Afrikaner nationalist 'self'. This proud and respectable Nationalist represents the high moral values of Christian-National Afrikanerdom and at the same time the ideal of true manhood. It is a simple visual portrayal of everything which at that stage was associated with hegemonic Afrikaner masculinity.

This portrayal of the Afrikaner man at the height of Afrikaner nationalist mobilisation in the centenary year of 1938 linked hegemonic masculinity to national identity. His words '*Ik bly Nasionaal*' and actions (walking the Nationalist road) showed his identification, not only with the National Party, but also with the Afrikaner *volk*. The 'manly ideal' had become a symbol of nationhood. Through the ideological coordination of nation, manhood, and whiteness a 'national manhood' had been established. Ten years later, after the ordeal of the Second World War, this national manhood would come into its own and, with the assumption of power by the National Party, become truly hegemonic in the broader South African society.

Notes

1 For ideology see: T. Dunbar Moodie, *The Rise of Afrikanerdom: Power, Apartheid and the Afrikaner Civil Religion* (Berkeley, 1975); W. A. de Klerk, *The Puritans in Africa* (Harmondsworth, 1975); I. Hexham, *The Irony of Apartheid: The Struggle for National Independence of Afrikaner Calvinism Against British Imperialism* (New York, 1981). For racial/ethnic mobilisation see: H. Adam and H. Giliomee, *The Rise and Crisis of Afrikaner Power* (Berkeley, 1979); J. P. Brits, *Op die Vooraand van Apartheid* (Pretoria, 1994). For formation of class alliances see: D. O'Meara, *Volkskapitalisme: Class, Capital and Ideology in the Development of Afrikaner Nationalism, 1934–1948* (Cambridge, 1983); M. Lipton, *Capital and Apartheid: South Africa, 1910–1986* (Aldershot, 1986).
2 R. W. Connell, *Masculinities* (Cambridge, 1995), p. 77.
3 See J. Tosh, 'What should historians do with masculinity? Reflections on nineteenth-century Britain', in R. Shoemaker and M. Vincent (eds), *Gender and history in Western Europe* (London, 1998), p. 76; Connell, *Masculinities* p. 77; D. Glover and C. Kaplan, *Genders* (London, 2000), p. 78.

4 O'Meara, *Volskapitalisme*, p. 63.

5 C. Enloe, *Bananas, Beaches and Bases: Making Feminist Sense of International Politics* (Berkeley, 1989), p. 44; E. Gellner, *Nations and Nationalism* (Oxford, 1983), p. 117; A. McClintock, *Imperial Leather: Race, Gender and Sexuality in the Colonial Contest* (New York, 1995), pp. 353, 355.

6 D. D. Nelson, *National Manhood: Capitalist Citizenship and the Imagined Fraternity of White Men* (Durham, 1998), pp. ix, 6, 11, 27.

7 The Great Trek was the organised migration in the 1830s of Afrikaner farmers from the British-ruled Cape Colony into the interior where they later established the Boer republics.

8 Connell, *Masculinities*, pp. 30–4.

9 Glover and Kaplan, *Genders*, pp. 60–1.

10 See, for example, E. C. Pienaar, *Onthou!* (Bloemfontein, 1936). Poets such as Totius, J. F. E. Celliers, and C. L. Leipoldt helped to keep the memory of Afrikaner suffering in and after the war alive.

11 The *bittereinders* were revered as symbols of the Afrikaners' struggle for self-determination and independence. By focusing on aspects such as the freedom struggle of the Boers, the republican ideal, the common religion of the burghers, and the allegedly egalitarian nature of the commando system the *bittereinder* metaphor was used to promote *volkseenheid*. See J. A. du Pisani, '*Volkhelde*: Die Boerekrygerbeeld en die konstruksie van Afrikanernasionalisme', *Literator* 20:3 (1999), 90–8.

12 In 1935 the family magazine *Die Huisgenoot* tried to record some of these anecdotes by writing out a competition for *oudstryder* accounts of their experiences in the Anglo-Boer War.

13 D. F. du Toit Malherbe, *Afrikaner-Volkseenheid* (Bloemfontein, 1942), pp. 113, 115.

14 A. Coetzee, *Die opkoms van die Afrikaanse kultuurgedagte aan die Rand, 1886–1936* (Johannesburg, 1937), p. 344.

15 S. G. Millin, *The South Africans* (London, 2nd edn, 1937), pp. 193, 195.

16 See J. L. Davies, 'Christian National education in South Africa: A study in the influence of Calvinism and nationalism on educational policy' (PhD dissertation, University of Wisconsin-Madison, 1978); R. Morrell, 'Of boys and men: Masculinities and gender in Southern African studies', *Journal of Southern African Studies*, 24:4 (1998), 617, refers to the role of Christian-National Education in bolstering the emerging Afrikaner hegemonic masculinity.

17 P. W. Coetzer and J. H. le Roux (eds), *Die Nasionale Party, deel 4: Die 'Gesuiwerde' Nasionale Party, 1934–1940* (Bloemfontein, 1986), pp. 78–9, 146–8; P. W. Coetzer (ed.), *Die Nasionale Party, deel 5: Van oorlog tot oorwinning, 1940–1948* (Bloemfontein, 1994), pp. 218, 611–12; B. K. Murray and A. W. Stadler, 'Van die Pakt tot die begin van apartheid, 1924–1948', in T. Cameron and S. B. Spies (eds), *Nuwe geskiedenis van Suid-Afrika* (Kaapstad, 1991), p. 262.

18 See J. A. Coetzee *et al.*, *Ons Republiek* (Bloemfontein, 1940).

19 'Naas God die helde' (next to God the heroes) stated *Die Huisgenoot* (May 1916), 12.

20 See, e.g. G. S. Preller, *Piet Retief: Lewensgeskiedenis van die grote Voortrekker* (Pretoria, 9th edn, 1917); G. S. Preller, *Voortrekkermense*, 6 vols (Kaapstad, 1920–1938); G. S. Preller, *Andries Pretorius* (Johannesburg, 1937); C. Potgieter and

N. H. Theunissen, *Kommandant-Generaal Hendrik Potgieter* (Johannesburg, 1938); H. B. Thom, *Die lewe van Gert Maritz* (Kaapstad, 1947).

21 W. A. de Klerk, *The Puritans in Africa* (Harmondsworth, 1975), pp. 194–5.

22 H. O. Terblanche, *John Vorster – OB – Generaal en Afrikanervegter* (Roodepoort, 1983), pp. 111–12.

23 C. B. Linder, *Christelikheid en nasionalisme in die opvoeding* (Johannesburg, 1946), p. 11.

24 See, e.g. *Die Burger* (4 October 1939), p. 2, *ibid.* (14 September 1940), p. 2; *ibid.*, (3 January 1940), p. 2.

25 P. de Klerk, 'Die ideologie van die Ossewabrandwag', in P. F. van der Schyff (ed.), *Die Ossewabrandwag: Vuurtjie in droë gras* (Potchefstroom, 1991).

26 When the government of Louis Botha, at the request of Britain, decided to invade German West Africa (now Namibia) during World War I, some Afrikaners led by former Boer generals rebelled in the hope of restoring an Afrikaner republic. The Rebellion was quickly suppressed by Botha's military forces.

27 W. A. de Klerk, *The Puritans*, p. 195; F. A. Van Jaarsveld, *Van Van Riebeeck tot Verwoerd 1652–1966* (Johannesburg, 1971), p. 250.

28 Murray and Stadler, 'Van die Pakt', pp. 257, 264.

29 P. Bonner, P. Delius and D. Posel (eds), *Apartheid's Genesis, 1935–1962* (Braamfontein, 1993), pp. 20–1; Murray and Stadler, 'Van die Pakt', p. 268.

30 H. J. Lubbe, ' "Swart gevaar" in beeld: Visuele propaganda in "Die Burger" gedurende die parlementêre verkiesingstryd van 1928 tot 1929', *Kleio*, 26 (1994), 27–44.

31 These include Geoff Cronjé's, *'n Tuiste vir die nageslag – die blywende oplossing van Suid-Afrika se rassevraagstuk* (Johannesburg, 1945); *Regverdige rasse-apartheid* (Stellenbosch, 1947) and *Voogdyskap en aparheid* (Pretoria, 1948).

32 G. Eloff, *Rasse en rassevermenging: Die Boerevolk gesien van die standpunt van die rasseleer* (Bloemfontein, 1942), pp. 90, 93, 101, 104.

33 *The Star* (5 May 1938), p. 11.

34 *Die Transvaler* (25 May 1948), p. 3. About the function of women's bodies in nationalist discourses as symbolical boundaries between self and other, see, for example, D. Stasiulis and N. Yuval-Davis, 'Introduction: Beyond dichotomies – gender, race, ethnicity and class in settler societies', in D. Stasilius and N. Yuval-Davis (eds), *Unsettling Settler Societies: Articulations of Gender, Race, Ethnicity and Class* (London, 1995).

35 F. A. van Jaarsveld, *Die Afrikaners se Groot Trek na die stede en ander opstelle* (Johannesburg, 1982), pp. 135, 146, 157. The white population on the Witwatersrand almost doubled from 233,000 in 1921 to 410,000 in 1936. See Murray and Stadler, 'Van die pakt', p. 257.

36 E. L. P. Stals (ed.), *Afrikaners in die Goudstad, deel 1: 1886–1924* (Pretoria, 1978), p. 178; A. Coetzee, *Die opkomst*, pp. 341–2; F. A. van Jaarsveld, *Stedelike geskiedenis as navorsingsveld vir die Suid-Afrikaanse historikus* (Johannesburg, 1973), p. 32; G. D. Scholtz, *Het die Afrikaanse volk 'n toekoms?* (Johannesburg, 1954), pp. 112–13.

37 See S. Swart, 'A conservative revolution: Republican masculinity and the 1914 Boer Rebellion' (Conference paper, colloquium on masculinities in Southern Africa, University of Natal, Durban, 2–4 July 1997).

38 G. Cronjé and J. D. Venter, *Die patriargale familie. 'n Kultuursosiologiese studie* (Kaapstad, 1958), p. 172; A. Coetzee, *Die opkomst*, pp. 385, 387–8, 397, 399.

39 J. A. du Pisani, 'Puritanism transformed: Afrikaner masculinities in the apartheid and post-apartheid period', in Robert Morrell (ed.), *Changing Men in Southern Africa* (London, 2001), p. 158.

40 These sentiments were expressed by the prominent poet N. P. van Wyk Louw in *Berigte te velde* (Pretoria, 1939) and *Lojale verset* (Kaapstad, 1939).

41 See Moodie, *The Rise of Afrikanerdom*, in particular and also T. R. H. Davenport, *South Africa: A Modern History* (Houndmills, 4th edn, 1991), p. 288. C. B. Linder's critique of Christian-National ideas in his *Christelikheid en nasionalisme in die opvoeding* (Johannesburg, 1946) provides an interesting example of the ideological contestation in Afrikanerdom in the 1940s. See also T. J. Hugo, *Die Afrikaanse universiteit en sy taak in die volkslewe* (Bloemfontein, 1941), p. 116.

42 Davenport, *Southe Africa*, pp. 290–1. For detailed accounts of the Afrikaner-Broederbond, see I. Wilkins and H. Strydom, *The Super-Afrikaners* (Johannesburg, 1978); J. H. P. Serfontein, *Brotherhood of Power: An Exposé of the Secret Afrikaner Broederbond* (London, 1979); A. N. Pelzer, *Die Afrikaner-Broederbond: Eerste 50 jaar* (Kaapstad, 1979).

43 D. F. Malan documented this process in his book *Afrikaner-volkseenheid en my ervarings op die pad daarheen* (Kaapstad, 1959).

44 J. H. Coetzee, *Verarming en oorheersing* (Bloemfontein, 1942), pp. 55–6, 59.

45 C. M. van den Heever, *Die stryd om ewewig: Opstelle oor ons strewe na kulturele selfstandigheid* (Kaapstad, 1941), pp. 267–9 discusses the strong emphasis in the Afrikaans literature on poverty.

46 Coetzee, *Verarming*, p. 122.

47 J. Taylor, 'Our poor: The politicisation of the Poor White problem, 1932–1942', *Kleio*, 24 (1992), 43.

48 These arguments form the main thrust of O'Meara's, *Volkskapitalisme*. See also Davenport, *South Africa*, pp. 288–9.

49 Scholtz, *Afrikaanse volk*, pp. 113–18; C. G. W. Schumann, *Die ekonomiese posisie van die Afrikaner* (Bloemfontein, 1940), p. 110.

50 Cronjé, *Voogdyskap en apartheid*, pp. 168–9.

51 Cronjé, *'n Tuiste vir die nageslag*, pp. 187–95.

52 L. Naudé, *Dr. A. Hertzog, die Nasionale Party en die mynwerker* (Pretoria, 1969) and O'Meara, *Volkskapitalisme*, discuss Afrikaner trade unionism from opposing perspectives.

53 Murray and Stadler, 'Van die Pakt', p. 260. See also Davenport, *South Africa*, p. 293.

54 W. A. de Klerk, *The Puritans*, pp. 113–14.

55 In July 1936 the concept was used for the first time when *Die Vaderland* referred to a Second Great Trek of the Afrikaner that was taking place to the Witwatersrand (cited in A. Coetzee, *Die opkomst*, p. 327).

56 Van den Heever, *Die stryd*, pp. 163, 266. For more information about the way in which ruralism and urbanism were blended in Afrikaner nationalist politics see, for example, A. Coetzee, *Die opkomst*, p. 327; D. F. du Toit Malherbe, *Afrikaner-volkseenheis*, p. 18; Davenport, *South Africa*, p. 292; O'Meara, *Volkskapitalisme*, pp. 165–6; Adam and Giliomee, *Rise and Crisis*, p. 156. See also S. Pauw, *Die beroepsarbeid van die Afrikaner in die stad* (Stellenbosch, 1946).

57 O'Meara, *Volkskapitalisme*, pp. 165–6.

58 Adam and Giliomee, *Rise and Crisis*, p. 156.

59 Cited in Van Jaarsveld, *Stedelike geskiedenis*, pp. 57–8.

60 See E. A. Messina, *Die Voortrekkereeufees, 1938* (MA dissertation, University of the Western Cape, Bellvile, 1982).

61 McClintock, *Imperial Leather*, pp. 370–8.

62 L. Korf, *Die sosiale identiteit van 'n groep stedelike Afrikaanssprekendes in die postapartheid Suid-Afrika* (PhD dissertation, Potchefstroom University, 1998), pp. 51–2, 67, 70, 71–2 discusses these traits in a later period and attributes authoritarian tendencies among Afrikaners to religious views based on Calvinist Protestantism, which endorse the principles of the sovereignty of God and predestination and start from the premise that there is only one correct way of thinking and behaving.

10

Temperate heroes: concepts of masculinity in Second World War Britain

Sonya O. Rose

I N Second World War Britain the requisites of manliness were evident everywhere and nowhere. They were 'nowhere' in that there was rarely explicit and concentrated attention paid to the topic of masculinity as there was to femininity. They were 'everywhere' because manhood, although not identified as such, was portrayed in a host of representations including the iconography of workers and their work, in armed services recruitment posters, and in wartime advertisements. The meanings of masculinity were also present in radio presentations and popular fiction as well as in wartime documentary and feature films.

This chapter examines how such representations fashioned hegemonic masculinity.[1] I suggest that they deployed and redefined crucial aspects of the post-First World War 'anti-heroic' masculinity and combined these traits with the seemingly antithetical heroic ones most clearly exemplified by combat soldiers. Further, this amalgam reveals a rough equivalence between the strictures of wartime masculinity and the Second World War constructions of Englishness and Britishness. Moreover, 'good citizenship' and masculinity were virtually the mirror images of one another. What follows, then, explores the gendering of the wartime nation as a complex and even conflicted masculine subject. It shows that hegemonic masculinity was constructed in opposition both to a hyper-masculine Nazi-like image, and to images of emasculated or effeminate men personified by old men and cowardly pacifists.

Britain declared war on Nazi Germany on 3 September 1939 following the German invasion of Poland. But although British soldiers were fighting on the Continent during the autumn of 1939 and the winter of 1940, the period the British at the time called the 'phoney war', it was not until spring, as Hitler's armies over-ran Norway and the Low

Countries, that the British truly began to confront the fact that they would soon be engaged in Total War. It was the evacuation of the British forces from Dunkirk just prior to the fall of France in June 1940 and the experience of the massive nightly bombing of London in autumn 1940 that gave rise to the representations of British nationhood that characterised the wartime period, and that have had a long life in historical memory ever since.

Tempered masculinity

What was new in the 1940s was the particular multidimensional and loose configuration of attributes associated with manliness that coalesced relatively early in the war – with Dunkirk and the Blitz – informing a sense of nationhood that, as Angus Calder has suggested, rapidly became mythologised.[2] The specific characteristics of the exemplary man or citizen were not in themselves brand new in the Second World War. Some had been in existence since at least the mid-nineteenth century; and some had a much longer lineage. Others were the product of new articulations from the inter-war period that were strengthened as they became enmeshed in newer wartime discourses.

Alison Light has argued that during the inter-war period, representations of the nation were feminised.[3] Home, 'the little man', and ordinariness replaced adventure in faraway places, great heroes, and challenging circumstances in the construction of Englishness.[4] The nation, identified as bearing these characteristics, was a more feminised or female nation than it had been before as it responded with revulsion to the devastation of the First World War and its aggressive and belligerent imagery.

Very early in the Second World War, however, the nation was remasculinised. Britain, in other words, was imagined as a profoundly masculine nation as it fought the People's War. But the virility of the nation was tempered. What accounts for such a restrained version of the masculine nation in the 1940s (restrained at least in contrast to representations of masculinity in the First World War)?

If both national identity and masculinity are constructed in opposition to an 'other', there was no more 'hyper-masculine' other than the Nazis against which to fashion nationhood and masculinity.[5] In his second *Sunday Postscript* radio broadcast in June 1940, J. B. Priestley, the widely known playwright and novelist, explicitly compared representations of the German military and the British military.

Yesterday morning I saw the Nazi film, 'Baptism of Fire', which deals
with the invasion and attempted destruction of Poland ... It's the
opposite of 'the Lion Has Wings' ... Our film didn't take itself too
solemnly; showed our airmen as likeable human beings, cracking jokes
with their wives and sweethearts. But this Nazi picture is all 'drums
and trombones' – gloom and threats. A loud German voice bullies
you through it all. There's a lot about destruction and death, and not
a glimmer of humour, or fun, or ordinary human relationships.[6]

The connection between the nation and a tempered British masculinity was evident in numerous other representations. The following
beer advertisement, for example, appeared in *Picture Post* in late
March 1940.

It is the custom of the English when there is serious trouble to be
faced, to lift their voices in loud and rollicking song ... it is part of
the English strength to deny all foreboding when the hour is grave ...
And if the waiting be hard, seek fortitude and clear, calm thought
over a Worthington-the golden brew that has nurtured generations of
the yeomen of England.[7]

The accompanying illustration was of a glass of beer with a man's smil-
ing face contained within it.

Recommending that men seek 'clear, calm thought' referenced
presumed national and masculine characteristics such as rationality and
emotional reserve that had a long history. As I have argued elsewhere,
'reason' had long been associated with both masculinity and good citizenship, or civic virtue.[8] And, more generally, the quintessential 'emotional
reserve' of the respectable British man, also had a long history which
was rearticulated in the wartime version of the 'stiff upper lip' represented
by the Blitz expression that London or Britain, 'Can Take It'.

John Tosh has suggested that the 'stiff upper lip', or emotional
reserve, characteristic of middle-class British men at the turn of the
twentieth century, had its roots in the Victorian dissociation of gender
attributes in which 'affection and tenderness' were associated with
mothers, while fathers were supposed to be 'stern and undemonstrat-
ive'.[9] He proposes that this was an outcome of the cultural significance
of domesticity to bourgeois men evident in the early Victorian period.
Tosh suggests that eventually this 'splitting' of gender characteristics led
to a masculine 'flight from domesticity' expressed in imperial adventure
and military heroism in the years prior to 1918.[10]

One reaction to the horrors of the First World War was the
'anti-heroic mood' of the inter-war years. Alison Light maintains that

this resulted in a realignment of sexual identities and a redefinition of Englishness.[11] Men became more 'homely', and the private, domestic sphere became the heart of the nation. Middle-class femininity, meanwhile, took on what had previously been 'regarded as distinctly masculine qualities: in particular the ethics or code of self-control and a language of reticence'.[12] I agree with Light that women were expected to be emotionally reserved, and during the war especially, they were to be good citizens by maintaining a cheerful demeanour and a 'stiff upper lip'. The well-publicised stoicism of British women in the Second World War highlighted the manly vigour of the British nation as a whole.

'Emotional reticence' or stoicism remained a masculine rather than a feminine characteristic, even as it was generalised to denote 'the good citizen' of the Second World War. If a woman did not maintain her good cheer and calm reserve, it would have been said she was being a silly girl or a foolish woman and not a good wartime citizen. In contrast, if a man lost control of his emotions, he was not being manly. This distinction was expressed graphically by the popular journalist and writer, Beverley Nichols in *Sunday Chronicle* in March 1941:

> How many grown men, achieving heroism ... realise that their toughness and their endurance stretch back ... back into the mists of childhood, when they ran crying to mother with a cut finger and she said ... 'Brave little boys don't cry!' How many women keeping a stiff upper lip during ... danger and difficulty, carrying on calmly during a raid when they feel much more like bursting into tears, realise that their behaviour was determined for them long ago by a quiet voice saying, during some childish tantrum, 'That's not a pretty face to make, darling ... and if the wind were to change it might stay like that.'[13]

This difference apparently also influenced male subjectivity. John Sweetland was eighteen when he wrote a memoir, based on his diaries, in the summer of 1945. He repeatedly described his mother as being 'terrified' during the Blitz while he calmed his own fears by listening to classical music.[14] His mother's participation in the war effort, he maintained, 'was not a success, and to the amusement of father', she found a job as far as possible from civil defence or factory work.[15] Sweetland's description of the difference between his mother's reaction and his own to the Blitz suggests how crucial the national 'stiff upper lip' was to manliness. The patronising depiction of his mother's discomfort with war work and his obvious identification with his amused father underscore the connections between masculine subjectivity and good citizenship.

Additionally, as Light suggests, the anti-heroic mood of the post-First World War era also was the source of the construction of the 'little men' as representatives of British identity, those who in the Second World War, became the 'ordinary people' of the home front.[16] Such little men were depicted by participants on a BBC radio discussion of the topic 'What is a Good Man?' One of the men proposed to the others:

> We've all been giving examples of men we've admired. [...] all the men we've singled out have been quiet men. I won't say soft, but quiet, stay-at-home, good, ideal husbands, good neighbours, but not forceful and not leaders. It isn't as if we hadn't been fighters ourselves. I used to fancy myself, in my younger days with the gloves a bit, and so did Walt, and Harry started life taking on all comers – there's nothing wrong in a fight, is there?[17]

Walt answered, 'No, there's nowt at all', and talked about a fighter who was a churchgoer, 'and I don't think he drinks, he enjoys life, he doesn't knock people about unnecessary'.[18] Then Harry reminded the others 'some people say . . . our "live and let live" and our staying at home, has let the Japs and the Germans go abroad and make themselves strong. Is it because we've lost a sense of the goodness we'd be prepared to impose on the world?'[19] After some discussion the men agreed that they shouldn't be imposing by force, but rather by influence, 'forceful influence'. One of them illustrated this idea with the example of a football centre-half who used to say, 'Come on, lads, come on lads', and they used to get their final goal from his forceful influence'.[20]

This exchange dramatises how the home-loving, quiet reticence of inter-war British national identity, which as Light suggests was a conservative and middle-class vision, could be rearticulated under the new wartime circumstance. It became a masculine construction, and one with which working-class men could identify by bringing into the discussion the distinctively masculine sports of boxing and football. This vision, as it was reclaimed for masculinity, contributed to how 'the people' in the People's War were imagined.

Deploying the construction of the inter-war anti-heroic masculine national identity, editor of the monthly publication of the Iron and Steel Federation, *Man and Metal*, wrote in December 1942 that 'arms alone are not sufficient to secure the weak from aggression,' and that Britain's special 'contributions to civilisation' were good humour and decency.[21] By 'good humour' the author meant being 'good tempered and light hearted'. Decency, he commented, is a baffling quality to analyse; bound up with it are the conceptions of fair play and consideration for others ... I believe that most foreigners would admit that Britain has shown the quality of decency, the sense of fair play and kindliness, more consistently than any other great nation in the contemporary world.[22]

Fair play and kindliness have roots in ancient notions of chivalry, and the more modern idea of 'character' – the manly code of behaviour taught to boys at public school.[23] Thus the masculinity of the 'good citizen' combined elements of an idealized lower and upper middle-class manliness, and one with which working-class men could identify.

The 'soldier hero'

But it was not just such 'moral toughness', and what we might identify on the basis of the earlier discussion of the British 'stiff upper lip' as 'emotional toughness' that was central to modern and especially wartime masculinity and nationhood. Not surprisingly representations of manliness also depicted military masculinity emphasising bravery, physical strength and endurance, and male bonding.

As Graham Dawson has argued, stories about male heroism in battle or in other arenas that test men's strength and fortitude, are, in a sense, training manuals for masculine identity.[24] There is ample evidence that young boys during the Second World War were fascinated by such stories, and fantasised about being fighting participants in the war.

For example, Mass Observation, the public-opinion research organisation founded in 1937, recorded the following exchange between the observer and children in Stepney that took place at the end of April 1940. The observer asked Betty if she would like a chance to go and fight on the Continent.

> Betty: Coo, I couldn't go up in an aeroplane. It would make my tummy go all funny like it does in a train only worse.
> Obs: What about you, Albert, would you like to join up?
> Albert: Would I? Oh boy, I'd like to take a crack at some of them jerries (sic).
> Obs: What would you join? Army, Navy or Air Force?
> Albert: Air Force. I'd just pull the catch and down they'd all drop, all the bombs (he demonstrates) pop, pop, pop, pop. My brother is a lorry driver. He has to drive with one hand and shoot with the other. ... I'd like to be in a tank. Zoom, zoom, up and down, knocking down everything in your way. I'd like to knock some of them jerries' houses down.[25]

Heroic narratives featuring feats in battle were regularly reported in the press. For example, a Cardiff newspaper published a story depicting the heroism of Squadron Sgt-Major Thomas who earned a medal for his bravery and initiative. The story portrays Thomas as being bold and adventurous, intelligent and efficient, courageous and patriotic. It also makes the point that Thomas, a railway worker in peacetime (one of the ordinary men), used his knowledge of trains to accomplish his heroic deeds. Thomas came up with a plan for destroying a large number of railway cars in Greece where Britain had attempted to stop the German advance. He had the preliminary assistance of the squad who worked under his direction. But then, acting alone and despite enemy gunfire, Thomas destroyed the trains.

This heroic narrative underscored another important aspect of the soldier-hero. He was a team player with strong bonds to his mates, but yet distinguished himself as an individual. Individuality, not individualism, was key to wartime masculinity. It was the bravery of individual men like Squadron Sgt-Major Thomas or specific units of men who were exemplary soldier-heroes.

Heroic epic tales also were told about civilians in dangerous jobs. For example, the Fire Brigades Union published an epic narrative depicting the heroic work of the Fire Service during the Blitz. The narrative presents fighting fires as even more dangerous than serving on the military front.

> Soldiers under bombardment take shelter; and under severe enemy pressure they withdraw. Firemen must hold their ground, however hot the bombardment. There is no possibility of evacuating untenable territory. Finally, soldiers . . . must preserve themselves, as they are fighting units. On the other hand, firemen in preserving the lives, the homes, and the means of life of others, cannot consider the risk to themselves as prime necessity.[26]

Commonly men in uniform were lauded for their heroism to inspire effort on the part of war workers on the home front. An issue of *Warwork News*, distributed by the Admiralty to shipyard workers, featured a picture of a group of men identified as members of the Merchant Navy. 'These men went through Hell for You.' They had been in an open boat for twenty-three days after their ship had been sunk by the Germans somewhere in the Atlantic. 'The men of the Royal Navy and Merchant Navy ask you to give every ounce of effort to speed up production.'[27] In such portraits the heroes were those who faced enemy fire in battle.

Other Admiralty posters, rather than distinguishing 'industry' from 'courage', equated them. One poster showed a shipyard worker's hands meeting the hands of a member of the Royal Navy with a U-boat drawn to resemble a shark being squeezed between them. The caption read, 'Put it there.'[28] Male heroism on the battlefront, and its rough equivalence on the home front were common representations, iconographically making the connection between masculine citizenship and heroic patriotism.

There also were numerous portrayals of heroic masculinity that reinforced the Second World War ideal of a temperate masculinity, one that did not display bravado. Tempered masculinity is illustrated in a vignette written during the so-called 'phoney war' in December 1939 by a contributor to the monthly publication of the Associated Engineering Union. It was entitled 'A "Black-out" Hero.' The story concerned a young man, Peter, whose girlfriend, Molly, was an avid fan of the 'pictures'. She liked the young man, 'but she liked the he-man in the pictures, too'.[29] She wished '*you* were a hero, Peter, I'd like you ever so much better'. Peter protested, saying People aren't heroes – nowadays – leastways, not ordinary civilians like me. Of course, out in the desert or the Wild West a fellow might get a chance. But here there's really nothing doing in the hero line.' But Molly persisted that there must be a way for him to be a hero if 'you really wanted to'. He confided in one of his workmates, and together they came up with the plan for the friend to lie in wait for them in the dark when they were on their way home from the movie theatre. He would demand their valuables; Peter would put up a struggle and beat him off. On the appointed evening as they walked home, they were accosted by a man with a rough voice, who punched Peter so hard that he became angry and rushed at his attacker. He fought the man while Molly screamed until a policeman showed up. The scoundrel, of course, turned out not to be his friend at all, and so the fight had been the 'real thing'. 'It was what Molly said – and did – which made Peter, bathing his eye at home, realise exactly how one of those tin-clad knights of chivalry felt when, after the battle, he claimed his prize.[30]

The story linked manliness and being loveable while at the same time the main character with whom the reader was to identify was one of the 'ordinary men' who was able to act heroically when necessary.

The many visual images of male heroism and verbal descriptions of men in action exemplify George Mosse's argument about the significance of the male body for conceptions of manliness in the modern era.[31] Its significance lay, he argues, in the tendency of moderns, since the Enlightenment, to associate physical attributes with inner qualities.[32]

Iconography suggesting endurance, effort, and/or strength would have been associated by the viewer with the physically fit male body – an ideal and a set of practices – that had been growing in importance throughout the century.[33] Keeping fit had an aesthetic dimension as well as being concerned with health and morality. As George Mosse commented, male beauty was 'confounded with strength and the developing of one's muscles'.[34]

It should not be surprising, then, that the importance of male physical fitness and muscular beauty continued on, and was reinforced by the militarisation of the home front. Advertisements for Charles Atlas, the fitness programme of 'The World's Most Perfectly Developed Man', appeared throughout the war.[35] Health products for men promised slimming and energy, such as Linia Belt to tone weak muscles and lift 'sagging organs to their correct position'.[36] In August 1940, *Picture Post* featured an article illustrated exclusively with numerous images of male civilians, 'Citizens Get Fit'. The theme of the article was 'the civilian is no longer behind the front. He is the front. So everywhere he is getting himself fit.'[37] Such advertisements and articles addressed an anxiety about the male body, historically rooted perhaps, in concerns about the manliness of the corporate, administrative, and professional activities of middle-class and elite men, heightened during the war in civilian men who remained on the home front.

A cartoon by Low, the famous British cartoonist, published while the Chamberlain Government was still in power, links fitness (or lack of it) and the war effort. In the background loomed a massive male figure, drawn more like a wrestler or a caveman than a Greek youth (Attila the Hun?), whose biceps and chest muscles bulge as he flexes his arms (untitled but representing Germany). In the foreground is a balding, middle-aged, paunchy man (labelled 'Allies' Potential Superiority'), holding weights, and wearing shorts made of the Union Jack. Behind him stands an older, frail-looking man labelled 'Simon' (referring to John Simon, Chancellor of the Exchequer), with a bit of thin white hair, holding a weight in one hand and pointing anxiously to the muscular figure behind him. A third figure, a small, balding man labelled 'Reynaud' (referring to the French Prime Minister), lifts weights and grins, seemingly unaware of the dangerous figure behind him. Low's caption reads, 'All you need is hard training.'[38] Low connected the male physically fit body with the military might and leadership necessary to win the war.

The emphasis on physical fitness had a corollary suggested in the Low cartoon; the hegemonic male was young. Hegemonic masculinity was constructed, in part that is, in opposition to old men. Six weeks or so after Chamberlain had resigned and Churchill had formed his Coalition Government, Edward Hulton, editor of *Picture Post*, wrote at the end of June 1940 about the turn the war had taken, and the importance of leadership on the home front as a consequence. His criticism of the previous government was unapologetic. 'Above all the leaders must be *men*. For the last twenty years they have been a lot of old women. The Old Woman Democracy of Neville Chamberlain, John Simon and Samuel Hoare has got to give way to the Leader Democracy of such men as Churchill, Duff Cooper, Bevin, Morrison and Amery.'[39]

Hulton's language makes clear the links between fitness and age on the one hand and masculinity on the other that were integral to the construction of the nation. He not only demeaned the former leadership for being old, but also for being womanish – feminising those whose views and policies were outmoded and weak.

Generally older men, who were not eligible for active duty, were represented in the media as doing something trivial. The Home Guard, for example, was not infrequently represented in a way that portrayed its members as having a lesser role in the war effort than younger men.[40] An advertisement for Four Square Tobacco in *Picture Post* began, 'Old soldiers never die! We just fade into the Home Guard, where we can still teach the youngsters a thing or two – how to smoke a pipe, for instance.'[41]

Letters to the press from the beginning of the war worried about the physical capacity of the old men in civil defence to do their jobs. 'I do not wish to be unduly critical of the ARP personnel, but after seeing some of the specimens who are wearing the uniform of the Auxiliary Police Force, I do suggest that a medical test of all prospective members should be enforced.'[42]

Another letter writer stated that he would prefer to take orders from the Boy Scouts than from 'once retired generals' who behave with 'conspicuous gallantry'.[43] As this letter suggests, older men, especially those who were given some official responsibility were especially singled out for ridicule.

I have been suggesting that hegemonic masculinity and wartime Britishness were of a piece. Hegemonic masculinity was concocted from a loose configuration of characteristics that combined the young, fit, heroic man with the ordinary, home-loving, emotionally reserved, good-humoured and sportsman-like team player.

Conscientious objectors

Masculinity, however, was/is not singular. Rather masculinities were shaped by and in interaction with, among other differentiations, those of occupation, class, and nationality as well as age. Hegemonic masculinity was formed in relation to femininity, and it also was counter posed to other masculinities with predominating characteristics whose fusion had different valences.[44]

Since the license to bear arms was reserved exclusively for men, it established about as clear a sexual division between men and women as the biological capacity to inseminate as opposed to giving birth. It was also reserved for men in the forces, and for men in the Home Guard (not even the police, of course, were given the prerogative of carrying a firearm). Given both this sex and military distinction, it is not surprising that the existence of a fair number of Conscientious Objectors (COs) during the Second World War challenged hegemonic masculinity. An examination of reactions by officials and the public to COs illuminates requirements of hegemonic masculinity that generally became evident only when they were perceived as being defied.

The 1939 Military Service Bill contained a 'conscience clause' allowing pacifists to be released from combat duties. Applicants' appeals for registration as COs were subject to rulings by tribunals established for the purposes of judging the validity of their claims for exemption. All told, there was an increase over the First World War in the numbers of people granted exemption on the basis of having a conscientious objection to war. In the Second World War there were 59,000 registered conscientious objectors, or roughly 1.2 per cent of the 5 million who were conscripted. In the First World War 16,000 or 0.125 per cent of the 6 million men who were conscripted were so registered.[45] Men of draft age thus could opt out of military duty if their claims to conscience were judged truthful.

Allowing claims of conscience to over-ride the obligations of military service was justified as a practice demonstrating British tolerance in contrast with Nazi persecution of pacifists. For example, during one of the numerous letters-to-the-editor exchanges about COs in one of the many newspapers in the country where they were published, 'Lawyer' wrote in response to someone who suggested branding COs, 'we must be careful our patriotism does not turn us into persecutors and purgers'. While some conscientious objectors might endure branding, he continued, 'it would reflect on the impartiality of the branders ... and remind the public that it is a German method to brand those they disagree with'.[46]

There was a variety of grounds on which Pacifists argued their case, but religion was the most common, and most commonly effective.[47] Jehovah's Witnesses, however, were frequently objects of abuse in Tribunals. The group was not generally publicly accepted as an established religious denomination, and thus their claims to conscience were vigorously challenged. At a Tribunal at Bristol in May 1943, Judge Wethered, the chair, for example, regarded them as doing 'very mischievous work; it was assisting the forces of evil. He could not understand how people accepted the nonsense.' Furthermore, he accused the group of 'going round undermining the confidence of people in their government at the present time'.[48]

The men who claimed exemption on the basis of conscience articulated alternative versions of masculine citizenship to the hegemonic one that required men to defend the country. The Witnesses, for example, claimed an allegiance to a higher authority than the state. They routinely said, 'I am not of this world; my citizenship is in heaven.'[49]

Not all COs, however, were the recipients of public disapprobation. Quakers often garnered public respect. The Friends supported alternative humanitarian service; many Quaker objectors served in the Friends' Ambulance Unit both during the bombings in London and on the battlefields abroad.

Those who, through alternative service, risked their lives to serve others, were recognised as 'good objectors'. Even though they refused combat, they were fulfilling the requirements of wartime masculinity by confronting risk and offering self-sacrifice. A *Sunday Pictorial* article of September 1942 underscores the distinction often made among COs, drawing on the language of wartime heroic masculinity.

It told the story of Nik Anderson who was shot while driving an ambulance in Tobruck during the North Africa campaign. The journalist used the incident to make a statement about 'other' COs – the 'wrong sort'. He wrote that Anderson could have found himself

> a job on the farm of some rich, easy-going pacifist – a nice funk hole somewhere in the country, miles away from bomb threatened cities ... His conscience would not have allowed him to skulk in the country – like so many other pacifists – while his fellow-countrymen suffered ... We know how they laze about their silly 'peace' farms and adopt an omnipotent and superior attitude to war-troubled Britain. We have seen them strolling in the quiet, peaceful lanes of England in their coloured corduroy trousers and shimmering silk shirts.[50]

The reference to 'coloured corduroy trousers and shimmering silk shirts' suggests effeminacy and intellectual eccentricity, and highlights the contrast with the self-sacrificing and brave Anderson. Such stories underscore the significance of bravery and taking risks to British wartime masculinity. Since illusions to homosexuality and effeminacy were commonly made about COs, these stories also suggest the centrality to hegemonic masculinity of heterosexuality.

The weekend of the evacuation from Dunkirk in June 1940, *Sunday Pictorial* declared 'war on the nauseating young men who pretend that they believe in "peace"'.[51] The editorial proclaimed: 'We don't like the elegant sissies who fester the restaurants of London, gossiping like girls about their "hearts" and "inner souls". They've got more scent than sense.'[52] And a scathing two-page article condemning pacifists appeared in *Sunday Pictorial* a week later under the headline PACIFISTS AND PANSIES. The article described the applicants for exemption as 'pale lilies', 'long-haired, mental perverts with no chins, no character, and no spirit', and 'national pansies', in contrast to a 'man who was a man, not a pansy'.[53]

It is, perhaps, understandable that in reaction to a devastating military defeat when the British were returning home there might be expressions of extreme intolerance for those who refused to fight on the basis of conscience. But the language of outrage concerning those who chose not to fight focused less on patriotism and more on male sexuality. COs seemingly exhibited an exaggerated version of temperate masculinity, a resemblance that threatened to cast the shadow of effeminacy over the entire nation, threatening the virility deemed necessary to defeat the Germans. Like young British girls who were chastised for endangering the future of the nation by being sexually irresponsible and promiscuous, pacifists were often constructed as irresponsible and sexually suspect anti-citizens.[54]

There were those who articulated the idea that standing up to the hostility to which COs exposed themselves was, itself, a mark of courage, further underscoring the importance of bravery for manhood. FMW, for example, who identified himself as a First World War veteran currently active in the Home Guard, wrote to the editor of a local newspaper in February 1941, 'The Christian CO – I emphasize Christian CO – is a "Great Man" to stand firm against public opinion.'[55] Predictably, the following week 'Disgusted' responded, 'Great men do not stand aside in one's hour of need.' 'Disgusted' thus trumped 'Great Man's' courage with willingness to sacrifice as a prerequisite for wartime masculine citizenship.

Although there were 'good objectors' who were seen as self-sacrificing and brave, it was also the case that COs, regardless of the grounds of their objection, were viewed as cowards. Members of the Tribunals and the public often implied that COs were so cowardly, so unmanly, that they would not protect women – even their loved ones. For example, a Chorley schoolteacher who was also a Methodist preacher was denied exemption after he was asked at the Tribunal if he had a girlfriend and she was attacked, what would he do. The man replied, 'I'd investigate.' Interrupting, the Chair said:

> No girl I know would think of having anything to do with a young
> man unless she felt sure he would be prepared to defend her. If a
> girl were assaulted would you not be prepared to defend her?
> [Answer:] I cannot answer.
> Chair: What! Do you mean to state you cannot say? I should not
> think there was any man in this country who would not be ready
> to defend his wife or any girl if she was being attacked.[56]

The stridently hostile article, 'Pacifists and Pansies', quoted above complained that the 'paternal, well-meaning Tribunal exempts the school-master on condition that he goes back to his job of spreading poison in the minds of the nation's children'.[57] Across the country there were numerous city and town councils that dismissed COs from their teaching positions, and from other city and town employment, even if they were already short of staff.

Although applicants for exemption from combat were often required to remain in their current positions, to work on farms or in the mines, and/or to take an active role in civil defence, the fireguards, or join the Royal Army Medical Corps, their attempts to fulfil these requirements often met with hostility. While parents may have objected to COs teaching their children, and tax payers resented tax money being spent to support pacifists in city or county government, their would-be fellow workers or members of civil defence units resented their presence. For them it was as if having COs in their midst was polluting. Journalist H. W. Seaman reported that Council offices in the Norwich Town Hall 'are infested by Conscientious Objectors'.[58] Similarly, the press reported that members of the Royal Army Medical Corp were deeply hostile to COs in their midst. 'Their enforced enlistment threatens to turn the "medicals" into the white-feathered corps of the Army. And the boys don't like it.'[59] Thus, although COs were publicly damned if they did not take on positions that put them at some risk, their doing so could also elicit hostility.

In April 1940 *Sunday Chronicle* carried an article by a regular feature writer calling himself 'Yorick'. It was written as a tongue-in-cheek commentary about COs.

> As most of you know, or have guessed, I am an out-and-out Pacifist with a horror of war and physical violence ... I was walking along the street the other day when a girl in khaki ... came up and handed me a white feather.
> Slapping her smartly across the face, I inquired politely, 'What's this for?'
> 'To clean your pipe, of course,' she said hastily, and hurried away.
> The following day, I was walking down the same street when another girl in navy blue slacks ... came up and handed me another white feather.
> Knocking her silly sailor hat, I said, 'What's this for?'
> 'I thought I'd like to tickle your ear,' she said hastily, and slunk off.
> The third day I was walking along the same street when a shy young man came up and handed me a white feather.
> 'It dwopped out of my new hat,' he explained very sweetly. 'Would you mind vewy much fixing it for me? It's a fwightful nuisance leaving my mirror at home.'
> Well, customers, I did warn you that I was an out-and-out Pacifist. Or did I?[60]

This essay certainly demeaned COs with satire, but it also had another meaning. Any male out of uniform (unless he was obviously too old to be in the military), regardless of what it was he was doing for the war effort, could be given a white feather to mark him as an effeminate, unmanly coward.

Throughout the war years, at least until the military began extensive demobilisation in 1945, men out of uniform were subjects of 'white feather campaigns' throughout the country. It is difficult to know, however, just how extensive was the practice, borrowed from the First World War, of people, apparently women, handing white feathers to those they suspected of being pacifists.[61] The press reported incidents such as the following: 'Another war hero gets "white feather".' The man reporting the incident said he was wearing the King's Badge for being disabled, and he had only recently begun walking again.[62] The newspaper claimed to be aware of many more such incidents. The article concluded with a drawing and complete description of the King's Badge to prevent misidentification, but warned that not all men who are discharged have been so disabled that they were awarded the Badge.

Most of the white-feather incidents reported in the press involved servicemen or ex-servicemen out of uniform and focused on the military heroism of those wrongfully identified as COs. This shaming ceremony and its media representations suggest the crucial importance of participation in the military to wartime hegemonic masculinity. Only men wearing military uniform could convincingly perform wartime temperate masculinity. Since the war was defined as a People's War, and victory depended on the active participation of civilian men, as well as women on the home front, hegemonic masculinity was unstable. Pushed too far in one direction it could be mistaken for a Nazi-like hyper-masculinity. Pushed too far the other way, it could mean being thought a cowardly and effeminate pacifist or an emasculated, decrepit old man.

Conclusion

In Second World War Britain, as this chapter has shown, hegemonic masculinity was composed of seemingly incompatible characteristics. It combined those of respectable and emotionally restrained manhood or what I have referred to as tempered masculinity, constructed in opposition to images of Nazi men, with those of the military soldier-hero. Conscientious Objectors challenged this hegemonic manliness, and were popularly envisioned as effeminate. Given the potentially subversive combination of military, heroic, and temperate masculinity, how did it become so dominant (if not uncontested) in Second World War Britain? As I have already suggested, the connections between masculinity and national identity made it crucial to oppose Britishness and Germanness. Additionally, some of the characteristics of this composite masculinity had longstanding historical connections to middle-class and elite Britishness.

But there is something that is also more fundamental to masculinity in British culture (or indeed Western cultures more generally) at play here. Military and heroic masculinity allowed for the assimilation to masculinity of what, in other contexts and articulations, might be considered soft, feminine traits. In the Gulf War in the United States, for example, Norman Schwartzkopf, the US Commander-in Chief, expressed sentimentality, and made it possible for grown men to cry and remain masculine. Being in military uniform was essential to successfully performing hegemonic masculinity.

The nation is linguistically gendered, although its gendering is unstable. As a 'homeland', as a space of belonging, the nation can either be masculine or feminine – fatherland or motherland.[63] So too as a subject of history the gendering of the nation is not fixed. When under attack the nation often is portrayed as a violated but supremely moral feminine body. But as the active subject of history, especially when the nation is waging war, it is cloaked in masculinity. But as this essay has suggested, the form of masculinity that defines the nation, is unstable. It is envisioned in relation to others – to the enemies without and within. In Second World War Britain, the nation-at-war was a masculine subject, but this was a temperate masculinity. Combining good humour and kindliness with heroism and bravery was an unstable mix. Pushed too far in one direction it could uncomfortably resemble the hyper-masculine Nazi enemy. Pushed too far in the other direction, it could slide into effeminacy.

Notes

1 For the concept of hegemonic masculinity, see R. W. Connell, *Masculinities* (Berkeley and Los Angeles, 1995).

2 A. Calder, *The Myth of the Blitz* (London, 1991).

3 A. Light, *Forever England* (London, 1991).

4 Joanna Bourke, however, suggests that demobilised soldiers of the First World War desired to return to normal life and to begin families because they were older, not out of disgust for war itself. She argues that there was continuity in men's lives over the period of the war. See J. Bourke, *Dismembering the Male* (London, 1996), esp. pp. 22–4, 155–70.

5 On masculinity and Nazism, see K. Theweleit, *Male Fantasies*, vols 1–2 (Minneapolis, 1989); G. L. Mosse, *Nationalism and Sexuality: Respectability & Abnormal Sexuality in Modern Europe* (New York, 1985) and *The Image of Man: The Creation of Modern Masculinity* (New York, 1996).

6 J. B. Priestley, 'Postscript', Sunday, 9 June 1940, in J. B. Priestley, *All England Listened: The Wartime Broadcasts of J. B. Priestley* (New York, 1967), pp. 11–12.

7 *Picture Post* (23 March 1940), p. 55.

8 S. O. Rose, 'Sex, citizenship and the nation in World War II Britain', *American Historical Review*, 103 (October 1998), 1147–76.

9 J. Tosh, 'Domesticity and manliness in the Victorian middle class', in M. Roper and T. Tosh (eds), *Manful Assertions: Masculinities in Britain Since 1800* (London and New York, 1991), p. 65.

10 Tosh, 'Domesticity', pp. 65–8. Also see J. Tosh, *A Man's Place: Masculinity in the Middle-Class Home in Victorian England* (New Haven and London, 1999), ch. 8.

11 Light, *Forever England*, p. 8.

12 *Ibid.*, p. 210.

13 B. Nichols, 'Is Your Child Your Own or the State's?', *Sunday Chronicle* (23 March 1941), p. 2.

14 Imperial War Museum, London, 97/21/1, J. L. Sweetland, 'Growing Up in Wartime London, 1939–45', pp. 20–1. Every effort has been made to obtain permission to quote from the copyright holder without success.

15 *Ibid.*, p. 21.
16 Light, *Forever England*, pp. 106, 211.
17 BBC Written Archives Centre, Reading, T 405, 'Living Opinion', p. 8.
18 *Ibid.*
19 *Ibid.*
20 *Ibid.*, p. 9.
21 Modern Records Centre, Warwick (hereafter MRC), Mss 38, *Man and Metal*, December (1942), 136.
22 *Ibid.*
23 Mosse, *Image of Man*, p. 23.
24 G. Dawson, *Soldier Heroes: British Adventure, Empire and the Imagining of Masculinities* (London and New York), pp. 11–13.
25 Mass Observation Archive, University of Sussex, Brighton (hereafter MOA), File Report 299 (microfilm), 'Children and the War', July 1940, p. 9. For similar evidence from Mass Observation at a date later in the war, see MOA, File Report 662–3, 'What Your Child Thinks of the War', April 1943.
26 Public Records Office, Kew (hereafter PRO), 47035, PIN 15/2792, National Fire Service, p. 23.
27 PRO, INF 2/72, 'Industry Publicity', *Warwork News*, 5 (1941), 3a.
28 PRO, *ibid.*, p. 8 (n.d.).
29 MRC, MSS 259/4/14/53, R. M. Fox, 'A "Black-out" Hero', *AEU Monthly Journal*, December (1939), 481.
30 *Ibid.*
31 Mosse, *Image of Man*, pp. 24–50.
32 *Ibid.*, p. 24.
33 For discussions of fitness at the end of the nineteenth century see J. Springhall, 'Building character in the British boy: The attempt to extend Christian manliness to working-class adolescents, 1880 to 1914', in J. A. Mangan and J. Walvin (eds), *Manliness and Morality: Middle-Class Masculinity in Britain and America* (Manchester, 1984), pp. 52–74; N. Vance, *Sinews of the Spirit: The Ideal of Christian manliness in Victorian Literature and Religious Thought* (Cambridge, 1985). For pre-First World War see Bourke, *Dismembering the Male*, ch. 4, and for the inter-war period see R. Graves and A. Hodge, *The Long Week-End: A Social History of Great Britain, 1918–1939* (New York, 2nd edn, 1994, reprint), p. 369.
34 Mosse, *Image of Man*, p. 137.
35 For example, *Picture Post* (8 July 1939), p. 6.
36 For example, *ibid.* (30 September 1939), p. 29.
37 *Ibid.* (14 August 1940), p. 20.
38 *Ibid.* (27 January 1940), p. 39.
39 *Ibid.* (29 June 1940), p. 33, emphasis in the original.
40 Penny Summerfield has suggested that a great number of representations of men on the home front featured older men rather than young, muscular workers. See P. Summerfield, *Reconstructing Women's Wartime Lives* (Manchester, 1998), p. 119.
41 *Picture Post* (30 November 1940), p. 4.
42 *Ibid.* (28 October 1939), p. 18.
43 *Ibid.* (29 June 1940), p. 34.

44 Connell, *Masculinities*.

45 R. Barker, *Conscience, Government and War* (London, 1982), p. 121.

46 *Evesham Journal and Four Shires Advertiser* (13 February 1943), p. 5.

47 See Barker, *Conscience*, p. 121.

48 Friends Library, London (hereafter FL), Temp MSS 914/11/2/1, 'Cuttings 1941–1947', *Bridgewater Mercury* (2 March 1943).

49 FL, Temp MSS 914/11/1, Clipping file, *Lincolnshire Standard* (8 October 1942).

50 FL, Temp MSS 619/11/2, Clipping file, *Sunday Pictorial* (6 September 1942).

51 *Evesham Journal and Four Shires Advertiser* (2 June 1940), p. 8.

52 *Ibid.*

53 B. Gray, 'Pacificists and Pansies', *Sunday Pictorial* (9 June 1940), pp. 8–9.

54 For a discussion of this phenomenon see Rose, 'Sex, citizenship'.

55 *Evesham Journal and Four Shires Advertiser* (13 February 1943), p. 5.

56 FL, MSS Temp 914/11/1, Album of Press cuttings from the Lancashire Tribunal, Manchester, 27 April 1940.

57 Gray, 'Pacifists', p. 8.

58 H. W. Seaman, 'City's "Conchies" Get War Bonus', *Sunday Chronicle* (21 April 1940), p. 5.

59 FL, MSS Temp 914/11/1, Political Objection Cuttings 1945 and earlier, *Berwick Advertiser*, 15 February 1940.

60 Yorick, 'Over the Garden Wall', *Sunday Chronicle* (14 April 1940), p. 7.

61 See N. F. Gullace, 'White feathers and wounded men: Female patriotism and the memory of the Great War', *Journal of British Studies*, 36 (April 1997), 178–206.

62 *The Coventry Evening Telegraph* (15 April 1943), p. 6.

63 See P. Duara, 'Historicizing national identity, or who imagines what and when', in G. Eley and R. G. Suny (eds), *Becoming National* (New York, 1996), p. 167.

PART IV

Analysing power relations:
the politics of masculinity

11

Translating needs into rights: the discursive imperative of the Australian white man, 1901–30

Marilyn Lake

I N 1907, Henry Bournes Higgins, the president of the newly established Australian Court of Conciliation and Arbitration, was set the task of defining a 'fair and reasonable' wage for unskilled male labourers. The case arose from an application by H. V. McKay, manufacturer of agricultural machinery, including the Sunshine Harvester, for exemption from excise duties as provided by the Tariff Act, if the employer could show that he paid his employees a 'fair and reasonable' wage. Higgins' historic judgment, which became known as the Harvester judgment, did more than prescribe a living wage of seven shillings a day for a six day week. It defined the condition of Australian manhood in terms of the worker's 'needs' as a 'civilised being' living in a 'civilised community', which included his obligation to support a wife and children.[1]

In his recent *Concise History of Australia*, Stuart Macintyre has assessed the significance of the Harvester judgment in these terms:

> The principles of Higgins' Harvester judgment became a fundamental feature of national life. Wages were to be determined not by bargaining, but by an independent arbitrator. They were to be based, not on profits or productivity, but human need. They were premised on the male breadwinner, with men's wages sufficient to support a family and women restricted to certain occupations and paid only enough to support a single person. Women contested the dual standard for the next sixty years.[2]

Macintyre's assessment speaks to the impact of feminist history which, since the 1970s, has tended to hold the Harvester judgment responsible for institutionalising the economic subordination of women.[3]

The determination of a minimum wage did not just reward manhood, however, it empowered white manhood. Aboriginal men were not awarded equal pay until the 1960s; and colonial and state legislation had already barred Asian, Afghan, Indian, and Islander men from entering a range of designated occupations. As Gail Bederman has pointed out in *Manliness and Civilization*, 'civilisation', 'manhood' and, 'whiteness' came to be defined at the turn of the century in terms of each other. Race became interwoven with manhood through discourses on civilisation: non-white men were considered neither manly nor civilised.[4] When Henry Bournes Higgins defined the average worker as a 'civilised being' living in 'a civilised community', he was signalling that Australia was to be, in the usage of the time, 'a white man's country'. Six years earlier in the debate on immigration restriction in the first federal parliament, when Higgins represented the electorate of North Melbourne, he had stated: 'We do not want men beside us who are not as exacting in their demands on civilisation as ourselves'; 'we do not want yellow and black faces in Australia'.[5]

In white post-colonial nations, such as the USA and Australia, manhood was an explicitly racialised, as well as a gendered condition. Although non-white men were considered neither manly nor civilised, they were nevertheless perceived to pose a powerful and dangerous threat to the 'white man'. In particular it was agreed that he needed 'protection' from 'Asiatics' through immigration restrictions. Their overwhelming numbers (they were always likened to a 'flood' or a 'tide'), their 'cunning' and their 'cheap labour' were said to threaten white men with annihilation. Yet the white man's manhood also required him to resist being represented as weak, dependent, or in need of protection. One response to this dilemma was to translate the prevailing discourse on his 'needs' into an assertion of political 'rights'. In the 1920s and 1930s, organised labour wrestled with the tensions inherent in the white man's vulnerability, when the living wage came under attack by feminists demanding equal pay and employers seeking to curb the cost of labour. By the 1930s, working men spoke of their entitlement in terms of their 'masculinity' (a newly invented concept as Bederman points out), adopting a more 'masculine' political discourse that spoke of their 'rights' rather than their 'needs'.[6] Whereas white men at the turn of the century spoke of their 'manly' virtues of 'frankness' and 'uprightness' to distinguish themselves from 'duplicitous' and 'servile' Asiatics, it was their 'masculinity' that was later invoked to justify their higher wages, their right to jobs and their power over women. Too many histories have simply conflated and equated these very different concepts.[7]

In tracing the story of the living wage and the white working man, this chapter seeks to show that representations of 'manhood' are not only constitutive of men's power over women, but are also integral to power struggles between men. In Australia, the 'white man' invoked his whiteness to justify the national exclusion of variously designated racial Others as well as his rule over Aboriginal 'natives', who were, from the turn of the century, positioned as 'wards of the state'.

In the 1920s and 1930s, organised working men invoked their rights as men in their struggle with employers over pay rates and employment and then in response to the perceived threat of women workers. As Michael Kimmel has pointed out manhood may often be a 'homosocial enactment', but it isn't always so.[8] Meanings of 'manhood' changed over time in response to challenges posed by other races and classes of men and also in response to the perceived power of women. In the process 'white manhood' came to articulate 'masculine rights' – understood as the prerogative of men as men – and 'masculinity' replaced 'manliness' as the dominant expression of manhood.

Deporting the black man

To recognise the way in which 'manhood' in the late nineteeth century was understood as a racial category, as well as a gendered one, we need to locate studies of 'gender relations' within the broader historical context of the relations of colonialism. As Catherine Hall has written in her study of imperialism in the Caribbean, the colonial project depended on 'the construction of a culture and the constitution of new identities, new men and women, who, in a variety of ways would live with and through colonialism, as well as engaging in conflict with it'. New selves were constructed, for those 'who were ruling as well as those ruled'.[9] One of those new selves was the 'white man' and we get a glimpse of his self-constitution in the first parliament of the Commonwealth of Australia, in 1901, in the debates on the legislation to deport Pacific Islanders, a measure that complemented the Immigration Restriction Act.

The Pacific Islands Labourers Act provided for the expulsion of the Islanders, or Kanakas as they were called, who had been brought from Melanesia in the late nineteenth century to labour in the Queensland sugar cane plantations. In introducing the legislation, Prime Minister, Edmund Barton explained the necessity of the measure in terms of the difference that separated the Pacific Islander from the 'white man':

> The difference in intellectual level and the difference in knowledge of
> the ways of the world between the white man and the Pacific Islander,
> is one which cannot be bridged by acts or regulations about agreements.
> The level of the one is above that of the other, the difference being

one in human mental stature – of character as well of mind – which cannot be put aside by passing 50 laws or 1,000 regulations ... He cannot be made to understand the condition of his engagement. He may be brought to a state of partial understanding, but it is impossible to say that he can have a degree of contracting capacity equal to that of the man who is dealing with him.[10]

Contractual relations were impossible between the Islander and the white man – a 'Higher Power' – having made them unequal and all attempts at co-existence or assimilation would surely end in degradation for both parties. The white man could not deal with the black labourer 'man to man'. This was the lesson Australian political leaders took from the republic of the United States of America.

In *American Ideals and Other Essays*, published just four years earlier, in 1897, future US president Theodore Roosevelt had offered this observation on white colonial democracies:

Nineteenth century democracy needs no more complete vindication for its existence than the fact that it has kept for the white race the best portions of the new worlds' surface, temperate America and Australia. Had these regions been under aristocratic governments, Chinese immigration would have been encouraged precisely as the slave trade is encouraged of necessity by any slave-holding oligarchy, and the result would in a few generations have been even more fatal to the white race; but the democracy, with the clear instinct of race selfishness, saw the race foe, and kept out the dangerous alien. The presence of the negro in our Southern States is a legacy from the time when we were ruled by a trans-oceanic aristocracy. The whole civilisation of the future owes a debt of gratitude greater than can be expressed in words to that democratic policy which has kept the temperate zones of the new and the newest worlds a heritage for the white people.[11]

According to Bederman, Roosevelt had consciously fashioned himself as an exemplary white man – indeed as 'a heroic and manly Western rancher' – in response to earlier taunts of effeminacy.[12] From the late 1890s he became an ardent advocate of imperialism as the white man's racial destiny. The spread of civilisation was the white man's manly duty. Australian political leaders shared much of this thinking. Furthermore, in the democratic societies of the temperate zones, white men considered they had a chance to pioneer a new type of civilisation.

The able and urbane Attorney-General in the new government, Alfred Deakin, conscious of being 'charged with the future of this country' also referred to the 'teachings from the experience' of the United States:

We should be false to the lessons taught us in the great republic of the west; we should be false to the never-to-be-forgotten teachings from the experience of the United States, of difficulties only partially conquered by the blood of their best and bravest; we should be absolutely blind to and unpardonably neglectful of our obligations, if we fail to lay those lessons to heart.[13]

Establishing a new civilisation for the white man was also the dream of Henry Bournes Higgins, lawyer and future president of the Commonwealth Court of Conciliation and Arbitration. In 1901 he was a member of the first federal parliament, representing the working-class electorate of North Melbourne. In 1904, he would serve as Attorney-General in the first Labor government. Higgins hailed the legislation to deport the Pacific Islanders as 'the most vitally important measure on the programme which the government has put before us'.[14] Its significance lay in the fact that it raised the question of whether 'northern Australia should be peopled by white men or not. I feel convinced that people who are used to a high standard of life – to good wages and good conditions – will not consent to labour alongside men who receive a miserable pittance and who are dealt with very much in the same way as slaves'.[15] In offering his 'strongest support' to the legislation to deport the Islanders, Higgins had confided that he 'watched its course with the deepest anxiety'. One way or the other, it would have 'a deep and lasting effect'.[16]

The Pacific Islands Labourers Act was complemented by the Immigration Restriction Act, both passed in 1901. 'The two things go hand in hand', advised Attorney-General Deakin. They were 'the necessary complement of a single policy – the policy of securing a "White Australia"'.[17] Drawing on the precedent of earlier colonial legislation, the Immigration Restriction Act was designed to prevent coloured aliens – 'those inclined to invade our shores' in Deakin's words – from entering Australia as future immigrants. There were already some 90,000 coloured aliens – variously named as Afghans, Assyrians, Hindoos, Chinese, Japanese, Manila-men, Malays, Islanders – within Australia, as members of parliament constantly attested.[18] White Australia became a consuming fantasy because it spoke to powerful anxieties. For Deakin, the issue was the cause of 'so much anxiety', because it called up 'the profoundest instinct of individual or nation – the instinct of self-preservation for it is nothing less than the national manhood, the national character and the national future that are at stake'.[19]

Protecting the white man

Why did these issues cause Australia's national leaders such profound anxiety? In what sense was their self-preservation at stake? To answer these questions we need to investigate the subjectivity of the 'white man' whose sense of self was so powerfully threatened. We need to attend to 'the practices of subjective self-constitution', 'the relation between the discursive and the psychic' (in Stuart Hall's words), and to locate the study within a post-colonial analytical frame.[20] There have been many histories of the 'White Australia policy', but none that have taken the constitution of the racialised, gendered identifications of the 'white man' as the focus of their analysis.[21] Earlier studies have argued about whether White Australia was the achievement of capital or labour, but the 'white man' was a racialised, gendered figure, not a subject constituted in class terms.[22] The anxiety of the white man, an anxiety which led to his demand for the 'protection' provided by the White Australia policy, was, I suggest, the anxiety of the colonial apprehending a post-colonial world.

When Prime Minister Barton rose in parliament in August 1901 to speak to the second reading of the Immigration Restriction Bill, he held in his hand a book that spoke to and shaped the white man's insecurities. Charles Pearson's *National Life and Character: A Forecast*, first published in London in 1893, and reprinted in London and New York in 1894, foretold of a future, 'not far distant', when white men would find themselves 'humiliated' and 'thrust aside'.[23] An Englishman, Pearson had been educated at Oriel College, Oxford and worked as Professor of History at King's College, before migrating in the 1870s, first to the colony of South Australia then to Victoria, where he enjoyed a career as a University lecturer, educational reformer, and a Minister for Education, championing, among other causes, women's education. In 1877 Pearson had formed a debating society at the University of Melbourne, where idealistic young men met to discuss the public questions of the day. Among their number were a young Alfred Deakin, future Prime Minister, and Henry Bournes Higgins, future president of the Commonwealth Court of Conciliation and Arbitration.

Barton read long passages from Pearson's book to the parliament self-consciously charged with the national future, including this clearly disturbing vision of a post-colonial world in which the erstwhile 'servile' classes had become masters:

> The day will come, and perhaps is not far distant, when the European observer will look round to see the globe circled with a continuous zone of the black and yellow races, no longer too weak for aggression

or under tutelage, but independent, or practically so, in government, monopolising the trade of their own regions, and circumscribing the industry of the Europeans; when Chinamen and the natives of Hindustan, the states of Central and South America, by that time predominantly Indian ... are represented by fleets in the European seas, invited to international conferences and welcomed as allies in quarrels of the civilised world. The citizens of these countries will then be taken up into the social relations of the white races, will throng the English turf or the salons of Paris, and will be admitted to inter-marriage. It is idle to say that if all this should come to pass our pride of place will not be humiliated ... We shall wake to find ourselves elbowed and hustled, and perhaps even thrust aside by peoples whom we looked down upon as servile and thought of as bound always to minister to our needs. The solitary consolation will be that the changes have been inevitable.[24]

In this passage, Pearson depicts the post-colonial world in piquant terms as a drama of white masculine humiliation – occurring in all the most manly of sites – on the high seas, in the halls of industry, at international conferences, in the salons of Paris, even on the English turf. He considered the changes inevitable, but were they? Was it not the duty of leaders of white men to defend their interests and to prevent these unsettling developments? Should not Pearson's forecast be received as a rallying cry?

Pearson's book caused a stir in England and the United States among men of public affairs. As his biographer has noted: 'Coming when it did at the full tide of imperialist sentiment, it produced the shock he had expected, and he became a celebrity'.[25] In London, Prime Minister Gladstone was reportedly 'full of Pearson's book', telling dinner guests at Downing Street that everyone should read it. In May, 1894, Pearson received a letter from the United States reporting that 'men in Washington' were greatly interested; few books had caused so many men to revise their 'mental estimate of facts'.[26]

The correspondent was Theodore Roosevelt, who also wrote a long review of *National Life and Character* in the *Sewanee Review*, in which he chided Pearson for being 'unduly pessimistic', but praised him for forcing the reader 'to ponder problems of which he was previously wholly ignorant, or which he but half understood'.[27] His own view, from the perspective of American experience with the Indian and the Negro, was that white control would never be jeopardised, because insurrections were always mercilessly crushed. But perhaps the time had come for the white man to assert his authority in the world at large?

In her study of Roosevelt in *Manliness and Civilization*, Gail Bederman identifies 1894 as the year in which he first began to advocate imperialism as the white man's racial challenge. She finds his interest in foreign policy first mentioned in a letter to Henry Cabot Lodge in October that year, but misses the significance of Pearson's book, which he read in May, and reviewed in August. As Thomas Dyer has suggested in *Theodore Roosevelt and the Idea of Race* his reading of Pearson was dramatically illuminating and clearly helped inspire Roosevelt's new imperial project.[28] In his review of *National Life and Character*, Roosevelt dismissed as a 'weakling' the 'man who cannot struggle with his fellow-men', though commended Pearson himself for being 'a man of strength and courage' for he faced the future with manly fortitude.[29]

The American statesman was altogether more sanguine about the state of the world than the gloomy Antipodean: 'At no period of the world's history has life been so full of interest and of possibilities of excitement and enjoyment as for us who live in the latter half of the nineteenth century.'[30] He was impressed, though, with Pearson's facts about the declining white birth rate and the implications for the world of 'the teeming population of China':

> Unquestionably, no community that is actually diminishing in numbers is in a healthy condition: and as the world is now, with huge waste places still to fill up, and with much of the competition between the races reducing itself to the warfare of the cradle, no race has any chance to win a great place unless it consists of good breeders as well as good fighters.[31]

Henceforth, as Bederman observes, 'race suicide' became one of Roosevelt's favourite themes.[32]

The American was perplexed, however, at Pearson's suggestion that 'once the tropic races are independent, the white peoples will be humiliated and will lose heart': 'this does not seem inevitable, and indeed seems very improbable'. With the insouciance of the already independent, Roosevelt continued:

> No American or Australian cares in the least that the tan-coloured peoples of Brazil and Ecuador now live under governments of their own instead of being ruled by viceroys from Portugal and Spain: and it is difficult to see why they should be materially affected by a similar change happening in regard to the people along the Ganges or the upper Nile.[33]

Taking his own condition of manly independence for granted, Roosevelt was unable to see that the independence of Africans or Asians might challenge the white colonial's very status as a man. Still under the protection of Britain, cast in the role of a dependent, how could the 'colonial' demand respect at international conferences, in Paris salons or on the English turf? He could, at least, retrieve his manhood in the confines of 'his own home'. As Roosevelt advised, 'in his own home', the white man 'can always protect himself, and as soon as he is seriously menaced, always will protect himself by protective tariffs and stringent immigration laws'.[34] In Australia, this combination of measures introduced in the first decade of the Commonwealth's existence, would be named New Protection – its novelty inhering in the insistence that tariff protection be accompanied by state protection of the adult male wage.[35] Australian national leaders would seek to protect the status of the Australian white man in the post-colonial world, not through heroic imperial conquest – they did not yet possess their own navy, as they were reminded when the impressive Japanese Training Squadron visited Sydney in 1903 – but through state action to guarantee his status in 'his own home'.

Henry Bournes Higgins, whose task it was to define the living wage in 1907, was an Irish immigrant to the colony of Victoria, opponent of the Boer War, and vigorous in defending the status of the white man in Australia against what he held to be imperial domination and bullying by the British. As Australians were at pains to point out, 'colonials' confronted different psychic challenges than those faced by the British in the metropolis. In *National Life and Character*, Pearson had observed that the 'Englishmen at home' found it hard to understand the 'fear of Chinese immigration which the Australian democracy cherishes', but it was simply 'the instinct of self-preservation quickened by experience' – the threat to the boundaries of White Australia was experienced as a threat to the self.[36] In the debate on immigration restriction in 1901, Deakin made a similar observation: European statesmen might 'well view with surprise the anxiety exhibited here in this respect'.[37] But as another member of parliament explained in the course of the same debate, the British could never grasp the importance of 'race' to the colonial, because 'it is not a question of manhood [for them] ... in the same way as it is for us'.[38]

In seeking to introduce the racial boundaries that they saw as essential to the preservation of their manhood, Australian political leaders ironically provoked their further emasculation by the British Colonial Office – being robbed of their manhood at the very moment they entered into their nationhood. The Colonial Office made it clear to Australian political leaders that they would not be permitted to

incorporate explicitly racist exclusions into federal immigration legislation as they proposed, but rather should follow the precedent set by
the colony of Natal in South Africa and specify a dictation test in a
prescribed language. There were loud complaints in the Australian
parliament that the Australian government was being 'trampled upon'
in 'submitting to the dictation of the Colonial-office'.[39] 'By giving us
our Constitution we have been treated as grown men with the responsibilities of grown men', observed Higgins. 'I hope the Government by
next week will reconsider the position.'[40] This would not happen.

In 1897, the colonial Premiers had been warned by Secretary of
State Joseph Chamberlain that they should seek to avoid giving offence
to other imperial subjects such as Indians and Chinese, but especially to
the Japanese, with whom the British had forged the Anglo-Japanese
Treaty in 1894. The Australians should 'bear in mind the traditions of
the empire, which makes no distinction in favour of or against race or
colour', announced Chamberlain, seemingly forgetting for the moment
that while some imperial subjects enjoyed the right of self-government,
others – subject races – were expressly denied it. To 'exclude by reason
of their race or colour all her Majesty's Indian subjects, or even all
Asiatics, would be an act so offensive to those peoples', continued Chamberlain, 'that it would be most painful, I am certain, to her Majesty, to
have to sanction it.' Moreover, Australians should remember that in
India there were hundreds of thousands of men who were every whit
as civilised as they were, 'who are, if that is anything, better born in
the sense that they have older traditions and older families'.[41] Was
Chamberlain reminding the colonials of their convict forebears? Could
a nation founded in convict transportation be regarded as civilised?

In his recent and controversial book *Ornamentalism*, David
Cannadine has sought to remind us of the complexity of colonial hierarchies, which were attuned to snobberies based on rank and status, as
well as racial and ethnic distinctions. To class-conscious British eyes,
he wrote, nineteenth-century settler colonies, such as those in Australia,
were full of 'the dross and detritus of the British metropolis: convicts
and their progeny ... poor rejects from the slums and back streets of
Birmingham and Glasgow; failed professionals in the law and the church
and the military'. Viewed as 'hicks and bumpkins and criminals', colonials
were, according to Cannadine, 'the white trash of their time'.[42] Or as
Ann Laura Stoler, in her work on the Netherlands East Indies, has
observed, white colonials were '*parvenus*', only 'fictive Europeans, somehow distinct from the real thing'.[43] Australians visiting Batavia had their
own reasons to doubt that Europeans there were 'the real thing', repeating

the British rumour that there was not one family of wholly Dutch descent, that 'the whole race is now riddled with the black element'.[44]

It was widely agreed, however, that the Japanese were a highly civilised and cultivated people, as the British reminded Australians in the debates over immigration restrictions:

> The Japanese belong to an empire whose standard of civilisation is so much higher than that of Kanakas, Negroes, Pacific Islanders, Indians, or other Eastern peoples, that to refer to them in the same terms cannot but be regarded in the light of a reproach, which is hardly warranted by the fact of the shade of the national complexion.[45]

They were also a powerful military force. Japan had emerged as a world power, proving its naval strength in its defeat of China in 1895. In this rapidly changing world, Attorney-General Deakin defended the government's decision to adopt the British suggestion of a dictation test.

To liken the Japanese to other coloured aliens was, he emphasised, understandably offensive to such a civilised, albeit 'high spirited' people:

> To lump all these peoples together as Asiatics and undesirables would naturally be offensive to a high spirited people like the Japanese, and surely, without any request from the British government or without representations from the Japanese people, mere considerations of courtesy, such as should exist between one civilised people and another, should lead us to make this distinction.[46]

In international relations, 'civilisation' could cancel out the effects of 'colour' or 'complexion', allowing the Japanese to be recast, in effect, as honorary white men.

Higgins, who advocated a new definition of civilisation based on the concept of the 'standard of living', would have none of it. He also admired the Japanese, he said, but it was their 'good qualities' that made them 'dangerous' to the white man:

> It is not their bad qualities, but their good qualities which make them dangerous to us. We frankly and openly say: 'You are thrifty, industrious, and you are willing to work from morning to night for the mere satisfaction of your physical wants, and for that reason we will not have you'. We frankly say that we want men with a higher standard of life, who will not be content with a low standard, or with low wages, but who are determined to get the best things the world can give them.[47]

In thus seeking to redefine the meaning of civilisation, Higgins also sought to cast doubt on Japanese claims to recognition as the equals of white men.

His reiteration of his preference for 'frank' and 'open' speaking also signalled his own identification as a 'white man' and his contempt for British unmanliness in their resort to subterfuge and duplicity – as instanced by their suggestion of the dictation test. To the colonial mind, the British were hypocrites, because while they claimed to disapprove of distinctions between peoples on racial grounds, they denied the rights of citizenship and self-government to their coloured subjects, notably in India. Alfred Deakin returned from a visit to India (whence he had journeyed to research irrigation schemes), deeply disturbed at the arrogance of the British administration and their 'almost contemptuous indifference' to the needs of the local population. Here was another lesson about the brutalising effects on whites of being served by a coloured servant class.[48]

The British, moreover, seemed to have no objection to the oppressions based on class that marked their own country. 'I am quite sure', said Higgins, 'that if any gentlemen, who form the Government of England, saw any chance of English slum children rubbing shoulders with their own children, they would soon take steps to stop it.' 'Slum children' were the unfortunate product of Old World class relations. In 1907, when required as president of the Commonwealth Court of Conciliation and Arbitration, to define a 'fair and reasonable' wage for the Australian worker, Higgins took the opportunity to define him as a 'civilised being' living in 'a civilised community'. Thus would New Protection secure the status of white Australian manhood in the New World.

Defending the living wage

In the 1920s, the idea that 'civilisation' required a man to be paid sufficient to maintain a wife and children came under challenge from feminists, who argued that such an arrangement kept women in dependent relations resembling 'serfdom' or 'slavery'.[49] Modern citizenship, they argued, required that all adults should enjoy a condition of independence as self-governing individuals. Men and women should be paid an income as individuals and the state should provide for the costs of maintaining children. Employers supported the challenge to the living wage for different reasons – they wanted to pay lower wages. The combined assault forced men to defend their higher wages, which they did before a Royal Commission appointed in 1927 by a Conservative government, to enquire into the desirability and feasibility of introducing a system of family endowment.

In defending their higher wage, men spoke of their needs, much as Justice Higgins had done in the Harvester judgement, but they became increasingly uneasy about articulating an identity defined in terms of need. For to be needy, to be defined by one's need, to be a person in need of care and assistance, was to be feminine or childlike or a native: it was not the condition of a white man. The living wage, they began to argue, was their right as men, a right that was understood to inhere not in their domestic needs or obligations, but in manhood itself. Men's 'needs' – their need of a wife, or a drink – had perforce to be translated into 'rights'. Such was the logic of the emerging concept of masculinity.

At the Royal Commission on Child Endowment or Family Allowances, appointed by the federal government in 1927, hundreds of witnesses from different occupations and classes, including the representatives of women's, employers', and labour organisations, came forward to make a case about the best way to organise the political economy and to distribute the national income.[50] Labor spokesmen represented the Australian Council of Trade Unions, several state branches of the Australian Labor Party, the Bricklayers' Union, the Builders' Laborers' Union, the Civil Service Association, the Clothing and Allied Trades Union, the Coal and Shale Employees' Federation, the Painters' Union, the State School Teachers' Union and the Trades and Labor Councils from New South Wales, Tasmania, Queensland, and South Australia.

Labor men found themselves on the defensive, forced to answer both employers and feminists, who proposed the dismantling of the living wage. Employers wanted to decrease their wages bill; feminists wanted the introduction of equal pay or the rate for the job, supplemented by a scheme of motherhood and childhood endowment paid from general revenue. According to feminists, mothers and children as well as workers, had a right to an individual income. As Lena Lynch, secretary of the Women's Central Organisng Committee of New South Wales told the Royal Commission, under the family wage regime 'women [were] not recognised as individuals at all, they are just appendages to men'.[51]

The Harvester judgment, in seeking to secure the power of white manhood by defining the worker as a 'civilised being ... living in a civilised community', had institutionalised a discourse on men's 'needs', which became crucial to their defence of higher wages, as employer representatives recognised. Thus T. R. Ashworth, president of the Victorian Employers' Federation told the Royal Commission: 'A fundamental weakness of compulsory arbitration is that it lends itself to wage distribution on the basis of needs, rather than deeds.'[52] In response to this charge, some Labor men replied that they would in fact prefer to be paid according to the work done – their deeds – rather than their needs. But they also assumed that men should be paid sufficient to support a dependent wife, while women in the workforce or at home should be paid a lesser, complementary, wage.

None of the Labor men who appeared in 1927 before the Royal Commission advocated the justice of raising women's wages; women were paid as women, men as men. Even a sympathetic witness such as David Davies, general secretary of the Australasian Coal and Shale Employees' Federation, took for granted that women would earn less than men, regardless of where they worked. Whether employed in a factory or office or at home caring for children, they should receive an income, albeit a lesser one. He explained his concept of the 'effective woman worker' to the Royal Commissioners:

> what I would say is that the ideal scheme, in my opinion, would be to fix a wage for an effective woman worker. In the event of her being married, she is worth so much per week to the nation, and she would carry that with her. She has only changed her occupation, but she is still working for the nation. If she is working in the home as a mother she is equally working for the nation and probably giving greater service than when she was sitting at the typewriter, or in the clothing factory or somewhere else. After she was married, I would recognize her social service to the community and she would carry the same wage as before. The husband would get his wage and each child who was born would get endowment.
> Q. How much is the single man's wage now? – A. 4.5.0.
> Q. How much is the single woman's basic wage? – A. Somewhere about 2.15.0.
> Q. Assuming that those figures are correct the married couple would get 7 a week? – A. That is what it should amount to.[53]

In his support of a separate, if lesser, wage for a wife working at home, Davies was in a minority in the labour movement, for although the Australian Council of Trade Unions and the Australian Labor Party supported the proposal for 'child endowment', they did not agree with the feminist proposal to render the wife independent of her husband through a scheme of 'motherhood endowment', that is an income paid directly to mothers by the state.

Although Labor men supported child endowment, they insisted that it should be paid by the federal government from general revenue on top of already existing wage levels. When asked about the contradiction in their position between supporting a 'family wage' for men in addition to a scheme of child endowment, most labour representatives simply said that the two issues should be treated separately. When pressed further on the matter, they conceded that although the introduction of child endowment might relieve industry of the responsibility for maintaining children, a man's wage must still provide for himself and his wife. For most of the witnesses this was the bottom line. A man needed a wife and had a right to a wage that supported a wife, as Sidney Bryan, representing the Queensland Trades and Labor Council made clear in the following exchange with the Royal Commission:

> Q. Have you considered whether a wife should be paid an allowance in respect of her services to the community? – A. No.
> Q. You do not suggest that any portion of the payment in the shape of wages by the employer or industry should be made to her in respect of her services? – A. We consider that the basic rate should be on a standard sufficient to maintain a man and his wife.
> Q. But it should be paid to him? – A. Yes.
> Q. You say that the basic rate should be sufficient to cover a man and his wife? – A. Yes.[54]

A working man needed a wife and there was no reason, according to Ernest Herbert Barker, general secretary of the Western Australian branch of the Australian Labor Party, why 'the wife should not be included as an obligation upon industry'.

> Q. Family endowment obviously includes a possible separate sum for the wife. We hear a lot about the immense services they render to the nation and our obligation to recognise them. Do you consider that the wife should be included in any possible endowment scheme? – A. No, for the simple reason that the wife is necessary to keep the husband working; if she does not do so the man cannot keep on working. There is no reason why the wife should be included as an obligation upon industry.
> Q. Why not include her and make a separate allocation for the wife? – A. For the reason that a man cannot work if he has not someone to look after him. In most instances it is the wife who does so, and she is just as necessary for the carrying on of industry as is the husband.
> Q. And therefore she should be paid? – A. She should be covered by industry under the wages paid to the man . . . The man has earned his money, and he is the person who should get it.[55]

Men should be paid for their 'deeds', but the wage should also be sufficient to meet their need for a wife, for she was necessary to 'look after him'. Uneasy about speaking their needs, Labor men re-defined the living wage as their right as men.

Men's right to domestic services was taken to be self-evident by Labor man and future Prime Minister John Curtin, who was one of the members of the Royal Commission. A single man required a higher wage as much as a married man, according to Curtin, because he had to pay for the domestic services provided 'gratuitously' by wives, 'that is to say the mending of his apparel, the cleaning of his room and house-keeping services which are not altogether to be met by his board'.[56] Others suggested that single men should be paid the higher wage because they had needs as 'potential husbands'. According to Thomas Howard, secretary of the United Trades and Labor Council in South Australia and vice-president of the South Australian branch of the Australian Labor Party, single men as 'potential husbands' worked to establish future households. As John Tosh has remarked of the influential Victorian domestic ideal, '*establishing* a household [was] a crucial stage in winning social recognition as an adult, fully masculine person'.[57] Witnesses often referred to single men's future domestic obligations of buying a house and furniture, however, because so many Australian men earning the living wage were, in fact, bachelors.

Men needed women to look after them, but when pressed about the proposal to replace the family wage paid to men with an individual wage, supplemented by a separate payment made to the wife, Ernest Barker turned need into masculine right, by referring to the situation of other (self-employed) men, such as doctors: 'If a doctor is called into my house to attend to me am I to be expected to pay him 10/6 and send the other 10/6 to his wife?'[58] Working men had to be treated with the same respect and accorded the same status as men of the employing class:

> Why should a single man working for wages have 10/6 taken off his income while the single employer has no such equivalent taken from him? . . . you have no more right to interfere with the income of a single man engaged in industry than you have to interfere with a single man who is not receiving wages.

'The man has earned his money', declared Barker,' and he is the person who should get it'.[59] Recognising that preserving the status of manhood necessitated treating all (white) men equally, Barker insisted that employees should be treated no differently from employers and single men should be paid the same wages as married men. The solidarity of white men was necessary to preserve their privilege as men.

Manhood entailed status, power and rights, but only white men were accorded the status of men. Continually asked about the proposal to take the portion of the family wage intended to maintain dependents and pay it to them separately, Barker declared: 'The single men of Australia would not stand it.' If the 483,175 adult men who were not heads of households, but in receipt of the family wage (on 'false pretences', feminists argued) were to have their wages reduced there would, warned Barker, be the 'utmost hostility, discontent and even open rebellion'.[60] The same observation was made by William Thomas, general secretary of the State School Teachers' Union of Western Australia: 'So independent of attitude is the Australian that if you attempted to take from him what he has been accustomed to receive and what is by no means a generous wage, I think you would have a rebellion.'[61] Men, including single men, had a right to the wage they earned, because they earned it as men, not as husbands or fathers.

Thus did the editor of the Sydney-based Australian Worker, H. E. Boote, strongly repudiate the idea that men's rights should be defined in terms of domestic need or obligation. He explained:

> I take the position that the remuneration of labour is a matter to be decided as between employers and employees, without any reference to the domestic condition of the latter, but in accordance with the value of the work they perform. A worker is not paid for producing children, but for producing wealth, or rendering other service to his employer. The living wage, when fixed to provide for the maintenance of a four or five unit family, does not indicate that employers are called upon to provide for the workers' children, as some have contended. It is simply a convenient method of formulating the standard of living that shall obtain in this country.[62]

Australian men – white men living in a civilised community – had a right to a decent standard of living, regardless of their family responsibilities, and in a further departure from the domestic model of manhood, Boote defiantly proposed that the single man needed a higher wage, because he set the 'standard of enjoyment' for the community:

> he has to help maintain the standard of enjoyment which is a very important aspect of this matter. A civilisation that does not provide its members with reasonable opportunities for enjoyment, is, in my opinion, built on a false basis; therefore the single man who sets the standard of enjoyment in this country is rendering a valuable service to the State . . .[63]

His assertion echoed the comment of a 'Westralian worker' reported in the local Labor paper as saying to a 'Jap standing outside a laundry': 'you don't get enough in a week to keep a white man in beer and tobacco for the same period'.[64] H. B. Higgins' list of items which the Australian worker could expect to purchase with his living wage, as outlined in the Harvester judgment, included alcoholic beverages and tobacco, as well as books and newspapers, union dues, life insurance, and tram or train fares. These were Australian men's 'demands on civilisation', the demands of men 'determined to get the best things the world can give them' as Higgins had told the federal parliament in 1901.[65]

The representatives of working men who presented themselves as witnesses to the Royal Commission advanced a variety of reasons for all men to be paid a higher wage, but they also supported the idea of child endowment. It is significant that they were prepared to hand over that aspect of men's traditional obligations, the obligation to support their children, to the state, but they would not forgo their right to support (and thus control) their wives. Men's rights included conjugal rights.

The Majority Report of the Royal Commission declined to recommend the introduction of any form of family endowment. Both the Majority and Minority Report argued explicitly against mother-hood endowment, for such a scheme would introduce 'a very powerful solvent' into 'family life as we know it'. The Minority Report, authored by Labor man John Curtin and feminist Mildred Musio, recommended the introduction of child endowment, but not motherhood endowment, because state payment for motherhood would 'revolutionize the organic unity of the family and involve a financial contract which the State would effect with wives and children in their individual right, apart from the husband and father'.[66] There would be no revolution in the family; white men's power was confirmed in their capacities as workers and actual or potential husbands. Their needs had been successfully trans-lated into rights, a triumph for their masculinity.

Conclusion

In white settler societies the 'white man' emerged as a figure defined explicitly in racialised, gendered and cultural terms. A discourse on 'civilisation' linked manliness to whiteness. In Australia, the meaning of white manhood in the early twentieth century was shaped in response to the legacy of complex colonial relations in which white settlers were positioned as both colonisers and colonials; they were beneficiaries of Aboriginal dispossession and assumed the right to govern the 'natives', yet at the same time they remained subordinate to and dependent on British imperial power. Granted the right of self-government in 1901, Australian white men were yet consumed by anxiety at the threat posed to their sovereignty – and to their manhood – by 'coloured aliens'.

When the living wage was institutionalised by H. B. Higgins in the Harvester judgment of 1907 it was justified in terms of the worker's 'needs' as an 'average employee' living in a 'civilised community'. By the late 1920s, when white working men were confronted by new challenges, from feminists and employers, who sought for different reasons to dismantle the family wage, the labor movement shaped a new political discourse which translated their 'needs' into 'rights', rights which, they argued, accrued to workers in their capacity as men.

As Gail Bederman has argued with regard to the United States, by the 1930s 'masculinity' had replaced 'manliness' as the aspiration of men across all classes and races. Whereas 'manliness' connoted an ethical code, celebrating such virtues as courage and candour, for example – 'masculine' referred to the characteristics, good and bad, of men as men and came to be associated particularly with the exercise of power. Crucially, 'masculinity' drew its meaning from the differentiation of men from women. This sense of polarity between the sexes was heightened by the 1930s Depression and the widespread perception that 'women were taking men's jobs'.[67]

It was now women workers, not coloured aliens, who were represented as invaders and usurpers, as the destroyers of men's manhood. Writing in the *Sydney Morning Herald* in 1934, one male critic of women's entry into the professions under 'feminism's shameless banner' proclaimed the doctrine of 'masculinism' to be Australia's only salvation.[68] The 'right to work' would henceforth be linked not to ideas of 'manliness', 'civilisation' or 'whiteness', but to the condition of masculinity, to men's power and status as men.

Notes

1 *Commonwealth Arbitration Reports*, 1907–8, vol. 11, ex parte H. V. McKay, pp. 3–4.
2 S. Macintyre, *A Concise History of Australia* (Melbourne, 1999), p. 151.
3 See, for example, E. Ryan and A. Conlon, *Gentle Invaders: Australian Women at Work 1788–1974* (Melbourne, reprint, 1989); P. Grimshaw, A. McGrath, M. Lake and M. Quartly, *Creating a Nation* (Melbourne, 2000, reprint).
4 G. Bederman, *Manliness and Civilisation: A Cultural History of Gender and Race in the United States 1880–1917* (Chicago, 1995), pp. 50–1, 214. See also G. K. Kaster, 'Labour's true man: Organised workingmen and the language of manliness in the USA, 1827–1877', *Gender & History*, 13:1 (April 2001), 24–64.
5 *Commonwealth Parliamentary Debates*, House of Representatives (hereafter CPD), 20 September 1901, pp. 5077, 5080.
6 Bederman, *Manliness and Civilization*, pp. 16–20; Macintyre, *Concise History of Australia*, ch. 4.

7 See, for example, M. Crotty, *Making the Australian Male Middle Class Masculinity 1970–1920* (Melbourne, 2001).
8 M. Kimmel, *Manhood in America: A Cultural History* (New York, 1996), pp. 7–8; see also M. Sinha, *Colonial Masculinity: The 'Manly Englishman' and the 'Effeminate Bengali' in the Late Nineteenth Century* (Manchester, 1995).
9 C. Hall, 'William Knibb and the constitution of the new Black subject', in M. Dauntin and R. Halpern (eds), *Empire and Others: British Encounters with Indigenous Peoples 1600–1850* (Philadelphia, 1999), p. 303.
10 CPD, 3 October 1901, p. 5571.
11 T. Roosevelt, *American Ideals and Other Essays* (London, 1897), p. 289.
12 Bederman, *Manliness and Civilisation*, pp. 170–5.
13 CPD, 12 September 1901, p. 4806.
14 *Ibid.*, 3 October 1901, pp. 6815–19.
15 *Ibid.*
16 *Ibid.*
17 *Ibid.*, 12 September 1901, p. 4806.
18 *Ibid.*, 6 September 1901, pp. 4634–5; 12 September 1901, p. 4805.
19 *Ibid.*, 12 September 1901, p. 4804.
20 S. Hall, 'Introduction: Who needs identity', in S. Hall and P. de Gay (eds), *Questions of Cultural Identity* (London, 1996, reprint 2002), p. 13.
21 See, for example, A. J. Yarwood and M. J. Knowling, *Race Relations in Australia: A History* (Melbourne, 1982); A. Markus, *Race Relations in Australia* (Sydney, 1994).
22 See, for example, V. Burgmann, 'Capital and labour: Responses to immigration in the nineteenth century', in P. Russell and R. White (eds), *Pastiche 1: Reflections on Nineteenth Century Australia* (Sydney, 1994).
23 C. H. Pearson, *National Life and Character: A Forecast* (London, 1894), p. 90.
24 Quoted by Barton in CPD, 7 August 1901, p. 3503.
25 J. Tregenza, *Professor of Democracy: The Life of Charles Henry Pearson, 1830–1894 Oxford Don and Australian Radical* (Melbourne, 1968), p. 231.
26 Quoted in *ibid.*
27 T. Roosevelt, 'National Life and Character', *Sewanee Review*, August 1894, reprinted in Roosevelt, *American Ideals and Other Essays*, p. 271.
28 T. G. Dyer, *Theodore Roosevelt and the Idea of Race* (Baton Rouge, 1980), pp. 144–5.
29 T. Roosevelt, 'National Life and Character', p. 274.
30 *Ibid.*, p. 273.
31 *Ibid.*, pp. 293–4.
32 Bederman, *Manliness and Civilization*, pp. 201–2.
33 Roosevelt, 'National Life and Character', pp. 290–1.
34 *Ibid.*, pp. 289–90.
35 Macintyre, *Concise History of Australia*, p. 150.
36 Quoted by Barton in CPD, 7 August 1901, p. 3503.
37 *Ibid.*, 12 September 1901, p. 4806.
38 *Ibid.*, 20 September 1901, p. 5073.
39 *Ibid.*, 20 September 1901, pp. 5066, 5070.
40 *Ibid.*, 20 September 1901, p. 5080.
41 *Western Australian Parliamentary Debates*, 1897, vol. 11, p. 423.

42 D. Cannadine, *Ornamentalism: How the British Saw Their Empire* (Oxford, 2001), pp. 124–5.

43 L. A. Stoler, *Race and the Education of Desire*, quoted in A. Woollacott, *To Try Her Fortune in London: Australian Women, Colonialism and Modernity* (New York and Oxford, 2001), p. 48.

44 D. Walker, *Anxious Nation: Australia and the Rise of Asia 1850–1939* (St Lucia, 1999), p. 186.

45 Cited in J. Bailey, *The White Divers of Broome: The True Story of a Fatal Experiment* (Sydney, 2001), p. 53.

46 CPD, 25 September 1901, p. 5136.

47 *Ibid.*, 20 September 1901, p. 5078.

48 Walker, *Anxious Nation*, p. 31.

49 M. Lake, *Getting Equal: The History of Australian Feminism* (Sydney, 1999), ch. 4.

50 For analysis of the feminist interventions at the Royal Commission see M. Lake, 'A revolution in the family? The challenge and contradictions of maternal citizenship', in S. Koven and S. Michel (eds), *Mothers of a New World: Maternalist Politics and the Origins of Welfare States* (New York, 1993).

51 'Royal Commission on Child Endowment and Family Allowances, Minutes of Evidence', *Australian Parliamentary Papers*, 1929, p. 923.

52 *Ibid.*, p. 819.

53 *Ibid.*, p. 976.

54 *Ibid.*, p. 83.

55 *Ibid.*, p. 348.

56 *Ibid.*, p. 915.

57 J. Tosh, *A Man's Place: Masculinity and the Middle Class Home in Victorian England* (New Haven, 1999), pp. 2–3.

58 Royal Commission on Child Endowment, Minutes of Evidence, p. 348.

59 *Ibid.*

60 *Ibid.*

61 *Ibid.*, p. 384.

62 *Ibid.*, p. 152.

63 *Ibid.*

64 *Westralian Worker* (26 October 1900), p. 6.

65 CPD, 20 September 1901, pp. 5078–9.

66 Royal Commission on Child Endowment and Family Allowances, Majority and Minority Reports, *Australian Parliamentary Papers*, 1929, p. 1392.

67 See M. Heagney, *Are Women Taking Men's Jobs?* (Melbourne, 1935), cited in M. Lake, *Getting Equal: The History of Feminism in Australia* (Sydney, 1999), pp. 178–80.

68 Lake, *Getting Equal*, p. 176.

12

Measures for masculinity: the American labor movement and welfare state policy during the Great Depression

Alice Kessler-Harris

ISTORIANS who have investigated how gender shapes the welfare state have paid a good deal of attention to the consequences of maternal claims, and the social movements organised around them. We now understand how such claims influenced the development of health insurance, protective labour legislation, mothers' pensions and aid to dependent children.[1] But we know less about claims made on behalf of manly ideals. In this piece, I suggest that ideas of gender may have a more subtle impact in shaping legislation than we have yet imagined. I argue that by constructing the imagination out of which the legislative agenda emerges, gender infuses the language with which individuals articulate demands for change. Notions of masculinity, I suggest, specifically influenced the nature of the US welfare state that emerged in the 1930s. Conceived in and through the American labor movement, images of masculinity governed the political possibilities and ultimately constrained the capacity of legislators to provide European-style benefits.

For most of the nineteenth century and the early part of the twentieth, American courts prohibited state intervention in the lives of individual workers. With the major exception of women and a few male workers on whom the public relied for its own safety and wellbeing (like railroad engineers), the federal government and most states had resolutely stayed out of the business of regulating the hours, working conditions, and wages of labour. Nor did the separate states provide much in the way of minimum standards for the health and wellbeing of any but women workers. Despite a good deal of pressure from socialist groups and reformers of various kinds, not until the 1930s did general labour legislation enable the US to join the ranks of the already-emerging welfare states of Europe. In what follows, I focus on how ideas about the relationship of manliness to democratic participation, which emerged in the late nineteenth-century American labor movement, helped to construct the framework within which an American welfare state could be imagined. The structure of these ideas influenced the fate of two important pieces of social legislation.

The influence of voluntarism

While many European industrial countries offered welfare benefits on the basis of residence or citizenship, the United States attached all of its most valuable benefits to wage work. Unemployment insurance and old age pensions, as well as private health insurance, emerged from the New Deal as the privileges of workers regularly employed in certain sectors of the economy. An emphasis on individual attachment to wage labour thus distinguishes the welfare policies of the US 1930s from those of most industrial countries. The pattern honoured the fears of organised labour which, weak as it was, sought to speak for all workers. In the late 1920s, organised labour represented only about 5 per cent of American workers, most of them skilled, white males. African-Americans belonged to a few mainstream unions like the United Mine Workers of America, and the Sleeping Car Porters' Union. If women organised at all, they joined unions in the garment, textile, and incipient electronics industries where the largest proportions of women workers concentrated. Still, the American Federation of Labor (AFL) was certainly the most powerful voice of workers, and when the depression of the 1930s inspired large numbers to organise, the AFL acquired a strong voice in labor legislation.

As represented by the American Federation of Labor, organised workers definitively did not want government intervention even when it seemed to be in their self-interest. Until the early 1930s, the AFL clung obdurately to the idea of voluntarism as it had been developed by its revered long-time leader Samuel Gompers. Voluntary organisation – the right of citizens to define and pursue their goals in free association – was both a call for action and a mantra for masculinity.

In the first guise, voluntarism embodied the economic self-interest of the trade union by assuring members that an investment in collective efforts would bring greater benefits and leave them less vulnerable than government intervention. Union strategy assumed that jobs were scarce resources to be distributed and protected by workers in defiance of employers' claims to control them. It invoked American ideals of individualism in defence of organisation and constructed solidaristic appeals to labor to preserve its collective self-interest in jobs without fear from, or benefit of, government intervention. Voluntarism presumed that wage earners had the courage, independence, and economic power, to protect their own interests. In the best of worlds, that included controlling the supply of labor in order to guarantee is price. Its advocates assumed that dignity – a man's dignity – resided in the capacity to do so.[2] Because it relied on the unified strength of skilled workers, partisans of voluntarism freely excluded those who might undermine labour's power, including the unskilled, most people of colour, and women.

In the second guise, voluntarism closely wove the liberty of members to pursue collective ends into a pattern that reflected manly identities. The labor movement marshalled words like courage, dignity, self-respect, and independence in defence of workers' liberty and freedom, associating them with manly conceptions of virility and economic power. It recognised that threats to liberty did not come only from clubs and rifles but from more subtle assaults on workers' conceptions of their own strength. And it found the idea of government regulations for male workers particularly threatening. Such regulation would inevitably privilege employers and undermine the manly character on which collective action rested, turning the worker into a cowardly and subservient creature forced to go hat-in-hand to the state for benefits. Fearful of the consequences, the AFL, under Samuel Gompers' leadership, consistently opposed even the most apparently beneficial interventions out of the fear that they 'would build up a bureaucracy that would have some degree of authority or control over all the workers of the state'.[3] It acquiesced reluctantly to workmen's compensation programs in the 1910s. But fear of government bureaucracy and administration led it to oppose reformers' efforts to introduce even such seemingly benign benefits as health insurance in the late 1910s.[4]

At the heart of voluntarism lay a uniquely American version of manhood. Closely tied to American faith in the possibilities of self-sufficiency and upward mobility for every individual, it was rooted in the notion that each worker could grow out of wage labor to become his own employer, by dint of skill and hard work. Those who gave up control over their own fate, workers who became deferential to bosses, who thought of themselves as servants rather than as equals, not only gave up a precious source of manhood, they stood to lose that liberty that made them equal citizens in a democratic polity. 'Socialistic' programs that created universal entitlements available to all American workers would inevitably rely on government planning and regulation, and so, in the view of many American trade unionists they threatened to undermine manhood by creating dependent and cringing males. In this respect, the stance of American workers differed from that of European labour movements which could comfortably support labor parties, ally themselves with many forms of social democracy, or encourage alliances between labor and social insurance advocates. Unlike some Europeans, who believed they could turn government to the purposes of male providers and their families, American labor leaders profoundly suspected government as the instrument of business and capital. As Samuel Gompers wrote: 'for the government to intervene would be wrong and harmful; wrong because such interference is destructive of personal (and inalienable) rights, harmful because it destroys initiative, independence, and self-reliance'.[5]

No equivalent inhibition guided the AFL's position on women's relationship to government. Many craft unionists supported special protective laws for women on the grounds that women could not organise effectively and that these laws protected male bargaining power and jobs. They shared with social feminists a commitment to maintaining male wages and believed, with them, that employers who took advantage of women's cheap labour would undermine the family-wage. AFL leaders acquiesced, as early as 1911, in plans to regulate the hours and wages of women and children in several states. By 1916, the Federation ardently supported them. Powerful voices saw labour legislation for women and children as a way of shoring up the family by discouraging employers from hiring women in the first place, while ensuring reasonable conditions for those who did enter the labor force. Regulating women's work also promised men less competition over jobs sustaining the solidarity and collective bargaining possibilities of men's unions. But unlike social feminists who often proclaimed labour legislation for women 'an entering wedge' that would ultimately lead to protection for all workers, the AFL's leaders continued to believe that labour laws would never do for men whose faith in collective bargaining embodied the manly force of working men's liberty. Yet both groups could agree on the central importance of family life and on male jobs to sustain it. Consensus on this issue may have enhanced the voice of a relatively weak AFL in national legislative councils.

Labor's goals

Ideals of manly liberty, never far from the labor movement's self-image, asserted themselves in campaigns for a shorter workweek, sought in the 1920s by many as a strategy for reducing unemployment. Acquired through collective bargaining, shorter working hours reflected the power of American labor. Achieved by legislation, however, they seemed to many to be a source of weakness. Legislative processes, labor leaders argued, never had and never would achieve progress for the labor movement. Instead, they invoked 'the great mass of workers' who had 'progressed successively from twelve to ten hours, then to eight hours, and in many instances, to forty-four or forty hours weekly through the power of their economic organizations.'[6] Some of labor's number disagreed. 'We have come to a point in the history of labor', argued one delegate to a 1932 convention of the Federation, 'when we must of necessity change our previous attitude and opinion of regulation of hours of labor by legislation ... I am not afraid of the United States government; it is bad enough, but it is not as bad as having 11,000,000 men walking the streets looking for work.'[7] Still, the convention roundly rejected a resolution to support a twentieth amendment to the US constitution mandating a thirty-hour workweek.

In the Federation's discussions, fear of the legislative quick fix prevailed. 'Do you know what it would mean to give this power to the Government to rule the hours of labor?' asked Andrew Furuseth of the Seamen's Union. 'How do you know that you will not get twelve hours instead of four hours?'[8] Thomas Donnelly of the Ohio State Federation of Labor pitched in: 'You attempt to fix the hours of labor for the working people of America, and just as soon as you do you take away from the adult worker his fundamental inherent right to work one hour, two hours, six hours or eight hours?'[9] AFL president William Green agreed. While he remained convinced that only shorter hours could permanently end unemployment, he wanted the labor movement to negotiate them. Anything less threatened labor's manly honour. 'It will ultimately rest upon labor to utilize its economic strength in a constructive and practical way in order to secure this great change', he roared to a standing ovation of union delegates.[10]

But the pressure on labor to change its stance escalated in the winter of 1932–33 when two members of Congress, Senator Hugo Black of Alabama and Representative William Connery of Massachusetts, introduced twin bills to forbid the shipment in interstate commerce of goods produced in any facility where 'any worker was permitted to work more than five days in any week or more than six hours in any day'.[11] With its ranks disrupted, its position as spokesperson for working people in question, and its own economic-self interest at stake, the AFL reluctantly shifted gears and supported the bill. Even as it did so, its leaders feared for the future of manly liberty. 'Personally', John Frey, told the Senate hearing called to consider the bills, 'I have always been opposed ... to regulating the terms of employment for adult males through legislation. I have believed', he went on, 'that free men should work out their problems instead of having the legislature endeavour to do for men what they were capable of doing for themselves; but I have reached the conclusion now we are in a position where men are not capable of doing these things unless Congress says.'[12]

Philip Murray, then a vice president of the United Mine Workers, picked up the theme. He was driven to support the bill, he said, by the need to 'sustain character' among those who would otherwise be idle. 'Men', he told the Committee 'want to keep their economic independence. They do not want to become objects of charity . . . they seek to maintain their relations as normal citizens toward society.'[13] Could they do that if they relied on government intervention? For many labor leaders confusion over a shorter hours bill reflected the distress of a complicated effort to solve the practical problem of unemployment while defending their vision of manhood as the last bastion of freedom and liberty.[14]

Energised by the optimism around President Franklin Delano Roosevelt's inauguration, hopeful that the wages issue could be resolved, in March 1933 its sponsors reintroduced a new bill to shorten the hours of labor. By early April, the bill had made its way through the Senate.[15] With Labor's reluctant backing and the issue of unemployment staring the administration in the face, shorter hours seemed like a popular and ready-made solution. Speaking for Roosevelt, Secretary of Labor Frances Perkins publicly accepted the principle of reducing unemployment by reducing hours, but insisted on making the bill 'more flexible and workable'.[16] In an act calculated to raise the worst fears of labor leaders, she proposed a three-member board empowered to 'license' a six-hour day in industries that met minimal requirements; minimum wages established by boards to determine appropriate wages in each industrial sector; enough flexibility to extend the thirty-hour limit to forty in some industries; and a relaxation of anti-trust laws where a thirty-hour week was imposed. This was everything that labor detested: a bureaucracy that could exercise discretionary powers over men's freedoms; loss of control over wages; untrammelled influence for industry. Fearing entrapment, the AFL withdrew its support, and the bill went down to defeat.

Would the bill have met such a precipitous end if labor had compromised over the imposition of bureaucracy, had its manhood not been offended by the very idea of a regulated wage? What if labor had swallowed its concern for voluntarism and exercised the power of a countervailing force? Would Congress have overcome business' objections to a rigid thirty-hour provision? We have of course no way of knowing. The AFL continued to make a reduced workweek the keystone of its collective-bargaining demands until the passage of the Fair Labor Standards Act in 1938 mandated a forty-hour workweek for most workers. Yet its continuing commitment to the manly qualities encoded in voluntarism restrained its enthusiasm for legislative regulation of hours. Though passage of a thirty-hours bill was never a foregone conclusion, once the proposal no longer fit the gendered imagination of a skittish labor movement, it became less likely.

Unemployment insurance

As it turned out, the struggle over a legislated thirty-hour workweek was a skirmish in the ensuing campaign for unemployment insurance. By the 1930s, unemployment insurance should have been an idea whose time had come and there were many advocates for a comprehensive and rational system. At one end of the political spectrum, socialists, communists, and radicals of every variety folded unemployment compensation into wide-ranging proposals to eliminate economic inequality and provide generous government support for the young, the aged, and the ill as well as the unemployed. At the other end, conservative voices of small business insisted that the federal government keep its hands off. Between these extremes lay more moderate groups whose members searched for stability and social justice within a business-oriented framework. Two proved particularly important in setting the tone of public conversations and in the policy debates within the subcommittees of the Committee on Economic Security (CES). The first consisted of reform-minded advocates of social insurance, many of them deeply influenced by European style programs; the second included proponents of employment stabilisation through the cooperative action of government, business and labor.[17]

The social insurance model had a good deal of support from ordinary workers as well as from social reformers of all kinds. Championed in the US by two somewhat controversial figures, Abraham Epstein and Isaac Rubinow, it took several different legislative forms. All of them offered to create a pooled fund from a combination of employer contributions and general tax revenues that would provide a minimum income to everyone who could not earn wages for reasons of sickness, disability, unemployment, or old age. The plans differed as to the level of income they offered and at least one offered maternity insurance for women workers; but they agreed on coverage for all workers, including the self-employed, farmers, professional workers, and wage earners.

AFL leaders quickly rejected the social insurance model, noting that it subjected all individuals equally to potential government supervision and control, and therefore suggested the helplessness of union members. The Federation's leaders sought a programme to which workers would be entitled by 'right' – whose benefits wage workers would have earned by virtue of their commitments to their jobs – rather than one that smacked to them of government charity or relief. So leaders threw their lot on the side of those who aimed for employment stabilisation.

In the US, John Commons had early conceived and campaigned for such programs. Commons was, in 1934, recently retired from teaching at the University of Wisconsin. His *Institutional Economics* had just been published, and the third volume of his *History of Labor in the United States* was about to go to press. In these books, he elaborated his notions of the economic institutions that sustained a democratic capitalism. Most forcefully, he advocated the notion that workers, like capitalists were 'citizens of industry', each with a stake in prosperity.[18] Industry's part of this compact was to provide employment: to stabilise work and ensure its availability. Commons believed that large employers should shoulder the responsibility for seasonal and technological employment fluctuations, arguing with most of his fellow-economists, that poor business practices caused most unemployment. Given adequate incentives, employers could, and should, be able to prevent it.[19] Commons conceived the right to work as essential to the exercise of citizenship, for, as he wrote early in his career, 'the right to work is the right of access to the land, the machinery, the capital, whose products support life and liberty'. And, 'the rights of liberty and property are the conditions on which personal character and responsibility are based'.[20] To this end he supported the collective individualism of the AFL, with its deep commitment to liberty earned through the manly freedom to work.

In practice Commons' ideas translated into a narrowly based unemployment insurance program rooted entirely in contributions from employers and therefore either directly or indirectly from workers' wages. He restricted his plan to large employers (those who could stabilise industry) and to regular workers (neither temporary nor part time), whose maintenance in the labor force would sustain industrial production as economic cycles changed. By charging firms with good records less than those that frequently laid off their employees, a practice known as experience rating, he hoped to discourage layoffs. And by paying workers benefits that lasted no longer than several weeks – the expected duration of a brief economic downturn – Commons promoted the rights of workers to retain particular jobs. Advocates of the Commons' point of view disagreed as to whether the funds contributed by employers should be controlled by industry or by state agencies, about the level of the unemployment stipend and the length of time it should be offered. But they firmly to agreed on the kinds of industries to be covered, and the need to exclude part time workers, and those, like women, who were only 'marginally' attached to the labor force.

For the AFL, what appeared to be a choice of technical solutions to a serious economic problem, represented far larger conceptions of who was and was not a man, and how the dignity and freedom of workers were to be preserved. As might have been expected, leaders objected vehemently to the demand that workers be required to contribute that constituted a feature of one such model.[21] They protested the inclusion of business in economic planning, the self-policing of employers, and the role of government intervention. These raised the threat posed by bureaucracy to manhood. Aiming at the idea of joint contributions, they asked why employers, who had created the unemployment problem, should be able to get off scot-free (they would after all pass costs on to consumers) while workers suffered from reduced wages? They objected to the helplessness of workers placed in this situation. But they supported the lesser reliance on the good will of employers in which the Commons based models were rooted, and the notion that every worker laid off through no fault of his own deserved to be paid. Even as they applauded the idea of pooled funds they protested the likelihood that government would collude with a coercive employer to exercise 'leverage over the employment term'.[22]

In distinguishing what kinds of wage work would promote eligibility for unemployment insurance and tying rights to particular patterns of labor force participation, the Commons' based programs conceptualised participation in ways that discounted the lives of the vast majority of African-Americans, members of other minority groups, and most women. If this was obscured with regard to African-Americans by a rhetoric that paid obeisance to the responsibility of industry and the rights of states, it was crystalline with regard to women. Only relatively large producing industries (where most women of any colour, and most African-Americans did not work) could conceivably regularise work or develop the individual insurance fund necessary to provide even minimal compensation. Only workers who remained in the labor force for lengthy periods could reap benefits. The idea of regularising work reflected a notion of rights to work that explicitly excluded women who were not providers, and tacitly dismissed all women as actually or potentially married. The employment stability plans thus promised to extend new citizenship rights to men, in particular (largely white) labour-force sectors, while denying them to other men, and to virtually all women in the labour force.

Still, even as the representatives of African-American organisations levelled sharp criticisms at the exclusions embedded in these proposals, most women did not challenge their exclusionary biases. Even when the Commons' plan became the bases for conversations within the CES, and ultimately the root of the unemployment compensation system adopted by Congress, women remained silent. Informed by popular beliefs about the significance of marriage in the lives of ordinary wage-earning women, most maternalists pursued social policies designed to reinforce women's continuing family roles. Instead of fighting for women's rights to work, they successfully placed motherhood at the centre of the legislative agenda for women workers, and encouraged and sustained prevailing conceptions of women's working lives as adjuncts to the family. Perhaps we should not fault them. For they acted on definitions of family developed through fights for protective labour legislation and won, in consequence, means-tested plans that would enable poor women to care for children without wage-work. Their relative failure to address work-related issues not only left the sphere of wage-work to men, but, arguably, allowed greater scope for the AFL's concern for manly liberty.

To be sure, maternalist and trade union leaders shared with other social activists a commitment to male providerhood, but they deeply disagreed over whether a government responsibility for male's economic functions would not undermine the self-respect and independence that defined manliness. While maternalists placed great faith in government's capacity to shore up the family, the AFL remained committed to the idea of manly independence. In support of this idea, successive AFL conventions had voted against government unemployment insurance, while supporting private union-employer plans and a negotiated thirty-hour week. What seemed like simple justice to many, felt to labor like an attack. 'You can't have unemployment insurance', declared President William Green, 'without agreeing to a set-up that will, to a large degree, govern and control our activities ... then you must be willing to give up some of the things you now possess. You can't have an unemployment insurance plan without registration. You must report, you must subject yourself in every way to the control of the law.'[23]

The AFL was no monolith, and pressure from several state federations and local and international unions led the AFL to reconsider its position beginning in 1929. Several years of long and heated disputes within AFL councils and on the convention floor followed. Opponents decried handouts from government and protested cowardly submission to state authority. Did American workers, asked a member of the 1930s Executive Council, echoing the language of the courts that justified protective labor legislation for women, want to follow the pattern of European schemes 'under which the worker becomes a ward of the state and subject to discipline by employers under state authority?'[24] In his view, unemployment insurance challenged the AFL to decide whether it should 'continue to hew to the line in demanding a greater freedom for the working people of America, or whether liberty shall be sacrificed in a degree sufficient to enable the workers to obtain a small measure of unemployment relief under government supervision and control'.[25]

At issue were some of the same things that had emerged in the labor movement's attack on shorter hours. First the creation of state bureaucracies that, as Gompers had put it, would undermine the principle of voluntarism by making 'the means for life and thus liberty dependent on government supervision of the conditions of leaving employment'.[26] Second, the construction of a fearful administrative apparatus. 'Every system', argued the Executive Council in a report that rejected the idea, 'contemplates supervision and control by both federal and state governments and will require registration, not only of the aliens among the workers, but of all workers.' And finally, the power it provided employers even over the jobless. Any compulsory unemployment insurance program, insisted AFL Vice President Mathew Woll, would remind a worker constantly 'that his employer holds what in effect amounts to at least a temporary veto power over his right to benefits when unemployed'. This would, he argued, inevitably increase the power of the employer and lead to 'a virtual surrender on the part of the workers . . . of their right to organize . . . Shall we be content to carry industrial passports because they have a government label?'[27]

Enmeshed in the fear of structures they could not influence or control, AFL leaders offered up a conception of liberty demanding defence by courageous men. Throwing down the gauntlet to the cowards among them who would place their faith in the false promises of government authority, Woll demanded to know if members had 'lost courage to the point where we regard freedom no longer as the greatest essential of life and the most necessary element in human progress?'[28] Nor did he shrink from religious symbolism: 'In return for a slice of bread – a mess of pottage, as it were – the workers are being asked ... to yield up their birthright, to practically surrender in their struggle for liberty.'[29] In this struggle over liberty, family support and personal well-being alike would take second place: 'Have we come to that position in our labor movement', asked Vice President Olander incredulously 'that we are about to say that one of the most precious liberties we have ... must be surrendered forsooth, because our people are hungry and they must eat?'[30]

To combat this strong language, supporters of unemployment insurance constructed an alternative conception of manhood. James Duncan, of Seattle's Central Labor Council, tried his hand at creating one. Invoking William Green's presidential address which had demanded a new right, 'the right of men to work', he insisted that if the government denied 'us the right to work' it 'must at least provide some means of feeding our families while we are waiting for the opportunity to work'.[31] Unemployment insurance, he suggested, far from degrading a man, would give him 'a chance to stand up and say, "No, I will not go in and work for less than my fellows get. I at least will not starve to death." '[32] Against the Executive Council's defence of freedom, liberty, and independence, Duncan, making common cause with social reformers, invoked a different form of manliness: solidarity with fellow workers and family provision. 'I want men to get the sustenance from somewhere so that they can stand up like real men and say, "No I am getting enough to get by on. I don't have to undermine my fellows, I will stick to my unemployment insurance until I can go to work with my fellows and maintain my self-respect." '[33] And Philip Ickler, of the Pensacola, Florida, Central Labor Council, offered yet another justification for the manliness of unemployment insurance. 'I don't believe', he argued, that 'we are making beggars out of all who need it ... it furnishes at least a little help to keep our fellow workers in the militant fighting spirit.'[34]

Would unemployment insurance contribute to beggary or fend it off? Some of the same labor leaders who had enthusiastically promoted legislation on behalf of women could not contemplate its negative consequences for manly independence. Andrew Furuseth of the Seamen's Union is a good example. Friend of Supreme Court Justice Louis Brandeis and enthusiastic supporter of special laws for women, Furuseth mounted a last-ditch resistance to unemployment insurance. After the 1932 convention finally accepted the idea, he rose to articulate what he called his unalterable opposition. No such law, he declared, had been enacted 'as will retain the working man his independence and courage ... I think you are making a mistake, men ... I can't stop you, but the road you are travelling is the road that leads to the destruction of humanity and the destruction of this nation and of all other nations that can find no other way than to make out of a man a pleading beggar and a man who must go for his goods to others.'[35]

By the time Furuseth spoke, the Executive Council had acted. Overwhelmed by pressure to combat existing unemployment, it reversed its position in November 1932, and persuaded William Green to reverse his. While it decried the continuing economic crisis, and once again repeated its conviction that a thirty-hour week would provide the surest solution to unemployment, it offered the convention an industry-funded plan that it thought it could live with.[36] In withdrawal, President Green tacitly aligned himself with the Commons' proposals. 'If compulsory unemployment insurance is forced upon our industrial, political and economic life, it will be because industrial ownership and management has failed to provide and preserve these opportunities for working men and women', he told convention delegates.[37] Workers, the Executive Council affirmed, 'are as much entitled to work security, to enjoy the opportunity to work, as the owner of capital are to returns from their investments'. Industry's failure should be charged to it by the imposition of compulsory unemployment insurance, paid for by employers alone. It should be 'clearly recognised as a legal right earned by previous employment within the state'.[38]

But no one was completely happy with this solution, and the Executive Council continued to be wary that the 'right' contained in unemployment insurance be absolute insisting, for example that drawing on unemployment insurance not infringe on rights of suffrage, or on other civil rights.[39] This would be a new, an added, an 'earned' right. 'We are going to propose and insist', Green told the AFL's leaders in the fall of 1934, 'that Congress and the State legislatures enact unemployment insurance legislation, old age pension legislation, the abolition of child labor, and the development here of a social order that will make for the highest degree of citizenship.'[40] The gesture meant little. By then, the President had already convened the CES to draft a social security program, and its staff and technical committees were hard at work. William Green, who had a seat on the Advisory Council, remained a largely silent member, leading executive director Edwin Witte to dismiss labor's role in the formulation of the final Act. It was not, he wrote later, 'a major player'.[41] But Witte was wrong. As much as anyone, the labor movement had set the terms within which the debate would be conducted.

On the table before the Committee on Economic Security in the autumn of 1934 was a proposal for a federal tax on payrolls, 90 per cent of which would be forgiven (or offset) for employers who contributed to either their own state-supervised reserve accounts or to state-wide pooled accounts. The offset, which removed the federal government from a direct relationship to the recipients of unemployment compensation, was meant to avoid questions of constitutionality; it also provided each of the forty-eight states with maximum discretion to develop whatever unemployment insurance program they wished. Employers' contributions were to vary with the employment records of the employer: those with stable work-forces would pay less. Everything else, including the level of benefits, possible employee contributions, and eligibility for coverage would be determined by the states. It was not a bill that labor could like very much for it left the states (and their most powerful employers) huge discretion. Yet Green reluctantly testified in favor of it when it was presented to Congress in the spring of 1934. 'We believe', he told the assembled legislators, 'a man will retain his independence and his manhood better if he is permitted to earn a living. In the absence of jobs we are inevitably forced to this position.'[42] The AFL continued to support it half-heartedly when a modified version entered the Social Security bill.

Organised labor, which disliked the flexible provisions that emerged, had little choice but to ally itself with the CES plan. The AFL had backed itself into a corner. Equally suspicious of state bureaucracies and legislatures, and of employer influence, uncertain whether unemployment insurance would cool workers' loyalties to their trade unions, Green had failed to take a strong stand either in the Council of the CES or before Congress.[43] Green would have preferred, he told the Senate Finance Committee, a plan that filtered contributions through the federal government in order that one entity could more readily impose standards for eligibility and benefits; he deplored the possibility of individual reserve accounts which failed to provide workers with security; he hoped no state would exact contributions of workers; he thought the payroll tax could easily be raised from 3 to 5 per cent so that a more generous benefit might be paid. Most especially, he wanted to ensure benefits sufficiently high to guarantee that labor could maintain its purchasing power.[44]

Though the AFL would have preferred to give vastly less discretion to the states (and might have allied itself with African-Americans to this end) its commitment to voluntarism bound it to a contributory programme. It did not believe employers could or would, given incentives, prevent unemployment. But it liked the idea that benefits were offered to workers in light of the contributions of their employers, and therefore available as of 'right'. It was more willing to hazard the risks of individual reserves than to fund a program with general revenues that might threaten to dilute the relationship of benefits to contributions and undermine male independence. If unemployment benefits were inevitable, they must be tied to employers' contributions. Everything else was secondary, including what the leadership quickly recognised as the unfortunate consequence of legislative discretion in excluding awkward categories of workers.

Conclusion

Labor had given up a lot to get benefits that sustained male dignity, available as a matter of right, without administrative or bureaucratic discretion. Bounded by a conception of unemployment insurance largely designed to provide incentives for employers to 'regularise' employment, the issue of who was appropriately defined as a 'worker' assumed paramount importance. Gender was a major constituent in that definition. At every turn it emerged as a dynamic agent. It participated in the initial conception of which jobs should be 'regularised' and which not. Its hand was strengthened by the issues of voluntarism prominent in the labor movement where notions of masculinity fostered suspicion of government intervention of every kind. It was sustained and enhanced by the attitudes of women reformers whose shared sense of the nature of breadwinning for the family blinded them to possibilities for supporting women's wage-work. And gendered understandings fuelled continuing contention over which workers constituted the regular labor force and therefore deserved to be covered by unemployment insurance and whether female workers with husbands should be considered available for work. Ambiguity over these issues lent discretion to the various state unemployment commissions that continued to debate them and in the end contributed to undermining the labor movement's desire for nationwide uniform regulations.

But by holding out for an insurance program that held employers responsible for funding benefits payable to regular workers without means-testing and without questions, the labor movement had preserved its image of masculinity. Its leaders could successfully argue that employers could exercise no discretion as to who got benefits, and trade union members could hold their heads up as they collected what was due them by right. If many were excluded from this and other welfare programmes because they lacked manly attributes, still the new American programmes preserved the ideology of the sturdy male provider whose benefits were due him because he had consistently done his bit, and they protected the families most likely to be within the union framework. And who is to say that the labor movement was alone in undermining a broader social insurance programme that might well have laid the foundation of a more generous welfare state?

Notes

1 These policies have sometimes been identified as the products of a two-channel state that assigned most women and men of colour to means-tested policies. See, for example, B. J. Nelson, 'The origins of the two-channel welfare state: Workmen's compensation and mothers' aid', in L. Gordon (ed.), *Women, the State and Welfare* (Madison WI, 1990), pp. 123–51; G. Mink, *The Wages of Motherhood: Inequality in the Welfare State, 1917–1942* (Ithaca, 1995). They were also the product of shared assumptions about wage-work, as is argued by L. Gordon, *Pitied but not Entitled: Single Mothers and the History of Welfare, 1890–1935* (New York, 1994); see as well, J. Goodwin, *Gender and the Politics of Welfare Reform: Mothers' Pensions in Chicago, 1911–1929* (Chicago, 1997); T. Skocpol, *Protecting Soldiers and Mothers: The Political Origins of Social Policy in the United States* (Cambridge MA, 1992).

2 On the history of voluntarism in the 1930s, see G. Gilmary Higgins, *Voluntarism in Organized Labor in the United States, 1930–1940* (New York, 1969, reprint of 1944 edn).

3 S. Gompers, 'Labor vs. its barnacles', *American Federationist*, 23 (April 1916), 270.

4 B. Hoffman, *Health Insurance and the Making of the American Welfare State: 1915–1920* (Chapel Hill NC, 1999); P. Brito, 'Protective labor legislation in Ohio: The interwar years', *Ohio History*, 88 (Spring 1979), 178–97.

5 L. Reed, *The Labor Philosophy of Samuel Gompers* (New York, 1930), p. 126.

6 *Report of the Proceedings of the 52nd Annual Convention of the American Federation of Labor* (Cincinnati, 1932), p. 245.

7 *Ibid.*, pp. 245–6

8 *Ibid.*, p. 246.

9 *Ibid.*, p. 246. The general discussion is on pp. 244–7. The quotes are on pp. 246–7. The comment of Andrew Furuseth continued: 'I cannot see any reason why we should follow some of the mad ideas of Europe when they set out from an entirely different point of view in dealing with governmental and social questions than we do', p. 246.

10 *Ibid.*, pp. 292–3. Also see D. R. Roediger and P. S. Foner, *Our Own Time: A History of American Labor and the Working Day* (New York, 1989), pp. 246–7.

11 Legislation quote from US Congress, 'Thirty-Hour Work Week', *Hearings before a Subcommittee of the Committee on the Judiciary, 72nd Congress* (Washington DC, 1933), 2d Session, p. 1. I found this story in S. Vittoz, *New Deal Labor Policy and the American Industrial Economy* (Chapel Hill NC, 1987), 83–5.

12 'Thirty-Hour Work Week', p. 426.

13 *Ibid.* He continued: 'During a depression, who can estimate the number of people who have become reconciled to charity, professional pensioners on the public bounty or professional hobos and criminals?'

14 This sense was fuelled by the fact that some of the same people who sought a thirty-hour week to expand employment and maintain citizenship attacked the rights of married women to work. Rank and filer Louis Draudt wrote William Green he thought it would be a 'God-send' if the AFL could 'get a 30 hour week for all wage-earners'. He then urged 'a national law passed eliminating all married women working where their husbands are working'. George Meany Memorial Archives, AFL-CIO papers, RG21, Box 44, file 46, Louis Draudt to William Green, 16 October 1933.

15 For more on the larger debate, see B. Kline Hunnicutt, *Work Without End: Abandoning Shorter Hours for the Right to Work* (Philadelphia, 1988), p. 154, and discussion, pp. 153–63. For the following discussion, see G. Farr, *Origins of Recent Labor Policy* (Boulder, 1959), pp. 63–4, 99–101.

16 'President Limits 30-Hour Week Bill', *New York Times* (13 April 1933), p. 2; Hunicutt, *Work Without End*, p. 153.

17 These two groups are frequently conflated under the 'social insurance' rubric in order to distinguish their proposals from those of the champions of assistance to the needy. See for example, L. Gordon, 'Social insurance and public assistance: The influence of gender and welfare thought in the United States, 1890–1935', *American Historical Review*, 97 (February 1992), 19–54. Despite their overlapping concerns, I have sharpened the distinctions for the purposes of examining the sources of the employment legislation.

18 J. R. Commons, *History of Labor in the United States*, vol. 3 (New York, 1935), xix.

19 Commons, *History of Labor in the United States*, p. xxvii.

20 J. R. Commons, 'The right to work', *The Arena*, XXI (February 1899), 134.

21 R. Lubove, *The Struggle for Social Security, 1900–1935* (Cambridge, 1968), p. 172; and D. Nelson, *Unemployment Insurance: The American Experience, 1915–1935* (Madison, 1969), 152ff. Within a year, by January of 1934, the plan had been considered by the legislatures of seventeen states. It would soon be adopted not only by Ohio, but, in modified version by New York.

22 Quoted in K. Casebeer, 'The workers' unemployment insurance bill: American social wage, labor organization, and legal ideology', in C. Tomlins and A. King (eds), *Labor Law in America: Historical and Critical Essays* (Baltimore, 1992), p. 232.

23 *Report of the Proceedings of the 51st Annual Convention of the American Federation of Labor* (Vancouver BC, 1931), p. 397.

24 *Ibid.*, p. 370.

25 *Ibid.*, p. 369.

26 Quoted in Casebeer, 'The Worker's Unemployment Insurance Bill', p. 232; this is of course exactly what protective labor legislation did to women. Gompers continued, 'The whole of our activity organized to assert and to live our own lives would be subject to every petty or high official . . . according to the government's conception of what is and what is not voluntary employment.'

27 *Proceedings of the AFL* (1931), p. 369.

28 *Ibid.*, p. 369.

29 *Ibid.*, p. 369.
30 *Ibid.*, p. 394.
31 *Ibid.*, p. 372.
32 *Ibid.*, p. 373.
33 *Ibid.*, p. 374; Quoted in Casebeer, 'The workers' unemployment insurance bill', pp. 236–7. Cf. also Florence Hanson, Teachers Union, who states: 'I believe … unemployment insurance will increase the freedom of the worker and his self-respect, and that unemployment insurance will be of great strength to trade unionists', *Proceedings of the AFL* (1931), p. 383.
34 *Ibid.*, (1932), p. 339.
35 *Ibid.*, p. 336.
36 *Ibid.*, pp. 40–1.
37 *Ibid.*, p. 346.
38 *Ibid.*, pp. 39, 43.
39 *Ibid.*, p. 43.
40 *Ibid.* (1934), p. 10.
41 E. Witte, 'Organized labor and social security', in M. Derber and E. Young (eds), *Labor and the New Deal* (Madison WI, 1961), pp. 252–3.
42 William Green testimony at US Congress, 'Ways and Means on H. R. 7659', *Hearings before a Subcommittee of the House Committee on, 73rd Congress,* (Washington DC, 1934), 2nd session, March 24, p. 256.
43 J. Douglas Brown, interview by Peter Corning, recalls a conversation with Green during which Green told him 'we will go along with you on joint contributions for old age insurance, but we will not make contributions to the unemployment insurance'. Columbia Oral History Collection, 4, J. Douglas Brown interview by Peter Corning, 5 February 1965.
44 US Congress, 'On S. 1130, Economic Security Act', *Hearings Before the Senate Committee on Finance, 74th Congress* (Washington DC, 1935), 1st session, January 22 to February 20, p. 167–73. Green had remained a reluctant supporter until the very end – a reluctance that undermined his influence. For example in the Wagner–Lewis hearings the year before (pp. 256–7), he testified to his wish that such unemployment insurance were not necessary, but that he would support it in order to protect the purchasing power of families. 'We have always believed that it would be far better for our social and economic order if employment could be furnished workers so that they could earn their living as decent, upstanding American citizens. We prefer that.' The male content of both work and citizenship is apparent as the statement continues: 'We believe a man will maintain his independence and his manhood better if he is permitted to earn a living, but we have found from experience that we have not yet mastered our economic forces, so that we can maintain an economic order which will guarantee and grant to the workers of this country even limited opportunities to earn a living.'

13

Masculinities, nations, and the new world order:
peacemaking and nationality in Britain, France,
and the United States after the First World War

Glenda Sluga

T HE landscape of the peacemaking processes that end wars is as
littered with men and the spectre of masculinity as are the battlefields and strategic centres of war itself, yet the history of peacemaking has only an anomalous place in the literature on gender and
war. As Andrew Williams has argued in the context of the end of the
First World War, war and peacemaking are together critical nodes of
the cultural history of politics. Just as 'the "canon" of war has been a
constant factor in defining and redefining our collective identities as
national groupings and in our definition of what we mean by "civilisation"', it played a critical background role in the way that those planning
a new world order 'saw their primary task, the taming or abolition of
war'.[1] We can add that just as gender is crucial to understanding the
canon of war, it is a critical aspect of the history of peacemaking,
the conceptualisation of post-war orders, and the definition of national
and collective identities. What is significant about peacemaking and
the 'new world order' that defined post-war aims among the victor
states in 1919, are the intersections between national and collective
identities and the overlapping histories of conceptions of masculine
and feminine selves.

Before the First World War had even ended, Britain, France,
and the United States made clear their intentions to effect a new world
order organised around the idea of national self-determination.[2] While
the war had encouraged a notion of citizenship rooted in martial duty –
to the extent that some women too argued for their rights as citizens on
the basis of their wartime contribution to national defence – national
self-determination resonated the Enlightenment political and philosophical ideal of the autonomous self-determining subject. The status of
national self-determination in the process of peacemaking relied too
upon a late nineteenth-century conception of self-determination as

the inevitable goal for peoples who had achieved consciousness of their national selves. Implicit in the organisation of the peace process was the assumption that this consciousness was only attainable by some peoples and some individuals – as dependent on their gender as their racial and cultural identities.

The modern politics of gender has a long pedigree stretching back into the eighteenth century. Among the representatives of the victor states involved in peacemaking in 1919, the predominant conceptions of sexual difference reiterated the preference for masculine political subjectivity that has long been part of that politics. But this preference was also renegotiated in the context of a new conceptualisation of nationality and of the self in science and in politics. In this chapter my aim is to explore the gender dimensions of the idea of national self-determination mooted as the basis for the transition from war to a projected democratic and permanent peace by representatives of specific-ally Britain, France, and the United States. Those gender dimensions are most evident in the consequences that the political legitimation of national self-determination at the end of the First World War had for selves distinguished as male and female: in the exclusion of women from peacemaking, in the denial of an intrinsic nationality to women, and in the predominance of masculinity in newly constituted national and international political arenas. This chapter tackles the gender history of the post-war definition of national and collective identities by revisiting the *longue durée* history of ideas about gender and national difference, and then examining peacemaking as a site where those ideas were nego-tiated and reaffirmed. As I will argue, accrued representations of gender difference contributed to the shaping of power relations between states and between individuals participating in the formation of a new world order in very specific ways.

This chapter then is structured around two seemingly distinct stories. In the first part I outline the late nineteenth-century gender history of the reconstitution of the self-determining subject as a national subject. In the second section I excavate the pertinence of this history of ideas to the history of peacemaking in 1919, a time when the political ideal of national self-determination had reached its international 'apogee'.[3] The gender history of conceptions of the self and self-determination provides a necessary background for understanding the (sometimes deceptively silent) gender resonances of the ideas of nation-ality and of self-determination evoked at the peace, and the significance of the ways in which those ideas were renegotiated in the course of peacemaking. By the turn of the twentieth century these conceptions had grown in popularity and influence, providing a critical discursive context for the ideas of nationality and self-determination espoused in post-war European politics.

The gender politics of self-determination

Representations of sexual difference are as historically specific as the political contexts to which they give meaning. Historians have argued that in the late eighteenth century, changing scientific definitions of embodied gender (or sex) differences – from the idea of the female body as an inversion of the male body, to the view of the female body as distinctive from and inferior to the male body – became crucial to the gendered imagining of unequal national communities and national selves.[4] By the end of the nineteenth century, psychology had added to the process of inscribing difference which focused on the visual and the physiological to create 'a grammar of the body'. It helped elaborate the inner self as a sexually, racially, and culturally differentiated self, and extended the sexed body into intangibly interiorised realms. Science naturalised sex difference, and provided a language of difference crucial to the imagining of collective identities. The decades preceding the First World War are of especial interest because of the manner in which the expansion in psychology across the European world influenced modern notions of the nation by locating national identity (as nationality) more firmly 'inside' the self, and made the self a more complex entity involving layers of conscious and unconscious subjectivity. Nationality was commonly described as a psychological phenomenon involving the expression of emotions and instincts, individual and group consciousness and will. Nationality expressed the expanded subjectivity of the individual as well as manifesting the objective characteristics of his group. In 1905, a reader of *La Femme Nouvelle* (The New Woman), a Paris weekly which aimed to educate and stimulate the modern young woman, could be apprised of the fact that national patriotism was no longer considered an expression of the territorial or political state of the *'patrie'*. Instead it was now understood to be 'a psychological reality, an affective disposition, such as filial or paternal love, which everyone could find in oneself and which it would be unnatural not to experience'.[5] Importantly, by contrast with this emotional quality of patriotism, the similarly interiorised concept of nationality was often described as manifest in the capacity to exercise will and, consequently, self-determination. As we shall see, it was in these particular manifestations that nationality presupposed masculinity with increasing authority and resonance.

Will was as critical as affect and emotion to the new language of the interiority of individual and national selves. In 1886, in his celebrated text *Qu'est-ce qu'une nation?* (What is a nation?), the French philosopher Ernest Renan emphasised will as a characteristic of the psychological nature of nations in contrast to the physiological qualities of races. Renan's view was reiterated in the following decades by French and English commentators on nationality eager to associate the concept of nation with the repudiation of biological determinism.[6] Representations of the capacity for self-determination of individuals and nations alike through their ability to exercise will was regarded as evidence of the individual's autonomy over the determinism of physiology and unconsciousness, and had become important for articulating democratic ideals. However, those representations were dependent on premises of national and racial differences and, in more subdued ways, class and sexual identities. In so far as the concept of self-determination *per se* involved the possession of will and of a normative inner self, it was depicted as the prerogative of certain male individuals and nations. As philosophers, scientists, and intellectuals made 'will' the crux of the association of liberty with nationality, they also moved women and certain specified peoples and races to the fringes of their emancipatory discourse.[7]

The relevance of gender to the history of nationality and the self becomes apparent if we consider that the masculinity of the subject of scientific study was usually only implied, in the same way that the intrinsic 'whiteness' of psychological man was rarely acknowledged or even deemed worthy of notice. By contrast, after the 1890s studies devoted explicitly to 'woman' and the nature of her psychological as well as physiological difference from 'man' flourished.[8] While men were not singled out for attention, science and philosophy (both critical domains of psychological thought in the late nineteenth century) entrenched women's difference and its political significance in a normative imaginary of the interiority of the male self – defined in terms of depth and will.

The ever-growing literature on women's difference drew on a well-stocked store of stereotypes, imbuing them with a new biological and psychological determinism. The emphasis placed in European scientific and philosophical discourses on women's lack of will or a weaker will, was complemented by depictions of women's more emotional or instinctive (but not 'deep') psychological life and their maternity. In the mid-nineteenth century, the sociologist Herbert Spencer stated that 'female energies' were 'directed toward preparation for pregnancy and lactation'; the result was that women ceased their individual evolution sooner.[9] In their influential tome *The Evolution of Sex* (1889) the English Darwinists, Patrick Geddes and J. Arthur Thomson, argued that females lacked 'the energy required to participate actively in society; their energy, such as it is, is entirely required for reproduction'. By consequence, women contributed to social and racial progress by their 'reproductive sacrifice'.[10] In his turn of the century investigations, the French anthropologist Charles Le Tourneau concluded that woman's greater intuition was directly derived from the animal stage of human evolution and was conserved in 'maternal instinct'.[11] Precepts situating women in an earlier phase of evolution, emphasising their maternalism, and accordingly establishing their social, national, and racial function as mothers, were repeated in German-language contexts. For example, in a medical article published in 1901, the physiologist Paul Moebius presented women's alleged mental incapacity as a necessary condition for the survival of the race, since it made women good mothers.[12] Moebius proposed that women who became more intelligent placed the 'race' at threat. Woman's natural conservatism was, in turn, regarded as a functional means of ensuring the continuity of the racially defined human species.

Representations of women's incapacity to exercise will were inextricable from representations of, and taken as evidence of, a masculine norm. As the sociologist Nikolas Rose has argued in his study of the impact of psychology on the history of subjectivity, 'since its invention the apparently sex-neutral subject-with-agency was a model applied to one sex and denied to the other; indeed it was dependent on this opposition for its philosophical foundation and political function'.[13] By virtue of the relational characterisations of masculinity and femininity, the authentic autonomous self – along with nationality, liberty, and politics in general – was made the provenance of white (and often specifically Western) European men. Thus Nietzsche not only celebrated masculine will, he situated the potency of that will in relation to the problematic nature of female will. Where 'woman' might not exercise volition, she might impose the power of her instincts, of her desire, over a man's own will.[14] Nietzsche emphasised what other philosophers, psychologists, and social scientists drawing on existing philosophical traditions at least implied, that the characteristics of the masculine self were dependent on representations of the relationship *between* men and women.

The concept of a female will, let alone a female self, was problematic not only because of the equation of women with maternalism, but because women's difference defined the norms and prerogatives of masculinity. In the increasingly influential publications of early twentieth-century psychoanalysts, from Freud to Adler, will to power, self-mastery, and sublimation were all characteristically masculine.[15] Similarly, mainstream Victorian psychiatrists influenced by theories of evolutionary psychology attributed to women desire and self-abandon, and to men will and self-control.[16] They diagnosed hysteria as the disease of both women who perverted their instincts by attempting to assert their selves and the male populations of less virile, more effeminate nations. Consequently, they rendered will the defining characteristic of the highly evolved British male self. Despite methodological and theoretical variations in developing national traditions of psychology, in general the concept of nation was uniformly and increasingly entrenched in the realm of the inside and the inner self was a characteristic of men, certain races and classes. Women, like 'the lesser races', were critical to the elaboration of a natural hierarchy which situated white, European, men at the top.[17]

The significance of women's alleged psychological attributes for their place in the nation was not merely coincidental. Rather it lodged in the mainstream language of masculine nationality and the racial bases of nationalism. In the decades prior to the First World War there was scope in this language for women's patriotism (as La Femme Nouvelle's interest in patriotism as a phenomenon suggests) but it was commonly identified with maternal and social responsibilities, not with a woman's 'self' or female self-determination. Women could not be presumed to have national subjectivities or to be national subjects or citizens (either philosophically or politically) in the same way as men. Their 'primitive qualities' and alleged instinctiveness potentially incorporated them into the emotional life of national patriotism, but it also associated them with an earlier phase in the evolution of nations experienced as a form of unconscious and intuitive attachment, rather than the form of national consciousness associated with masculine political maturity and self-consciousness, and the capacity for national self-determination.[18] These conceptualisations of sexual difference coincided with the reinforcement of exclusivist laws on nationality. In the nation-states of Europe, including Germany, France, and Italy, the pre-eminence of the patriarchal family was legally established as a national characteristic. Women marrying foreigners lost their existing nationality without any certainty that they could assume the nationality of their husbands. Even though common law had imposed nationality on both men and women born in England as an irrevocable 'obligation', from 1870 English women who married foreigners forewent their right to English nationality, and the patrilineage of nationality was similarly reinforced.[19] Such laws attest to both the relevance of sexual difference for determining forms of political agency or power, and the growing political importance of the nation and nationality as sites for the elaboration of power relations.

With the outbreak of war in 1914 national self-determination became a significant political theme among British, French, and United States politicians and intellectuals concerned to define the democratic possibilities of a post-war new world order. As I have argued, by this time scientific discourse had extended the nation into a deeper, layered, inner self and made the capacity for self-determination, like will itself, normatively masculine. The concept of the self-determining national citizen privileged masculinity on the basis of representations of an Enlightenment notion of the self-conscious subject as 'a being with inner ideal ends, to which it freely acknowledges responsibility'.[20] At the same time, self-determination was only by agitation or exception an attribute of women, who, according to mainstream scientific and philosophical discourse, were ineluctably subject to the determinism of their physiology. Ironically, national self-determination appealed particularly to liberal-minded intellectuals who deplored the determinism that accompanied developments in the biological and racial sciences. With the benefit of hindsight we might observe too that national self-determination potentially cast the idealised terms of citizenship adrift from the wartime mooring of military or warrior representations of masculinity and of national identity. Instead, it anchored post-war citizenship in an idealised, collective, if still masculine, national subjectivity.

Peacemaking and masculinity

The reconstruction of gender order is now viewed by historians as a significant corollary of post-war political and economic demobilisation.[21] Just as gender norms framed images and discussions of the war, in the transition from war to peace gender relations and identities were critical to attempts by each of the victor governments (Britain and the United States and to a lesser extent France) to regain a social equilibrium at the same time as contributing to a 'new world order'. Contemporaries employed gender conventions to signal the acceptable limits of revolutionary or radical political change, and gender identities were at issue in the national and international formulations of post-war reconstruction. The wartime disorientation of conventional gender roles only heightened concern about sexual difference in the post-war.[22] On one level, wartime propaganda had polarised representations of men as soldiers and women as mothers.[23] On another level, the exigencies of war had required that women occupy positions in the public sphere on the home front while men were reduced to the ignominy of the trenches, a kind of warfare that in practice denied them their warrior masculinity more than it virilised them.

The often-anomalous nature of wartime gender conventions, roles, and relations was hardly exceptional, reflecting instead the irregularity and unpredictability of representations of difference in creating and maintaining relationships of power. For example, in the post-1919 political order gender anomalies were evident in the strange juxtaposition of, on the one hand, the legal and political status quo of the older states, and, on the other, of the constitutions of the new nations of Eastern and Central Europe, which were to some extent 'created' by Allied experts and delegates at the peace. The new constitutions usually gave equal suffrage rights to women and men (while also emphasising the need to legally cater for the especial maternal role of women by introducing protective labour laws). In contrast there was no formalised acknowledgement of such rights in the states and legislatures of Britain, France, or the United States themselves. Indeed, representatives of the Great Powers determining the contours of the peace did not presume in all cases that women would be given the vote, or should participate in plebiscites.[24] In an extension of widespread late nineteenth-century views of women's social and legal status in relation to men, the plebiscite was in principle not extended as a right to married women, and nationality was not a right for women in the states represented by the victors – in both cases this was to prevent any potential conflict between the woman's vote and that of the male household head. Women were neither regarded by experts and delegates representing the Great Powers as intrinsic nationals in terms of political entitlement (whether suffrage or nationality), nor was their self-determination depicted as relevant for the democratic new world order. This was despite the fact that mainly middle-class organisations such as the Women's International League for Peace and Freedom, the International Council of Women, and the Allied Women's Suffrage League campaigned intensively during the peace for female suffrage and for the right to participate in the creation of the new world order.

By the 1919 peace process existing representations of women's different political subjectivity were affirmed in the question of who could represent nations in the international community, and in attitudes towards women's political agency. The expert bodies established by the victor states to decide the terms of the peace were exclusively male (despite offers of assistance from women with scholarly expertise in the areas under study and the recruitment at lower levels of female support staff). Liberal internationalist women attempted to intervene in peace proceedings in support of a feminist version of the Wilsonian agenda, writing to and speaking with key male figures at the conference with whom they had professional and personal links (including Woodrow Wilson himself, the French leader Georges Clemenceau, and the influential British delegate, Jan Smuts). But the presence of women was barely tolerated, unless in the formalised modes of secretaries, mistresses, or wives. The all-male British Foreign Office delegation in Paris, comprising men who were well known for their progressive political views and even theoretical support for female suffrage, commented favourably on the invisibility of French women in Paris as evidence of the depth of French femininity. They compared this situation with London where they alleged that predominance of women in the public sphere marked the extent of social disorder.[25] The expression of such attitudes towards women after the European experience of women's unprecedented contribution to wartime economies did not help improve the status at the peace of those women who did attempt to become involved in proceedings. As the British Prime Minister Lloyd George dramatised in his post-war memoirs: 'The suffragette campaign was then at its height. All meetings attended by Ministers were interrupted by female shrieks and screechings about "Votes for Women". The interruptions were indiscriminate ... To avoid disturbance all women were now being excluded from functions of this kind.'[26] Lloyd George's comments suggest women's groups were purposely excluded, sometimes through the conflation of pre-war images of suffragette violence and of the delegations at the peace process, and more generally through the presumption that it was improper and unnatural for women to assert their selves and their self-interest at the peace. Underlying the sense of female impropriety were conventional conceptions of the masculinity of political subjectivity and the public sphere.[27]

Nationality may have been the prerogative of masculinity by virtue of the normative status of men as citizens and self-determining subjects, but a range of definitions of masculinity were also operative in the process of peacemaking. The acceptable bases for political agency in the context of international relations included images of masculine chivalry which established the male as protector and patron, and arbiter of peace, the latter a function that women's groups had been eager of course to associate with their *feminine* qualities. The English Fabian and co-founder of the British League of Nations Society Leonard Woolf contributed to wartime discussions of how problems of international relations were to be resolved in the post-war by comparing the competition between nations to that of men fighting over women: 'Thus two men may each desire exclusive sexual relations with a single woman; two men may each desire exclusive possession of a single material object; or two national groups may each desire exclusive control of a single portion of the material earth.'[28] Woolf outlined the need for an International Court of Arbitration and International Government of the kind that would translate into a League of Nations by likening the ways in which 'primitive man' in the past and 'stags' in the present 'fought for the exclusive possession of a female', to the manner in which 'nations to-day fight to "impose their wills" upon one another'. Following the analogy through to its logical conclusion he argued that just as in modern society courtship was regulated by custom or general social rules, international relations too could be remade to operate on principle of arbitration rather than force, as a more 'gentlemanly' option.

When it came to the actual peace a similar comparison with its evocations of a primal masculinity and gentlemanly codes of honour defined through the exercise of will and subjection of the feminine was deployed to a contrary purpose. The British Under-Secretary of State, Sir Eyre Crowe, argued on behalf of the British Delegation to the peace conference *against* the idea of international arbitration, drawing on an example of gentlemanly behaviour:

> The national honour would be involved in issues which raise consideration of the moral law, religious convictions or general principles of political conduct. There are in private life things which a free man will not allow to be questioned or discussed, things to which he will not submit, even if it cost him his life – religious coercion, the honor of his wife for instance. These [sic] are analogous matters in international relations ... a proposal to join Ireland to the French republic would violate an English vital interest.[29]

The differences between Crowe and Woolf highlight the range of representations of masculinity and ways in which the consequences of representations of difference and identity were not always predictable. But the fact that representations of the distinctive roles of men and women and the relationship between them were used to support contrary political arguments indicates the legitimacy of the representations themselves, the conceptualisations of difference that they insinuated, and their political potency.

While the peace process reaffirmed women's different subjectivity and the normative masculinity of self-determination, maternalism too was appropriated by men as a means of legitimating the paternalistic aspects of the peace itself. As we have seen, at this time scientific and philosophical literature associated maternal instinct definitively with women and with their especial social and political role as nurturers and mothers, rather than as citizens or agents exercising direct political power. During the war and after, women who attempted to influence the formation of the anticipated new national world order and argue for their equal inclusion in the creation of a new peaceful and democratic order, alternated their emphasis on female self-determination with invocations of their specific national status as mothers. On this view, motherhood was the antithesis of the masculine world of war. However, during the peace process even this antithesis was resolved in the naturalisation of the national basis of the new world order in the image of a masculine maternalism. In a published account of his peace diary, Harold Nicolson, a junior British delegate to the Paris conference, refers to the elation he shared with his 'expert' colleagues in their task of creating and fortifying 'the new nations whom we regarded, with maternal instinct, as the justification of our sufferings and of our victory'.[30] Nicolson goes so far as to add that 'the Paris Conference will never properly be understood unless this emotional impulse is emphasised at every stage'. Ironically, as Nicolson's quote suggests, at the same time that women were sidelined from any substantial role in the peace process, male 'experts' at the peace had appropriated both peacemaking and 'maternal instinct,' rendering the latter a fundamental 'emotional impulse' among men in their task of creating, or literally giving birth to new nations through their unprecedented roles as scientific 'experts'. The historian Marilyn Lake has pointed out that in the post-French Revolutionary era of citizenship, national reproduction was a masculine preoccupation, placing men in competition with the regenerative and reproductive powers of women: 'all men, not just fathers, can generate political life and political right. Political right is defined in terms of sex-right. Political creativity belongs not to paternity, but masculinity. Men give birth to nations.'[31] In the Nicolson example we can see the idea of masculine responsibility for the reproduction of nations actually being translated into the international responsibility of a certain intellectual class representing the Great Powers. This masculine capacity for creating or birthing nations was reinforced by the exclusion of women from the sphere of peace-making, by the emphasis on nationality as the foundational principle of political association and of political representation, and by the naturalisation of a new international order in the psychological language of instinct, impulse, and emotion.

The history of peacemaking then is marked by the iteration of assumptions regarding normative political subjectivity and its masculinity that we cannot directly link to specific intellectual influences. However, we can situate these assumptions in a broad context of the contemporary history of ideas as a means of estimating their possible resonances and their consequences. Contextualising political evocations of 'will', maternal 'instinct', and emotional impulses in the specific history of the scientific and philosophical struggle to gender individual subjectivity brings to our attention the ideological work taking place in the post-war political sphere to reaffirm those norms, and to renegotiate the borders of sexual difference and its political significance. Importantly, there were national variations even among the Allied states in the political conclusions that were drawn from the mobilisation of the language of sexual difference. The French delegation, for example, represented a state which after the war gave married French women the right to retain their nationality for reasons of nationalist pragmatism, that is the fear that in the face of a shortfall of French men, French women would turn to foreigners for husbands and, by law, their children would become the nationals of another country. But French government representatives were blatantly determined in their opposition to the influence of women on the post-war international sphere that they were helping create. Leon Bourgeois, the grand old man of French republicanism, committed internationalist, and deemed 'father' of the League of Nations, challenged the powers of the League's Advisory Commission for the Traffic in Women and Children (an issue placed on international agendas to placate the demands by women's organisations for international involvement) to even discuss the abolition of state-regulated prostitution. This was because, Bourgeois argued on behalf of the French government, such issues were 'exclusively national, interior, and not international', they were questions of 'unique relevance to territorial authority' and of a state's 'nationality itself'.[32] As if to highlight the difference between French and English society, Bourgeois also expressed his disdain at the ways in which he felt that English delegations to the League of Nations bowed to the influence of feminists, particularly over the issue of state-sanctioned prostitution.[33]

The place of women at the peace marks the masculinity of new world order politics and nation-making. It returns us to the theme of implicitly gendered political subjectivity and its reaffirmation in the principle of nationality. Meetings of the Council of Ten (which included most vocally representatives of Britain, France, Italy, the United States, and Japan) and their documented attitudes towards the place of women in the new national world order provide evidence of a post-war trans-national consensus among the victor nations regarding women, even if in practice it manifested itself in diverse ways in different nations: Women did not automatically exercise the right of self-determination within nations, and the ascription of female political self-determination to the realm of an international 'principle' potentially jeopardised the autonom-ous identity and sovereignty of nations. Women could act as symbols of the national collective, as proponents of an unconscious and emotional national patriotism, and in their capacities as biological mothers of the nation. After all it was on the basis of the rhetoric of maternalism that some European women were given the vote. But on this same basis women could not be presumed to have national 'consciousness' or to be national subjects or citizens (either philosophically, politically, or legally), or have responsibility for the political life of nations in the same way as men. As a disillusioned former American 'expert' Walter Lippmann commented in the messy aftermath of the peacemaking process, the principle of nationality exhibited 'a deeper prejudice', a preference for masculine identity: 'Unless the female line happens to be especially remarkable descent is traced down through the males. The tree is male. At various moments females accrue to it as itinerant bees light upon an ancient apple tree.'[34] Well into the interwar period, the British government regarded the opinion that nationality 'in so far as it is transmissible or inheritable through generations is only inheritable through the male line and not through the female line' as 'one of the great principles of English law'.[35] In post-war discussions of nationality there were even more precise invocations of the language of self that had undergirded scientific and philosophical elaborations of women's difference in the late nineteenth century. In an analysis of the various viewpoints on the topic of women's nationality in 1934, an English member of the Grotius Society for International Law explained that: 'the difference between this claim of woman to equality of rights with man [i.e. nationality] and the other claims she has made lies in the fact that it is a claim to exercise a right against the State itself . . . it cannot lightly be expected to permit the individual to opt for or against the rights of citizenship at her own unfettered will'.[36]

Women's exclusion from peacemaking and their uncertain national status in the inter-war period reflected available and prevailing representations not only of femininity and women's 'selves' in relation to men and in the context of nations, but of the nature of masculinity. The irrelevance of the status of women to the new world order agenda of self-determination and greater democracy contrasts starkly with the significance of women's status as a question for nations (represented by men), and as definitive of national order. In terms of power relations between men and women, the presumed interiority of nationality not only implied a masculine subject/agent, it made control of the destiny of its female constituents a marker of national autonomy and sovereignty, and of masculinity.

Conclusion

The history of peacemaking at the end of the First World War reveals critical aspects of the gender dimension of power relations in the victor states. It also reveals the gender implications of the new international sphere grounded in the ideal of national self-determination. The creation of a new world order at the end of the First World War closely wove together national with gender identities and new conceptions of citizenship. It was also a process which coincided with the reinforcement of relational pre-war conventions of femininity and masculinity, and changing scientific representations of the relationship between gendered selves and of nationality. The history of peacemaking, like the history of self and nationality in which I have contextualised it, is indicative of the extent to which the potency of masculinity was negotiated around the positioning of women. Evocations of nationality, like national will, relied on and implied unequal gender – as well as national and racial – differences; when women went against 'their nature' by demanding rights as individuals with 'selves' in public domains, it was seen to be at the expense of men as well as the nation and race; when men claimed a maternal instinct towards nations, or the role of arbiters of peace by gender custom, they appropriated the potency of women's capacity for biological reproduction and for pacifism.

Adding gender to the history of the end of the First World War reminds us of the relatively unspoken masculinity of the nationally and racially hierarchical international sphere forged in the peace process and the principle of nationality that underlay its design. While some historians associate the post-war with new possibilities for women in the public sphere created by the experience of the war – including the 'reward' of suffrage and equal constitutional status for women in the new nation-states – the national(ist) motif of the new world order also led to a renewed denial of nationality rights for women in a majority of established and new European states, and the widespread privileging of masculinity in respect to the concept of nationality.[37] Even where suffrage was granted after the First World War, gradually in Britain, and in the pre-war period in the United States and Commonwealth states such as Australia, it did not guarantee women nationality rights in principle. The new importance of nationality to women's political and legal status in the post-war was made evident in the expanded (and unsuccessful) interwar campaign by women's organisations to have nationality rights for married women legislated throughout the world. Too often, women whose countries denaturalised them as citizens because they married foreigners were unable to gain national citizenship from their spouse's country, with political, legal, and social consequences, including the legal and cultural obstacles to their independent travel outside national borders.[38]

Gender historians of nationalism have commented on the five fundamental ways in which women are symbolically and actually involved in ethnic and national processes: As biological reproducers of national collectivities; as reproducers of the boundaries of national groups; as transmitters of national cultures; as signifiers of national difference; as participants in national struggles.[39] Yet the episode of peace-making also illustrates the importance of masculinity to nations, and by extension to power relations within nations and between them: masculinity is definitive of accepted conceptions of national subjectivity, whether through evocations of the citizen-soldier or, as at the end of the First World War, of the self-determining autonomous subject exercising their will; and it is men, rather than women, who are imbued in discourse and in practice with the capacity to create or give birth to politically legitimate nations. It may be hardly surprising, but it is also worthy of historical investigation that, as a result, national self-determination and peacemaking were rendered overwhelmingly masculine affairs.

Notes

I would like to thank the editors for their extremely helpful comments and the Australian Research Council for its generous funding of the research that informs this article.

1 A. Williams, *Failed Imagination? New World Orders of the Twentieth-Century* (Manchester, 1998), p. 180.
2 L. E. Gelfand, *The Inquiry: American Preparations for Peace, 1917–1919* (New Haven, 1963), p. 158.

3   The term 'apogee' is taken from Eric Hobsbawm's study, *Nations and Nationalism since 1780* (Cambridge, 1990), ch. 5.
4   For more discussion of this earlier period, see G. Sluga, 'Identity, gender, and the history of European nationalisms', *Nations and Nationalisms*, 4 (1998), 87–111.
5   D. Cabane, 'Education et patriotisme', *La Femme Nouvelle* (1 October 1905), p. 794.
6   This discussion is based on G. Sluga, *What is a Nation? A History of Ideas of Nation and Nationality in Britain, France, and the United States, 1872–1921* (forthcoming).
7   J. Finot, *Race Prejudice* (London, 1902, reprint 1969), p. 182.
8   G. Richards, *Putting Psychology in its Place* (London, 1996), pp. 151–2.
9   See S. A. Shields, 'Functionalism, Darwinism, and the psychology of women', *American Psychologist*, 30:7 (July 1975), 749–50.
10 Cited in L. Duffin, 'Prisoners of progress: Women and evolution', in S. Delamont and L. Duffin (eds), *The Nineteenth Century Woman* (London, 1978), pp. 63, 74.
11 C. Le Tourneau, 'La Femme a travers les ages', *Revue d'Ecole Anthropologique de Paris*, 11 (1901), 273–90.
12 P. Moebius, 'The physiological mental weakness of woman', *Alienist and Neurologist*, 22 (1901), 631; See also Shields, 'Functionalism', 742.
13 N. Rose, *Inventing Our Selves* (Cambridge, 1997), p. 6.
14 R. Diprose, 'Nietzsche and the pathos of distance', in Paul Patton (ed.), *Nietzsche, Feminism and Political Theory* (London, 1993), p. 20.
15 J. Le Rider, *Modernity and Crises of Identity* (New York, 1993), p. 118.
16 E. Showalter, *The Female Malady* (London, 1985), p. 106.
17 C. Eagle Russett, *Sexual Science* (Cambridge MA, 1989), p. 14.
18 Ch. Letourneau, *La Psychologie Ethnique* (Paris, 1901), p. 72.
19 See B. Bicknell, 'The nationality of married women', *Transactions of the Grotius Society*, Vol. XX (London, 1935), pp. 106–22.
20 W. James, 'Person and personality', *Johnson's Universal Cyclopedia* (New York, 1895), reprinted in W. James, *Essays in Psychology* (Cambridge MA, 1983), pp. 318–20.
21 S. Kingsley Kent, *Making Peace* (Princeton, 1993), p. 3.
22 M. L. Roberts, *Civilization without Sexes* (Chicago, 1994).
23 For more on the force of the warrior masculinity, see J. Horne, 'Social identity in war: France 1914–1918', in T. G. Fraser and K. Jeffery (eds), *Men, Women and War* (Dublin, 1993), G. L. Mosse, *The Image of Man* (New York, 1996) and K. Theweleit *Male Fantasies, Vols 1–2* (Minneapolis, 1987–88).
24 See G. Sluga, 'Female and national self-determination: A gender re-reading of the "Apogee of Nationalism"', *Nations and Nationalisms*, 6 (2000), 495–521.
25 R. C. V. Bodley, *Indiscretions of a Young Man* (London, 1931), p. 105.
26 L. George, *The Truth About Peace Treaties* (London, 1938), p. 258.
27 On one occasion a delegation of Allied Women Suffragists was received by the peacemakers, see Sluga, 'Female and national self-determination'.
28 L. S. Woolf, *The Framework of a Lasting Peace* (London, 1917), p. 13.
29 Public Record Office, London, FO608/240 Peace Conference British Delegation 1919, Sir E. Crowe, 'Memorandum on Compulsory Arbitration', 9 January 19, p. 13.
30 H. Nicolson, *Peacemaking 1919* (London, 1945), p. 26.

31 M. Lake, 'Mission impossible: How men gave birth to the Australian nation – nationalism, gender and other seminal acts', *Gender and History*, 4 (1992), 312. See also the discussion by L. Kramer in *Nationalism* (New York, 1998), pp. 93–103.

32 Archives Ministère des Affaires Etrangères, Paris (hereafter AMAE), *Societé des Nations*, I-M Protection des Femmes et des enfants, Vol. 1709, 'Note de M. Bourgeois sur la question de la Reglementation de la Prostitution', May–Nov. 1922, pp. 60–2.

33 AMAE, *Societé des Nations*. I-M Protection des Femmes et des enfants. Vol. 1709, 1ère session de la Commission Consultative 1922, Bourgeois Rapport presenta à M. le President du Conseil, May–Nov. 1922, pp. 110–11.

34 W. Lippmann, *Public Opinion* (New York, 1922, reprint 1947), p. 146.

35 Committee of the House of Commons on The Nationality of Married Women, *Report by the Select Committee appointed to join with a Committee of the House of Commons on The Nationality of Married Women* (London, 1923).

36 Bicknell, 'The nationality of married women', p. 121.

37 See B. Caine and G. Sluga, *Gendering European History* (Leicester, 2000), ch. 6.

38 C. Lewis Bredbenner, *A Nationality of Her Own* (Berkeley, 1998), p. 196.

39 For more detail see N. Yuval-Davis and F. Anthias, *Women-Nation-State* (Basingstoke, 1989), Introduction.

PART V

*Including the subject:
masculinity and subjectivity*

14

The political man: the construction of masculinity in German Social Democracy, 1848–78

Thomas Welskopp

W HEN labour history rediscovered the 'subjectivity' of workers, after a long period dominated by 'working-class histories' occupied with collectivities, 'masculinity' soon entered the agenda as well. This added a new complexity to the picture historians had drawn of the workers in the past. It showed that identity formation was not just a matter of 'class interests' but a complicated process of active construction involving and linking many different dimensions. In this context, 'masculinity' did not appear as just another 'add-on' to the analysis of 'subjectivity'. In labour history we often find that 'masculinity' served as the very mode in which multi-faceted identities such as 'workers', as 'breadwinners', or as 'citizens' were expressed. This means, however, that there was no uniform workers' 'masculinity' in the same sense as there was no uniform 'class identity'. This chapter analyses a distinct labour movement milieu – that of German Social Democracy between 1848 and 1878 – under the hypothesis that its specific social, cultural, and political characteristics translated into an equally specific form of masculinity which, in turn, became the basis of group identity formation and revolutionary politics.

The profoundly male character of most nineteenth-century labour organisations has become common knowledge in recent histories of labour and gender relations. Yet the different modes and practices which workers and their unions, cooperatives, and workingmen's parties employed in representing masculinity as both means and end of their organisations need further exploration. There was no 'one paradigmatic way' workers understood themselves and their comrades as 'male' or 'manly'. Ava Baron has demonstrated how American printers virtually 're-invented' their profession as a purely male occupation, drawing on a bogus 'tradition' centred around the self-image of well-educated 'artists'.[1] German and American steelworkers took pains to show off their 'manly' skills and physical strength as attributes of a 'man-sized job'.[2] Both groups of workers located the workplace as the arena to showcase their masculinity. In contrast, Anna Clark's research has unearthed the 'making of the British working class' as a project of artisans and skilled textile workers, who developed a mixture of patriarchal household behaviour and hard-drinking club life to justify their claims to political participation. Their masculinity rested on a rude 'manly' habitus *vis-à-vis* their wives, instead of the modest material decency which 'respectable' workers strove for in order to meet the standards of full citizenship based on pecuniary independence as set by bourgeois liberalism.[3]

This chapter introduces a spectrum of the German labour movement that constructed masculinity neither as a workplace requirement nor as an attribute of household life. The young journeymen, petty artisans, and radical outcasts of bourgeois extraction who made up the bulk membership and leadership of early German Social Democracy situated the representation of their masculinity in the public sphere of political discourse. This discourse had the professionally unspecific political 'workers' clubs' – the local units of Social Democracy – as its background. Lacking both occupational cohesion and the privacy of a family household, German Social Democrats turned toward their clubs as centres of fraternisation, emotional gratification, drink, and political passion in order to express themselves as men. Not surprisingly, the rhetorically brilliant public orator, the charismatic leader of peers and the courageous defender of steadfast political principles became the apotheosis of Social Democratic manliness. In consequence, women were barred from club life to an extent that even surpassed restrictive German laws governing the public sphere. The exclusion of women was a prerequisite for male Social Democrats to express themselves as political citizens and revolutionary subjects.

This practice translated into discourse. In a mixture of misogyny and chivalry, Social Democratic speakers depicted women both as the victims of an immoral capitalism and as the retarded half of humanity that had to be liberated and educated by the men's political action. Yet Social Democrats defined their masculinity not so much in contrast to women as in relation to the imagined 'other'.[4] The male bourgeois liberals with their different notions and norms of masculinity, condescending to the workers, served as their actual counterparts. Social Democrats thus attacked an hegemonic ideal of masculinity based on both private property and patriarchal household bonds. This ideal was embodied by urban notables of middle age. The young Social

Democrats replaced this unattainable norm with their own vision of 'true' masculinity centred around the political citizen and his energetic activities within the public sphere.

The specific social and political profile of early German Social Democracy

In contrast to other nations, the German labour movement constituted itself early as a political party. This did not reflect a comparative lead or progressive state of maturation as interpreted by orthodox Marxism. To the contrary: in 1848 and again in the 1860s, German Social Democracy originated as a variant of the labour movement that was virtually forced into party politics from the start. On the one hand, a trade union movement, based on informal social networks on the shop-floor, the neighbourhood or the ethnic or confessional community, was only beginning to present itself as an alternative model of organisation. On the other hand, all organisational life among artisans and workers was driven into the public sphere of associations, clubs, and rallies simply because of a profound lack of alternative sites for sociability. And since the public sphere in 'civil society' – which was just emerging in Germany – carried heavy political connotations from the outset, any form of organisation operating there would take on a political character. Moreover, the association or club served as *the* social infrastructure of party politics in nineteenth-century Germany, and, in turn, became the central stage for political debate. In this process, it was both their specific social composition and their specific internal culture that made *workers'* associations a basis of party politics. Their radically democratic character proved far superior to the bourgeois model of a liberalism of notables.[5]

Where the basic conditions are favourable, labour movements tend to emerge as *trade union* movements rather than as parties. In the first place, strong social bonds on the shop-floor make fertile ground for trade union organisation. Many elitist craft unions developed on the basis of pride in skill and work group solidarity.[6] Ethnic and neighbourhood ties in some industries compensated for a lack of craft cohesion, although workplace socialising often determined that such ties could be transformed into organisational structures. The British and US labour histories furnish excellent examples of this mechanism. In Germany, however, a shop-floor or ethnic basis for the formation of trade unions 'from below' did not – yet – exist during the second third of the nineteenth century. The only notable exceptions to this general lack of 'pre-organisational' structures were the German printers and cigar makers. Autonomous work in close groups and tightly knit travelling networks for the journeymen of these trades allowed for an exceptionally early constitution of unions. The journeymen of either trade formed national unions as early as 1848. Yet even in these crafts workers tended to join both trade unions and workingmen's parties.

Most crafts in Germany, in contrast, had not yet outgrown the stage of small workshop production under the command of self-employed masters. Although the traditional guilds had eroded under the pressure of capitalist commercialisation, the small unit structure of the guild era remained intact. Lack of capital prevented the smooth transition from workshop to small factory which was so typical of the English and American path of industrialisation. Commercialisation forced craft production into the manifold bonds of dependency on capitalism. Yet in the short run, capitalism in Germany stabilised the craft structure, 'colonised' working arrangements, and retained the small-scale workshop composition of most trades. During the 1860s and early 1870s, a more and more commercialised world of small workshops and a still limited but thriving factory sector flourished side by side. It was the first realm that became the cradle of the German labour movement.

In consequence, German Social Democracy originated not so much as a movement of wage workers in factory settings but as a movement of journeymen in traditional crafts. Early Social Democrats continued to herald the status of master artisan as their supreme ideal. The independent producer and not the life-long wage worker was central to their concerns.[7] This also explains why German Social Democrats portrayed capitalism as an external enemy that undermined this independence. Capitalism seemed external to production – and therefore an object for elimination through political revolution. Socialism, in turn, came to mean producer cooperatives. The voluntary 'association' of producers was the fundamental alternative to a capitalism that isolated the artisans, held them in the bondage of dependency, and destroyed society in a Hobbesian war of all against all.

Mutual isolation of journeymen in small workshops prevented shop-floor solidarity vis-à-vis a common employer. In many instances, furthermore, journeymen and small masters, toiling side by side, shared the experiences of capitalist dependency. Traditional guild structures, which could have compensated for shop-floor ties, had eroded. Where they were still intact, they were subject to control by wealthy masters. They rather served as an instrument of patriarchal hierarchy than as a source of anti-capitalist craft loyalty. Therefore, in the revolution of 1848 and again in the 1860s, the Workers' Educational Societies, the workers' associations and clubs, became the focus of organisational energies. The associations were as anti-capitalist as they were hostile to guilds. They were distinct enough from the guilds to be accepted as a 'modern' organisational model designed for the future. It was because of this anti-guild hostility that German workers' associations insisted on allowing men of all trades to join. A producers' consciousness and not an abstract class consciousness in the Marxian sense bridged the gaps of inter-craft rivalries.[8] Moreover, the associations not only served as a stage for political action. They became the centres of social life for those who joined up. German Social Democracy united recruits from a vast array of social backgrounds. Yet members of the traditional artisanal trades formed the largest contingent among them. Journeymen and small masters made up the majority of the associations' membership. Tailors, shoemakers, cabinet makers, carpenters, and weavers clearly predominated. The trade of cigar making, organised in artisanal settings yet lacking a guild history, was also over-represented. The number of Social Democratic elementary school teachers, literati, journalists, doctors, and pharmacists was also larger than Marxist theory can account for. On the other hand, factory workers or casual labourers only formed a tiny minority in the radiating urban centres of the movement.[9] Early Social Democracy in Germany was not a class movement in the strict theoretical sense. Rather, it originated as a movement of small producers and radical 'marginal men' united both by a shared organisational life-world and the common opposition against the 'bourgeoisie', the reactionary state, and the church.

'Worker', 'citizen', and 'man': identity formation in organisational culture

The adoption of the term 'workers' movement', therefore, did not reflect a process of social levelling. It signalled the construction of a *political identity* on a post-guild basis, which placed the commonwealth of independent producers in the centre of all notions of citizen rights. Not only journeymen figured as 'workers' according to this definition. The term 'worker' also applied to small masters if they did not employ more than five journeymen and thereby proved that they lived off the labour of their own hands, rather than from the exploitation of other men. Moreover: 'Not only the labourer is obedient to the bourgeoisie, the scholar as well, the physician, the poet, the journalist, all of them are its servant.'[10] German Social Democracy began as a political movement on the basis of a rather artificial, ideological identity. Yet this identity was not a free invention. It did have a basis in social practice and experience. It was self-consciously acted out in the world of associational culture. Politically charged sociability in this context became the bedrock for a specific model of 'strong' masculinity, featuring the virtues of active citizenship and brotherly consciousness. The very term 'worker' in this sense stood for an alternative vision of what a man could and should be.

The young tailors, master weavers, cigar makers, yet also the equally young teachers, literati, and shop owners – the core of Social Democracy – experienced the associational life and the political gatherings as the only self-controlled sphere in which they could act out 'honour' and 'respectability'. Here they debated on equal terms, socialised, and presented themselves as refined personalities with broad interests and skills. This was the sphere where they translated needs into rights, weakness into strength, obedience into masculine independence. Elsewhere this was impossible: in the small workshops, the patriarchal artisanal household was still intact. Many journeymen continued to reside in their master's house and remained subjects of draconian household regimes. The state treated journeymen not as citizens but subjugated them as immature servants. Small masters in cottage industries often experienced an erosion of traditional gender roles when their wives contributed to production. Roughly fifty percent of the urban journeymen were still bachelors and, consequently, without a household of their own that could be used to make claims to citizenship on the basis of 'respectable' patriarchy. Many of them voiced surprisingly conventional, almost 'bourgeois' imaginations concerning the relations between sexes that were idealisations without a background of real experiences. The habits of male-bonding in the workingmen's lodging houses and of journeymen's misogyny informed the representations of 'manly modesty and self-composure' Social Democrats put forward time and again in their meetings.[11] This was the result of experiences made under the circumstances of forced bachelorhood. It explains why young Social Democrats nourished an ideal of masculinity beyond the confines of husbandry and fatherhood. Yet their version of 'contentious masculinity' easily encompassed the self-image of their more seasoned comrades as 'male breadwinners'. Their visions coalesced in the primacy of producerism and a most traditional view of the role of women as the domestic supporters of the men's active citizenship:

> Bring about conditions, under which every mature Man can marry a wife, so that there will be none of the poor creatures any more that falls prey to the isolation of the desperate, that sins against herself and

nature, that brands 'civilisation' by prostitution and trade with live human flesh ... To the wives and mothers belong the duties of the home and family, the nursing, care for, and first education of the children, doubtlessly provided that the wives and mothers are themselves adequately educated. The wife and mother shall stand for the comfort and poetry of family life, complementing the solemn public and family duty of the Man and father. She shall bring grace and beauty into social life and cultivate the pleasure of life of humanity.[12]

For all these reasons the self-determined public sphere of associations, clubs, and gatherings became the guarded hoard of masculinity for German Social Democrats. They brought about a specific type of masculinity based on active participation in public affairs and a youthful but cultivated public appearance as orators. This combined with their urge to act out their imaginations of a complete personality as embodied in the vision of the political citizen. In associational meetings and public rallies political zeal, quest for identity, and fraternal sociability formed an indissoluble unity. Here one would not only meet as political comrades, but as friends and drinking buddies who mutually assured one another of their 'manly' qualities. These were the places where one would stage his 'respectability', sites of engagement in passionate debates, of listening to powerful – and empowering – speeches. In associational meetings and public gatherings an emotionally condensed atmosphere spread, further condensed by cigar smoke and beer fumes, petrol lights, and the tense collective body of the audience. This atmosphere provided social gratification, comfort, emotional release – or simply entertainment – for all participants.

On his travels through Austria as a journeyman, Social Democratic ace speaker Johann Most, for instance, a young book binder from Augsburg in southern Germany, was introduced to this spell-binding atmosphere. Over the following years he became completely absorbed by this public political culture and began to work for the party professionally as a travelling orator and journalist. After an unhappy marriage to a 'dark-eyed girl from Chemnitz' he consciously decided to live as a bachelor, fully devoted to the party. As editor of party newspapers and a fiery speaker he spent day and night on the road for Social Democracy. By the early 1870s his life oscillated between editors' offices, meetings, rallies, the *Reichstag*, and jail: 'I plunged into [this movement] with such an energy that I became totally absorbed by party life. Although I had to work from early morning to late night for a meagre wage, I ran from one workers' rally to the other on Sundays or as soon as work was over.'[13]

This emotionally charged leisure activity, performed to display political respectability and democratic steadfastness, proved extraordinarily attractive to young journeymen, small masters, and bourgeois radicals. A report on a Viennese rally from May 1869 stated:

> He who has given up hope of the people's energy should go to such a gathering, and he can easily convince himself that democratic blood indeed is still circulating in the people's veins. Look at these Men of Labour, who, after having worked all day long, still follow the deliberations with utmost attention, giving evidence with their glances and expressions that the democratic spark has ignited their hearts. Listen to these orators who are virtually mushrooming [everywhere] and surpass in passion, force, and flow of speech everything accomplished by our regular parliamentary eloquence. Here you find this truthful and excelling eloquence that is rooted in the brain as it is in the heart.[14]

German Social Democrats portrayed their political mass rallies, understood as 'assemblies of the people', as the future body politic representing a process of direct legislation by the people. Correspondingly, they staged their public debates in a pathetically 'respectable' manner, driving home the values of radical democracy. The Men of Labour, in their dark Sunday suits, presented themselves as the 'people proper', the creative, working, intellectually distinguished 'complete personalities' they were not able to be in the workshop or at home. Their competence in a 'parliamentary' public became the core of their 'democratic version' of true masculinity: 'As early as two o'clock the people convened at the gathering site which became overcrowded already by three o'clock. The garden and adjacent beer halls were densely packed with sturdy men, whose calm solemnity reflected the meaning of an assembly of the people. At least 3,500 men were present.'[15]

As reports about rallies in the style of battle accounts showed, Social Democrats experienced these assemblies sometimes breathlessly thrilled and sometimes turbulently agitated. The back-and-forth of the debate created an atmosphere of passion. Participants might leave the battlefield stirred and disunited, but never unaffected. Yet the emotions invested had to be justified as respectable behaviour, as passionate dedication to the just cause of the working people. The 'honourable' self-image of German Social Democrats called for such a representation. Their notion of 'honour' and 'respectability' rang with allusions of a solemn but somewhat belligerent and rebellious masculinity. This gesture was even more elevated on occasion of the numerous festivals the labour movement staged. Here, playful entertainment, drinking sociability, and the pathos of a 'higher mission' combined in ennobling fraternisation and male-bonding the celebration of which left the male audience visibly touched:

> [After the formal address] gifts of joy and the most harmless pleasantry followed en suite, and the banquet carried the air of a refined sociability, that some of the assembled never had experienced before. Some recited poems and songs, Others pleased the audience with humorous sketches of folklore, and in cheerful change with all of this the songs and music performed by the members raised our festive mood. Not less visible to the eye of the beholder was the spirit of concord, the sentiment that enlightens the physical world of society from a higher, refined standpoint, the spirit of true manly zeal.[16]

It was decidedly manly to take part in the associations' debates. It was almost the apotheosis of masculinity to engage in public discourse and to stand for one's principles in an intrepid manner. Correspondingly, the ferocious public orator became the paramount hero in the self-imagery of Social Democratic manhood. To speak publicly was a lustful passion for both orator and audience. In this context, rhetorical competence was taken as a masculine property. This 'rhetorical masculinity' rang with connotations of duels, victory, and defeat. It was possible to 'win' the debate. The speakers aimed at ridiculing the opponent, at driving him from the floor, at 'routing him off balance'. In 1870, a Schwäbisch-Hall member of the Social Democratic Workingmen's Party reported to August Bebel in a letter brimming with pride about his rhetorical victory over 'bourgeois' members of the Southern German *Volkspartei*:

> I took the floor and opened the assembly at 3.30 p.m. Schwend was appointed chairman, and I presented the Eisenach platform in a lengthy speech. Roddo did [the same with his platform], he was refuted by Schwend and shaken thoroughly in his social and political views. Now followed [the separatist] Auer who completely lost track in his flattering aberrations. The same was disrupted by 'oho'-calls and hissing and suddenly stood there as if petrified and did not know how to go on. Hereupon I entered the stage and exposed these chaps and their theories as they deserved it. Grinding their teeth and grimacing they heard the applause, and I came forth with the following motion . . . With long faces the Stuttgart chaps bailed out, and they will most likely shun Hall for the time being and will not easily forget of the Social Democrats there.[17]

Rhetorical skills, intrepidity, and steadfastness in principles combined to form a decidedly masculine posture. 'It is disgraceful for a Man to deny his persuasions; it is even more shameful to embrace their opposite openly', Brunswick grain tradesman Wilhelm Bracke wrote to August Bebel in 1875.[18] Steadfastness in fundamental principles, hardened in numerous debates, proved a manly warrior's heart. In contrast to this, compromise not only rang with associations of 'female' but of 'effeminate'. This reproach was not directed against women. Rather, it targeted the male political opponents present in assemblies held together. It was the political opponent, the liberal 'bourgeoisie', that was depicted as one-dimensional personalities, calculating 'humans of fish blood', and not sturdy men.[19]

Social Democrats developed a challenging appearance, rebellious against all kinds of established authority. They ceremoniously staged this appearance by dressing impeccably and stylish, by demonstrating faultless manners, and by excelling in a fiery rhetorical competence. For Social Democrats, these attributes and habits combined to be the only legitimate form of masculinity in their eyes: the politically active producer citizen who skilfully moved in the public sphere and whose speckless habit reflected both inner values and honourable principles.[20] In order to present themselves as defiant, belligerent, self-conscious, and superior vis-à-vis their opponents, Social Democrats cultivated a decidedly masculine self-image. Conversely, this posture required that similar masculine qualities be denied in their opponents. In order to brand these opponents as 'effeminate', they unwillingly devalued the women as well. The 'gathering of the people' appeared as a theatre of combat, in which one had to remain master as if on a battleground or on top of the barricades, in a struggle for life or death. 'The people's party unites Men, not babblers and comedians', Wilhelm Liebknecht proclaimed in 1869 in a retrospective of the Reichsverfassungskampagne (campaign for the Reich constitution) in 1849; 'as Men who knew how to die for their cause, the victims of the May revolution have erected an immortal monument for themselves in the hearts of the people's party. They are legitimately entitled to the tribute these lines shall pay them today.'[21] In the small-scale war of debate 'manly' true-heartedness stood against simple emotional 'partisanship' identified as 'effeminate' sentimentality. To be sure, the Social Democratic Man as a 'complete personality' had to be passionate. Yet what was artfully sublimated as 'love' in relation to the other sex had to become determined passion in political battle. For this reason women had no active role in the public sphere:

To the Men

Enough has been written for womanhood,
Sentimental and mellow with love;
On Germany's hopes and Germany's affection,
We abound in verse and prose.
For Men shall sound my tune,
Urge them on to courageous deeds,
Urge them on to daring endeavours,
So that they *themselves* steer the wheel of the world.[22]

The Social Democrats' passionate – yet strictly formal – 'respectability' as represented in associations and assemblies had the exclusion of women as its reciprocal value. This was only a superficial transformation and elevation of the misogynist journeymen's culture. Seemingly, the presence of women disturbed the solemnly staged elevated atmosphere of the assemblies by inserting 'profane' elements. This image sometimes rang with open sexual allusions:

> It is only too good that we do not allow ladies to come to our sessions, like last time on the occasion of Tauscher's speech. That day – to tell the truth – at least 500 of them were on the scene, and there was no talk of the labour movement, rather different sorts of movements were performed on the *Stiftsgarten's* galleries.[23]

Gender troubles in Social Democratic club culture

In the debating culture of Social Democratic associations and assemblies, the eloquent and fiery public orator literally personified the ideal of the political citizen. And this ideal was equivalent to true masculinity. Hence the exclusion of women from the debates became an outright prerequisite for creating an atmosphere of 'parliamentary dignity' that helped keep up manly self-consciousness. Within the Chemnitz Lassallean General Workers' Association (LADAV, a splinter organization derived from Ferdinand Lassalle's ADAV), a small group of women sympathisers, led by Auguste Wunderlich, planned an evening of entertainment for the local party lodge in the fall of 1868. They contemplated 'arranging a show programme since – as women – we do not have an association, and we want to invite the men in order to raise funds for the party's public agitation'. The women intended to present their project at a formal session of the local LADAV. Yet the majority among the male membership of the party refused to let the women take the floor.

Auguste Wunderlich and her female companions received little support:

> Mr Schultheiss, whom I call an honourable fellow [he was at the age of 24 at that time], who combines the Beautiful with the Useful, who excels in uniting Austerity and Kindness, he engaged in all of the eloquence he commands and spoke in our favour; the same did Mr Reuther who had taken us oppressed women under protection so many times.

The way the majority of male members justified their rejection resounded with open misogynist clichès:

> Messrs Helfrig, Eichhorn, Berthold, and Fischer spoke out against [the women's presence]. Mr Eichhorn brought us to reason with a drastic vocabulary, and it was not at all flattering to hear that we had to stay home; as long as he and Berthold were members of the board they would not tolerate women speaking, even if Mende and Försterling had ruled otherwise; 'we do not tolerate that since the women are no more than our guests'.[24]

Underlying the men's position was a tacit consensus that the full participation of women in associational life threatened to 'effeminate' the sturdy 'Men of the Assembly'. Allegedly, women impaired the 'respectable' atmosphere of 'gatherings of the people' by making unqualified statements and breaking 'parliamentary' rules. Even Auguste Wunderlich herself drew on such images of the females 'lacking education' when she defended her cause: 'Be assured that if we indeed had taken the floor, we would have spoken with prudence and consideration. No silly babbling would have come to the fore, they could have listened to us and then judged for themselves.'[25]

Women remained unwanted in the associational meetings and public assemblies. It was the political opponent who occupied the position of the 'feminine' in Social Democratic practice and discourse in the first place. Female intrusion into this masculine world would have disturbed an atmosphere where 'honour', 'respectability', and 'self-composure' dominated as performatively constructed elements of collective (male) identity. Finally, women threatened to break in to the painstakingly cultivated sphere of 'masculinity' that compensated for the lack of opportunities to present oneself as a 'Man' elsewhere. The public realm of associations and assemblies was the only sphere in which Social Democrats could nourish their claims to 'manliness' and 'citizenship'. By engaging in public debate, they could stage themselves as 'men' clearly superior to women and opponents alike. Social Democrats cultivated the self-image of the 'truly educated' precisely against the background of 'uncultivated' women and 'bourgeois' liberals. Since living together as couples did not seem to warrant a 'natural' superiority of the men involved, the artificial and idealised life-world of the associations and assemblies needed protection if it was to prevent this sphere from degenerating to an object of profane wrangling: 'The lady who proves unreceptive to the Man's lessons will prove even more uncivilised in a public locality, where He rightfully dwells, and where she would be confronted with a much bigger world than she is already in her home.'[26]

If the party press made any mention of the presence of women at gatherings and festivities, this happened in order to highlight the Social Democrats' conscious defiance of the state's draconian associational laws that, among many other restrictions, explicitly prohibited female participation in political meetings until 1908. It was rare that the papers called to notice such instances; this and the fact that women were addressed explicitly hints at the presence of women in formal meetings as a rather marginal phenomenon. If women indeed left traces in the various reports about gatherings, these as a rule stressed their passive role as listeners: Women were guests, tacit admirers of the men, mere 'camp-followers'.[27]

As mentioned above, women did play an important role at the entertainment shows, tours, Lassalle commemorations, and founder's days of German Social Democracy. Yet they did not enter centre stage. The female 'guests' of such events remained in the background: busy with preparing such festivals, as an audience impressed by the speakers and by the overall cultural skills of the associations – ornaments, in fact, that added to male self-elevation. It was their task to make Social Democratic festivals unprecedented experiences for the (male) members. The women formed part of a resonating audience that applauded the rhetorical aces delivering the formal address – undoubtedly the highlight of every commemoration. The eloquent orators within the movement utilised these addresses to prove rhetorical competence and thereby to present themselves as refined 'Male Beauties' to a breathlessly listening audience:

> The culminating point of the festival was the formal address delivered by Mr *Motteler*. This steadfast fighter for commonwealth and human rights, quick-witted as ever, showcased his rhetorical talent to the best that evening. He spoke with sweeping enthusiasm about the task of the people's party and the noble aims of Social Democracy. His truthful, clear cut and potent words radiated into the mass of participants, tightly packed head to head, like sparkling flashes of lightning, and they made an everlasting impression on the minds of our ladies as well.[28]

Such moves to address wives and other women in the context of Social Democratic festivals and commemorations did not serve the purpose of really integrating them into labour movement culture. Rather, Social Democrats aimed at tearing down the female walls of resistance against the political engagement of their husbands and sons. Furthermore the celebratory staging of the festivals was designed to persuade women that Social Democracy was a just cause worth fighting for by men and women alike. This act of persuasion took place on an emotional rather than an intellectual level. Only if the women were won, could they be expected not only to tolerate but actively support the men's activities.[29] Women's activities in favour of the associations also served as an appeal to the male members' 'honour' not to let themselves be surpassed in their courage but to prove themselves as 'true Men'. Thus Wilhelm Bracke wrote in 1868:

> We must not underestimate how important it is to enlighten the women politically. I would truly like to know how we could impress this upon the tender sex better than by means of our shows and dances. Here in Brunswick I know several cases where husband and wife almost picked a quarrel as soon as the husband intended to go to a lodge meeting or to an assembly. Yet after we had celebrated Christmas, Lassalle's birthday, and the anniversary of his death – where the women were present, everything was different. When it was eight o'clock on Mondays or Saturdays, the wife made her appearance and said: 'Husband, you have to go to the lodge where you belong.' This alone, everything else discounted, readily justifies such entertainment. . . . Scum is the name for someone who deserts this banner and lets himself be ashamed by the women's courage.[30]

Finally, this appeal to the women for their support of the men's cause did not fail to address their obligation as mothers to educate their sons as recruits to the movement.

The utopian conundrum: the woman and socialism

This patronising and chivalrous position, generated in an all-male and decidedly manly environment, placed German Social Democracy in an ideological dilemma. A central element in the Social Democratic outlook on the world was to present the 'miniature republic' of the workers' association as *the* institutional model for the future socialist state.[31] The attraction such an image of 'associational socialism' could stir up in early German Social Democracy heavily depended on the ability of the members to experience the association in its role as a promise for the future as a central part of their real life-world. Seemingly, this promise was already fulfilled at least in their immediate environment. The association was not only the arena where the struggle for the just cause took place. It was also the site where members socialised as 'associational Men', where they satisfied social needs in a community of 'manly' comrades, and where they remained undisturbed.

Yet when Social Democrats viewed these artificial 'micro-worlds' as a blueprint of future society, they in fact excluded the women and, in doing this, half of the populace. This contradicted the universalist claims they made in ideology. It now became a serious problem that German Social Democrats had to link their self-image as 'Men' so closely to this public sphere as the only forum where they could act out this role. Neither the 'rough' shop-floor nor a patriarchal household could compensate for this public sphere. In consequence, balancing gender relations in ideology was exceptionally difficult for the early German labour movement. To be sure, this problem unfolded fully only after the close ties between existing associations and the ideology of 'associational socialism' had begun to loosen in the early 1870s. Now ideology took a utopian turn that forced Social Democrats to spell out in detail the contours of future socialist society. This necessarily implied coming to terms with the ideological conflict between universal humanism and male exclusiveness.

How could German Social Democracy develop a vision of socialism which on the one hand was based on a gender comradeship much unlike bourgeois marriage but that on the other hand perpetuated an inequality of sexes on which male images of supremacy rested? How could the movement reconcile ideological pressure to further women's liberation with the urge to keep the associations intact as all-male institutions – at least for the present-day era of struggle?

This very dilemma caused August Bebel in the middle of the 1870s to choose the 'women's question' as a topic of theoretical and utopian considerations. In the first edition of his book *Die Frau und der Sozialismus* (Woman and Socialism), which was published in Zurich in 1879, he found a pseudo solution to this problem that was deeply informed by explicit references to Darwinism, yet gave it a historical twist. According to Bebel, the oppression of women in human society, sustained over so many centuries, had subjugated women to a degree of immaturity that prevented them from participation in Social Democracy's political struggle on equal terms. The institution of marriage – in bourgeois society – had particularly fostered this immaturity, since it forced women to surrender their personalities to the rule of money in order to secure their livelihood – just like prostitutes. Only in future socialist society would gender relations develop on the basis of emancipation and comradeship. Economic independence would uplift marriage ethically. This, in turn, would break the ground for a better education of women. And only this, finally, would prepare women for proper participation in public associational life. The extension of cooperative forms of communal life would help relieve the partnership between the sexes from economic and household constraints. This reasoning, in sum, enabled Bebel to justify the persistent exclusion of women from the associational life of the present. August Bebel did support women's suffrage, together with a rather slim minority of prominent Social Democrats, in contrast to 'grassroots' sentiment. Yet he did this for mainly tactical reasons: he aimed at forging a coalition between Social Democracy and the infant women's movement especially in his hometown, Leipzig. This meant that he envisaged a functional alliance between institutions in which men and women continued to be organised separately.[32]

This 'Darwinisation' of gender relations allowed German Social Democracy to project the solution of the women's question into a far away future. Gender equality was seen as the long-term *consequence* of a political revolution brought about by the collapse of fully developed capitalism and no longer by the deliberate action of Social Democratic revolutionaries. Party leaders like Johann Most stated that future developments of associational life might provide new solutions to the problem of gender partnership that eluded anticipation by contemporaries. Therefore it would be an academic exercise to speculate – and one which would invite unnecessary conflict in the process.[33] It was unfair to blame the present associations for maintaining gender inequality, since it was the enemy itself, the reactionary state, that decisively restricted women's rights in public life. In the long run, the specific problem of gender relations, which deeply penetrated the Social Democratic self-image of revolutionary universalism, contributed to the transformation of 'associational socialism', virulent from the 1840s to the 1870s, into the evolutionary 'state socialism' typical of the Wilhelmine era. Over the last two decades of the nineteenth century, German Social Democracy converted from a party fighting the existing 'relations of production' to a party applauding the expansion of the 'forces of production' – in the hope of ultimately profiting from the alleged future collapse of the system. The party, almost imperceptibly to contemporaries, changed from an active revolutionary perspective, which nourished expectations that the revolution was imminent, to a tacitly reformist stance. From the 1890s on, only the Marxian term 'class struggle' continued to bridge more and more pragmatic day-to-day politics and the utopian promise. The eventual solution of the gender question became part of this promise. By dodging the present-day problems of gender relations, German Social Democrats managed to conceal the fact that they did not have an answer to this problem clearly distinct from both traditional misogynist and conventional bourgeois positions. And their 'contentious masculinity' vanished with the demise of the Anti-Socialist Law in 1890. When the 'heroic days' of the movement were over, a more conventional figure – the skilled metalworker of middle age, displaying his muscular build under a leather apron and clearly representing the male breadwinner – stood for a Social Democratic 'counter masculinity' that highlighted sturdiness in the ongoing battle for integration into Wilhelmine society.

Conclusion

This chapter has shown how closely questions of masculinity were interrelated with other dimensions of identity formation among German Social Democrats in the 1860s and 1870s. Their subjectivity as 'workers' and 'citizens' rested on a specific quality of 'manhood' which translated into the sovereign appearance of the competent orator in the public sphere of society and politics. This notion of masculinity became the very basis for their wide-reaching claims to full political citizenship. Yet this did not mean playing by the rules of bourgeois liberalism then dominating public life.

Social Democrats did not imitate bourgeois 'hegemonic masculinity'. They did not let themselves be victimised as servants displaying a subaltern type of masculinity. Nor did they retreat into an autonomous niche of society where they could have cherished a somewhat anti-bourgeois version of a 'rough' 'counter-masculinity'. Since they embraced most bourgeois values but considered themselves as the only legitimate heralds of these values – as producers and active citizens – their gender project can best be termed as 'contentious masculinity'.

Notes

1 A. Baron, 'Gendered subjects: Re-presenting "the worker" in history', unpublished paper, The Centre for the History of Business, Technology, and Society, Hagley Museum and Library, Wilmington, DE, 12 December 1995.

2 T. Welskopp, *Arbeit und Macht im Hüttenwerk: Arbeits- und industrielle Beziehungen in der deutschen und amerikanischen Eisen- und Stahlindustrie von den 1860er zu bis den 1930er Jahren* (Bonn, 1994).

3 A. Clark, *The Struggle for the Breeches: Gender and the Making of the British Working Class* (Berkeley, Los Angeles and London, 1995).

4 K. Canning, *Languages of Labour and Gender: Female Factory Work in Germany, 1850–1914* (Ithaca and London, 1996).

5 S. Na'aman, *Der Deutsche Nationalverein: Die politische Konstituierung des deutschen Bürgertums 1859–1867* (Düsseldorf, 1987); T. Offermann, *Arbeiterbewegung und liberales Bürgertum in Deutschland 1850–1863* (Bonn, 1979).

6 D. Montgomery, *The Fall of the House of Labour: The Workplace, the State, and American Labour Activism, 1865–1925* (Cambridge MA and New York, 1987).

7 This is a statement against Richard Biernacki's argument that German workers experienced 'pure' wage work earlier than their British counterparts and that this experience facilitated their reception of Karl Marx's theory. See R. G. Biernacki, Jr., *The Fabrication of Labour: Germany and Britain, 1640–1914* (Berkeley and Los Angeles, 1995).

8 H.-J. Zerwas, *Arbeit als Besitz: Das ehrbare Handwerk zwischen Bruderliebe und Klassenkampf 1848* (Reinbek, 1988).

9 My analysis is largely based on T. Welskopp, *Das Banner der Brüderlichkeit: Die deutsche Sozialdemokratie vom Vormärz bis zum Sozialistengesetz* (Bonn, 2000).

10 *Protokolle der sozialdemokratischen Arbeiterpartei, Vol. I (Eisenach 1869–Coburg 1874), and Vol. II (Gotha 1875–St. Gallen 1887)* (Bonn and Bad Godesberg, 1976, reprint) (hereafter *Protokoll 1869* etc.), *Protokoll 1872*, p. 17.

11 *Protokoll 1872*, p. 8.

12 Quoted in W. Thönessen, *Frauenemanzipation. Politik und Literatur der deutschen Frauenbewegung 1863–1933* (Frankfurt am Main, 2nd edn, 1976), p. 19.

13 J. Most, 'Memorie I', in S. Riesenfellner (ed.), *Arbeiterleben: Autobiographien zur Alltags- und Sozialgeschichte Österreichs 1867–1914* (Graz, 1989), pp. 13 ff.

14 *Demokratisches Wochenblatt*, no. 18 (1 May 1869), p. 200.

15 *Demokratisches Wochenblatt*, no. 41 (18 September 1869), p. 465.

16 *Deutsche Arbeiterhalle*, no. 6 (25 March 1868).

17 Stiftung Archiv der Parteien und Massenorganisationen der DDR im Bundesarchiv (hereafter SAPMO-BArch), NY 4022/96, Wilhelm Atz to August Bebel, Schwäbisch-Hall, 14 March 1870.

18 SAPMO-BArch, NY 4022/101, Wilhelm Bracke to August Bebel, Braunschweig, 31 March 1875.

19 *Nordstern*, no. 292 (14 January 1865).

20 SAPMO-BArch, NY 4022/114, Johannes Renk to August Bebel, Munich, 7 November 1869.

21 *Demokratisches Wochenblatt*, no. 21 (22 May 1869), pp. 227 ff.

22 W. Hasenclever, *Liebe, Leben, Kampf: Gedichte von Wilhelm Hasenclever* (Hamburg, 1876), p. 151.

23 SAPMO-BArch, NY 4022/114, Johannes Renk to August Bebel, Munich, 7 November 1869.

24 SAPMO-BArch, RY 15/6/69, Auguste Wunderlich an Fritz Mende, Chemnitz, 15 November 1868.
25 *Ibid.*
26 *Social-Demokrat*, no. 74 A (26 June 1868).
27 *Demokratisches Wochenblatt*, no. 24 (12 June 1869) p. 264.
28 *Demokratisches Wochenblatt*, no. 31 (31 July 1869), p. 351.
29 *Social-Demokrat*, no. 142 (3 December 1869).
30 *Social-Demokrat*, no. 70 (17 June 1868).
31 D. Dowe (ed.), *Protokolle und Materialien des Allgemeinen Deutschen Arbeitervereins* (Berlin, Bonn, 1980, reprint), p. 150.
32 A. Bebel, *Die Frau und der Sozialismus* (Zurich, 1879), in *August Bebel: Ausgewählte Reden und Schriften*, Vol. 10/1 (München, 1996, reprint).
33 J. Most, 'Die Lösung der sozialen Frage', in V. Szmula (ed.), *Johann Most: Dokumente eines sozialdemokratischen Agitators*, Vol. 3 (Grafenau-Döffingen, 1990), p. 46.

15

Making workers masculine: the (re)construction of male worker identity in twentieth-century Brazil

Barbara Weinstein

POCKETS of large-scale industry, mainly devoted to textile manu-facturing, began to form in Latin America in the early twentieth century, provoking often contradictory responses from both propertied and labouring populations. Especially contradictory were opinions about industry and its impact on women and the family. As mill-owners throughout Latin America scrambled to hire women workers for the 'light', repetitive tasks required for textile manufacturing, wage-earning women gained a new visibility. Employers valued women because their gendered position within society made them cheap to hire, and their supposed docility made them easy to fire. And many families of modest means welcomed the additional wages a working wife or daughter contributed to the household.[1]

At the same time, large-scale employment of women and girls in industry generated a series of censorious responses. Critics of industry from the middling and upper classes cited industrialists' employment of women as threatening to disrupt traditional family structures and expose the women, and by extension, the family, to a variety of per-nicious influences. Among them would be the undermining of male authority in the home – a source of particular anxiety in the Latin American context where few households actually conformed to the classic bourgeois model of a family with a wage-earning father and a stay-at-home mother, but where 'nation-builders' viewed such a model as crucial to the construction of honorable, hygienic and productive national populations.[2]

Such anxieties, moreover, were by no means confined to govern-ment officials and elite segments of society. Early labour leaders – most of them male – decried the employment of women and children as impairing men's efforts to improve their wages and retain control of the work process. Not only was female employment denounced for depriving male breadwinners of job opportunities, but with their supposed lack of skills and, hence, weak bargaining position, the presence of women in the factory was seen as degrading industrial labor generally, and making it unfit for manly men.[3] Thus, from the outset, the questions of skill and apprenticeship emerged as central themes in debates about who should work in factories, what factory labour meant for worker identities, and what kinds of citizens these new workplaces would form. In effect, the tendency was to associate skill with the maintenance of manly dignity in the workplace, whereas unskilled labour was marked as degraded and feminine.

This chapter will examine the intersections of debates about skill, working-class masculinity, and citizenship in Brazil. It will examine the efforts – principally by industrialists and their spokesmen, but also by government officials and labour leaders – to construct 'modern' masculine subjectivities in which skilled industrial employment and household headship were the crucial ingredients. While acknowledging the considerable overlap in the discursive strategies of these different groups, this article will also indicate the ways in which the dominant discourses about masculinity, skill, and citizenship opened spaces for male workers to contest industrialist politics and policies. These are issues of national, even transnational, scope, but most of the material below will address the specific case of São Paulo (a designation that refers to both city and state), the most important locus of industrialisation in twentieth-century Brazil, and a region that would eventually gain the distinction of being Latin America's largest manufacturing centre.[4]

By the 1920s, a circle of industrialist-intellectuals and engineers had formed in São Paulo that, despite close cooperation with the immigrant textile magnates (pejoratively dubbed 'the Italian Counts'), actively sought to construct a different public image for themselves, in the eyes of both other elite groups and the rapidly forming working class.[5] For this circle of aspiring entrepreneurs and budding technocrats the large-scale employment of women and children in factories signalled all that was problematic about Brazilian industry: low levels of skill in the workforce, the weakness of basic (especially metallurgical) industries, the lack of rational organisation in the workplace, and the low moral and cultural level of the working class. In addition, as these new industrial spokesmen aggressively sought effective protectionist measures from the central government, they became keenly aware that a poor public image could dampen enthusiasm for government-sponsored industrialisation, or worse, premise 'favours' for manufacturers on the introduction of coercive forms of state intervention into industrial relations. Impelled, in part, by this concern with their credibility and authority in the larger Brazilian political sphere, but also by their own Fordist project for the construction of a rational and productive society, they sought to foreground the skilled male worker as the future citizen and beneficiary of a modern, industrialising Brazil.[6]

Gender, skill, and vocational training

Skill acquisition in these early decades involved the gradual accumulation of knowledge through observation of older, more experienced workers on the shop floor. Though this system of casual apprenticeship did not rigidly exclude women, it made it likely that gendered divisions of labour by skill would be reproduced within the factory, with men continuing to monopolise positions defined as skilled (rather than semi-skilled or unskilled) even in the textile industry. There were, however, efforts from a variety of quarters to provide more systematic training for aspiring industrial workers, and these efforts led to the founding, in 1911, of São Paulo's first two major 'professional schools': the *Escola Profissional Masculina* and the *Escola Profissional Feminina*.[7]

The simultaneous creation of vocational schools for both girls and boys might be interpreted, at first glance, as an endorsement of women's employment in the industrial sphere. But it is essential to note the dramatically different configurations of the two schools, with the *Escola Masculina* being designated explicitly to offer industrial training, while the *Escola Feminina* studiously avoided any association with factory labor. The former, in its architecture and operations, was designed to approximate conditions on the shop floor, and to exemplify a rational, orderly workspace, with manual instructors drawn directly from the industrial milieu. In contrast, the latter was housed in an old residential structure, offered only artisanal forms of instruction, repeatedly tried to incorporate domestic arts into the curriculum, and employed only normal school graduates from 'good backgrounds'.

Furthermore, the man who served as the first director of the two professional schools was a staunch defender of adult male skilled workers and vehemently denounced the hiring of women and minors for factory work, citing their unwelcome presence as the main explanation for (men's) depressed wages. Treating women and children as equivalent categories, Aprígio de Almeida Gonzaga called for their 'removal' from the factory workforce, a process that he claimed would 'rebound to the benefit of the race, of the society, and of the nation'.[8] Gonzaga's position on this matter, moreover, transcended a simple notion of cheap female labour driving down the value of manly work since he saw the feminisation of industrial labour as intimately related to the menace of de-skilling. Although he did not regard rational organisation and the valorisation of workers' skills as entirely incompatible, he nonetheless regarded de-skilling as a grave danger, and one that was magnified by the employment of women and children in industry. In Gonzaga's opinion, unskilled factory workers were 'morally dead, physically inadequate, mere human machines in the service of capital'.[9] And Gonzaga claimed that the very presence of women was promoting the de-skilling of industrial labour. Therefore, it was not just a matter of constructing industrial labour as masculine, or representing the factory as a dangerous or inappropriate space for women, but of associating manly dignity with skill, associating skill with rationalised and modern methods, and making the exclusion of women a prerequisite for protecting the value of manual skills within industry.

The question of female employment was particularly vexing for industrialists and their spokesmen. Factory owners were hardly eager to drive women out of the mills and thereby deprive themselves of a cheap source of labour. But the 'new-style' industrialist-engineers, eager to diversify Brazilian industry and increase productivity, were highly self-conscious about the image of the factory in Brazilian society, and how unrestrained employment of women might tarnish it. Convinced that industrial growth in a late-developing nation such as Brazil required at least some form of state intervention and protection – thus making it a *political* question – associations such as the Center for Industry in São Paulo State (inaugurated in 1928) had to portray industrialisation as benefiting all Brazilians.[10] Yet, such claims were difficult to substantiate if industry was seen as undermining the already fragile family and exploiting the most vulnerable members of the emerging working class. Therefore, in terms of 'public opinion', it was vastly more sensible to associate the future of industry with an image of the male/skilled 'worker-citizen', than with a female textile operative, even one who worked in a well-ordered, paternalistic environment.

Attuned to the Fordist message of productivity as the key to a stronger nation and better society, these new industrialists and industrial engineers (led by Roberto Simonsen and the Swiss-born advocate of vocational training, Roberto Mange) saw the good worker as inseparable from the good citizen who would work hard for a brighter future, and know his place in both the political and economic hierarchy of Brazilian society. Indeed, this greater potential for compliance, in their eyes, was one of the few advantages offered by the Brazilian worker; he might be less literate and less skilled than his European counterpart, but he was also less likely to resist new work processes or reject new technologies.[11]

Nationalising and masculinising apprenticeship

The rise of Getúlio Vargas, who seized power in 1930 through a largely bloodless revolution, and who would preside over an authoritarian but reform-minded regime for the next fifteen years, stimulated even greater interest in vocational instruction among educators and employers. Vargas' nationalist and proto-populist appeal to urban workers meant that he would foreground such issues as 'nationalising' the workforce and providing practical educational opportunities for the growing industrial working class.[12] Such opportunities were not defined as exclusively intended for male workers, but over time, vocational training became ever more identified with skilled *male* factory work. And even though Vargas did not exclude women from his conceptualisation of the Brazilian citizen, his populist promises to workers typically envisioned a proletarian culture in which men worked and women remained in the home.[13]

Several alterations in the vocational education landscape were indicative of this masculinisation process. By the early 1930s the state of São Paulo had passed a new educational code that further hardened the distinctions between male and female vocational instruction. Among other things, it forbade any mixed gender classes in professional schools, and made home economics a requirement for female students.[14] As a 1934 report by a leading group of vocational educators argued, domestic education should be obligatory in vocational schools throughout Brazil, 'because a woman's professional life should be considered as merely a transitional phase: destiny designates her for ... the role of wife, mother and housewife'.[15]

Shifting to the federal level, where debates about vocational instruction were more heated and conflictive, we can identify as a key unifying assumption the view that the typical skilled worker would be a man, not a woman, and that vocational instruction should be oriented toward his transformation into a good citizen as well as a productive worker. Beyond that, however, there was little agreement on the precise shape that industrial training should take. Employers were particularly resistant to the idea, proposed by some government spokesmen, that all (male) workers receive vocational instruction. Indeed, employer representatives portrayed this as an unaffordable luxury since a rationally organised industrial sector would require extended training for a mere 15 per cent of new workers, according to Roberto Mange's calculations.[16] Instead, industrialists proposed a system in which only a minority of the working class would enjoy access to apprenticeship. The vast majority of workers, they contended, needed only a good general education 'that enriches ... the personality, gives them basic knowledge, awakens qualities of initiative, of cooperation, of loyalty; that creates habits that promote health, hygiene, thrift, hard work, discipline; that develops their capacity to reason, to observe, and to understand; and that makes them conscious of their duties as a worker, head of a family, and citizen of a country of which they form an integral part'.[17] In other words, the most 'able' workers could aspire to skilled status, but an industrial worker did not *have* to be skilled to be manly or a good citizen.

Vargas, meanwhile, felt increasing pressure to announce a major initiative in the realm of vocational instruction. Brushing aside a chorus of objections, on May Day 1939 Vargas issued decree law no. 1238, which required every factory employing five hundred or more workers to establish 'courses for professional improvement for minors and adults'.[18] Widely regarded as unworkable, this decree mainly served to goad the industrialists and educators into coming up with a more reasonable alternative. What is interesting for our purposes is the way in which its opponents attacked decree-law no. 1238. The principal rationale for its rejection was that it illogically associated plant size with skill demand. The federation of *paulista* employers argued that the vast majority of firms with over five hundred workers were textile mills, plants that typically required low levels of skill. Position papers on this matter did not explicitly identify the gender of textile operatives, but the unchallenged assumption that there was no need to provide extended training for workers in these plants indicates the extent to which textile work, long gendered female, was automatically defined as semi- or unskilled labor. Representatives of the Vargas administration who were given a guided tour of Paulista industry readily acknowledged that the only plant with a high proportion of skilled workers – a mechanical goods factory – had well under five hundred employees.[19]

The lack of references to gender in this documentation is itself revealing – in effect, it had become unnecessary to specify that the primary targets of industrial training were men since none of the participants seriously considered expending significant resources on the apprenticeship of women workers, who were defined (by 'nature') as unskilled or temporary workers who needed training for the home, not the factory. Further reinforcing this trend was the growing attention to apprenticeship in metallurgical, electrical and mechanical trades – categories that were unimpeachably masculine. All sides agreed that industrial labour, and especially skilled industrial labour, should be the province of men.

The consensual view of skilled labour as a masculine domain did not, however, resolve the question of what constituted proper working-class masculinity. The ongoing differences over this issue did not amount to diametrically opposed positions – there was a great deal of overlap in the conception of the good worker-citizen, whether the point of reference be the spokesperson for industry, the professional educator allied with the state, or the militant labour leader. But there were, nevertheless, some significant distinctions in the way working-class masculinity was being envisioned. Even at the height of Vargas' repressive policies toward unions, the working-class press characterised the accumulated knowledge required for certain crafts as a source of (worker) authority, and identified working-class interests as only partially compatible with those of industrial employers.[20] Similarly, personnel from the Ministry of Education extolled vocational training, not only as a source of discipline and productivity, but also as the 'great protective armour' of the male worker.[21]

Industrialists and the (re)making of the skilled male worker

Not surprisingly, industrialists and their allies envisioned proper working-class masculinity in a somewhat different light. Concerned that workers, and especially hard-to-replace skilled workers, 'know their place' within industry, they sought to establish a system of industrial training that would produce craftsmen who were technically, politically and psychologically compatible with the needs of a rationalised (and ever-rationalising) industrial economy. While acknowledging that a certain degree of conflict between labor and capital might be inevitable, they aspired to create an industrial community in which workers identified with industrialists' goals, presumed that labor and capital engaged in collaboration, not conflict, and together would work to construct a greater Brazil.[22] In this projection of the industrial community, the worker demonstrated his manliness through hard work, self-discipline, and a constant effort to improve his skills so as to serve industry better and expand his family's participation in modern consumer culture.

Industrialist associations readily agreed with government educators and labor leaders that Brazil needed a systematic source of 'national' (not imported) skilled workers, but they were eager to ensure that workers' training made them fit for and fit with the goals of industry.[23] Thus when negotiations over the future of industrial training appeared to be at a standstill in the early 1940s, Simonsen convinced Vargas to form a committee openly weighted in favor of employer interests to craft an alternative proposal on industrial apprenticeship. This *comissão de empresários* produced a proposal that designated industrial employers as responsible for the (mandatory) funding of the apprenticeship system, but by the same token placed industrial training almost entirely under the direction of the regional industrialist associations. Eventually dubbed the *Serviço Nacional de Aprendizagem Industrial* (SENAI), this national training service was designed to provide extended training to a minority of aspiring/adolescent industrial workers, as well as rapid courses to upgrade the skills of adult workers already employed in industry. And it was organised so that the industrialists would have a nearly free hand to define the programmes, to decide who was eligible, and to classify jobs as skilled, semi-skilled or unskilled.[24]

As one would expect, the new entity provided few opportunities for girls or women who aspired to jobs in industry, even though girls accounted for the majority of factory workers under the age of eighteen well into the 1960s. To be sure, it did not exclude females entirely: as SENAI's own national magazine described it, 'there are trades that are indicated for young female apprentices. In the graphic arts course, the job of stapling is an example.'[25] But even within the textile industry, where female workers were so numerous, courses defined as apprenticeship training tended to be reserved for boys – which indicates that girls were being systematically excluded. Moreover, once the war ended, SENAI curtailed its rapid training courses for 'semi-skilled' occupations and thereby eliminated most of the female students from its rosters.[26]

In effect, SENAI functioned as an apprenticeship programme for a small but essential segment of the male workforce, and concentrated its efforts on transforming what it saw as poorly-educated, disorderly, and unwashed working-class boys into disciplined, respectable, and productive working men.[27] One of the most striking aspects of SENAI's operations, at least in São Paulo, was the considerable effort and resources devoted to remaking the Brazilian worker not only in terms of his technical skills and abilities, but also with regard to his personal character and hygiene. Simonsen, Mange and the other leading lights of SENAI in São Paulo always insisted that the organisation had to provide its students with something more than just manual skills; they were producing not just competent, honest workers, but good citizens.

In his 1944 annual report on SENAI activities in São Paulo (where he was the founding director), Mange declared his 'absolute conviction that, without a social service especially designed for the student-apprentices, and which provides them with medical and dental care, proper nutrition and social assistance, the efficiency of the professional courses of instruction will be minimal'.[28] Moreover, the young worker was challenging, according to Mange, not only because he typically came from an indigent household, but also from a culturally deprived one.

> In the social and familial atmosphere inhabited by the SENAI student, he finds little encouragement to improve his general culture and to elevate his civic and moral precepts ... [Thus his] preparation will be incomplete unless placed within a context of order and discipline, morality and happiness in work, that would seek to create in these youths, who are the workers of tomorrow, a sense of responsibility and an elevated interest in the progress of technology and the national labour force.[29]

Or as one staff psychologist put it, SENAI would do for the student 'what his family was too ignorant or too incompetent to do'.[30] Moreover, as the composition of São Paulo's working class shifted away from (white) European immigrants and their descendants and toward mixed-race migrants from the Brazilian Northeast, Mange insisted that SENAI had an even greater obligation 'to be concerned with the formation of a healthy mentality, firm and conscientious, within the new labouring generation'.[31] Armed with this racially-inflected construction of the Brazilian working class, SENAI situated itself as a crucial civilising force within the emerging 'industrial community'.[32]

What SENAI imagined for these supposedly flawed but remediable future workers was a respectable masculinity based on the promise of steady industrial employment (as opposed to the more precarious rural and service occupations), on self-improvement through industrialist-funded training courses, and on the dignity of being the head of household and chief breadwinner. But by lamenting the defects of the Brazilian working class on the one hand, while avoiding all direct criticism of industrial employers on the other, the personnel of SENAI had to walk a very fine line in which workers' faults were portrayed as the result of cultural defects rather than, say, exploitation by factory-owners.[33] Indeed, crucial to SENAI's discourse was the claim that industrial employment, in and of itself, promised a better, more dignified life for the male worker, who could aspire to mobility within industry by gaining the confidence of his supervisor and/or acquiring a skill. But few workers had the kinds of skills that allowed them to parlay their training into higher wages and job security. In short, there was the nagging problem of the limited reach of the SENAI system and the persistently low wages for workers not classified as skilled. Despite its warm embrace by organised labour, the national training service could hardly function as a vehicle for *mass* socialisation or for collective improvement in the standard of living for the Brazilian 'working masses'.

The working man and the skilled housewife

In the face of mounting worker discontent and social discord at the end of the Second World War, a cohort of Brazilian industrialists (many of them previously involved in the creation of SENAI) began discussing the pressing need for an entity structured along the same lines as SENAI that would be geared toward the provision of educational and welfare services to *all* urban/industrial workers – including members of the workers' families. The eventual result of these discussions was SESI – the *Serviço Social da Indústria* (Industrial Social Service), founded in 1946. As with SENAI, the SESI decree-law designated the regional industrialist associations as entirely responsible for defining the organisation's goals, priorities, activities and structures.[34]

SESI's mission, however, was far broader than SENAI's, and its premises more explicitly ideological. The welfare and educational services offered by SESI were remarkably diverse and wide-ranging. The former category included medical and dental clinics, recreational centres, vacation colonies, discount food posts, and worker kitchens. In the latter category were courses in basic literacy, sewing, labour legislation, human relations in the workplace, public speaking, home economics, and accident prevention. Simonsen, one of SESI's founders, outlined its educational mission as 'the full civic development of the Working Man, integrated into his professional and social group'.[35]

As with SENAI, the figure who stood at the center of the SESI mission was an archetypal 'Working Man'. But SESI, even more than SENAI, was committed to remaking the Brazilian worker outside as well as inside the factory, and hence SESI's participation in this process would mean offering services to women as well as men. Some of SESI's facilities, such as the recreational centers and literacy classes, attracted clients of both genders. More typical of SESI operations, however, was a sharp separation by sex, and the gendering of SESI services as relevant either to the domestic (female) sphere, or to the public (male) sphere. Thus, the publications and courses of the Division of Social Guidance, oriented toward workplace, union, and political issues, figured its clientele as overwhelmingly male, while the Division of Social Assistance appealed to women within the home and family, and was staffed almost entirely by female social workers.

The heavily female composition of the 'caring' professions quickly emerged as a problem for SESI. Women social workers might be perfectly suitable for sewing and conversation with working-class housewives, but SESI's directors felt uneasy about sending women to factories to fraternise with workers and to inform them about SESI programmes related to work and shop-floor conditions. To address this problem, SESI created a new professional category: the social educator. These 'soldiers of social peace' had a similar educational background to the more conventional social worker, but were given supplementary training in labour law, rational organisation of work, and Christian-democratic/anti-Communist doctrines. And whereas virtually all the social workers were women and were oriented toward domestic problems within the working-class milieu, many of the social educators were men, and had as their primary function visits to factories, unions, and other work-related locales.[36]

SESI's campaign to de-feminise social work served to reinforce the representation of the factory as a masculine social space. Moreover, who better than these quintessential middle-class professional men to disseminate SESI's prototype of masculine respectability? The manly qualities that SESI underscored were not strength or independence, but those associated with steady industrial employment – the potential for a good wage, for mobility within the factory, and for recognition as the chief breadwinner within the household. The emphasis was on discipline and self-control; according to an article in a SESI magazine, 'discipline is essential to a man's development'.[37] The worker was to be encouraged to seek self-improvement but also, above all, to respect the hierarchy of knowledge and authority within the factory.[38]

In effect, SESI sought to re-define industrial employment, in and of itself, as a mark of manliness when paired with the prestige of being a head of household. Skilled or not, a Brazilian man working in a factory could count himself among those contributing to the modernisation and transformation of Brazil into a great nation, according to SESI publications and pronouncements. Through his hard work, discipline, and cooperation, he earned the right to be regarded as a full citizen of the nation and respected as a head (or future head) of household. And employment in industry, even in an unskilled position, offered endless vistas of self-improvement for the worker who knew his place and conformed to the factory hierarchy, thanks to the organisations founded and funded by industrial employers.

The flipside of this masculinising coin was the erasure of the woman worker from the imagined industrial community. This was not unrelated to demographic trends – censuses of the economically active population in the post-war period showed the percentage of adult women in the industrial labour force to be in sharp decline. But even so, almost a quarter of industrial workers continued to be women, and over half of minors working in industry were female.[39] Yet SESI, as an organisation, always positioned working-class women as current or future housewives, and the many services and courses it provided exclusively for women were organised around this assumption.

Not only did SESI position the working-class woman as a housewife, but it also delegated her responsibility for cultivating a comfortable and hygienic home environment that would ensure respectability and help civilise the working-class male. In the pages of SESI's 'women's magazines' social workers and hygienists exhorted working-class women to stretch their husbands' wages, make themselves and their homes attractive so that their men would be more inclined to spend their leisure time at home, cook balanced and tasty meals to combat 'nutritional deficiency', and take measures to ensure that they and their future husbands did not become victims of venereal disease.[40] While SESI authors assumed that *men* would drink to excess, and *men* would be the carriers of syphilis, it was nonetheless *women's* responsibility to see that these scourges of working-class life were eliminated. To be sure, many of the services SESI provided for male workers valorised sobriety and clean living, but neither SESI nor SENAI regularly exhorted men to behave in specific ways within the private sphere. SESI publications provided very detailed guidance on how industrial workers should deal with their colleagues and supervisors, avoid industrial accidents, improve personal productivity, understand labour legislation, register to vote, and participate in labour unions. But rarely did SESI or SENAI presume to intervene directly in men's behaviour beyond the realms of work and politics, recognising this sphere as a 'private' terrain that, according to the unstated division of power and authority, had to be treated as the male worker's domain. Not that SENAI and SESI refrained from intervening in this terrain, but instead of direct 'interference', they sought to re-orient male workers' private lives through the indirect influence of their wives and mothers.

In pursuit of the model worker

By the 1960s, the Brazilian industrial labour force had undergone a process of masculinisation, with men heavily outnumbering women in factories and other urban workplaces. Even more striking, a mere 3 per cent of all skilled workers were women.[41] Not that industrialists shunned women workers altogether; factory-owners continued to employ large numbers of young women in low-wage, semi-skilled occupations. But as we have seen, the industrialist vanguard that created SENAI and SESI harboured ambitions that went beyond immediate concerns for productivity and profitability; they sought to promote a certain notion of 'social peace', which they construed as requiring the cultivation of disciplined, responsible worker-citizens. Masculinisation of the workforce on the one hand, and the training of better working-class housewives and mothers on the other, eminently suited this purpose.

The industrialists' objective, moreover, was not just to transform the image of the factory operative from the exploited and pathetic female worker to the robust and respectable male worker, but to attach a particular notion of manliness to the latter. To celebrate its image of the ideal worker, SESI, together with the Rio newspaper *O Globo*, launched an annual model-worker contest in 1964 that publicly rewarded industrial employees who embodied the desired qualities. Candidates for the title of '*Operário Padrão*' had to demonstrate not only skill, discipline and cooperation at work, but also provide evidence of devotion to family and exemplary behaviour as husbands and fathers. Women workers were not excluded from the competition, but the standards by which the model worker was to be judged – skill, upward mobility, length of employment, recognition in the home and neighbourhood – tended to eliminate most women from consideration.[42]

SESI and SENAI's emphasis on the value of manual skills and of being the primary wage-earner certainly squared with the vision of the manly worker embraced by union leaders throughout industrialising Brazil. But SENAI and SESI went further, defining the manly worker as cooperative, as knowing his place, as exercising self-control, and as a good citizen who would subordinate his own preferences and aspirations to the exigencies of 'national development'. That is precisely where industrialist spokesmen parted company with organised labour, whose leaders persisted in regarding skill and hard labour as earning working men the right to demand a degree of respect, authority, and security – notions that informed the discourse of labour unionism independent of ideological inclinations.[43]

Back in 1931, Roberto Simonsen publicly praised rationalisation and declared that this 'veritable social doctrine' would neutralise the 'fundamental ideas of Marxism' and moderate class conflict.[44] Indeed, many of the industrialists and educators involved in SENAI and SESI expected the services and courses offered by these organisations to produce compliant workers inoculated against the temptations of labour militancy. Yet the very programmes that the industrialists funded produced a variety of unintended consequences. Nothing demonstrates better the failure of their efforts to produce the compliant worker than the labour insurgency of the late 1970s, led by São Paulo's metalworkers whose most militant representatives, typically, had learned their trade in a SENAI school.[45]

Even before the dramatic events of this era, which led to the formation of the Workers' Party and helped undermine military rule, there were signs that the training and culture provided by the industrialist organisations bolstered a masculine identity that was not exactly what employers intended or desired. In the mid-1970s, a study of 'worker consciousness' in Brazil noted the tendency of skilled workers to be more activist (even in the constraining conditions of the military dictatorship) than their unskilled colleagues. In the words of one metallurgical worker, 'Normally, the workers who belong to a higher category are those who are most interested [in labour activism]. They are the ones who go to the union and make strikes. I believe that it's a matter of culture. The fellow who has a craft, perhaps a course in SENAI, has more experience and greater facility to speak.'[46]

In the 1931 discourse cited above, Simonsen claimed that rationalisation would promote 'the continual development of technical and professional culture', and allow partial 'worker control in the solution of economic problems'.[47] By the 1970s, SENAI and SESI had contributed substantially to the first phase of Simonsen's formula; a study of metropolitan São Paulo during that decade noted the 'enormous growth in technical and vocational schools, in night courses, and generally even in the educational level of the working classes',[48] A rapidly growing cohort of male workers, especially in the metallurgical sector, was developing a sense of pride in its skills and an estimation of its importance in the production process. But the second phase of Simonsen's formula – the role of 'worker control' in some spheres of the economy – utterly failed to materialise. Instead, a 1978 study of large metallurgical plants in São Paulo revealed the dominant mode of organisation to be a Brazilianised Taylorism. Factories were organised in a markedly hierarchical fashion; workers had little contact among themselves and almost no participation in decisions affecting production. Considerable emphasis was also placed on simplification of tasks, thereby allowing for easy substitution of workers, and in place of the monetary incentives and bonuses that characterised classic Taylorism, firms substituted close supervision and the threat of dismissal.[49] Metalworkers at all points of the production process chafed at these conditions, but they were particularly incompatible with the skilled worker's sense of pride and expertise. The anger and frustration of these lathe operators and tool-and-die makers proved strong enough to fuel the most important labour insurgency in Brazil's history.

Elsewhere I have argued that SESI's programmes and publications for women had considerable success because the ideal of femininity and feminine respectability that SESI purveyed had genuine appeal for working-class women (and men), and did not have to compete with a strong alternative/class-based femininity.[50] Moreover, the cross-class association of women with the 'private' sphere allowed SESI to present its domestic programmes as politically neutral and universally applicable.[51] Some aspects of the SENAI/SESI construct of working-class masculinity did have genuine appeal for male workers – especially the opportunity to acquire a skill and become the chief breadwinner.[52] But the SENAI/SESI vision of the compliant worker/citizen, and of 'hierarchical solidarity' between labour and management, had to compete with a very different working-class notion of masculinity that associated industrial labour with horizontal solidarity and viewed the acquisition of manual skills as a source of power and authority for (male) workers.[53]

To further illuminate this distinction, it would be useful to hark back to the masculinised language of class one can already discern in the São Paulo printers' newspaper in the early decades of the twentieth century. According to multiple articles published in *O Trabalhador Gráfico* during that era, only the well-trained worker, steeped in the technical know-how of his craft, could be *'consciente'* (conscientious/conscious) – that is, both a productive worker *and* a good defender of his class. In this formulation, skill and masculine dignity, work and class identity, were inextricably linked.[54] Whereas SENAI and SESI, in their discursive constructions of the good worker, sought to reduce the meaning of *'consciente'* to conscientious, male, skilled operatives in key industries continued to imbue the term with a double meaning that implied that the good worker was both conscientious *and* conscious.

Notes

1 On women in the early textile mills see A. Farnsworth-Alvear, *Dulcinea in the Factory: Myths, Morals, Men, and Women in Colombia's Industrial Experiment, 1905 – 1960* (Durham NC, 2000), and J. Wolfe, *Working Women, Working Men: São Paulo and the Rise of Brazil's Industrial Working Class, 1900–1955* (Durham NC, 1993).

2 On anxieties about female factory employment, see E. Q. Hutchison, *Labors Appropriate to their Sex: Gender, Labor and Politics in Urban Chile, 1900–1930* (Durham NC, 2001); and the introductory essay, 'Squaring the circle: Women's factory labor, gender ideology, and necessity', in J. French and D. James (eds), *The Gendered World of Latin American Women Workers* (Durham NC, 1997), pp. 1–30. On issues of family and nation-building, see S. Caulfield, *In Defense of Honor: Sexual Morality, Modernity, and Nation in Early Twentieth Century Brazil* (Durham NC, 2000).

3 On male worker critiques of women in industry, see K. Rosemblatt, *Gendered Compromises: Political Cultures and the State in Chile, 1920–1950* (Chapel Hill NC, 2000), esp. pp. 27–94.

4 The classic study of industrialising São Paulo is W. Dean, *The Industrialization of São Paulo* (Austin Tex., 1969).

5 R. Simonsen, 'Pela Administração Scientífica', in *O Trabalho Moderno* (São Paulo, 1919), p. 37. For a study of the quintessential 'Italian count', see J. de Souza Martins, *Conde Matarazzo: O Empresário e a Empresa* (São Paulo, 1973).

6 On industrialist-engineers' efforts to deploy their technical authority in the political sphere, see B. Weinstein, 'The discourse of technical competence: Strategies of authority and power in industrializing Brazil', *Political Power and Social Theory*, 12 (1998), 137–75.

7 The discussion of the two vocational schools is drawn from B. Weinstein, *For Social Peace in Brazil: Industrialists and the Remaking of the Working Class in São Paulo, 1920–1964* (Chapel Hill NC, 1996), pp. 33–6, and C. S. Vidigal Moraes, 'A Socialização da Força de Trabalho: Instrução Popular e Qualificação Profissional no Estado de São Paulo, 1873–1934', PhD dissertation, Universidade de São Paulo, 1990.

8 Arquivo do Estado de São Paulo, Escola Profissional Masculina, 'Relatório', 1920, p. 6.

9 *Ibid.*, p. 22.

10 Simonsen's speech is reprinted in P. S. Pinheiro and M. M. Hall (eds), *A Classe Operária no Brasil, 1889–1934*, vol. 2 (São Paulo, 1981), pp. 224–8. On complaints lodged against industry by spokespersons for commerce, labour, and an ill-defined middle class, see M. H. Capelato and M. L. Prado, *O Bravo Matutino* (São Paulo, 1980), pp. 79–81, and N. Vilela Luz, *A Luta pela Industrialização do Brasil* (São Paulo, 2nd edn, 1975), pp. 140–63.

11 P. Nogueira Filho, *Ideais e Lutas de um Burguês Progressista*, vol. 1 (Rio de Janeiro, 1958), pp. 128–9.

12 In a 1933 speech Vargas declared that 'the education we need to develop to the extreme limits of our possibilities is the vocational and technical kind'. *A Nova Política do Brasil*, vol. 1 (Rio de Janeiro, 1938), p. 25. The fundamental work on Vargas and populism in Brazil is J. D. French, *The Brazilian Workers' ABC: Class Conflict and Alliances in Modern São Paulo* (Chapel Hill NC, 1992).

13 On Vargas, the Estado Novo and gender norms, see S. K. Besse, *Restructuring Patriarchy: The Modernization of Gender Inequality in Brazil, 1914–1940* (Chapel Hill NC, 1996), pp. 5–7.

14 H. da Silveira, *O Ensino Technico-Profissional e Doméstico em São Paulo* (São Paulo, 1935), pp. 21–3, 43. When the *Escola Feminina* first opened, several home economics courses had to be cancelled due to insufficient enrolment. B. Weinstein, 'Unskilled worker, skilled housewife: Constructing the working-class woman in São Paulo, Brazil', in J. French and D. James (eds), *The Gendered Worlds of Latin American Women Workers*, pp. 77–8.

15 Fundação Getúlio Vargas, Centro de Pesquisa e Documentação, Rio de Janeiro, (hereafter FGV/CPDOC), GC/g 34.11.28, 'Organização geral do ensino profissional'.

16 R. Mange, *A Formação dos Técnicos para a Indústria* (São Paulo, 1940).

17 FGV/CPDOC, GC/g 38.04.30, Doc. IIa-1, J. Faria Góes Filho, 'A aprendizagem nos estabelecimentos industriais', pp. 4–6.

18 S. Schwartzman *et al.*, *Tempos de Capanema* (Rio de Janeiro, 1984), p. 235.

19 FGV/CPDOC, GC/g 38.04.40, Doc. III-2, 'A viagem de estudos e observações ao estado de São Paulo'.

20 'Salàrio, Questão Social', *O Trabalhador Têxtil* (November–December 1939), 4.

21 FGV/CPDOC, GC/g 41.09.13, Doc. I-6, 21 July 1942.

22 'Carta da Paz Social', in E. Carone, *A Quarta República, 1945–1964* (São Paulo, 1980), pp. 399–403.

23 There were some industrialists who despaired of the capacity of 'national' (i.e. non-white) workers for modern industrial labour, and called for renewed European immigration. Arquivo Geral do SESI-São Paulo, P109, Correspondência, 31 March 1948.

24 On the founding of SENAI, see Weinstein, *For Social Peace in Brazil*, pp. 95–100; on friction between industrialists and the Ministry of Education, see S. Schwartzman *et al.*, *Tempos de Capanema*, pp. 238–41.

25 *Informativo SENAI*, 13 (November 1946), 2–3.

26 SENAI's reclassifications usually lowered the percentage of jobs *classified* as skilled in all industries, but reductions were sharpest in textiles where the percentage of skilled positions dropped (1950–60) from 38 per cent to under 8 per cent. On the changing composition of the industrial labour force, see Weinstein, *For Social Peace in Brazil*, pp. 193–4.

27 'O Aluno SENAI', *Informativo SENAI*, 1 (September 1946), 3.

28 SENAI-São Paulo, *Relatório* (1944), p. 3.

29 *Ibid.* (1945), 75; also R. Mange, *Planejamento e Administração Unificada da Aprendizagem Industrial no Brasil* (São Paulo, 1949).

30 SENAI-São Paulo, *Curso de aperfeiçoamento para Instrutores: Noções de Psicologia do Adolescente* (1953).

31 SENAI-São Paulo, *Relatório* (1945), 10. On the changing racial composition of the industrial workforce, see G. R. Andrews, *Blacks and Whites in São Paulo, Brazil, 1888–1988* (Madison Wis., 1991).

32 See, for example, E. Lodi, *Positivos os Indícios de que a Criação do SENAI foi um Ato Acertado da Indústria* (São Paulo, 1949), p. 5.

33 A striking example is a study carried out by SENAI on the causes of the high drop-out rate among its apprentices. SENAI-Departamento Nacional, *Pesquisa sôbre Evasão Escolar: O Problema da Escola de Aprendizagem no Brasil*, 6 vols (1952).

34 On the founding of SESI, see Weinstein, *For Social Peace in Brazil*, pp. 100–13.

35 Reprinted as 'O Problema Social no Brasil', in R. Simonsen, *Evolução Industrial do Brasil* (São Paulo, 1973), p. 449.

36 SESI even created special 'men only' fellowships to encourage men to take up social work. Weinstein, *For Social Peace in Brazil*, pp. 148–60.

37 *Educador Social*, 3 (March 1953), 1.

38 *Educador Social*, 6 (June 1953), 1.

39 On post-war masculinisation of industry in Colombia and Mexico, see Farnsworth-Alvear, *Dulcinea in the Factory*, pp. 209–28, and S. Gauss, 'Working class masculinity and the rationalized sex: Gender and industrial modernization in postrevolutionary Puebla, Mexico', in J. Olcott, M. K. Vaughan, and G. Cano (eds), *Engendering Revolution: Gender, the State, and Everyday Life in Twentieth-Century Mexico* (Durham NC, forthcoming). Women were not necessarily disappearing from the paid-labor market. According to Elizabeth Hutchison, Chilean labour censuses understated the presence of women as waged labourers since they typically excluded sweatshop and home workers. See Hutchinson, *Labors Appropriate to their Sex*, pp. 36–58.

40 Whenever workers failed to pay the small fees for SESI services, a social worker would be dispatched to find out (in the words of SESI president Antonio Devisate) 'why the workers' wives were not able to make their husbands' wages go as far as they should.' Weinstein, 'Unskilled worker, skilled housewife', p. 85.

41 This percentage reflects the number of women whose jobs were *classified* as skilled, an operation that is itself subject to gendered notions of what counts as skill, what requires extended training, and who would be difficult to replace. J. W. Scott, *Gender and the Politics of History* (New York, 1988), esp. pp. 93–177.

42 B. Weinstein, 'The model worker of the Paulista industrialists: The "Operário Padrão" campaign, 1964–85', *Radical History Review*, 61 (1995), 92–123.

43 Weinstein, *For Social Peace in Brazil*, pp. 283–7.

44 Reprinted as 'As finanças e a indústria', in R. Simonsen, *Á Margem da Profissão* (São Paulo, 1932), p. 217.

45 At least one early SENAI official, interviewed in 1990, put a different spin on this outcome. According to Oswaldo de Barros Santos, SENAI graduates' prominent role in the new unionism was evidence that the organisation truly trained the 'cream' of the working class. Interview, SENAI-São Paulo, Projeto Memória (12 June 1990).

46 C. Frederico, *Consciência Operária no Brasil* (São Paulo, 1978), p. 46. See also J. Humphrey, *Capitalist Control and Workers' Struggle in the Brazilian Auto Industry* (Princeton, 1982), p. 162.

47 'As finanças e a indústria', p. 217.

48 E. Sader, *Quando Novos Personagens Entraram em Cena* (Rio, 1988), p. 87.

49 A. C. Corrêa Fleury, 'Rotinização do Trabalho,' in A. C. Corrêa Fleury and N. Vargas (eds), *Organização do Trabalho* (São Paulo, 1983), pp. 84–106; J. F. Springer, *A Brazilian Factory Study*, Cuaderno no. 33 (Cuernavaca, 1966), ch. 2.

50 This is not meant as a universal generalisation about working-class femininity. Daniel James shows that Argentine women were able to mount a serious critique of 'bourgeois femininity', aided in part by the figure of Eva Perón. *Doña María's Story: Life History, Memory, and Political Identity* (Durham, NC, 2000), esp. pp. 244–80.

51 Union newspapers that were often critical of SESI typically printed its domestic advice columns without hesitation or comment. See, for example, 'Vida no Lar', *Voz do Metalúrgico* (December 1958), 2; and 'Economia Doméstica', *O Trabalhador Gráfico* (March 1960), 6.

52 This notion of manliness differs from the images of masculinity, based on physical strength and sexual autonomy, that T. M. Klubock cites as circulating among Chilean copper miners in the early twentieth century (with the difference stemming, perhaps, from mining's almost exclusively masculine image and isolated locations). *Contested Communities: Class, Gender, and Politics in Chile's El Teniente Copper Mine, 1904–1951* (Durham NC, 1998), esp. pp. 155–87.

53 The phrase 'hierarchical solidarity' comes from a social educator's 1956 report following a visit to a multinational firm where 'from the director to the doorman, everyone works in a spirit of hierarchical solidarity'. Arquivo Geral do SESI-São Paulo, Processos, P9/2573, 9 October 1956.

54 'O Nosso Trabalho', *O Trabalhador Gráfico* (April 1905), 2; 'O Memorial', *ibid.* (21 February 1923), 3; 'Direitos e Deveres', *ibid.* (7 February 1926), 2.

16

Maternal relations: moral manliness and emotional survival in letters home during the First World War

Michael Roper

A FTER witnessing the death of his 'faithful friend' Jim Noone as they were leaving the front line, Lance-Corporal David Fenton wrote to Noone's mother, giving her details: 'I held him in my arms to the end, and when his soul had departed I kissed him twice where I knew you would have kissed him – on the brow – once for his mother and once for myself.' Prior to Noone's burial where he fell, Fenton had 'tried hard to get you a lock of his hair, Mrs Noone'. He had now parcelled up Noone's possessions and would see that they were sent on. 'If there is anything of his which you could spare for me to wear, I should be greatly favoured', he added.[1]

Fenton's direct expression of his feelings for his friend is a striking feature of his letter. However, it also testifies to the profound significance of relationships between young men and mothers on the Western Front. It was after all to his friend's mother that Fenton confessed his feelings, as the person that would best appreciate and share the love he felt for Jim. As he concluded his letter, 'I join my tenderest sympathy with you in your great loss.'[2] Fenton's letter is all the more striking given that his own mother and stepmother were deceased. Sensitised perhaps by his own past losses, Fenton strove to sustain the maternal connection for his friend through and beyond death, whilst at the same time appealing for a mother's help. When Fenton asked Noone's mother to send items of clothing to him, he drew her into a relationship of practical support such as existed between mothers and sons.

The importance which Fenton attached to the individual mother–son relationship, and the manner in which his letter located it within communities of men and mothers, is not uncommon. The vast majority of letters which unmarried officers wrote home from the Western Front during the First World War were addressed to mothers.[3] Yet, despite the fact that letters home remain one of the most widely used sources to document their experiences, the maternal relationship itself has received little attention. The problem here is that, within the Anglo-American context at least, the attention of military historians has been fixed on the immediate surroundings of the trenches, whilst gender historians have focused on the activities and representations of mothers on the home-front.[4] The *men's* view of mothers has been less well illuminated.

Drawing largely on subalterns' accounts of the front line, this chapter investigates the nature of young middle-class men's emotional attachments to their mothers.[5] Such a project brings into question some of the established accounts of masculinity and trench soldiering. Work in the late 1970s by Paul Fussell and Eric Leed, whilst not explicitly adopting the language of gender, opened new questions about men's subjective experiences of mechanised war, and its effect on cultural norms of manliness.[6] The nature of the psychological boundaries which frontline soldiers drew between home and front was a key theme for these writers. They focused on the incommensurable nature of the experiences of those at home and at the front. 'Civilian incomprehension' of trench warfare was widespread, Fussell argued, and could hardly have been otherwise, since 'its conditions were too novel, its industrialised ghastliness too unprecedented'.[7] Frontline soldiers as a result came to perceive the world in binary terms, the troops versus 'everyone back in England'. 'Estranged' from the domestic, bonds between men developed in particularly intense ways.[8] Similarly, for Leed the figure of the soldier is always 'presumed to lie "outside" the boundaries of domestic experience'.[9]

More recently in the light of feminist and gender studies, this conception of a distanced, even antithetical relationship between home and front has been re-evaluated. Joanna Bourke, in *Dismembering the Male*, has argued that for men the significance of the domestic was if anything enhanced by trench warfare. Home 'remained the touchstone for all their actions'.[10] Its significance was enhanced through the carrying out of feminine duties such as washing, mending, cooking, and washing. Men also 'mothered' each other; for example in nursing the sick and wounded.[11] For Bourke such sentiments furnished a source of stability which helped men to cope with physical hardship and emotional disruption. In *Women's Identities at War*, Deborah Grayzel also questions the assumption of divided fronts. She notes the importance of correspondence in wartime fiction. Letters, leave, and the traffic in gifts, she remarks, 'enabled the men and women of wartime Britain and France to transcend the gender-bound categories – to bridge the gap between divided fronts – in which they had been placed'.[12]

Letters home furnish much of the evidence of life at the front for these historians. Yet they have not by and large considered them as testaments to an ongoing relationship, in which the content was shaped by men's perceptions of what mothers might wish to read and of what they ought not to know, as well as by interior, psychological needs.[13] Grayzel focuses on depictions of letter-writing in war literature, but this gives little indication of its extent. By 1917, the army on the Western Front was sending 8,150,000 letters home a week.[14] The traffic was not just in letters but parcels, with over a million a week being sent to the British Expeditionary Forces (BEF) during 1917.[15] Parcels provided a vital means of improving the men's experience of the front. Food, clothing, and small luxuries were treasured. The listing of items needed, and descriptions of the contents and of how they were used, constituted perhaps the principal topic of letters. Officers in particular, because of the relative wealth of their families, were well-provided. Supplying the men's needs required time, energy, and organisational skills. Whilst fathers generally arranged the finance, it was mothers and daughters who baked and tailored, ordered and purchased, and who parcelled up goods for sons and brothers.[16]

Given the scale of such activity it seems astonishing that military historians have not acknowledged more often the role of communication from home in sustaining men at the front. Most historians of the war it seems remain locked into a presumption of geographical and psychic divide which, whilst parasitic upon the gender scripts of Edwardian society, does not even acknowledge the ways in which for contemporaries, the sending and receiving of goods and letters brought separated spheres into a relationship. At the same time, letters did not allow the sender to – as Grayzel asserts it – 'transcend' the constraints of geography and gender. Even a cursory look at what men actually wrote signals this. Letters home were always conditioned by the tension between being at the front and writing to those who had no direct experience of it. Rather than chronicling a chasm of misunderstanding or an easy crossing of the fronts, this chapter asks how, in the physical absence of mothers, men nurtured and negotiated the maternal relationship through writing.

Letters home can tell us about the subjective experience of the front, if understood as a double process, in which men both sought to communicate to the mother in the here-and-now, and respond to feelings and fantasies which were themselves shaped by the earlier relationship with the mother. The maternal figure was always simultaneously 'external', the principal symbol of and contact with home, and 'internal', a primary influence in the men's psychic make-up. For the historian of masculinity, the value of such correspondence – particularly that composed after traumatic experiences – lies in the complex evidence it gives of this double image, and its characteristic shifts between the self as soldier and man, and a self shaped by a sometimes more primitive and dependant maternal relation. In what follows I will look firstly at the place of sons and mothers within the gender scripts of middle-class Edwardian society, and at how conventions of letter-writing reflected these scripts. Part two presents a case-study of a subaltern's letters home after battle as a means of exploring the emotional aspects of the maternal relation. The final section considers the psychic and cultural roots of the conflicts exposed in letters home, between prescriptions of manliness and the emotional situations of sons.

Mothers, sons, and middle-class masculinities

The regimental officers on whose letters I shall draw were born in the 1890s and were in their late teens or early twenties during the war. For men of this class and cohort the maternal relation was characterised by distance and intimacy in equal measure. The fact that they were unmarried meant that, for most, familial relationships probably remained among the most intimate in their social circle. By comparison with the Victorian upper class, middle-class mothers were very involved in the emotional and moral guidance of children. In Evangelical households in particular, her role in instilling a sense of 'moralised home' was seen as crucial to the development of manly character. As John Tosh argues, this generated close affections between mothers and sons, all the more so given the growing tendency for fathers' employment to be located away from the home.[17] For both the middle-class mother and son, the moment of leaving of home for school or employment was especially fraught.[18] Sons were also highly valued within the family. They were comparatively well educated compared to their sisters. Eldest sons occupied a unique place in the family structure between siblings and the authority of the father, because of their future role as a provider and because of their assumed responsibility for care of parents in old age.[19] Indeed these responsibilities were already in play in households where the father was dead. The affections of mothers towards sons were tinged with considerations about his future role, as were those of sons towards their mothers. In the gender scripts of middle-class Edwardian Britain it was the duty of sons to provide emotional support for the mother, as they might for a future wife. The capacity to reassure and be constant in times of difficulty was seen as an important quality for a prospective husband, father, family head and carer of parents.

Cutting across these elements was the inculcation among this generation – through their schooling, reading and leisure activities – of precepts of manliness designed precisely to loosen the maternal bond. Tosh has noted how the perceived necessity to remove sons from the feminising influence of home grew during the second half of the nineteenth century, in tandem with the expansion of public schools. In the Spartan conditions of the late nineteenth-century public school boys were trained in endurance, stoicism, and the homosocial life of team sports and group loyalty.[20] Such training encouraged a distance from, even a disparagement of, feminine values. It fostered a disposition of 'suppressing the need to give or receive affection, and the impulse to express feelings'.[21] Late Victorian sons, in Tosh's view, suffered from particularly acute contradictions between this rigorous training in manliness, and their early upbringing, which was largely the responsibilities of mothers.

Tosh's analysis, although it does not continue into the Edwardian period, is nevertheless suggestive about the immense significance of war service for this generation in the negotiation of adult masculinity, and some of the tensions this created. On the one hand, particularly in the early years after 1914, war seemed the culmination of lessons in independence, adventure and public service which schooling and university had prepared them for. Symbolising its significance in this passage, the moment of leaving for France was one which many preferred to handle on their own, foregoing the well-wishes of family.[22] Ex-public school boys, by contrast with many working-class recruits, were also used to coping away from home. Whilst this did not *lessen* their need for maternal support, the conditions and demands of army life were at least somewhat familiar to them. On the other hand, the capacity of war to make the man could be as much a source of worry as of excitement. Subaltern officers carried heavy responsibilities: a Second Lieutenant might be barely eighteen, but in command of sixty men or more, most of a different social class, and often older than he. Such responsibilities, the men's self-expectations, and the significance of war service in the passage to adult masculinity could encourage a reliance on mothers as confidantes and as resources of moral and spiritual strength. The characteristic admixture of anticipation, manly pride and anxiety is conveyed in Urwick's last letter to his mother before embarking for France: 'All my ideals England is fighting for. That I may not disgrace her is my constant prayer.'[23]

Sending and receiving letters

In the First World War, as Jenny Hartley has observed of the Second, it was women who acted as the principal bridge from home to young men, performing 'mothering at a distance'.[24] Many mothers wrote daily to sons whilst they were at the front.[25] Their letters contained news of all the family, and they often communicated messages from other family members. In addition, they prevailed upon others to keep up correspondence. Reflecting the role of the mother in matters of care, sons assumed her obligation to write, and freely requested alterations in her supply of letters according to their needs. By comparison the father's role as correspondent was less clearly defined. Most fathers wrote less often than mothers, and when they did write, it tended to be in a subsidiary fashion, for example enclosing notes or a postscript in the mother's letter. The asymmetry between the men's expectations of mothers and fathers is captured by Wilfred Owen, who, after a particularly gruelling first experience of the front line, wrote to his mother: 'nothing but a daily one from you will keep me up. I think Colin [his brother] might try a weekly letter. And Father?'[26] Since fathers' duties were presumed to lie in the public sphere, regular correspondence was not expected, even if desired. Fathers were assumed not be natural letter-writers, as Captain Gibbs revealed when thanking 'dada' for his letter, as 'I know you aren't fond of letter-writing'.[27] If the form itself was not seen as a feminine one, mothers were certainly regarded as the more skilled and comfortable practitioners, reflecting the identification of the mother with responsibilities for emotional support.[28]

The fact that geographical distance from the mother was not new to many of the men did not lessen their enthusiasm for news of home. The moment of arrival of the mail bag occasioned great excitement amongst officers and men alike. As Marchant explained: 'We all look forward each day to the post bag as the great event of the day.'[29] Men not only weighed up the time of arrival, but the amount of correspondence: 'I can't tell you how much I enjoy getting your letters so often', wrote Hall.[30] Delays occasioned great disappointment. Hutt's early correspondence after reaching the front for the first time expressed disappointment about the lack of letters from his mother. Over the following days this slid over into a sense of impatience, and finally grievance, though he cannot have been sure whether the lack of communication from home was due to the post or his mother's failure to write: 'I have written you lots of letters it seems to me, but I haven't had a single one from you, or the parcels I am expecting so much. I need some Gold Flake cigarettes badly.'[31] That Hutt should move between these two sentences from a comment about letters to the physical sensation of deprivation, suggests the way in which such communication from home was felt as nourishing the men. The material functions and emotional work of caring were closely related. Letters, like tobacco, were felt to be basic necessities.

Traumatic experiences, illness, or generally low spirits intensified the men's desire for letters. The moment at which morale was lowest was that in which they most needed the image of home to be renewed. Gibbs, writing from hospital after he was wounded in the hip, confessed that 'I have never wanted a letter so badly before, but I knew that I couldn't possibly get one.'[32] The postponement of Webb's leave occasioned 'bitter disappointment', and a plea for further letters, as 'my only comfort will be in receiving letters from you'.[33] It was as much the fact of their arrival as their content that mattered. Love operated in the material of exchange; care was gauged in the number of letters sent and received.[34] The strength of the expressed need for correspondence show us that, far from the realities of trench warfare making the home increasingly irrelevant, if anything its significance was enhanced.[35]

When men wrote home, it was usually to the mother. A typical case was Gibbs, who addressed 120 letters to his mother in the twelve-month period after his arrival in France in December 1915, and eleven to his 'dada'.[36] Mothers were assumed to be the first repositories of news from the front, and the principal conduits of it amongst family and friends. Sons' letters might be read aloud, a practice which, like the reading of books (which men sometimes recalled when writing home), would be performed by the mother.[37] When men were short of time, one letter had to serve many. E. F. Chapman wrote to his sisters and his mother, but as he explained to his mother, 'when I only have time to write one letter, I like it to go to you.'[38] Men also addressed their mothers at moments of extreme difficulty: when Arnold was injured at Le Cateau and then captured by the Germans at the end of August 1914, the secret account he kept in his Field Pocket book began 'My own darling little mother'.[39] Such comments suggest a perception of the mother as the primary emotional connection for young men, and the embodiment of the family. Upon marriage, many of these functions seem to have transferred to wives, who then became the conduits of news to and from the front.[40]

Although any assessment of the men's letters must take censorship into account, its effects were not predictable or uniform. Men were not supposed to give details of location, effects of hostile fire, the physical and moral condition of troops, and details of defensive works.[41] Officers, unlike other ranks, were trusted to censor their own letters. As Hutt put it, 'we are on our honour to put in nothing that the enemy wants to know'.[42] This gentlemanly code gave rise to considerable variety in practice. Most, although careful not to give away information about location, sometimes broached topics which were formally subject to censorship. The perception that mothers would be anxious for their safety had a far greater influence on the content of officers' letters than formal censorship. Indeed, perhaps the main purpose in writing was 'not to worry her'.[43] At the bottom line, letters were a sign of life. Field postcards, often sent from the front when shelling, cramped, wet, and cold conditions made it difficult to write, allowed the acknowledgement of this, simply confirming that 'I am well'.

Given the demands for circumspection, and the obligation to convey signs of life and good spirits, writing home must often have been a psychically-laden activity. The process of writing itself might encourage a desire for reflection in response to distressing events.[44] At the same time there were countervailing internal and external pressures *not* to confess or dwell on how they felt. The men's felt needs and their social obligations were often in conflict, most acutely in the aftermath of battle, as we shall now see.

Second Lieutenant E. K. Smith

FIRST BATTLE

Ernest Smith's family was from North London and broadly middle class (his father was an ex-mining engineer and entrepreneur). Born in September 1892, Ernest was the eldest of five children. He embarked for France in late December 1914, was selected for officer training in early April 1915, and in July began service as a regimental officer with the 1st Battalion of the East Kent Regiment. He immediately assumed command of a platoon in 'A' Company. Just over a week later, with Smith still feeling uncertain of his command, his Battalion was engaged in a major offensive.[45] Smith wrote to his mother warning her not to expect to hear from him, as 'I may not be able to write in the trenches'.

At the commencement of the attack 'A' Company was in reserve and had to dig themselves in and await orders to consolidate their position. Meanwhile they witnessed 'a truly terrific bombardment' from their own and enemy guns. Smith found this 'passive part . . . rather trying' since it was impossible to avoid the shelling. After the trenches were taken his company was moved up to help the wounded, bury the dead, and carry out repairs. There they stayed for two nights, resisting attacks from the flanks by German bombing parties. During this time the officer with whom he had trained at cadet school, Ferguson, was hit. Smith then took over command of his part of the line, a particularly '"jumpy" job' as the Germans could 'crawl up almost onto you without being seen'.[46]

His letter describing these events was written on 13 August, the second day of rest after the attack. It was over double the length of his usual letters; a fact that his mother must have noted, since Smith felt obliged to explain it in a later letter. His tone is almost apologetic about the strength of his *own* felt need to write: 'I am afraid no credit is due to me for writing such a long letter that time, as I was longing to tell someone all about it, and also I did not write till the second day of rest.'[47] His comment indicates a commonly felt tension between a personal need to reflect on events, and the mother's need for reassurance. Smith's account of how he felt during the battle expresses a sense of radical disjunction between the fronts: 'The taking over of that line seemed an unreal sort of dream to me, I am not going into details, but it seemed as though there was an infinity of time and space separating us from anything beautiful or desirable and the weird effect was increased by the half light and mist.'[48]

Far from the 'infinity of time and space' between the fronts making understanding impossible, the events encouraged Smith to construct a long narrative to his mother. However his narrative was highly circumscribed. This was due in part to the demands of formal censorship. Smith prefaced his description of the battle by saying 'I will now tell you as much as is permissible about our part in the affair'. Danger is routinely down-played. He refers to the battle as the 'excitement', and of being 'annoyed by bombs and things'. Even so, he gives clear signs to his mother of the emotional impact of events. Through its very reference to things unsaid, the phrase 'I am not going into details' communicates something of the horror he has witnessed. His sense of having been in a dream state during battle is not unusual. Gladden wrote of wandering into an 'unreal world'; Andrews, a reporter in civilian life, described going through battle at Neuve Chappelle 'like a sleepwalker'.[49] For Smith, in this context, the capacity *not* to elaborate shows his mother that he retains control over memory, and is not subject to involuntary recall.

Throughout the letter Smith downplays his part in and reactions to the attack. Comments which might be interpreted as referring to his individual experience are turned mid-sentence into testaments to the spirit of the men. Having explained to his mother how they could not 'relax our watchfulness for a moment' during the two-day ordeal, he explains how 'this resulted in a great strain on the nerves which the men stood wonderfully well'. After being relieved 'I had time to realise that I had a bit of a nerve shaking and was hungry and thirsty, but the men never had their tails really down the whole time.' His letter focuses on the heroism and bravery of fellow officers such as Ferguson: 'leading his own men under the most excessively trying conditions, he did more than his duty, hurling bombs and holding the men together in the most wonderful way, the Captain cannot say too much for him'.[50]

Throughout Smith attempts to minimise self-scrutiny, placing others' achievements first:

> Personally I soon got used to seeing nasty things, and one seemed to forget everything else, but a desire to help as much as possible. I wish I had been able to do more real good, but anyone else's efforts seemed to pale before the absolutely marvellous energy of these men, surely there is some good even in war if it provides scope for things of this sort!! Anyhow, that is the way I prefer to look at it.[51]

Why does he concentrate his narrative on others' actions? In part it may be because his experience of battle was at odds with the expectation of heroic action. His battle had consisted of passively enduring shelling, and then of dealing with the bloody aftermath of action. Writing about the exploits of his fellow men enables him to supply what a war narrative should; a sense of agency and of selfless sacrifice. It allows him to appropriate the identity of the regimental officer, whose responsibility is to commend men on their good work and look after their welfare. Writing constructs memory around the altruism of the officer and, by simply forgetting 'everything else', it contains the difficult aspects of his first encounter within the realms of the dream.

The use of writing to minimise self-reflection is apparent above all in the effort to maintain the *mother's* morale. He seems to review his prose as he writes, reading it as his mother would, searching for anything that might cause unnecessary anxiety. The description of rescuing wounded men is followed by a statement that his mother 'must not run away with the idea that our own losses were exceptionally heavy'. Later he asks her to keep in mind his earlier descriptions of 'delightful furnished and peaceful trenches', instilling a memory of peace and repose.[52] He is seeking to manage not only his own but his mother's emotional state.

This letter performs a delicate balancing act. On the one hand, as Smith acknowledges, it is written out of his own need to put experiences into symbolic form. On the other, the point of writing is to reassure the mother, providing a sign of life and of good morale. Linking the two is the maternal figure, the address to whom can tell us something of Smith's emotional state. His letter draws the mother into an understanding of terror, whilst at the same time advising her not to dwell on it. Writing allows him a means of nurturing a reparative urge. It performs an interior function – through an altruistic emphasis on the actions of other men, and attentiveness to the mother's feelings – of assuaging his anxiety.

MUD AND DREAMS

Smith's second prolonged experience of the front line was from early October until mid-November 1915, during which time he was in trenches with barely a night's relief. Although there was no major attack, the weather was exceptionally bad. As with the letter he wrote after his first experience of battle, 'Once again I am moved to commence a letter to you at a time of more than usual unpleasantness'. 'My luck is out', he explained, as the trenches were 'quite noisy at times' and he was finding 'it very hard work'. At the same time, he controlled the expression of being fed-up: 'of course it is awfully jolly, with plenty of diversions of all sorts, but I am getting a little bit blasé now and would be quite satisfied with a humble and uninteresting billet!'[53]

His descriptions focus on the conditions of the trenches and his duties in enabling the men to stay alive in them. These were the kinds of duties with which his mother would have been familiar: the conditions of his sleeping quarters; washing and shaving; difficulties in keeping clean and keeping the men clean; and in staying warm and dry. His 'house-keeping' also included burying the dead and maintaining the walls of the trenches, which under the incessant rain were 'forever falling in unexpectedly'.[54] Although couched in the terms of domestic duties, such descriptions conveyed the radical difference between home and the front. Typically, the mention of death hints most at the overturning of domestic standards, moral and physical. The Germans had begun pumping the water from their own trenches into the British ones: 'It would not matter so much if it were ordinary water, but unfortunately, it has passed a good many corpses on the way and stinks most horribly!'[55]

The other main topic of Smith's letters during this time was his relationships with the men in his platoon and company. After three months as platoon commander he had developed a strong sense of duty towards his men. He described in detail the conditions under which they had to live, in flooded trenches with inadequate cover from the rain. In such circumstances he felt he should share the same hardships: 'I am out a good deal as one does not feel comfortable sitting in one's dugout small and insignificant though it is – when the men have practically none'.[56] On 27 October he discovered some men asleep on watch:

> when they should have been on the look-out and – weakly I suppose
> – brought them up for 'inattention only' as I knew they had hardly
> had any sleep at all for a long time and could not bring myself to take
> the worst view of the case – the punishment for which of course you
> know. Of course, if this were known, I should be hauled over the coals
> pretty severely . . . This is a thing I have always dreaded – (not being
> a real soldier I suppose).[57]

On the following evening he recorded that 'I have been having horrible dreams about my entire platoon convicted of something dreadful and being left out in the filthy rain all night with practically nothing on!!'[58] In the closing passage of his next letter, he mentioned them again: 'More tomorrow. I must lie down now and hope not to dream of finding all my men lying out in the pouring rain with only underclothing on – as I did the other night!'[59]

Duty towards the men is the central theme of both Smith's actions and the dream. The dream has obvious associations with his worries about the difficulties the men were going through in the wet and cold. It expresses extreme altruism. The punishment for Smith's misdemeanour of turning a blind eye is visited upon his men, who lie fully exposed to the elements. In so far as the dream registers anxiety about his own possible punishment, it does so through association to the men. It is his failure to protect *them*, the fact of their vulnerability, which makes the dream unnerving.

In part I think he narrates the dream out of the hope that putting it into words will lessen the likelihood of its return. But why share it with his mother, just as he is about to go to sleep? The dream reveals important similarities between the mother-son relationship and that between the officer and his men. In *Instinct and the Unconscious*, the wartime psychologist William H. R. Rivers comments on the intensity of the officer's interest in the welfare of his men, which 'could not be greater if those under his command were his own children'. Rivers regarded the bond as 'more nearly resembling that of father and son than any other kind of relationship', although his wording suggests that the paternal did not quite capture its quality.[60] In letters we see how the officer's duties towards his men might also encourage identification with the mother, through her role in the men's own earlier history of care.

An important aspect of this earlier history concerned the mother's role in dealing with the anxieties of the infant. The men's mothers would often have been in the position of performing what the Kleinian psychoanalyst and First World War veteran Wilfred Bion calls a 'containing' function for their sons. By this, Bion means the mother's ability to experience with the infant its terror, to empathise with it and process it in such a way that the infant comes to recognise that its fears are not life-threatening.[61] Through her capacity to endure the child's distress, and not to feel overwhelmed by it or project it back as unbearable, the mother plays a role in developing the child's capacity to tolerate fear.

Traces of this earlier containing function can sometimes be detected in letters home. In recalling his dream, Smith may have been soliciting his mother's concern for him, as well as evoking the similarities in their positions. We might assume that in his mother's association to the dream, it would be Smith himself who lay grossly exposed in the mud. In this sense the narration of the dream might have functioned as a means of self-containment, reminding and re-assuring him, as perhaps his mother had earlier in life, that it was after all, 'only a dream'. Rivers talks of similarities between the vivid and unnerving dreams experienced by shell-shocked soldiers and childhood nightmares.[62] Such dreams must have re-kindled primitive and powerful anxieties from earlier life. In relating his dreams to his mother, not once but twice, as he prepared for sleep, Smith was perhaps reaching for a maternal presence which could hold his anxieties, process them, and give them back in a manner shorn of terror.

The maternal relation

War removed men from the company of mothers and family. As such it gave a physical dimension to the gender scripts characteristic of late Victorian and Edwardian society, in which manliness was defined less against womanliness than domesticity, and motherliness in particular.[63] Despite this, the conditions of trench warfare did not create an unbridgeable gap between soldiers and home.

That the mother occupied perhaps the central place in the men's affective lives was widely recognised, as the social practices surrounding home visits, death, and injury suggest. On Smith's death, his batman wrote to his mother, offering his support and seeking to draw the fronts into a meaningful relationship: 'When I do get home I will come and visit you and I will be able to explain better. I live at Hammersmith – not far from you. I had got all his clothing ready for him to come home on leave.'[64] The letter of condolence sent to Smith's mother by his non-commissioned officer, Sergeant Mould, explicitly associated the affections among men with those between mothers and sons: 'Dear Mrs Smith, I know within a little how you feel by my own feelings, as Mr Smith confided in me in everything.'[65] The closeness of the mother–son tie was something which men replicated in their relationships with each other at the front. The bonds between men were not forged in *opposition* to home. Men acknowledged the depth of the maternal attachment, and mothers remained important figures in emotional relations amongst men.

In their letters, officers developed forms of description which could sustain the maternal relation. Writing home prompted them to observe their physical surroundings with a mother's eye. Domestic functions offered a vantage point recognisable to the mother, from which the horror of conditions could be apprehended. The men's physical and social situation intensified the choice of this domestic frame, and thus, the significance of writing to mothers. Firstly, the primitive conditions of trenches heightened the men's sensitivity to basic human functions of survival. Such things as hygiene or adequate diet could not be taken for granted, but had to be ensured. Men were in a position of taking responsibility for the physical and material aspects of personal survival, just as their mothers once had. In this they continued to rely heavily on services performed by the mother, in forms as various as the provision of food, clothing, and practical advice. Secondly, subaltern officers occupied a position akin to the mother in that they managed such tasks, not just for themselves, but for a wider social group. When they wrote of illness among the men, or of the men's difficulties in eating, sleeping, or keeping warm and dry, they were expressing the kinds of concerns which the mother probably had towards them in earlier life. The similarity in their roles at the front created a close bond between mothers and sons. The connection was doubly resonant in the case of subaltern officers, whose responsibilities to others may well have intensified their own felt need for care and protection.

Whilst the men's situation in the here-and-now strengthened such identifications, the emotional content of those identifications often reveals a more primitive perception of the mother. When Chapman wrote to his mother about the dysentery he was suffering in the aftermath of Mametz Wood, he made an explicit comparison with earlier sickness: 'This time last year I was in bed with typhoid; what a very happy time that was for me, at all events. For you it was anything but a holiday, I am afraid.'[66] This quality of 'pastness' in son-mother correspondence contrasts markedly with letters addressed to lovers or wives. In the letters between German soldiers and their wives and lovers examined by Christa Hämmerle, she remarks on how often writers express anxiety about the others' affections, anxieties reflected for example in tensions over the frequency of letter-writing.[67] In letters between couples the future was at stake: physical separation placed the burden upon writing as a means of nurturing fledgling relationships. In letters to mothers, by contrast, it is the stability and continuity of the relationship that is appealed to. Its longer history and significance in early life often shows – as, for example, in the way men alluded to the mother as the nurse of the child.

If in their letters home men often appealed to this longer history of care, at the same time mothers could do nothing to alleviate the immediate anxieties which men felt. Yet even this very incapacity might consolidate the son's identification with the mother. After all, both mothers and their subaltern sons were in the position of having little ultimate control over the fates of those in their care. When Smith narrated his dream to his mother, he expressed a mutual understanding of what it meant, emotionally, to be in such a position. Writing about the care of men allowed empathy with the mother's own sense of helplessness. For other men, the mother's inability to contain only wrought frustration and despair. When Lyndall Urwick wrote to his mother from hospital of the attack of diarrhoea which had forced him to withdraw from the front line just prior to a battle which decimated his platoon, he explained that 'I suddenly found myself curled up with a stomach-ache that put the best efforts of my childhood to naught.'[68] His comments cast his mother back to an earlier moment when his pain had also been literally uncontainable, as a means of communicating something of the horror of his recent experiences. At the same time, he insists that the two experiences are incomparable: she cannot know, he intimates, the utter wretchedness of his recent predicament, and she can therefore do nothing to process it for him.

Masculinity and the diminution of the self

Whilst the physical and emotional situation of men at the front encouraged men to confide in mothers, writing home also involved them in negotiations about what would remain unsaid. Officers did not express themselves unreservedly. In particular, they attempted to re-gain composure by directing concern from their own predicament to the care of others. Setting aside the issue of censorship, there are two aspects which might help explain the tendency to try and minimise the self and sustain a focus on others. One is the significance of war in the passage to manhood. Men were anxious to communicate to mothers their capacity not only to endure the stresses of battle personally but to exhibit appropriate soldierly qualities. When the volunteer Smith wrote enthusiastically about becoming a platoon commander, it was in a manner that linked what he called the 'housewifery' of the job with its capacity to develop qualities of manliness: 'one is held personally responsible for the comforts and good spirits of the men and [must] try to make them respect one as a man as well as a soldier'.[69] The way in which subalterns scrutinised their reactions after battle, and strove to overcome the sense that they did *not* 'yet ... feel very grand', suggests the importance for manliness of sustaining the focus on others.[70] However, far from success signifying the rejection of domesticity, the men's rectitude was as much motivated by the desire to sustain the pride of the mother.

The indirect way in which men conveyed their feelings about battle also reflected the notion, integral to the emotional economy of the middle-class family, that the son must protect the mother. The point of writing was precisely to demonstrate concern for her and to allay her anxieties. A further cultural element added to the demands of this gender script. The men's attempts to place the mother's needs first reflected more than the desire to show fitness as a prospective family head. It was also evidence that they had not descended into psychological malaise. Rivers, in his work on shell-shocked officers, pointed out that they tended not only to suppress the expression of fear, but fear itself. He attributed this to early socialisation in public schools, where the capacity to avoid fear was instilled in games and contests.[71] Sentiments such as the heightened desire to care for the men resulted in part from sublimation, the channelling of fear into altruism. We can observe this process at work in letters, as men seek firstly to minimise self-reflection, and then to re-orient themselves towards the care of others, especially the mother. When mothers read men's letters, we might assume that they were anxious for signs of how they were feeling, and yet might be relieved that they retained a capacity to *not* write about the traumas they had witnessed. The significance of the mother in the early moral training of sons would have given them a particular appreciation of the capacity to minimise self-absorption.

Stefan Collini gives a way of understanding this emotional complex in his work on the culture of public moralism in Victorian Britain, although in a manner that does not fully acknowledge the complexity of its gendered connotations. Collini argues that altruism – the assessment of self-conduct in terms of its contribution to the social good – was a 'dominant' moral sensibility amongst Victorian intellectuals.[72] This ideal retained a strong personal hold partly because of the psychological consequences that were thought to follow from absorption in purely 'selfish aims'.[73] Altruism provided the best defence against the 'emotional entropy' associated with self-reflection. Psychological health was seen to lie in the capacity to place others' needs first; despair, in the failure to do so. Public moralism had a psychologically 'deep hold'.[74]

Collini observes at one point that women, especially mothers, were regarded as particularly likely to possess such a moral sensibility, having 'special gifts for "feeling" and "concern for others"'.[75] Elsewhere, he identifies 'self-forgetfulness' as an aspect of the tradition of Christian manliness stemming from Thomas Arnold and others, concerned with moral qualities rather than athleticism.[76] Looked at from the perspective of the young subaltern, both these interpretations have validity, suggesting in turn something about the ambivalently gendered masculine identity of the soldier-son.[77] In showing attentiveness to the mother and her predicament, men fostered a connection with a feminine sensibility. In the aftermath of destruction, they sought to restore the mother's moral world as a touchstone. At the same time the avoidance of personal disclosure was seen as an indication that they had not descended into egotistical despair, and thus showed their success as men and soldiers. Personal reflection may have been curbed out of empathy with the mother, but was also a means of enacting culturally vaunted qualities of manliness.

Writing home after battle, subalterns confronted a profound difficulty. Writing encouraged introspection. In so doing it threatened to bring difficult experiences back to memory, and re-kindle anxiety. Yet write they must, since the well-being of those closest to them depended on news. How subalterns negotiated this dilemma tells us not only about the tensions within middle class Edwardian scripts of masculinity, but something about what these *felt* like. In letters home men veered between the mother-centred existence of their early years and the precepts of manliness associated with school and the military. The extreme anxiety of battle threw them back on both of these, equally formative, senses of self. In this context, diminution of the self was not merely a pervasive cultural form, but was a response to anxiety that functioned at the very deepest psychic levels. War placed men beyond the protection of mothers and faced them with anxieties ultimately beyond assimilation, since death was no mere fantasy, but in their midst. Confronting the extreme difficulty of containment, they strove to re-focus their emotional energies on the care of others. Writing home, whilst it gave clues as to the turmoil they were experiencing, functioned as a means of recovering the reparative urge in which both moral manliness and emotional survival were seen to consist.

Notes

I am extremely grateful to staff at the Imperial War Museum Document Collection and the Special Collections department of Leeds University Library for their assistance. They have made research for this project a pleasure. I would also like to thank Andrew Briggs, Anne McElroy, John Tosh, the editors Stefan Dudink and Karen Hagemann, and participants in the Centre for Psychoanalytic Studies Seminar series at the University of Essex for their insightful comments on this chapter.

1 Imperial War Museum (hereafter IWM), 87/13/1, D. H. Fenton and W. C. Fenton, letter from D. H. Fenton to the mother of a fellow soldier, n.d.
2 *Ibid.*
3 Evidence in this chapter is primarily drawn from twenty-three such collections, located at the IWM and Liddle Collection, University of Leeds (hereafter LC).
4 On mothers and the British home front, see especially S. Ouditt, *Fighting Forces, Writing Women: Identity and Ideology in the First World War* (London, 1994) and D. Grayzel, *Women's Identities at War: Gender, Motherhood and Politics in Britain and France During the First World War* (Chapel Hill, 1999). For a collection of essays on the German context which explores relations between the fronts, see K. Hagemann and S. Schüler-Springorum (eds), *Home/Front. The Military, War and Gender in Twentieth Century Germany* (Oxford, 2002).
5 All correspondence drawn upon here is from Second Lieutenants unless indicated otherwise.
6 P. Fussell, *The Great War and Modern Memory* (Oxford, 1977); E. Leed, *No Man's Land: Combat and Identity in World War I* (Cambridge, 1979).
7 Fussell, *Great War*, p. 87.
8 *Ibid.*, p. 86.
9 Leed, *No Man's Land*, p. 204.
10 J. Bourke, *Dismembering the Male: Men's Bodies, Britain and the Great War* (London, 1996), p. 23.
11 *Ibid.*, pp. 133–6.
12 D. Grayzel, *Women's Identities*, p. 49. Grayzel cites a passage from Henri Barbusse's novel *Under Fire* (published in 1916 and the most widely read war novel in England in 1917 and 1918): 'He has gone home', Barbusse comments as he observes a soldier writing. *Ibid.*, p. 14.
13 Bourke, for example, cites Fenton's letter in *Dismembering the Male*, but she views it as an example of male bonding, rather than as a letter appealing to a mother's sentiments, conjoining the affections of mothers and men, and appealing for maternal care. See Bourke, *Dismembering the male*, p. 137.

14 P. B. Boyden, *Tommy Atkins' Letters: The History of the British Army Postal Service from 1795* (London, 1990), p. 28.

15 E. Wells, *Mailshot: A History of the Forces Postal Service* (London, 1987), p. 63.

16 See also A. Woollacott, 'Sisters and brothers in arms: Family, class and gendering in world war I Britain', in M. Cooke and A. Woollacott (eds), *Gendering War Talk* (Princeton NJ, 1993), p. 140.

17 L. Davidoff and C. Hall, *Family Fortunes: Men and Women of the English Middle Class 1780–1850* (London, 1987), pp. 340–1, p. 103. On evangelicals and the mother's responsibility for the manliness of sons, see J. Tosh, *A Man's Place: Masculinity and the Middle-Class Home in Victorian England* (New Haven and London, 1999), pp. 112–14.

18 Davidoff and Hall, *Family Fortunes*, pp. 344–5.

19 *Ibid.*, p. 345.

20 Tosh, *A Man's Place*, pp. 177–8.

21 *Ibid.*, p. 184.

22 Urwick discouraged his mother from seeing him off: 'really we men do not understand these things. If, as I say, you feel that to see me will help you, come'. In private possession, 'war letters', Lyndall Urwick to mother, 7 August 1914. E. K. Smith, *Letters Sent From France* (London, 1994), letter to mother, 31 December 1914.

23 Urwick to mother, 11 August 1914. On the significance for mothers and sons of enlistment and separation from home, see J. Damousi, *The Labour of Loss: Mourning, Memory and Wartime Bereavement in Australia* (Cambridge, 1999), ch. 2.

24 J. Hartley, 'Letters are *everything* these days': Mothers and letters in the Second World War', in R. Earle (ed.), *Epistolary Selves: Letters and Letter-writers 1600–1945* (Aldershot, 1999), p. 185.

25 Survival rates of mothers' letters are, however, low, a product of the difficulty which men experienced in preserving them; also perhaps of the fact that the relationship, unlike that between lovers, was secure and needed no proof, but certainly because correspondence from home did not – and still is not – considered of equal historical worth to the testimonies of men actually *at* the front. See also Hartley, 'Letters are *everything*', p. 186 for an insightful discussion.

26 J. Bell (ed.), *Wilfred Owen: Selected Letters* (Oxford, 1998), letter 481, to Susan Owen, 19 January 1917, pp. 214–15.

27 Gibbs to father, 2 January 1916. Responding to a letter from his father, Smith's gratitude – and the sense that writing was not an activity his father took naturally to – is clear: 'My Dearest Father, I was so glad to get a letter from you as I quite appreciate the difficulty you have in writing. Even if it were not for this press of work which I am delighted to hear about' (Smith, *Letters Sent From France*, Letter to father, 26 March 1915). Hartley remarks on the 'low' expectations of men as letter-writers in the Second World War. 'Letters are *everything*', p. 185.

28 For a discussion of gender and letters as a genre, see Earle, 'Introduction', *Epistolary Selves*, p. 6; and Hartley, 'Letters are *everything*', p. 185.

29 IWM, DS/MISC/26, E. Marchant to mother, 11 July 1915.

30 IWM, 96/57/1, L. Hall to family, 12 March 1917.

31 IWM, 90/7/1 and 90/7/1A, E. R. Hutt to mother, 19 May 1915.

32 IWM, P. 317, A. Gibbs to mother, 12 April 1918.

33 IWM, 90/28/1, M. Webb to mother, 22 August 1915.

34 The functions performed by mothers can be illuminated by looking at cases where the mother was dead. In such cases, female relatives took over the functions of keeping up correspondence with men, and arranging for their needs to be met.

35 For similar comments in the Australian context see Damousi, *Labour of Loss*, pp. 27–8.

36 In only one of the collections I have looked at do letters to fathers outweigh those to mothers. Some men wrote to both parents, but the majority addressed the mother.

37 See Earle, 'Introduction', pp. 6–7 on women's role in the reading of novels and letters; E. F. Chapman, 'I look forward to *tea in the garden*, and . . . hearing you read some quiet tale aloud to us.' See IWM, 92/3/1, Chapman to mother, 14 February 1917. Writing from Mesopotamia, A. Hooper wrote, 'Another thing I long for, is to hear you read aloud.' See LC, DF 066, L. Hooper to K. Hooper, extract of letter from A. Hooper to mother, 21 April 1916.

38 Chapman to mother, 31 October 1916. Chapman's father had died in 1914, which might have intensified the only son's sense of duty towards his mother.

39 LC, POW 036, 'Field Pocket Note Book', K. Hooper, 30 August 1914.

40 See for example IWM, P471, J. H. Merivale, letters to Mrs Blanche Merivale; and LC, DF 088, Lady Macleod to N. Macleod. On 19 June 1915 Lady Macleod wrote to her son, 'My Dear Norman, It is an age since I put pen to paper to you, but you see with Irma [his wife] writing daily I have felt you got all my news as well as hers.'

41 Boyden, *Tommy Atkins*, p. 30.

42 Hutt to mother, 5 May 1915.

43 Looking back at these letters, preserved by his mother, Noakes remarked that it is 'the memories which they revive of the things I did *not* say' which strikes him most. F. E. Noakes, *The Distant Drum: The Personal History of a Guardsman in the Great War* (Tunbridge Wells, 1952), p. 56.

44 On the functions of writing in encouraging interiority and managing psychic states, see Walter J. Ong, *Orality and Literacy: The Technologising of the Word* (London, 1982); M. Roper, 'Splitting in unsent letters: Writing as a social practice and a psychological activity', *Social History*, 26:3 (October 2001), 318–40; and 'Re-remembering the Soldier Hero', *History Workshop Journal*, 50 (Autumn 2000), 181–209. On how writing might draw servicemen into emotionality, see also Hartley, 'Writing is *everything*', p. 191.

45 On assuming command of his platoon, Smith had delivered 'a speech in a severe tone which was very largely assumed, had they known it'. Smith, *Letters Sent From France*, Smith to mother, 6 August 1915.

46 *Ibid.*, 13 August 1915.

47 *Ibid.*, 21 August 1915.

48 *Ibid.*, 13 August 1915.

49 Cited in D. Winter, *Death's Men: Soldiers of the Great War* (London, 1978), pp. 188–9. On the 'anaesthetic quality of combat' see also N. Ferguson, *The Pity of War* (London, 1999), p. 366.

50 Smith, *Letters Sent From France*, letter to mother, 13 August 1915.

51 *Ibid.*, 13 August 1915.

52 *Ibid.*

53 *Ibid.*, 1 November 1915.
54 *Ibid.*, 28 October 1915.
55 *Ibid.*, 28 October 1915.
56 *Ibid.*, 27 October 1915.
57 *Ibid.*, 28 October 1915.
58 *Ibid.*, 29 October 1915.
59 *Ibid.*, 2 November 1915.
60 W. H. R. Rivers, *Instinct and the Unconscious: A Contribution to a Biological Theory of the Psycho-Neuroses* (Cambridge, 2nd edn, 1924), p. 217. Captain Irving Wilson confessed to a fellow officer that losing men was 'something like losing one's children'. Cited in M. Brown, *The Imperial War Museum Book of the Western Front* (London, 1993), p. 193.
61 See especially 'Attacks on linking', and 'A theory of linking', in W. R. Bion, *Second Thoughts* (London, 1967).
62 *Ibid.*, p. 243; see also W. H. R. Rivers, *Conflict and Dream* (London, 1923), p. 66.
63 Karin Hausen makes a similar observation about late nineteenth-century Germany, where 'motherliness' was 'juxtaposed to a pattern of orientation for being a man which was geared not to fatherliness, but to "manliness"'. Cited in R. Schulte, 'Käthe Kollwitz's Sacrifice', *History Workshop Journal*, 41 (Spring 1996), 209.
64 Smith, *Letters Sent From France*, Charles Smith to Mrs Smith, 4 January 1916.
65 *Ibid.*, Sergeant G. Mould to Mrs Smith, 24 January 1916.
66 Chapman to mother, 27 August 1916.
67 Christa Hämmerle, 'You let a weeping woman call you home?' Private correspondences during the First World War in Austria and Germany, in Earle (ed.), *Epistolary Selves*, p. 158.
68 Urwick to mother, 26 September 1914. For a discussion of how this event was re-composed in recollections across Urwick's life, see See Roper, 'Re-remembering the Soldier Hero'.
69 Smith, *Letters Sent From France*, Smith to mother, 21 April 1915; Smith to father, 22 June 1915.
70 Chapman to mother, 27 August 1916.
71 Rivers, *Instinct and the Unconscious*, Appendix IV, 'War neurosis and military training', p. 209.
72 S. Collini, *Public Moralists: Political Thought and Intellectual Life in Britain 1850–1930* (Oxford, 1993), pp. 63–6.
73 *Ibid.*, p. 74.
74 *Ibid.*, p. 89.
75 *Ibid.*, p. 87.
76 *Ibid.*, p. 187.
77 I am indebted to the editors, Stefan Dudink and Karen Hagemann, for this insight.

Index

Note: literary works can be found under the author's name.

Breinigsville, PA USA
13 December 2009
229151BV00003B/2/P